Red Scorpion

RED SCORPION

The War Patrols of the USS *Rasher*

Peter T. Sasgen

BLUEJACKET BOOKS

Naval Institute Press
Annapolis, Maryland

Naval Institute Press
291 Wood Road
Annapolis, MD 21402

First Bluejacket Books printing, 2002

Library of Congress Cataloging-in-Publication Data
Sasgen, Peter T., 1941–
    Red scorpion: the war patrol of the USS Rasher / Peter T. Sasgen.
    p. cm. – (Bluejacket books)
    Originally published: Annapolis: Naval Institute Press, 1995.
    Includes bibliographical references and index.
    ISBN 1-55750-404-0 (alk. paper)
    1. Rasher (Submarine)   2. World War, 1939–1945—Naval operations, American.   3. World War, 1939–1945—Naval operations—Submarine.   4. World War, 1939–1945—Campaigns—Pacific Area.
I. Title. II. Series.
D783.5.R37 S27 2002
940.54'5973—dc21

2002070343

Printed in the United States of America on acid-free paper ∞
09 08 07 06 05 04 03 02 9 8 7 6 5 4 3 2 1

Statistics from John D. Alden, *U.S. Submarine Attacks During World War II* are reprinted by permission of the United States Naval Institute. Photo credits: *Sasgen,* collection of Peter T. Sasgen; *Hutchinson,* collection of Peter J. Sasgen; *Laughon,* courtesy of Capt. William Norrington, USN (Ret.); *Munson,* official U.S. Navy photo; *Adams,* collection of Peter J. Sasgen; *Nace,* courtesy of Rear Adm. Charles D. Nace, USN (Ret.).

To the officers and men of the USS Rasher

Contents

Rasher: *Sebastes miniatus.* A venomous vermillion and white scorpionfish (or rockfish). Its habitat is the sandy bottom and rocky coastline from British Columbia, Canada, to Baja, Mexico. Rashers grow to 30 inches in length and thrive in water up to 150 fathoms deep. Their poison glands lie under the base of deeply grooved spines and transmit a paralyzing sting.

From a standard work on marine biology

USS *Rasher* (SS 269): a *Gato*-class attack submarine laid down on 4 May 1942, by Manitowoc Shipbuilding Company, Manitowoc, Wisconsin; launched 20 December 1942; commissioned 8 June 1943.

From *The Dictionary of American Naval Fighting Ships*

Preface

A series of events that helped make this book a reality must be mentioned. When my father, Peter J. Sasgen, was undergoing treatment for cancer in December of 1991, I telephoned his old friend, Rear Adm. Charles D. Nace, whom I'd never met but most certainly knew from Dad's war stories. I was aware of their mutual high regard for each other, developed when both were aboard the *Rasher* on her seventh and eighth war patrols, Dad as an engineering officer, Chuck in command. I explained the situation to the retired admiral and suggested that a letter to Pete might be just what was needed at that juncture. Chuck agreed; he was delighted to have located his old shipmate, having lost track of him in the seventies. He also took the time to contact some of Dad's other shipmates to apprise them of the situation. Needless to say, Dad was overwhelmed ("flabbergasted," one of his favorite words, would be more like it) when he received Chuck's letter. The letter precipitated a phone conversation between the two. It was, quite literally, all Pete talked about for weeks afterward. Fortuitously, the letter arrived just before the January 1992 *Rasher* reunion, held in Lakeland, Florida, and set in motion a visit by several of Dad's shipmates to his home in Spring Hill, Florida. It was like a private reunion. A month later, Dad passed away. I find it difficult even now to know how to express my thanks to all those who visited him or later wrote to express their sorrow at his death.

Afterward, I began to peruse the *RASHER REPORT* newsletters that someone thoughtfully had given him, along with some pictures and letters from the Lakeland reunion. I was so taken with the depth of involvement with the *Rasher* and her exploits by former crew members that I got in touch with Bob Mathewson, who filled me in on reunion activities, particularly the one planned for Manitowoc in 1993 to celebrate the fiftieth anniversary of the *Rasher*'s commissioning. Next, I talked to Bill Norrington, and he piqued my interest even more. Then in March, I got the notion that it would be interesting to locate the *Rasher*'s original builder's plans and blueprints and . . . well, you get the idea.

Being a closet submarine buff, I was impelled by my father's death to pull together the disparate parts of the *Rasher*'s story. That story is an adventure of the first order, replete with perils and triumphs, heroics and tragedy; an adventure that has always held a powerful fascination for me.

Writing a book about the *Rasher* was quite a challenge. For one thing, the events took place more than fifty years ago. For another, having been born in 1941, I wasn't aboard when she went to war in 1943. But my father was, and that fact has been a part of my life since the day in 1942 when he reenlisted in submarine service and was assigned to the *Rasher*, then under construction in Manitowoc, Wisconsin. So in a way I've always felt that I was aboard.

I was unprepared for the mountain of information relevant to the *Rasher*'s war years that had to be digested. Flipping through my father's memorabilia and scrapbooks was one thing; reading and understanding patrol reports and deck logs was quite another, to say nothing of the individual reminiscences and personal papers of her former crew members, declassified Navy documents, submarine history, submarine tactics, charts, letters, pictures, fleet submarine technical manuals, old service records—and that was just the easy part. For instance, Edward Hutchinson's reports are tersely written descriptions lacking the minutia of day-to-day patrolling, while Willard Laughon's are minute-by-minute (sometimes second-by-second), blow-by-blow accounts that read like a novel; Henry Munson's are supplemented with detailed attack diagrams. How to use this stuff and how best to convert it into a narrative of my own? That was only one of many problems I confronted that made the challenge all the more exciting.

To my amazement, much of the material I needed was readily available in government archives and libraries. At times I likened the search to an archaeological dig in which I'd occasionally come across a treasure in the flimsy, crumbling documents in some long-forgotten file.

Always over my shoulder as I started to weave the story together, I felt the presence of the *Rasher*'s crew. Would they approve of my efforts, would they agree with my interpretation of things, much less my technical grasp of tactics and events that took place nearly half a century ago? Could I count on their memories being foggy enough to overlook distortions and outright mistakes should they creep in? And also, was it "okay" for me to do this as opposed to someone who served in the *Rasher*? I knew my dad would have approved, but what about everyone else? These were real concerns. As for the issue of my authoring this work, my wife, Karen, asked, "Who better to do it?" Bill Norrington essentially said the same thing. So, I decided I would take a direct and steadfast approach; I would write it the way I wanted it to be written, and I would decide what was important and what was not. The interpretations would be mine alone, and I would try to make it rich in detail and exciting to read.

Creating an armature on which to build this narrative was the most difficult part because I did not want merely to rehash the bald facts or tediously recite torpedo gyro angles and target bearings. Rather, I wanted to create a story that was first and foremost a good yarn, one which happened to be about the USS *Rasher*.

To do this required a thorough search through other sources, both official and unofficial, for how things were done, why they were done —cause and effect, if you will—and how things looked, or what I call "atmospherics." It also required a bit of time crawling through the retired submarines *Becuna* in Philadelphia and *Pampanito* in San Francisco, checking out the details and soaking up the unique qualities that only a fleet boat exudes. (If only it had been the *Rasher* herself!) It also meant getting an unofficial tour of Hunters Point, standing at the head of the abandoned submarine dry docks and surveying the weeds growing around the old submarine barracks. While the *Rasher*'s official patrol reports are loaded with facts, and while the reminiscences of her crew members enliven them, those things were not in and of themselves sufficient to power a story that can stand on its own. There are so many peripheral elements—naval history, command structures, personalities, submarine doctrine, communications, weather, and day-to-day procedures at sea, to name just a few—that influence the way submarine war patrols are conducted. It would have been impossible to ignore them. Finally, there is the leitmotif of the war itself, the background to all of this.

The ultimate problem was that these vital ingredients do not always appear in the *Rasher* documents. So some of them had to be recreated by investigating how it was in similar circumstances and hazarding an educated guess as to how it may have been with the *Rasher*. It was not possible, of course, to reconstruct the conversations and day-to-day interactions of her crew, except in the broadest fashion. Also, there was no way to know who handled the TDC chores, who ran Plot, who was the assistant approach officer, who operated radar, sonar, engines, etc., during each patrol run, and certainly there was no way to know who said what when or to whom. Therefore, I've used the simple device of allowing the action to flow around the skippers, Hutchinson, Laughon, Munson, Adams, and Nace. In so doing, I tried my best to be as accurate and faithful to the record as possible. Any errors or omissions of fact are strictly mine and have undoubtedly occurred due to an overzealous imagination, not from any attempt to embellish or revise the truth.

Since my dad had put his own memories to paper and since I wanted this book to be a tribute to him as well, I decided to use as much of his material as possible. Thus, he plays a major role in this book. With this point of view in mind I got started and quickly found myself caught up in the drama of the *Rasher*, her days and nights in the Makassar Straits* and the Celebes Sea, bone-rattling depth charges and heroic deeds—all the elements needed for a compelling tale if ever there was one.

It took physical and mental courage to venture into enemy waters to destroy the Imperial Japanese merchant fleet at a time when the Empire was at its height of power. Though fleet-type submarines like the *Rasher* were state-of-the-art warships, it still meant engaging a tenacious, deadly, and cunning foe, one well-equipped for defensive undersea warfare. The fact that most of the fifty-two American submarines lost during the war were victims of the Japanese Navy's antisubmarine measures attests to their potency. The fact that U.S. submarines swept the sea lanes clear in spite of those measures attests to superior American submarining and fighting ability.

The *Rasher* and her crews own an impressive combat record. Examining the official chronicle of her eight war patrols reveals a submarine with a history of dogged determination in the face of tough opposition. Her famous fifth war patrol, a tactical tour de force, bears this out most emphatically. Impressive, too, are the citations she was awarded for her achievements.

Amazingly, she accomplished what she did in just eleven months.

---

*Many of the regions, countries, territories, islands, and bodies of water throughout the Pacific and Far East have undergone numerous name changes in the years since the Second World War. Where possible I have used the names they were known by during that period. Otherwise I have used the names currently found on maps and charts. The patrol track charts accompanying the text show a highly simplified layout of the *Rasher*'s actual track. The locations of sinkings are approximate.

She was officially credited with sinking eighteen ships and 99,901 tons*; impressive indeed, since many boats had a big head start on her. One has to wonder what her score might have been had she arrived in SoWesPac six or nine months earlier, or if the Navy's infamous torpedo problem had been solved sooner.

It came as somewhat of a surprise to realize that the *Rasher*'s almost two and a half-year combat deployment was but a small part of her history. Looking at it another way, from Manitowoc, Wisconsin, in 1943, to Staten Island, New York, in 1945—twenty-nine months—represented a mere 7.5 percent of her 387-month life, keel laying to scrapping. After the war she was called back to active duty—albeit in a different guise—for another twenty years before she was finally stricken from the list in 1971. It was actually twenty-three years if one counts the time she spent in the Bremerton, Washington, junk fleet before being auctioned for $266,666 to American Ship Dismantlers in Portland, Oregon, in August of 1974. In addition to her World War II awards and citations, the *Rasher* won two battle stars for service off Vietnam in 1964. So from the day she was laid down to the day she was reduced to ruins at the breaker's yards she'd been in existence for thirty-two years, three months—a very long time indeed for any naval vessel.

Unremarkably, though, time moves on, and so does the Navy. Technology accelerates. Ships are built, and, regrettably, when no longer needed, they are scrapped. After a long career, the *Rasher* is gone. But her men are with us still, either in fact or in spirit. They will always be remembered.

This project would not have been possible without the help of many interested and supportive individuals and institutions. I am grateful to my mother, Isabelle Sasgen, who experienced the *Rasher*'s eight war patrols in a different but no less arduous fashion than did my father. I thank my wife, Karen, for her usual cool and objective advice and her computer wizardry. Former *Rasher* commanding officer Rear Adm. Charles D. Nace, USN (Ret.) provided keen insights into submarine personnel and training, submarine operations and war patrolling, and allowed me to use his extensive written notes on these matters. I also am grateful for the loan of his personal copies of patrol

*According to the JANAC (Joint Army-Navy Assessment Committee) tally of 1947. The book *U.S. Submarine Attacks During World War II*, by John D. Alden, published in 1989 by the United States Naval Institute Press, credits the *Rasher* with twenty ships and 114,732 tons sunk.

reports, for the time he generously gave me during our long telephone conversations, and for the sage advice he offered after reviewing a copy of the manuscript. Capt. William Norrington, USN (Ret.), former executive officer under skippers Munson and Nace and resident *Rasher* historian, graciously permitted me to quote from his diary, supplied me with patrol reports and other documents that would have otherwise taken months to obtain from government archives, helped me with many small but important details of the *Rasher's* patrols, and took time to read and comment on the manuscript's factual and technical accuracy. I also thank Bob Mathewson, editor of the *RASHER REPORT*, who encouraged me to write this book and shared his thoughts and submarine experiences with me, and Kenneth E. Tate, who loaned me his personal diaries, notebooks, and publications and provided the answers to many, many questions via our weekly correspondence.

Also, the researchers at the National Archives in Washington, D.C., and Suitland, Maryland, the Portsmouth Naval Shipyard, Portsmouth, New Hampshire, and the Naval Historical Center Operational Archives Branch at the Washington, D. C. Navy Yard; the personnel at the Public Affairs Office of the Philadelphia Naval Shipyard; the staff of the United States Naval Institute, the William W. Jefferies Memorial Archives at the United States Naval Academy, and the United States Naval Academy Alumni Association, in Annapolis, Maryland, all of whom supplied me with or helped me find information, documents, and photographs relating to the *Rasher* and her commanding officers; Ms. Anne Witty, Curator of the Columbia River Maritime Museum in Astoria, Oregon, for her loan of pictures and copies of *Rasher* documents and plans; Dr. Eric Berryman of NavSeaSysCom, who guided me through the thicket of bureaucracy surrounding the search for various declassified documents; Steve Hettenbach, my old chum and college classmate, who cleverly arranged for me to visit Hunters Point in San Francisco; Comdr. John D. Alden, USN (Ret.), who supplied me with computerized information on the *Rasher's* war record; Thomas A. Bell, Esq., who loaned me books on military affairs, many of them long out of print, from his personal library, and who reviewed and offered constructive comments on a late draft of the text; present and former employees of Schnitzer Industries, Portland, Oregon, the parent company of the one-time American Ship Dismantlers, who took the time to search their files for *Rasher* memorabilia (alas, in vain) and to discuss with me the business of scrapping submarines.

I am indebted to the former officers and enlisted men of the *Rasher* who responded to my letters and phone calls soliciting information and who helped me unravel many a confusing episode: T.W.E. Bowdler; Dean C. Brooks; David P. Brown; Charles L. Delbridge Jr.; Howard E. Geer; William F. Inskeep; Chester M. Kenrich; Walter E. Muller; J. P. Paris; Leonard Pavelka; Michael Pontillo; Charles G. Reuff; Roland J. Soucy; James A. White; Norval D. Wilson; and Wallace D. Woode. I am grateful to graphic designer William B. Bird for his beautiful patrol track charts; my good friends Neal Blank and L. George Parry, who read the manuscript, and now know as much about submarines as I do. A special thanks to editor Bruce G. Guthrie, who straightened me out and asked the right questions; to Greg Alesiani, G. Jeremy Cummin, and to those who helped or contributed in so many ways. Most important of all, however, I thank my dad.

Peter T. Sasgen

A Remembrance

PETER JOSEPH SASGEN, LT. (JG), USNR
11 MARCH 1913–25 FEBRUARY 1992

"Hell, I figured none of those depth charges had my name on it."
Indeed none did.

My dad seemed the ultimate submariner, let alone the ultimate father: big, indestructible, fearless, no job too tough, yet loving and generous. He started out in S-boats in the thirties when Pearl Harbor was still a way-stop to the greater Pacific. He and my mother even honeymooned there.

He went to the *Rasher* in 1942 and stayed with her until she put in to Tompkinsville, Staten Island, in 1945. He made every dive and all eight war patrols. Along the way he won the Silver Star. His citation reads:

> For conspicuous gallantry and intrepidity in action in the line of his profession as Chief of the Watch and Hydraulic Manifold Operator of the U.S.S. RASHER during the Third War Patrol of that vessel in restricted waters of the Pacific Ocean Area. Cool and courageous under intense enemy shellfire on the surface and frequent bombing

and depth charge attacks while submerged, Ensign (then Chief Machinist's Mate) Sasgen operated the ship's main engines and auxiliary machinery with unfaltering skill and efficiency, thereby rendering invaluable assistance to his commanding officer in the execution of many hazardous missions. By his aggressive spirit and superb mechanical ability throughout, Ensign Sasgen contributed materially to the extensive damage inflicted on Japanese shipping lines and his zealous devotion to duty in the face of strong opposition was in keeping with the highest traditions of the United States Naval Service.

When Dad returned to civilian life and I grew up, his recitation of his exploits (told only after some coaxing) made me come to think of him and the *Rasher* as one and the same entity. I never tired of hearing about how he spotted a Zero diving on the boat out of the sun just as he was leaving the bridge. Or how, while on a boarding party, he got his treasured Japanese flag trophy. He and the *Rasher* certainly shared two common traits: confidence and success.

Later, when he was in charge of Pennsylvania Railroad diesel locomotive maintenance, he brought those same *Rasher* traits to that job, never taking no for an answer, always looking for a better way to do things despite an obstructionist management hierarchy. Similarly, a few years ago when he rounded up the men of his congregation to help him build furniture for their struggling parochial school, it was as if he were in charge of the *Rasher*'s machinery spaces again, giving orders, checking the main induction, and firing up the diesels.

After he retired the war faded into nostalgia for Dad. He would often say that he wasn't interested in the past; he had just done his job, the same thing any American would have done when the country went to war. And yet . . . in his late seventies he suddenly felt the prick of interest (or was it pride?) in what he and the *Rasher* had done together. He even took to wearing a *Rasher* cap emblazoned with his submarine combat pin with three stars and the old, battered twin dolphins I found for him in the boxes of memorabilia he'd given me.

Finally, near the end of his life, he wrote a memoir of his years in submarine service, entitled *A Submariner's Story*. That document is a fitting legacy for a man and a submarine that to this day, even though they are both gone, are inseparable still.

Red Scorpion

Part 1

From Wisconsin to the Celebes Sea

"I hear so many comments from old-time submariners about how they miss the boats, and I confess that I miss them more than anyone. But what we really mean is that we miss being with the people who served in them."

Rear Admiral Charles D. Nace, USN (Ret.),
the *Rasher*'s Commanding Officer,
seventh and eighth war patrols.

Prologue

Through the attack periscope, the captain of the *Rasher* can just make out the masts and smokestack of an enemy ship peeking above the silver horizon line. Unless one knows where to look she can easily be missed, since she's still hull down, 15,000 yards away. As the submarine speeds up to close in, the skipper makes observations at regular intervals to plot the target's course and speed and assess the situation.

Lumbering into full view at 6,000 yards, the target is identified as a large, heavily laden transport, blotchy with rust, topsides cluttered with cargo-handling equipment. On either beam and slightly astern, what first appeared as two thin masts now reveal themselves as two well-armed escorts. Following standard Japanese convoy procedure, the trio is zigzagging off its southerly base course, offering port and starboard sides to the *Rasher*'s periscope.

"She has escorts. *Chidoris*," announces the captain. Sound reports their distant echo-ranging.

The *Rasher* maneuvers silently, ventilation, air conditioning, and other machinery not vital to the business at hand secured. The conning tower is stiflingly hot. The only sounds are those of the whirring Torpedo Data Computer (TDC) and, when the skipper motions "up" with his thumbs, the periscope hoist motors.

"Range?"

"Two-seven-double-oh, Captain," answers the TDC operator as the range counters click down. The *Rasher* is closing with the target rapidly.

"Distance to the track?"

"Twenty-one hundred yards."

Thumbs up, and the periscope hums out of its well. Squatting on his heels, the captain snatches it off the deck, snaps the handles down, rises with it, and quickly sweeps the sky and sea, checking for intruders. Then he settles on the target. "Bearing—mark! Range—mark! "

" Zero-four-zero. Nineteen hundred."

"The near escort will pass astern. Down periscope!"

3

The malevolent sound of the *Chidori*'s thrashing screws grows louder and louder. Inside the submarine the men rivet their attention on the overhead; they stare as if they could follow the enemy's progress with their eyes. The escort crosses from port to starboard, "pinging" all the while, propeller declivity fading rapidly as she sweeps by overhead. The *Rasher* has not been detected inside the enemy screen.

Now the submarine is maneuvered to fire a spread of three torpedoes from the bow tubes on a 90-degree track. The big transport is approaching, broadside on. The skipper makes his final shooting observation. "Open outer doors on One, Two, and Three! Standby forward! Standby One!" The periscope crosshairs are on the target's big, black stack.

"Shoot any time, Captain," he is advised as the TDC's Correct Solution Light comes on.

The captain gives the order to fire at intervals of ten seconds. Three times the *Rasher* jolts as torpedoes whine out of the tubes, running hot, straight and normal. The skipper watches their smokey wakes streak for the ship; momentarily, he's mesmerized by them. Just before they reach the end of their timed runs, he twists the periscope around to check on the *Chidori* that passed astern.

"Escort's seen the fish." His voice is calm but clipped. "Take her deep! Use Negative! Three hundred feet! Rig for depth charge! Here she comes!"

With a frighteningly steep down-angle and her rudder hard over, the *Rasher* goes deep to escape. The *Chidori*, alerted to the attack by the telltale torpedo wakes, heels about and rushes in at full speed to counterattack. Sonar pulses zing like bullets; depth charges are sure to follow. The sharp reports from exploding torpedo warheads crackle through the water, but there's no time to rejoice over the hits. The *Rasher* plunges deeper and deeper, until she is far below her test depth. And it is only the beginning of her ordeal.

The Rising Sun

Shortly after World War I, America's sixty-odd-year friendship with Japan began to deteriorate. Ever since Commodore Matthew Perry and his Black Ships visited Yokahama in 1854 to negotiate steamship coaling privileges and other matters important to international trade, there had been an atmosphere of mutual respect and trust between the two nations. But because her expansionist strategies conflicted with U.S. interests in the Far East, the Empire was seen as the most likely military threat America would face in Asia in the future. Adding to this belief was the fact that the Treaty of Versailles signed after the war gave Japan the Mariana, Caroline, and Marshall Islands (the so-called "Mandates"), all former possessions of Germany. President Wilson and his naval advisors feared that these possessions, if developed as military bases, would be future stepping stones to the conquest of New Guinea, the Philippines, the Malays, eventually Australia, thence the whole of the western Pacific.

To counter this potential threat, the United States developed "Plan Orange," a complex and, in light of the technical abilities of the day, unwieldy tapestry of troop and ship deployments designed not only to retake these islands from Japan, but also to completely destroy the Imperial Navy in one mighty sea battle. Plan Orange required a large, fast, mobile fleet of warships that could project America's power quickly and emphatically over the great breadth of the western Pacific. Submarines, their offensive ability amply demonstrated by the German Navy in World War I, were to be integrated into this plan in the role of forward reconnaissance units, screen protection for the main U.S. battle fleet, and major offensive weapons against enemy naval vessels.

Unfortunately, an exercise held in 1921 to prove the feasibility of the submarine's role in support of Plan Orange quickly and decisively demonstrated that the Navy's submarines were woefully unable to do what was expected of them. Lack of speed, disastrous breakdowns, and poor seakeeping qualities conspired to relegate them to their traditional coastal defense roles. Despite the fact that German U-boats proved beyond a doubt that no navy could be a world sea power without submarines, the role played by U.S. submarines in the defense of the Pacific would have to be rethought, if not flat out discarded, by Navy planners.

Still, it was obvious to younger, less hidebound officers that the Navy needed modern submarines that were capable of operating far from home. They had to be equipped with large fuel and torpedo capacities and endowed with total mechanical reliability—traits heretofore unknown in the submarine service. The search for such a submarine began in earnest after the Navy digested the hard lessons learned in 1921. And once the chronic problem of diesel-electric propulsion could be mastered (how to build reliable and powerful diesel engines eluded the Navy for decades), the successful design and construction of true fleet submarines would manifest itself in the massive V-boats of the late twenties: *Barracuda*, *Bass*, and *Bonita*. Or so the Navy thought.

As expected, the naval arms limitation conference of 1921 had far-reaching effects. Being in a pacifist frame of mind, notwithstanding Plan Orange (renamed Rainbow Five in 1941), the United States agreed to scrap its surface warship building program and to vastly reduce its submarine fleet. Some delegates to the conference went so far as to demand that submarines be outlawed altogether because they were thought to be immoral; others considered them obsolete, what with the recent invention of ASDIC (the British version of sonar) and the advent of bombing aircraft. Though submarine tonnage limitations suggested at the conference were never adopted, the attitude of Congress and the nation slowed submarine development and construction to a snail's pace.

The big V-boats were finally completed in 1926. Three more— *Argonaut*, *Narwhal*, and *Nautilus*—soon followed. While there were technical difficulties associated with these big boats—among others, leaky tankage and balky diesels—they were a crucial advance in the evolution of some of the world's finest warships: the *Gato*-, *Balao*-, and *Tench*-class fleet-type submarines.

The world situation changed drastically in the thirties. On 18 September 1931, Japan's Kwantung Army invaded Mukden in Manchuria. Two years later, German Chancellor Adolf Hitler launched a massive U-boat building campaign. By 1937, both Germany and Japan had repudiated the Naval Armament Limitation Treaties. President Franklin Roosevelt understood that these events warranted a new naval building program to counter the dual threat of a rearmed, Nazified Germany and a militarist Japan. Congress immediately planned for the building of 200 ships totaling 1,350,000 tons, which included 7 battleships, 8 carriers, 27 cruisers, 115 destroyers, and 43 submarines.

From these events was born the Navy's *Gato* (SS 212)-class fleet-type submarine, the prototypical attack boat of World War II. The

Gato's development lineage actually began with the P-class and *Salmon* (SS 182)-class submarines, laid down in 1933 and 1935. These were smaller, more maneuverable boats than the Vs. The design was refined further in the *Tambor* (SS 198)-class adopted by the Navy's General Board and the Submarine Officers' Conference for the 1939 program.

Credit must go to three naval officers, Comdr. Charles A. Lockwood, who was later admiral and Commander Submarines Pacific, Lt. Comdr. Andrew I. McKee, planning officer at Portsmouth Navy Yard, and Lt. Armand M. Morgan, head of the Navy's submarine design section. Working together, these men overcame the inherent bureaucratic and technical difficulties of such a complicated undertaking and were the masterminds behind the design and construction of the boats that would eventually be deployed against the Japanese.

One key to the *Tambor*'s success was the development of a compact diesel engine designed in concert with the American railroad industry, which enthusiastically embraced the benefits of diesel-powered locomotives (and was delighted by the Navy's willingness to fund the huge research and development costs associated with their creation).

Thus, as the *Tambor*-class evolved into the *Gato*-class in the fall of 1940, the United States had at last a submarine whose performance transcended its specifications. The trouble was, the Navy had not thought to order nearly enough boats. And when the sky over Pearl Harbor was peppered with flak on 7 December 1941, America needed submarines, and lots of them.

The Silent Service

Nobody seems to know with any degree of certitude the derivation of the appellation "Silent Service." Perhaps, some say, it developed in peacetime when submarine sailors had a certain mystique about them, as though schooled in some black art or possessed of some arcana unknown to their surface counterparts. During the war it was an apt description of a service that resisted pressure from Congress, the news media, and even the White House to release information about its operations, its engagements, its losses, and even its victories. Silent or not, among submarine sailors there existed an esprit de corps, camaraderie, and pride that did not exist in any other branch of the military service. And why not? After all, it was dangerous to take a pre-World War II submarine to sea, much less submerge in it.

Charles D. Nace, later one of the *Rasher*'s commanding officers, had firsthand experience in these matters:

> The older boats were full of rust, and they leaked a lot of sea water. It was disconcerting to dive a very old submarine, look aft to the engine room and see water cascading down through a warped hatch which would only seat when the boat was deep enough for sea pressure to slam it shut.
>
> Incidents like these built character and fostered a condition of togetherness. And these sorts of happenings were very common in peacetime operations for many years, along with the sweat and stench which was the result of no air conditioning, diesel fumes, and oil in the bilges.
>
> Only those who served in these older submarines could truly appreciate the hardships which the crews endured, particularly submerged, when temperatures ran over 100 degrees and the standard uniform was usually skivvy shorts, a Turkish towel around the neck, and sandals to squish through the puddles of sweat on the painted canvas decks.

These veterans would be the nucleus of the crews that would man the submarines that fought the Japanese.

The submarine service took only volunteers because the duty was demanding and hazardous. Those who volunteered did so for varying reasons. Some saw opportunities for faster promotion, since the force was minuscule compared to the surface fleet. Many wanted to be part of an elite group. Others were attracted by the extra pay. And others just felt that submarines were a challenge that demanded their best. For whatever reason, they reported to submarine school at New London, Connecticut.

Before training commenced, students were screened by medical officers to ensure they did not suffer from claustrophobia (certainly a debilitating affliction for any submariner), that they had good night vision, and that they would be mentally suited to the environment of a submarine.

Even before Pearl Harbor, it was necessary to shorten submarine school from six months to three months for officers and to one month for enlisted personnel because the submarine building program had been accelerated and the fleet was expanding at the rate of seven or eight new boats per month. Training covered everything from torpedoes, diesel engines, storage batteries, and electric motors, to submarine operations themselves. Inside the water-filled training tower all students were required to make an ascent from a 100-foot depth using a Momsen Lung breathing device to acquaint them with the difficulties of escaping from a sunken submarine. The most realistic and most interesting training took place aboard the old school boats—mostly decrepit O-class and R-class submarines better suited for the scrap yard.

After submarine school the primary objective for each officer and enlisted man was to earn the designation "qualified in submarines" and to wear the coveted "Twin Dolphins," which signified he was a full-fledged submariner. To achieve this status required long hours of intense study outside of regular work and duty hours. Each man had to become familiar with the location and operation of practically every piece of machinery on board. The submariner needed to know about loading and firing torpedoes, charging batteries, the operation of diesel engines and main propulsion systems, the location of water and hydraulic piping systems and their valves, control of the boat during diving and surfacing, and the details about what to do in every conceivable type of emergency.

This regimen of training, rigorous in peacetime, gained a much greater sense of urgency when war broke out. Every new man had to learn his responsibilities in less time than normal. It became routine procedure for every submarine to conduct intensive training—"school of the boat," as it was known—every day during a war patrol. The training was essential to enhance the combat performance of each ship. In addition, it helped provide the crews for new construction; after each war patrol a submarine gave up about 20 percent of its crew and took on new and mostly inexperienced officers and enlisted men.

Additions to the submarine fleet required that the regulars who were in the boats at the start of the war be augmented with reserves. These men volunteered for submarine service possessed of a vast range of badly needed skills. Many had technical, electronic, and engineering backgrounds, and in short order they were as proficient as the men who had been there since before Pearl Harbor. By the end of the war nearly 75 percent of submarine personnel were reserves. Each man, regular or reserve, knew his shipmates' and his own life depended on his knowledge and actions: in submarines, there was no margin for error.

These were the men who took the *Rasher* to war.

The Bosun and the Bear   /

> TRANSFERRED: to Manitowoc, Wisconsin, and report to
> Supervisor of Shipbuilding for duty in connection with fitting
> out of the USS RASHER.
> DATE TRANSFERRED: 11 November 1942.
> DATE REPORTED ABOARD: 13 November 1942.
> Submarine Maintenance Activity, Manitowoc, Wisconsin.

So read the orders.

Congress passed the $5 billion 70 Percent Expansion Act (also known as the "Two-Ocean Navy Act") on 19 July 1940. President Roosevelt signed the appropriation bill on 9 September, and within a day or two the Navy awarded contracts for the ships to practically every building yard in the country. As part of the submarine building program authorized under the act, ten contracts for *Gato*-class boats were let to the Manitowoc Shipbuilding Company in Manitowoc, Wisconsin, a highly respected shipbuilding concern owned by Charles C. West. Manitowoc, known as the "Clipper City" for its long history of Great Lakes shipbuilding, was located eighty miles north of Milwaukee. West's facility was situated on a peninsula in the twisting Manitowoc River, virtually on the shores of Lake Michigan, and was shortly to become famous for its beautifully built submarines and innovative construction methods. All told, Manitowoc turned out twenty-eight boats for the Navy during the war: fourteen *Gato*-class and fourteen *Balao*-class.

To win the contracts, West and his engineers had to overcome two thorny problems relevant to building submarines in fresh water, 1,500 miles from the sea. The first was fairly easy to solve. No one at the Manitowoc Shipbuilding Company had ever seen a modern submarine, much less built one. Manitowoc was essentially a "follow-on" yard to Electric Boat Company of Groton, Connecticut, building the *Gato*-class submarines according to the plans and detailed drawings provided by Electric Boat with only a few modifications necessary to adapt them to Manitowoc's facilities. At first the shipwrights worked with the Electric Boat staff that was present on-site to provide technical assistance. In no time at all, however, Manitowoc's workers, who possessed varied skills and had vast experience with naval architecture, mastered the complexities of submarine construction. Manitowoc even introduced improvements to the original designs. Among these was an improved 3,000-pound high-pressure air manifold, a method for packing and silencing propeller shafts, advanced methods for casting bronze torpedo tubes, and a variable-speed radar training motor. The most important improvement from a purely operational standpoint was the change in the rigged-in angle of the bow planes from zero to full dive, giving them a sharper bite in the water when submerging, thus making the boat dive more quickly.

Manitowoc's second problem—how to get the boats to sea—turned out to be a bit more difficult. But West's fertile and creative mind found a solution.

There were three possible avenues to the ocean from Lake Michigan: the St. Lawrence River via the Welland Ship Canal and a network of six smaller canals with twenty-one locks leading to the Gulf of St. Lawrence; the Erie Canal, which connected Lake Erie with the Hudson River at Troy, New York; and the Illinois and Mississippi Rivers flowing to the Gulf of Mexico at New Orleans, Louisiana.

It was not feasible to use the first two routes because the locks were too short to accommodate a 300-foot-long submarine. The third route had drawbacks too, particularly the shallow water and the multitude of fixed bridges over the rivers and canals. West's solution was to run the submarines into a shallow-draft floating dry dock of his own design and deliver them by towboat to New Orleans. The Army Corps of Engineers would work with local authorities to adapt the bridges to the Navy's needs.

Manitowoc's ten submarine contracts were signed and delivered to the Bureau of Ships in December 1940. They called for one of the boats to be completed and commissioned by the end of 1942, the other nine during calendar 1943. One of them was assigned hull number 269 and later named, without fanfare, in Navy-regulation alphabetical fashion, USS *Rasher*. The other nine boats were named *Peto* (SS 265), *Pogy* (SS 266), *Pompon* (SS 267), *Puffer* (SS 268), *Raton* (SS 270), *Ray* (SS 271), *Redfin* (SS 272), *Robalo* (SS 273), and *Rock* (SS 274).

At Manitowoc, submarine hulls were built from prefabricated sections constructed in erection sheds along the building ways out of the weather. One of the yard's premier innovations was to rotate the sections in jigs as they were welded so the workmen were always stationary and so used their torches with the work moving under and away from them, a technique called "down welding." This accounted for the great strength of the Manitowoc hulls. The sections, sixteen in all plus the conning tower, were brought to the site on crawler-tractors, then lifted onto keel blocks with a crane and welded together. Because the building yards were located along the banks of the narrow, twisting

Manitowoc River, the boats had to be launched sideways, a technique heretofore unheard of in submarine construction and a cause of concern to the Navy. But it proved to be totally safe and efficient.

The *Rasher*'s contract number was NOD 1514 CF, and her estimated cost, like her sister ships, was $3,021,000. Her keel, or her first hull section, depending on how one looked at it, was laid—lifted into place, actually—on 4 May 1942 on building ways "A." It was assembled from steel plates manufactured by the Lukens Steel Company in Coatesville, Pennsylvania, the only mill in America capable of making plates in the necessary fifteen-foot lengths.

Construction progressed rapidly, and on 20 December 1942, Mrs. G. C. Weaver, wife of the supervisor of shipbuilding at Manitowoc, Navy Lt. Comdr. George C. "Buck" Weaver, stood by on the speakers' platform to break the traditional bottle of champagne on the *Rasher*'s bow as she was christened. Workmen gave Mrs. Weaver a target to aim for by rolling back part of the red, white, and blue bunting that draped the bow and chalking an "X" inside a circle. The weather was subzero. Photographs taken that day clearly show tugs had been at work in the river breaking up the ice. An hour earlier yard workers had driven oak wedges between the supporting cradles and the submarine's hull to lift it just enough so the cradles could be removed. The ship was resting on the greased 16-inch by 24-inch fir launching ways and held in place by 8-inch diameter manila "trigger lines."

Holding a bouquet of red roses in one hand, the petite Mrs. Weaver gave a mighty swing, whacked the wrapped bottle on the ship's hull, and declared, "I christen thee *Rasher*." With that, the trigger lines were severed by a brace of pneumatic cutters, and starting jacks at the bow and stern of the vessel gave her a gentle nudge. The new submarine slid sideways thirty feet and, with a crash of flying timbers, cribbing, and icy spray, hit the water, heeled over 48 degrees to starboard, hesitated a moment, and righted herself. Applause, whistles, and cheers burst from those assembled for the occasion. With the aid of a tug, yard workers quickly tied her up to the bulkhead.

Gato-class submarines like the *Rasher* were virtual duplicates of the *Tambor*s on which their design was based, but with updated propulsion machinery and fire-control systems. A look at the *Rasher*'s Submarine Characteristics Card, dated 8 June 1943, reveals the classic *Gato* specifications: overall length 311 feet, 6 inches; beam 27 feet, 3 ¾ inches; full load displacement 1,806 tons; maximum draft 17 feet. The *Gatos*' internal layouts were refined from the original *Dolphin* (SS 169) and *Tambor*-class boats and in final form included a bulkhead between the two engine rooms that made them less vulnerable to flooding.

From fore to aft there were nine watertight compartments. The forward torpedo room had six 21-inch torpedo tubes in its forward bulkhead, handling equipment for sixteen torpedoes and mechanisms for loading and firing them. Tubes One, Two, Three, and Four were above the platform deck, while tubes Five and Six were below it. The sonar gear, pitometer log, escape trunk, and crew berthing facilities for fifteen men were located in this compartment, plus a head for the officers.

Next came the forward battery compartment. The lower portion housed 126 rechargeable Gould or Exide cells, also known as *"Sargo-type"* batteries. This powerful storage battery was developed by the Navy's Bureau of Engineering and had a much longer performance life than did earlier ones. Its first successful installation was in the submarine *Sargo*. The upper portion of the forward battery compartment held the sleeping quarters for the officers and chief petty officers in spaces no larger than a Pullman roomette like those aboard the 20th Century Limited. The ship's office and officers' shower were located on the starboard side of the passageway. The officers' wardroom and serving pantry were located forward of the staterooms.

Going aft, the adjoining compartment was the control room. It housed the master gyro compass, periscope wells, steering stand, high-pressure air manifold, hydraulic manifold, 600-pound main ballast tank blowing manifold, bow and stern plane diving station, radio room, decoding equipment, main ballast tank vent controls, and much more. Above the control room was the 8-foot by 12-foot conning tower, where the Torpedo Data Computer (TDC), radar stacks, periscopes, sonar equipment, gyro compass repeater, and various pressure gauges and electrical apparatus were located. The conning tower connected to the control room below and the bridge topside through watertight hatches. These two compartments—control room and conning tower—were the operations center of the ship.

Below the control room was the pump room, which housed the trim pump used to transfer water from various tanks to control the trim of the ship. Under normal conditions, a one-degree dive angle was kept on the submarine by use of the trim pump and bow and stern planes. The boat could be trimmed so precisely that the effect of a man moving from bow to stern could upset it. Two air compressors delivered air at 3,000 pounds per square inch. Stepped down, this air was crucial for several systems: the impulse air flasks for firing torpedoes required 300 p.s.i.; 600 p.s.i. was needed for blowing ballast tanks; starting the diesel engines took 500 p.s.i.; and 225 p.s.i. supplied ship's service air for miscellaneous use. The pump room also housed two air conditioning compressors, a refrigeration compressor, low-pressure blowers, and a hydraulic pump for operating the rudder, diving planes, periscopes, and ballast tank vent valves.

Beyond the control room was the after battery compartment. Below its main deck were another 126 battery cells. Above it were the galley, crew's mess, crew's quarters with bunks for thirty-five men, heads, showers, and a washing machine. Below decks was the ship's freezer and cold room. Enough provisions could be stored aboard ship for ninety days of operations, although fresh stores such as milk and vegetables would last only two weeks.

The crew's mess, with its four stainless steel tables and eight benches, could accommodate thirty-two men at a time for meals. It was a convenient place to study, play cards, write letters, and pass the time when not standing watches. At sea there was always a cribbage or pinochle game going. Fresh coffee, cold cuts, cheese, and homemade bread, biscuits, and rolls, were available twenty-four hours a day. At mealtime the cooks used the compact but super-efficient galley to whip up delicious steak dinners, roasts, chicken, ham, soup, cakes, pies, and delicate desserts, some topped with frozen strawberries and whipped cream. Sub crews had only the best. The mess was *the* place to come after standing a watch to grab a bite to eat and get a cup of coffee. During war patrols it doubled as a classroom for "school of the boat." Taught by the leading chief petty officers, the wide-ranging "school" included written exams, question-and-answer sessions, and practical work through which the student had to show his proficiency in operating the submarine's thirty basic systems. Drawings and sketches of these systems were also required for qualification.

The next two compartments were the forward and after engine rooms. Each engine room contained two 16-cylinder, 2-cycle General Motors Winton Model 16-248A diesel engines that each produced 1,600 horsepower at 750 rpm. The engines were cooled by fresh water, which in turn was cooled by sea water after its passage through the engine. The diesels were connected to four air-cooled D. C. generators rated at 1,100 kilowatts and 415 volts. The forward engine room also housed two Kleinschmidt distillers for making fresh water from sea water at the rate of about 5,500 gallons a week. That included water for the batteries, which consumed 500 gallons a week. An auxiliary eight-cylinder engine with an output of 750 horsepower was located below decks between the two main engines in the after room; it could be used for topping off batteries or carrying the "hotel load" while in port. Additionally, there were engine fuel and lube oil centrifuges, air induction valves, and hull ventilation supply lines in the engine rooms.

Aft of the engine rooms was the maneuvering room, which housed the electrical controls, switches, rheostats, and the control cubicle. In the control cubicle were the levers for arranging the current flow from the four main diesel-powered generators to the four air-cooled main motors below deck. The motors were rated at 1,375 horsepower at 1,300 rpm. They were connected in pairs to reduction gears that drove the two propeller shafts. Submarine diesel-electric drive was very flexible. On the surface, any combination of diesel engines and electric motors could be used for propulsion or battery charging, or both. The maneuvering room also had a crew's head, oxygen flasks, and a six-inch metalworking lathe that was one of the most important pieces of equipment aboard ship.

The last compartment was the after torpedo room, which had four tubes in its after bulkhead, stowage for eight torpedoes, and sleeping and locker facilities for fifteen crewmen. The hydraulic steering rams were positioned on the port and starboard sides of the hull. This compartment also contained the stern diving plane tilting mechanism, external air salvage connections, and an escape trunk.

Submarine complements, like their surface counterparts, were structured along lines of command and seniority. The lines tended to blur a bit in the boats because of their tight-knit nature. The *Gatos* were originally specified to have a crew of six officers and fifty-four men. But as more fire-control equipment, radar, radio, and sound gear was added during the war, the complements grew to ten officers and seventy or seventy-one men. In command of the ship was a Naval Academy graduate (there were no Naval Reservists qualified for command until late in the war), usually a commander or lieutenant commander. His executive officer, a lieutenant or lieutenant commander qualified for command, was in charge of navigation, served as the assistant approach officer, and generally took charge of running the ship's daily routine. Other officers, from lieutenants and lieutenants junior grade to ensigns, headed the departments, such as torpedo, engineering, communications, and commissary. The last was traditionally the purview of the most junior officer aboard.

The enlisted men, most of them experienced submariners, included six or seven chief petty officers who ran the ship's departments on a day-to-day basis and oversaw the actual operation of the ship. Usually the most senior chief aboard was designated "Chief of the Boat." He was a key man in that he was in charge of enlisted personnel. His battle station was at the hydraulic manifold. Other chiefs were in charge of the engine rooms and torpedo rooms and oversaw the electrician's mates, machinist's mates, torpedomen, gunner's mates, quartermasters, and ordinary seamen and firemen. The last two rates were called "strikers" because they were working, or striking, to become proficient in a specialty rating. In addition to these rates, there was also a pharmacist's mate, radioman, radarman or two, a yeoman, two cooks, and two stewards.

At battle stations, the diving officer—usually the engineering officer—was stationed in the control room to supervise the dive and relay orders to the diving station. Most of the other officers, especially the commanding officer, were busy in the conning tower handling the approach and attack, coordinating information, working the Torpedo Data Computer, and generating the navigational plot.

Enlisted personnel also were part of the tracking and fire-control parties and handled sonar and radar. Quartermasters recorded information and kept the logs; torpedomen manned the torpedo rooms; and all men without regular battle station assignments turned to for torpedo reloads. Machinist's mates and electrician's mates, who with torpedomen made up the bulk of the crew, handled chores related to diesel and battery propulsion and electrical functions. Telephone talkers relayed orders and information through the ship. Their job was an important one; those not in the conning tower were dependent on them to form some idea of what was going on outside the hull.

All hands except the captain and executive officer stood standard Navy watches of four hours on and eight hours off, depending of course on where and how they were operating. The work was incredibly demanding. During an approach and attack of many hours' duration, everyone on board was seemingly on watch or at battle stations continuously.

◆ ◆ ◆

The *Gato*s were long, slender, beautifully proportioned vessels that to this day still impress with their functional good looks. Builder's photographs taken of the *Rasher* in Lake Michigan in the spring of 1943 bear this out. She lies low in the water with a 12-foot, 5-inch freeboard at the bow, 3 feet at the stern. Limber holes forward give way to one long, graceful opening over the curve of her ballast tanks starting at the conning tower and running aft the length of her superstructure, a different look altogether from the boats built at Portsmouth, New

Hampshire, and Mare Island, California, which had large, multiple, horizontal perforations to allow free flooding of the superstructure.

Some wartime publications listed the *Rasher* and her sisters as "Repeat *Albacore*-class" submarines rather than *Gato*s. That unusual classification ("group" rather than "class" would be more accurate, as the *Albacore* was herself a *Gato*) was a misnomer caused by the Navy's constant modifications to specifications.

Topside, the *Rasher's* conning tower underwent several changes. Photos taken when she was on the builder's ways show a streamlined fairwater with a smidgen of tumble-home (not unlike the sails on modern nuclear boats) but with holes in the fairwater for the outdated and soon to be eliminated glass viewing ports called "bull's-eyes." Later, her fairwater was cut away fore and aft to reduce her profile in the "covered wagon" style and to accommodate 20- and 40-millimeter guns. Photos taken of the *Rasher* after her 1944 Hunters Point refit show that radar antennas and other gear were repositioned abaft the periscope shears as new equipment was added, while the SD radar mast became free-standing. Her *"Trigger*-style" bridge modifications enhanced personnel protection and provide a good example of changes dictated by experience in action.

Also, in late 1944, her high-pedestal "pea-shooter" 3-inch deck gun mounted forward was replaced by a Mark-17 5-inch/25 wet mount installed aft. For years the Navy's General Board resisted heavier armaments to dissuade submarine skippers from engaging in gun battles with the enemy. Wartime experience proved them wrong; surface gun engagements played a major role in submarine operations late in the war. And as boats returned from war patrols, other features once thought to be essential to a fighting submarine—the main ballast tank flood valves, the bridge steering station, marker buoys, propeller guards, ship's boat, periscope cladding, and much more—were eliminated, too. Despite the changes the *Rasher* underwent during the war, she remained a handsome-looking ship in every respect.

The *Rasher*'s maximum designed speed was 20 knots on the surface, 9.5 submerged. And while her maximum designed operating depth is not listed in the Characteristics Card, it would be well documented during her eight war patrols that she could dive far below 400 feet. To allow for even deeper diving, submarines built beginning with the *Balao* (SS 285)-class had even stronger pressure hulls (so-called "thick-skinned" boats) than did the *Gato*s. In fact, postwar data proved conclusively that the change from the 11/16-inch mild steel hulls in the *Gato*s, to the 7/8-inch high-tensile steel in the *Balao*s would have allowed the *Balao*s to dive to 925 feet without fear of hull collapse.

Even so, being rather conservative in matters of safety, the Navy set the *Balao*s' official operating depth at 450 feet. But because the Bureau of Ships normally designed submarine hulls with a safety factor of 2 1/2, the *Rasher* and submarines like her could have dived safely to more than 600 feet. In fact the old *Salmon*, launched in 1937 and restricted to a maximum operating depth of 250 feet, reportedly descended to 600 feet to escape a severe Japanese depth-charging off Kyushu during her eleventh war patrol. This matter of deep diving would figure prominently in the *Rasher*'s fifth war patrol.

With a full load of 89,362 gallons of diesel fuel aboard (118,000 for wartime patrolling, when a main ballast tank group would be converted to fuel ballast tanks), the *Rasher* had a cruising radius of about 13,500 miles. Thus, boats of this class could operate thousands of miles from their bases on the Japanese side of the Pacific. Her fuel consumption at maximum speed was 18 gallons per mile.

Finally, the Characteristics Card includes a list of small arms. Along with the .30-caliber Browning machine guns and Thompson .45-caliber submachine guns (two of each allotted) is a High Standard .22-caliber pistol. Indeed, the fleet-type boats were well designed and fully equipped for the war of attrition the Navy would have to fight.

The *Rasher* would be under the command of thirty-nine-year-old Comdr. Edward S. Hutchinson, a veteran submarine officer ordered to Manitowoc from the *Grampus*. He had skippered that submarine on three war patrols. On one, the *Grampus* sank an 8,636-ton Japanese tanker that managed to fire a few rounds from her deck gun in protest as she went under. (His hometown newspaper, the *Philadelphia Evening Bulletin*, reported his exploits under the dramatic headline, "SUBMARINE HERO ESCAPED SHELLS.") "Hutch" was 5-feet, 9-inches tall, with a stocky build and full, expressive face. He came from a well-to-do Philadelphia family. His proud mother told how as a youngster, Edward sat enraptured at the feet of a family friend, Adm. Richard P. Hobson, listening to stories from the Spanish-American War. Now he had his own to tell.

The *Rasher*'s other commissioning officers were: Lt. Comdr. Stephen H. Gimber, executive officer, and former engineering officer of the *Trigger*; Lt. Comdr. Ellis B. Orr, engineering officer; Lt. Theodore F. Grefe, torpedo and gunnery officer; Lt. William E. Norrington, first lieutenant and communications officer; Lt. (jg) Arthur Newlon, commissary officer; and Ens. Peter N. Lober, assistant engineering officer. With few exceptions, they were very young.

Most of the *Rasher*'s commissioning crew—her "plank owners"—had assembled in Manitowoc about mid-November 1942. Norval Wilson, a thirty-three-year-old chief motor machinist's mate, was the first man to report for duty. There were a total of seven officers and sixty-seven enlisted men, including seven chief petty officers.

Upon arrival in Manitowoc, some of the sailors with families moved into scarce government housing, while others rented apartments. Twenty-nine-year-old Pete Sasgen, the second man to report for duty, brought his family from Evanston, Illinois. Being a native midwesterner, he was not fazed by the snow, ice, and blustery weather of a Wisconsin winter.

Sasgen was a veteran submariner. He'd been in the Navy from September 1931 to September 1937, most of the time aboard the old *S 33*, based in Pearl Harbor. He was discharged as a machinist's mate first class at the Philadelphia Navy Yard and went home to Illinois. After working briefly for the National Biscuit Company as a machinist, he took and passed the test for a job as a fireman and was soon a tillerman on Evanston's big American-LaFrance hook and ladder truck. The day the war broke out he was lounging in the firehouse, feet propped on a chair as he listened to the Chicago Bears beat the Chicago Cardinals at Comiskey Park, when he heard the chilling, "We interrupt this program to bring you a special news bulletin!" He was stunned; being familiar with Pearl Harbor, he thought it impregnable. By spring of 1942, the Navy desperately needed experienced submariners, and over his wife Isabelle's vehement objections he reenlisted as a chief machinist's mate, USNR.

Single enlisted men like Dean Brooks, a radioman third class, and eighteen-year-old Robert "Feets" Mathewson, a fireman third class (and future *Rasher* Fuel King), lived in a drafty Navy barracks that was part of a factory that made 20-millimeter shells. A boatswain's mate who was the master-at-arms held reveille every morning with the help of a trained black bear. "Boats" was a former circus performer who had been called up from the reserves and had brought his ursine companion with him to Manitowoc. Even after the men had been out late at their favorite hangouts, such as the Five O'Clock Club, The Pit, and the American Legion bar, the bear never had any difficulty getting the sailors out of their racks in the morning, Brooks recalled. Mathewson said he would never, ever forget having a bear's hot, foul breath in his face at the crack of dawn.

Before the *Rasher* was launched, her future crew members had the opportunity to see her being completed on the building ways and watch the workmen installing the torpedo tubes, decks, and other gear. They could also watch this work being done nearby on her sister ships, the *Redfin* and *Raton*. It gave them an appreciation for the complexity of a modern submarine and the sheer amount of labor involved in its construction.

After she was launched, the *Rasher* was moved to the outfitting docks near the warehouse on the other side of the Soo Line bascule bridge spanning the harbor. Once there, pipefitters, electricians, installers, shipfitters, and mechanics set to finishing her up with such loving care and attention to detail, one would have thought they were her crew. Scaffolding was erected around her conning tower, welding lines were snaked aboard, temporary ventilation ducting was installed, and more gear was deposited dockside. Her huge batteries were lowered in place (as a safety precaution the Manitowoc boats were launched without their batteries) and her engines buttoned up. Lights blazed twenty-four hours a day on the dock and above and below decks. Tools were everywhere. Her teak decks were partially laid over the perforated superstructure even while large access patches were still open in her hull to allow bulky equipment to be installed. The sound of power tools and the acrid odor of hot metal floated from the *Rasher* day and night.

Yet even in such a disheveled state—patchy yellow chromate paint here and there, ungainly exterior fitments sprouting from her topsides—there was no mistaking the *Rasher* for anything but the sleek and powerful warship she was. And though she and her crew were strangers, it would not be long before they got to know each other. She would come to life, her character would be formed, she would develop a soul like all ships do. A lifetime bond between sailor and ship would soon be forged.

The Navy's original plan was for Mr. West's submarines to be delivered to the submarine base at New London, Connecticut, by Manitowoc's civilian crews. There the freshly trained Navy crews would take over the boats and prepare them for sea. The outbreak of war changed that plan, however. Instead, it was decided to hold trials and train the submarine crews in Lake Michigan. The boats and their crews would then be delivered to New Orleans, and they would sail to Panama, receive further training, and head for the war zone. Despite the cold and the presence of fresh rather than salt water, the lake trials worked out well. With the building yard nearby, any repairs found necessary during shakedown could be undertaken immediately. And even though the crews could not work with torpedoes, they received rudimentary approach and attack training. More intensive training in

Panama with real torpedoes would follow. Small details like equipping an auxiliary vessel with submarine rescue equipment and negotiating with Canada to suspend treaty provisions that prohibited warships from operating in the Great Lakes were quickly worked out.

The Manitowoc commissioning crews arrived fresh from sub school, the fleet, or Navy technical schools where they had worked on trainers designed to teach them about shipboard submarine systems, radio, radar, and sonar. Still others had learned about air conditioning, refrigeration, and the like. Many senior petty officers had spent time at the various manufacturers' plants to gain firsthand experience with engines and propulsion machinery. Pete Sasgen not only had attended air conditioning classes at York, Pennsylvania, but also had spent two intense weeks in Cleveland, Ohio, at the General Motors Cleveland Diesel plant learning about the *Rasher*'s Winton engines.

After the *Rasher*'s crew assembled in Manitowoc, the leading petty officers organized their divisions and prepared the Watch, Quarter, and Station Bill, which set out each man's battle station and watch-standing responsibilities. The myriad personnel assignments aboard such a complicated vessel created dozens of problems. But they were quickly sorted out, and the *Rasher* began to take on the atmosphere of a functioning warship. Chief Sasgen described the activities:

> The crew was divided up into three watch sections and each section had similar duties. Now that the submarine was in the water, we could operate the diesel engines, charge batteries, and assume the normal duties as you would if you were out to sea. It was time well spent getting acquainted with the operation of fresh water evaporators, fuel and lube oil centrifuges, air compressors, ice machines, and air conditioning equipment. The crew worked diligently, studying the various manufacturers' manuals. It's surprising what can be done with a green crew in six months to make them a smooth operating team.

Day after day, dry dives and drills, starting with the simplest and working up to the more difficult ones, were held dockside until the *Rasher*'s crew was proficient in every phase of her operation. And while the men got acquainted with their boat, they also got to know each other. It was standard procedure to afford the crews an opportunity to go aboard the boats that were already completed. Thus, some *Rasher* sailors went along when the *Puffer* underwent trials in Lake Michigan to see how that boat was operated and organized.

Commander Hutchinson's daily reports detailed the myriad problems associated with recalcitrant equipment, parts shortages, missing gear, faulty workmanship, and disagreements between builder's representatives and BuShips over running design changes. For instance, when the time came to augment the ballistic protection around the bridge with Special Treatment Steel, both the plans and armor plating were missing. And when the decision was made to eliminate the external conning tower door, it was discovered that the welded patch would be impossible to position properly because reinforcing bracketry would interfere with equipment that had been installed months earlier. That modification was cancelled. Still pending was the delivery of chrome-plated cylinder liners for the four diesel engines. They were finally installed after the *Rasher* completed her acceptance trials. Obviously, there was a lot of work to be done.

Correspondence between the Supervisor of Shipbuilding and the Chief of Naval Operations dated 4 January 1943 outlined the inevitable delays in the *Rasher*'s completion date—first from March to April, then finally to June. The main problem was that work on her sister ship, the *Pogy*, which was scheduled to be finished first, fell behind; workers and equipment needed to build the *Rasher* were tied up with the *Pogy*. In fact, the entire 1943 submarine building program at Manitowoc had to be revised due to the limitations of the yard's production capacity. It simply could not turn the boats out as fast as BuShips wanted.

Nevertheless, with the yard working round the clock, fitting out was completed, and the *Rasher* was ready for trials on 1 June 1943. Cardboard protection covering the freshly laid linoleum throughout her compartments was removed. Cables and hoses were disconnected from shore, and loose gear was stowed. Books and manuals not already aboard were fetched from the *Rasher*'s office in the yard building. Prior to departure, Hutchinson and Weaver, the supervisor of shipbuilding, personally inspected all compartments. When they were satisfied, the special sea detail was stationed for getting under way. With expert use of rudder and props, the *Rasher* was maneuvered out of the small harbor, down river past the two railroad bridges, and into Lake Michigan. The Coast Guard cutter *Tamarack* accompanied her as a safety precaution. Manitowoc's builders, manufacturers representatives, and Navy officials were aboard the *Rasher* to observe and to lend a hand in the event something went awry.

Chief Sasgen described the *Rasher*'s first dive.

Trials included the first static test dive in fifty feet of water to ensure the ship was watertight at all hull openings and hatches. This was done by sitting dead in the water and opening the ballast tank flood valves and allowing sufficient water into the tanks until the sub slowly sank beneath the surface.

Further tests were conducted underway as in a normal dive, which was good training for all hands. It was a thrill to put the sub through its paces, especially when we went to flank speed. Finally, we took the submarine out to deeper water and made our test depth submergence to 312 feet.

To dive a submarine while under way on the surface, the large main ballast tanks and the special ballast tanks—bow buoyancy and safety—are flooded until enough weight is taken on to overcome the boat's positive buoyancy. To dive rapidly, a tank called the negative tank is flooded to provide instant negative buoyancy. Routine submerged operations are usually carried out with the boat in a state of neutral buoyancy, which is achieved by blowing negative tank shortly before reaching the desired depth. In that condition, depth is easily controlled by the diving planes and propulsion motors. Just as on the surface, horizontal maneuvers are controlled by the rudder. Vertical maneuvers are controlled by varying the angles of the diving planes and adjusting ballast. The bow planes influence depth, while the stern planes control angle. The effect of the diving planes is proportional to the submarine's speed.

To surface a submarine, water is blown out of the tanks through the flood ports by compressed air. Two sub-systems of the main 3,000-p.s.i. air system are used: the 600-pound main ballast tank blowing system and the 10-pound low-pressure blowing system. Safety tank, which is always kept flooded when submerged, is blown first to restore positive buoyancy. Blowing safety tank at any time immediately imparts positive buoyancy to the ship unless she is damaged and badly flooded. Next, bow buoyancy tank is blown to give the boat a rise angle. The low-pressure system, referred to as the "turbo blow," is used when the ship is surfaced. It completes the work of the 600-pound system and conserves high-pressure air. The turbo is used to blow the main ballast tanks dry when greater freeboard is needed; this reduces drag and increases the submarine's speed. The variable ballast tanks are not blown, since they control the submarine's overall trim.

In addition to their water ballast tanks, fleet boats like the *Rasher* had three fuel ballast tanks. Filled with fuel, they extended the boats' range by many thousands of miles. As with water ballast tanks, they had to be completely full for the boat to submerge. Hence, as diesel fuel was consumed, water entered through the flood ports to keep them filled. The fuel floated on top of the sea water and thus could be pushed up into the fuel intakes by additional flooding. A centrifuge removed any water in the fuel. After the fuel was consumed, the tanks were converted back to water ballast tanks and flooded or blown as required. When they were used as fuel tanks their flood valves were locked shut, the vents blanked off, and the tanks isolated from the main ballast tank blowing system until manually changed over to water ballast tanks. Miscellaneous tanks for battery water, torpedo alcohol, lube oil, sanitary discharge, and the like were located through-out the ship. But none were as voluminous as the main ballast tanks.

At sea, these manipulations of tankage and ballast were conducted either on the surface or while submerged, depending on the situation—whether the submarine was patrolling, attacking, or evading the enemy.

In Lake Michigan, the object of the static dive was to take on enough weight to submerge the *Rasher* to a depth of 46 feet so the tops of her periscope shears would be even with the surface, all the while keeping about 5 feet of water under her keel as a safety margin. It was, as Sasgen described, a standard test of watertight integrity for new submarines. The diving procedure itself was relatively simple.

On the surface, fully loaded with fuel, lube oil, fresh water, stores, and her crew, a typical *Gato*-class submarine like the *Rasher* displaced 1,806 tons. In this condition her draft was 17 feet, and the distance from the waterline to the tops of her periscope shears was 29 feet, 6 inches. In this condition the boat was in a state of positive buoyancy and her marked waterline was even with the surface. Because Lake Michigan's fresh water had a lower density than salt water, the submarine had been specially compensated and ballasted at Manitowoc with less lead.

To submerge, water would be flooded into the seven main ballast tanks as the air in the tanks was vented off. The tanks would hold a total of 359 tons of water. With her main ballast tanks full, the *Rasher* would displace 2,109 tons and draw 22 feet of water. Sitting 5 feet lower in the water, her decks almost awash, she nevertheless still would have positive buoyancy. Next, the special ballast tank group—safety and bow buoyancy—would be flooded to add 55 more tons of water. But even with this extra weight, she still would have enough positive buoyancy to keep her on the surface. Another 55 tons of water would be added to the variable ballast tanks. Using the trim pump, this water would be distributed evenly throughout the variable ballast tanks to maintain the boat's fore and aft (front-to-back) and athwartship (side-to-side) balance. With this added weight, the *Rasher* would slowly submerge to the proper depth.

Technically speaking, at this point the submarine was in a state of neutral buoyancy, hovering over the bottom. Any additional weight taken aboard would put her in a state of negative buoyancy, and she would continue to submerge until she came to rest in the Lake Michigan clay.

About to undergo the test just described, the *Rasher* lay to in the cold lake water.

"Standby to dive!"

The crew stood ready at their stations under the watchful eye of the Navy's experienced trial officers. Commander Hutchinson was ostensibly in command, but in the event of an emergency he could be overruled by the senior officers; after all, the *Rasher* was still owned by Manitowoc Shipbuilding, which was ultimately responsible for her safety and satisfactory operation. Hatches were dogged and all induction and exhaust valves were closed.

"Bleed air in the boat!"

Compressed air roared into the ship's compartments. Watching the barometer, the diving officer, Lt. Comdr. Burt Orr, held up his right hand, palm and fingers open. Abruptly, he clenched his fist and ordered, "Secure the air!" Immediately the stop valve was shut, cutting off the air, halting the rise in pressure.

The Hull Opening Indicator light panel mounted over the vent control manifold displayed a glowing green board. It was commonly referred to as the "Christmas Tree" because its red (open) and green (closed) lights showed the status of all hull openings.

The barometer was inspected. It registered about a half-inch rise in atmospheric pressure and, more importantly, held steady. The submarine and her welded seams were airtight.

"Pressure in the boat, Sir!" Hutchinson was informed.

The *Rasher* had successfully passed her first big test.

"Very well. Take her down!"

For real this time, rather than for a dockside drill, the klaxon diving alarm sounded twice, followed by, "Dive! Dive!" over the 1MC announcing system.

With that, Chief Torpedoman Tom Herrmann, the chief of the boat, yanked the vent control handles. The vents popped open with a *whoosh* of air escaping from the forward and after ballast tank groups. The rudder was already amidships, and the two engine order telegraph handles were pointing to "All Stop." Earlier, the maneuvering room had switched from diesels to battery propulsion when the *Rasher* had reached her diving position. Now she was stationary in the water.

As the air in the ballast tanks was displaced by water, the bow began to tilt downward. Orr, standing behind the bow and stern planesmen at the diving station in the control room, adjusted the boat's trim by pumping water into the variable ballast tanks so the *Rasher* would settle evenly fore and aft. The burble of water sluicing into the superstructure, then breaking over the decks and climbing the conning tower, drowned out the sound of venting and pumping. In the conning tower, Hutchinson "walked" the periscope around. He announced that both bow and stern were under simultaneously as the submarine settled. Gurgling around the conning tower gave way to the rush of water swirling into the bridge cavity and up the periscope shears.

"Secure flooding!"

The diving officer adjusted the ship's final trim with more pumping and venting until he and Hutchinson were satisfied. All compartments reported they were watertight except for a small trickle here and there around a packing gland or a valve that was not fully seated.

Hearing that, Hutchinson congratulated the Manitowoc shipbuilders and thanked them for a well-constructed ship. Then the *Rasher* was surfaced and taken into the deep-water test area off Sheboygan, Wisconsin, to make dives while under way, including the all-important one to test depth.

At Sheboygan, with just enough way on the boat to carefully control her descent, the *Rasher* was taken deep.

Tension in the boat was palpable as the needles on the shallow-water depth gauges slowly crept around and reached their stops at 165 feet. Attention in the control room shifted to the depth gauge mounted above and between the bow and stern plane wheels. When its sea valve was opened, the needle headed straight for the 300-foot mark, salt water depth to keel.

The pressure hull creaked and popped from the enormous physical forces at work on it. Before the dive to test depth, moveable battens marked with graduations had been installed athwartship and from the overhead to the deck in each compartment. Every fifty feet on the way

down, the battens were inspected as the hull was compressed and dis-
torted by the sheer weight of water. At 312 feet—test depth—it was
duly recorded that the pressure hull had compressed inward five-
eighths of an inch. When the *Rasher* surfaced, the hull returned to its
normal shape, just as it was designed to do. The tests were a complete
success.

There was no rest when the *Rasher* returned to Manitowoc. All
sixty-four cast iron cylinder liners in the four diesel engines had to be
replaced with the new chrome liners that had arrived. Also, the crank-
shaft main bearings had to be inspected. The chrome liners were a
design upgrade instituted by General Motors; the bearing inspection
was necessary because quality control problems at the bearing manufacturer's plant had led to scored and damaged crankshafts in other
submarines' diesels. Three work gangs labored around the clock to
tear down and rebuild each engine for the changeover and inspection.
The leading chiefs strained and sweated alongside the strikers.

With the engines back on line, drills and training resumed in Lake
Michigan non-stop. In lieu of torpedoes, the fire-control parties practiced shooting water slugs at the *Tamarack,* which always accompanied
the *Rasher.* Each of the ship's three sections had to be able to dive, trim
the boat, and operate her on the surface and submerged. The officers
had to be proficient in all phases of fire control, propulsion, navigation, and the like. As the grueling days wore on, the *Rasher* and her
crew developed that special rapport sailors and ships have with each
other.

The *Rasher* was officially delivered to the Navy on 7 June 1943. That
day, with officers from BuShips and Manitowoc Shipbuilding looking
on, she successfully passed her Dock Trial and Inspection, a rigorous
examination and performance test of all shipboard systems. As
expected, the diesel engines rolled over, fired up, and easily produced
full power; the electric motors functioned correctly on both generator
and battery power; engine induction and exhaust valves opened and
closed properly; bow and stern planes were tested and their operation
approved; air, hydraulic, electrical, refrigeration, water, and lube oil
systems all passed official scrutiny. The Navy's acceptance documents
praised the overall high quality of the *Rasher*'s construction, cleanli-
ness, and general condition.

Inspection complete, an AirMailGram setting out the Navy's official position regarding the new submarine was sent to the interested
parties:

JUNE 7, 1943
FROM: INSURV MANITOWOC WIS
ACTION: VICE CH OPNAV
INFO: INSURV WASH BUSHIPS COMSUBLANT—
                  USS RASHER—COMSUBDIV 162—COM 9
ACCEPTANCE RASHER ON JUNE 8 AUTHORIZED

INSURV was the Navy's Board of Inspection and Survey, which was in charge of supplying ships and materiel. The local board was now informing INSURV Washington, D.C., the Bureau of Ships, and Commander Submarines Atlantic that it was approving the *Rasher* for acceptance. Based on the information supplied by INSURV, the Vice Chief of Naval Operations authorized her acceptance.

On 8 June 1943, the *Rasher* was commissioned an active unit of the United States Navy. She was beautifully turned out for the ceremony, her black paint flawless; gear was properly stowed, bunks triced up, decks fresh from a clampdown, every compartment immaculate.

On deck, flanked by West, Commander Weaver, and the Right Reverend St. Clair, a local Protestant minister who offered the invocation, Commander Hutchinson read his orders and ordered the watch stationed. Then he addressed the crew, assembled dignitaries, and guests. Next, the commissioning pennant was broken, the union jack and Stars and Stripes were hoisted, and a band struck up the national anthem, followed by "Anchors Aweigh." Officers and enlisted men alike, standing in ranks, saluted the colors. Resplendent in their uniforms, they then assembled on the *Rasher*'s main deck and conning tower for the official commissioning photographs. Motor Machinist's Mate 1st Class Robert Rayl, posed with his young son, *Rasher* mascot Bobbie Rayl Jr., who was dressed in a miniature sailor's dress blues, complete with thirteen-button fly. Afterward, families and friends of the crew were treated to a tour of the ship, followed by a party at the downtown Elks Club hall. Many of the girlfriends who attended were destined to become wives of *Rasher* crewmen who would return to Manitowoc to live after the war.

After commissioning, the men moved aboard the *Rasher* permanently and began loading. Chief Wilson recalled being momentarily taken aback by the size of the task facing him and his shipmates:

When our food supplies and equipment were delivered to us on the dock, we all took one good look at this mountain that was twice the size of the ship. We all decided that the only thing expected of us was the impossible.

After three more days of outfitting, a mailgram was received by the commandant of the Ninth Naval District at Great Lakes Naval Training Center, near Waukegan, Illinois:

C O N F I D E N T I A L
FROM: CO USS RASHER
TO: COM NINE
THIS IS PARAPHRASE OF CO USS RASHER TWX MESSAGE 081755.
MESSAGE FOLLOWS:
ORIGINATOR CO USS RASHER. USS RASHER REPORTING FOR DUTY. SOPA MANITOWOC RECOMMENDS THREE DAYS FOR LOADING STORES AND EQUIPMENT. UNLESS OTHERWISE DIRECTED WILL BEGIN SHAKEDOWN AND TRAINING PERIOD 12 JUNE. COM NINE REQUESTED TO RETRANSMIT TO INFO ADDRESSES. COMMANDING OFFICER USS RASHER.

Via mailgram, Commander Hutchinson was announcing that his ship was ready for the final phase of her preparations for combat. SOPA (Senior Officer Present Afloat) was Hutchinson himself.

As expected, the *Rasher*'s final shakedown in Lake Michigan disclosed a few minor deficiencies. They were repaired when she returned to port. As problems both big and small were eliminated one by one, and as she became more and more familiar to her crew, the boat began to assume the feel of a seasoned naval vessel rather than a newly constructed ship.

The crew considered Commander Hutchinson an excellent skipper. He in turn showed great confidence in his officers and crew, often congratulating them on their performance. And he afforded his officers plenty of time to learn. For example, he gave each of them a chance in turn of seniority to take the conn when leaving and entering Manitowoc harbor, both in fair weather and foul. One such opportunity was not soon forgotten.

A junior officer, Lt. Ted Grefe, had the conn when the *Rasher* came in from exercises in the lake. To make a smart landing, all he had to do was reverse the props to slow down and stop and then, with a small change in rudder, put her alongside the pier.

Officers and enlisted men on the anchor detail forward could hear his order, "All back one-third," as she approached. Next they heard,

"All back two-thirds!" Instead, the submarine headed forward, straight for a mud bank at the end of the harbor. She seemed to pick up speed. "All back full!" Grefe bellowed. The *Rasher* speeded up some more. "All back emergency!" he ordered, to no avail. It was obvious the ship was going to run aground. The anchor detail braced themselves as she rode up on the river bank with a screech, damaging two forward torpedo tube shutters and packing the openings with mud and gravel.

Sure enough, the backing orders were being answered by ahead bells on the engines. A warning system designed to alert the maneuvering room to engine orders had been dismantled and reassembled improperly. No reprimands were issued, however. Instead, Hutchinson treated the episode as a learning experience. Since he and Supervisor Weaver were Naval Academy classmates, Weaver put the *Rasher* in dry dock that night and had the mud and debris cleaned out, the shutters repaired, and the boat back in the harbor the next morning ready to go. The engine telegraph warning mechanism was repaired, and nothing more was said about the incident.

After the *Rasher*'s commissioning, Isabelle Sasgen had gone home to Evanston. But to see her husband off to war, she returned to Manitowoc on 25 June and checked into the Hotel Manitowoc ("New and FIREPROOF"; room rate $4.00 per night).

Chief Sasgen suspected the *Rasher* was shipping out to Australia: most, but not all, of the Manitowoc boats went "down under" to SoWesPac. But nobody knew whether they were bound for Brisbane or Perth/Fremantle. Basing at Pearl Harbor was also a possibility. Knowing that the Navy censored the mail, he and Isabelle worked out a code that would at least give her a rough idea of where he was. It was simple: if he started a letter with "My Darling Isabelle," it meant he was in Brisbane; if he started with "Isabelle, My Love,"it meant Perth; if he started with "Dearest Isabelle," it was Pearl; and if she got a letter that said, "My Darling Wife," it meant a refit stateside. Now all she had to do was wait for his letters. And worry.

With final shakedown completed on schedule, the *Rasher* departed Manitowoc on 27 June 1943. Those men who wanted to could take leave to see their families before shipping out, then meet the ship in New Orleans. Many of them did.

To provide clearance under the low bridges spanning her route, the *Rasher*'s periscope shears, Kollmorgen periscopes, and radar masts were removed and securely stowed on deck in crates. Late in the afternoon of the twenty-seventh, after all the goodbyes were said and best wishes and good luck bestowed, the *Rasher* cleared the Manitowoc breakwater and headed south to make a brief courtesy call at Great Lakes, as had all the new boats.

At 0500 on the twenty-eighth, assisted by two tugs, she entered the Chicago River via the control lock at Lake Michigan. The tugs maneuvered her through the Loop (downtown Chicago's business district), then the trio headed down the Chicago Sanitary Canal to Lockport, Illinois. There the boat was eased into West's floating dry dock, built by Chicago Iron and Bridge Company. The fully equipped dry dock even had a crane to reinstall her periscopes at New Orleans. Secured to the stern of the dry dock was the *Minnesota*, a powerful 230-foot tow boat belonging to the Federal Barge Line, a subsidiary of the Inland Waterways Corporation. Then the "tow," as it was called, proceeded down the Illinois River to Grafton, thirty-eight miles above St. Louis, where it entered the Mississippi River. Spectators lined the bridges and river banks in cities and small towns like Peoria and Meridosia for the unusual sight of a submarine traveling on a river in a floating dry dock.

During the trip the *Rasher*'s crew remained aboard attending to various items of maintenance and small repairs. Workers from Manitowoc detailed to accompany the ship gave her hull a touch-up coat of paint while she was on keel blocks in the dry dock.

The only untoward event occurred when a chief electrician's mate was badly burned in an electrical cabinet fire. Hutchinson laid aft to the maneuvering room to look at the man's injuries, then radioed from the *Minnesota* to Cairo, Illinois, requesting a doctor meet them there. When the tow arrived, the physician came aboard and, after an examination, insisted that the chief come ashore for treatment. But being an old salt, the chief would have none of that. The doctor looked at Captain Hutchinson, shrugged, and went ashore without his patient. The tow got under way and headed south again.

An entry in the diary kept by Lt. William Norrington described a modern-day Huck Finn adventure:

> Arrived New Orleans after a swell, lazy trip down the "Old River." Ship was painted and cleaned up on the way down and we spent the rest of the time taking it easy.

It was 3 July when the *Rasher* arrived in New Orleans. She was refloated and her periscopes and radar masts were reinstalled and tested alongside the dry dock. Topped off with fuel, torpedoes, fresh water, and provisions, she was made ready for sea.

While this was being done alongside the pier at the Algiers Naval Station, Bob Mathewson and Merle Rosenbrook, a fireman third class, were down in the superstructure near the bow tracing the layout of topside equipment for their submarine qualification logs when someone—the culprit remained unidentified—accidentally opened the vent on one of the forward ballast tanks. Air whistled out through the vent risers, and the bow suddenly dropped, flooding the area under the deck where the two men were working. The upper and lower forward escape trunk hatches were open, and, despite the immediate danger to themselves, the two men managed to slam and dog the upper hatch. Had they not done so, the forward torpedo room would have flooded.

With everything squared away, and after the Shore Patrol delivered some of the *Rasher*'s sailors from the French Quarter, she cleared New Orleans on 10 July 1943. She made her first dive in salt water south of the fresh water line flowing into the gulf from the Mississippi. Panama was her next port.

Down Under

The *Rasher* got under way from New Orleans with the warning to beware of both German U-boats *and* friendly aircraft. Allied planes patrolling the Gulf of Mexico often shot first and asked for identification later. (The *Dorado*, a new submarine out of Electric Boat, would be sunk by U.S. aircraft off Panama in October 1943.) All friendly forces in the region were notified of the *Rasher*'s schedule and passage south, but the daily communiques sometimes failed to reach the air patrols, so the *Rasher* was ultimately responsible for her own safety.

Meanwhile, U-boats seemed to ply the Caribbean and the gulf from the southern coast of the United States to Panama with impunity. Their skippers were highly experienced and fearless; rumor had it that they even dared to come up the Mississippi River as far as Dalcour. And they were known to cut through the well-patrolled Straits of Florida that crooked around the Florida Keys and Cuba. So the *Rasher* navigated a zigzag course and doubled her lookouts just as soon as she cleared Port Eads, Louisiana. Her lubbers line was pointed due south through the gulf, the Yucatan Channel between Mexico and Cuba, and the Caribbean. The five-day passage transpired without incident, and a hundred miles from Panama, the *Rasher* met her escort.

The patrol craft accompanied her into the sheltered harbor at Coco Solo, where the submarine tied up at the naval base and took on 26,300 gallons of diesel fuel and 2,500 gallons of fresh water. As soon as this was completed, she was ordered to Cristobal for locking through the canal to Balboa, on the Pacific side.

Pete Sasgen recalled the last time he'd seen the Canal Zone. It was 1937, and he was aboard the *S 33*. Her commanding officer was then-Lt. Dick Voge, now a captain and ComSubPac operations officer. The *S 33*, on her way to the Philadelphia Navy Yard from Pearl Harbor for decommissioning, put into Colon with a bent port prop shaft sustained in a collision with a pier in San Diego. Limping along at three knots on one screw, Voge and his crew had jury-rigged a canvas awning as a sail to provide more motive power.

Just inside the breakwater at Cristobal, a pilot came aboard for the *Rasher*'s forty-mile-long canal transit. She anchored a short while in Limon Bay near the entrance to the canal (a perfect place for a swim) to wait while a battleship passed through. When it was her turn she was dwarfed by the 1,000-foot-long locks with their vaulting sides. After she completed the all-day passage she had officially passed from control of SubLant to SubPac.

The *Rasher* docked in Balboa, unloaded her war shots—torpedoes with live warheads—and in their place took on torpedoes with yellow practice warheads. Then she began a nineteen-day training period off Las Perlas Islands in the Gulf of Panama.

The weather was hot and tropically muggy. The work was exhausting. Training went on day and night and covered every aspect of submarine combat operations, from approach problems and man overboard drills to damage control, chlorine gas drills, collision drills, and gunnery exercises using helium-filled balloons for targets. Practice torpedoes were fired over and over at a small patrol craft that accompanied the *Rasher* every day and provided target services. The torpedoes surfaced at the end of their runs when the low-pressure flask valve opened and blew the water from the exercise head. A tug accompanying the *Rasher* recovered them. Later, in an anchorage, the torpedoes were winched aboard the submarine and the torpedomen prepared them for firing again the next day.

More bugs were eradicated, and the boat's systems and machinery got a thorough workout. More importantly, all hands learned from their mistakes. Taught by experienced men qualified in submarines, the new men quickly mastered the complexities of their profession. And little by little the days of drills had the desired effect. When the musical chimes signaled battle stations, they were manned and ready in record time. By the end of the training period every man aboard had developed the most important ingredient of submarine warfare: self-confidence.

◆ ◆ ◆

It was not all hard work. Occasionally there was time for a swimming call in Gatun Lake or around the offshore islands. And there was some serious fishing, too. The after capstan was pressed into service as a giant reel with heavy-duty tackle for trolling. One day a shark was caught, killed, and thrown to other circling sharks, which tore it to pieces. Suddenly, swimming was no longer popular.

Exercises were completed on 16 August. The *Rasher* went back through the canal to Coco Solo to be loaded. Then she returned to Balboa and, in accordance with her orders, sailed for Brisbane, Australia. There she would join other SoWesPac submarines, undergo a brief refit and combat indoctrination, then commence her first war patrol.

The *Rasher* and her crew were prepared for what lay ahead. To be sure, there was fear; fear of the unknown and of the Japanese who, to the uninitiated, seemed invincible. What was the enemy like? How good were their anti-submarine forces? How bad would depth-charging really be? Would they be able to take it? Each man harbored a fear greater than death itself—the fear of being a coward, of not being able to function under fire. As the men prepared to go to war with all the uncertainties and risks it held, the answers to these questions lay far over the horizon. The rigors of their training had imparted an appreciation, if not a full understanding, of the danger and the great physical and emotional stress they would face in combat. So they put their faith in themselves, in each other, and in Commander Hutchinson, who was the personification of the prewar-trained submarine skipper. He was experienced, self-confident, demanding of performance, and genuinely concerned for the welfare of his crew, officer and enlisted alike. More importantly, he was combat-tested and had the respect and trust of his men.

The days and nights of hard work and intimate contact had had its effect; the *Rasher* and her men were now one entity.

Unrestricted Warfare

On 7 December 1941, there were about fifty-one U.S. submarines, both fleet types and S-boats, in commission in the Pacific. Some were in the Philippines, some on practice war patrols near Wake Island. Still others were in Pearl Harbor, or on their way to it from the States.

The submarines were at that time divided between two commands: Submarines Scouting Force Pacific Fleet—later to become Commander Submarines Pacific (ComSubPac)—with headquarters at the submarine base at Pearl Harbor, and Submarines Asiatic Fleet—later Commander Submarines South West Pacific (ComSubSoWesPac) — headquartered on board the tender *Canopus* in Manila Bay. The big problem both commands faced was that since its creation in 1903, the submarine force had no combat experience; it had never sunk a ship in anger.

With the outbreak of hostilities, the fleet commanders at first envisioned a submarine offensive founded on a prewar strategy designed to destroy enemy warships. Unfortunately, this strategy relied upon a tactical doctrine thrown suddenly and horribly out of date by the vagaries of geography in the western Pacific and by an enemy whose combat forces were widely dispersed and not disposed to conform to the Navy's assumptions about their units' strength, motives, and abilities. It was immediately obvious that new and completely different methods would be required to win the war against Japan. It was essential that the Japanese home islands and Japan's widely dispersed military units be cut off from the supplies needed to sustain them. Therefore, the United States placed the highest priority on the destruction of Japan's merchant fleet. The destruction of her navy would play a decidedly secondary role in the overall submarine strategy.

To effect the changes in tactics as quickly as the situation dictated was simply not possible because there was no previous experience with war patrols of this nature from which to draw. Submarine doctrine, expounded year after year in peacetime, was based on the precepts of caution and reserve, the reliance on passive sonar, minimal periscope exposure, and the firing of torpedoes from deep submergence. These were methods that would, if used against the Japanese, result in tactical failure and the loss of submarines, though in late 1941 few naval officers realized it.

For starters, it was assumed that Japanese anti-submarine forces would compel U.S. submarines to stay submerged during the day while in enemy waters and permit them to surface only at dusk to charge batteries. At dawn they would be forced to submerge again. It was a given that patrol area coverage would be severely limited under these conditions. It was also assumed that it would be prudent to remain well away from any enemy coastline and that it would be necessary to operate at deep submergence in any area where enemy aircraft were operating. Since most peacetime training exercises had been based on these assumptions, most commanding officers were very cautious when conducting the pioneering war patrols. Additionally, early in the war, submarines were not equipped with radar, and there was very little experience with night surface attacks because peacetime safety restrictions thwarted any attempt to reproduce realistic conditions.

Said Admiral Nace,

> It was truly dangerous business to run around at high speed on a black night with all ships darkened, and no better way to measure distances than by seaman's eye.

So the early months of the war were a learning period. The submarine fleet commander at Pearl Harbor, Rear Adm. Thomas Withers Jr., quickly recognized the situation the submariners faced and did his best to get his boats ready for war by throwing away the doctrine book and urging his skippers to be aggressive and innovative.

It was also necessary to take another look at the commanding officer situation. The first submarine skippers who ventured into enemy waters were operating in an environment that was unfamiliar to them. The meager results of the first patrols created serious concern that the commanding officers were too old for combat operations.

In December 1941, the average age of a submarine skipper was about thirty-seven. As the war progressed the average age dropped dramatically. For example, Edward Hutchinson was thirty-nine when he commissioned the *Rasher* in 1943; two years later, Charles Nace took command of her when he was only twenty-eight. The fact that most skippers were older at the start of the war was simply the result of there being too few commands available and the amount of time required to attain the rank of lieutenant commander or commander required for submarine command. After the war started, the trend toward younger commanding officers was inevitable as the building program accelerated and as it became apparent that the physical and mental demands of combat—lack of sleep, climbing up and down ladders, mental fatigue and stress—took their toll on older men. And with younger officers in command of the boats there was a marked improvement in results and in the aggressive, resourceful manner in which war patrols were conducted. Ironically, had officers shown a proclivity for such a style before the war, they would have been severely censured, if not relieved of command. But in war, much that was carved in stone is quickly reduced to rubble.

It did not take long for the submarine skippers to discover the many faults inherent in their peacetime doctrine. Coverage by Japanese air and surface anti-submarine forces was not all-encompassing. This allowed the boats to stay on the surface longer during daylight hours, especially during transits to and from patrol areas, but even in the patrol areas themselves. The skippers discovered that Japanese anti-submarine tactics were often ineffective. Moreover, they found that submarine sonar could provide accurate target ranges—the distance in yards from the periscope to the target—without necessarily revealing the submarine's whereabouts to the enemy. The greatest discovery was that it was often easier to attack at night on the surface than submerged during the day. At night the targets were less alert and the submarine was hard to see. Staying on the surface greatly increased maneuverability and allowed the submarine to gain a more favorable initial attack position and, if necessary, a re-attack position. When it was prudent to submerge on a brightly moonlit night, sub skippers discovered that the targets could be seen very well through the periscope.

With this knowledge, submarine tactics gradually moved away from the prewar doctrine and evolved into to a more aggressive, wide-open style. And as each patrol revealed new discoveries and forced the skippers to develop new methods, the lessons were passed along to other boats.

The *Rasher* soon would epitomize this new doctrine.

The *Rasher*'s only contact during the three-week, 7,600-mile run from Panama to Brisbane was with a panicked American freighter that fired three rounds from its deck gun in her direction at a range of four miles. Farther south, a pair of abandoned barges drifting in the middle of the Mid-Pacific Basin provided an opportunity for gunnery practice. They proved immune to hits.

It was a long run to Australia, and careful navigation was required to remain within the moving submarine sanctuary, a rectangle fifty miles long and twenty miles wide in which the *Rasher* was ordered to steam. Accurate calculations of speed and fuel consumption were vital to ensure her arrival at particular points of her track at the proper times.

Adding to the complexity of the trip was the fact that she was a new boat. Despite the run from New Orleans to Panama, which provided her engineering officers with a base line for a fuel consumption curve, it was still a guess as to just how much fuel she would use getting to Brisbane. There were damn few fueling stations along the way.

The *Rasher*'s first official equator crossing took place submerged. The pathetic Pollywogs—sailors who had never crossed the equator—became bonafide Shellbacks and joined those who had been across the line. In Brisbane, they would receive their coveted certificates, decorated with languid, bare-breasted mermaids and signed by Neptunus Rex, proclaiming to the world in florid prose that they were now Shellbacks:

> To all sailors wherever ye may be (and to all Mermaids, Sea Serpents, Whales, Sharks, Porpoises, Dolphins, Skates, Eels, Suckers, Lobsters, Crabs, Pollywogs, and other Living Things of the Sea)

> Greetings:

> Know Ye That on this date, in Latitude 00000 and Longitude 100-05-00 there appeared within the limit of Our Royal Domaine, bound southward for the Equator, the

> U.S.S. RASHER.

> BE IT REMEMBERED That the said Vessel and Officers and Crew hereof have been inspected and passed on by Ourselves AND LET IT BE KNOWN By all ye Sailors, Marines, Land Lubbers and others who may be honored by his presence, that (name) has been found worthy to be numbered as one of our Trusty Shellbacks and duly initiated into the SOLOMN MYSTERIES OF THE ANCIENT ORDER OF THE DEEP.

> Signed, Neptunus Rex, Ruler of the Raging Main

During the passage to Brisbane, Pete Sasgen began his runup to the self-proclaimed title of Undisputed Cribbage Champion of the Southwest Pacific. He boasted that he'd never been double-skunked. There was a lot of good-natured ribbing about this. When he set up shop in the crew's mess with his cribbage board, pegs neatly aligned in their holes, only the dumb, uninitiated, or masochistic would dare challenge him; he was that good.

Plenty of hot, strong coffee, fresh baked goods, and thick steaks prepared on the electric galley ranges by Dave Brown and the other cooks made for a happy group of submariners. Chief Cook Dave Ball, reputed to have been at one time President Roosevelt's personal steward, worked the wardroom and kept the officers' Silexes bubbling between meals served on white linen tablecloths with real china and silverware.

Since there was always the possibility of encountering a Japanese submarine even in the Mid-Pacific Basin, the *Rasher* zigzagged at standard speed—about fifteen knots—when she was on the surface, day or night. Drills were conducted at all hours, and trim dives were made each morning. Trim dives allowed the crew to take steps to compensate for changes in the boat's weight and trim caused by the consumption of fuel, fresh water, the firing of torpedoes, or even changes in the salinity of the sea water. It was an important part of submarine routine because it kept the ship in the proper condition of buoyancy should she have to dive quickly.

The passage of the miles was marked solely by the change of time zones on the ship's chronometers. Otherwise the ocean's vast expanse seemed endless. The only adverse event was the weather. At first, the days were beautiful and balmy. But then the towering cumulus clouds changed to cirrus, or mackerel clouds, the kind that resembled wave-rippled sand on a beach. The old seafarer's proverb, "Mackerel skies and mare's tails / make tall ships carry low sails," held true for submarines as well. The farther south the *Rasher* worked, the uglier the weather turned. A storm front and heavy rain overtook her. Pete Sasgen noted,

> On the trip to Brisbane we ran into extremely rough weather. We were unable to sit down for chow. These were days when you got your sea legs. Most everyone got seasick but eventually got over it.

The wildly rolling and pitching decks forced many a man to make a dash for the nearest head or slops bucket. The sailors complained about having six meals a day—three down and three back up.

As the seas made up to Force 7, the *Rasher* was lifted to the tops of huge waves, where she hung suspended until she pitched over their crests and skidded headlong down into deep troughs, burying her bow up to the 3-inch gun. Then she would recover and lurch upward, shedding white water, beginning the agonizing climb to the pinnacle of the next wave so she could slide down its backside and crash into the valley again. The boat was nearly swamped by seas that roared across her deck and burst over the conning tower. Three engines were needed just to maintain speed and position. The main air induction valve below the conning tower cigarette deck had to be kept shut lest the intake piping and engine rooms be flooded. This made the diesels pull air, at gale force, through the upper conning tower hatch. But whenever seas threatened to swamp the bridge, the hatch had to be slammed shut to keep water from flooding the conning tower. The engines, deprived of air, pulled an ear-popping vacuum throughout the ship. Hardly a man could function under such conditions.

When darkness fell, the *Rasher* was virtually blind. Black mountains of storm-driven water rose up on all sides. It hammered in and out of the superstructure and pounded on the hull. There was so much sea return that radar was useless. Navigation was mostly guesswork. Watch-standing was nearly impossible. After a few days of this torment, the men were dazed and physically exhausted. A seasoned veteran suggested that seasickness was all in the mind, and that if a sailor could only see the moon and stars he would be cured. Hearing this wisdom, men sprawled in their damp, sour-smelling bunks just moaned.

Six hundred miles east of Rarotonga the weather finally moderated. The barometer's rise signaled good weather was on the way. Hot chow was piped down again three times a day, and clean dungarees, khakis, and hot showers had a revivifying effect. The ship settled into a normal routine once more, and everyone was glad to be back at work.

◆ ◆ ◆

After the *Rasher* surfaced from a trim dive one morning, word was passed from the bridge to test the torpedo firing circuits fore and aft, a routine procedure. Torpedoes are fired by compressed air. The inner tube door is closed, the tube flooded, the outer door opened, the impulse flask charged with air under very high pressure, and the torpedo is blasted out of the tube. The system itself, the safety interlocks and the mechanisms, is complex. The tests ensure that everything is working properly without actually launching torpedoes. They also exercise the fire-control party and torpedomen.

The bow tubes were tested successfully. But unknown to the torpedomen in the after room, there was pressure in the 300-pound impulse flasks of Tubes Nine and Ten when they were test-fired. The torpedo in Tube Nine was expelled; it smashed open the outer door and shutter and was gone. The torpedo in Tube Ten bolted, forced open the outer door and shutter, got jammed halfway out, and made a "hot run" in the tube, filling the compartment with choking blue exhaust smoke. The torpedo's turbine and props emitted a deafening shriek until the high speed governor shut them down. Total chaos ensued as shouting, cursing men reacted to the emergency. Not waiting for orders, the engineers rang up All Stop on the engine order telegraphs, then pulled a suction on the boat to ventilate the after torpedo room.

With the *Rasher* laying to in the heavy swell, Hutchinson rushed aft from the bridge to assess the situation.

Both outer doors and shutters were wrecked, the tubes flooded. A 3,000-pound torpedo with a quarter-ton of explosive was sticking out of the ship's stern underwater, jammed firmly in place by the ruined outer door. It could not be pulled back into the tube because there was no way to seal the tube and drain it. If the inner door was opened to attach handling tackle to the torpedo's afterbody, sea water would rush in and flood the compartment. The big question was whether or not the tin fish had armed itself. For that to happen, the impeller under its nose would have had to have been activated by forward motion through the water. The consensus was that, since the torpedo was facing aft, it probably had not armed.

The bow was flooded down to raise the stern, and the executive officer, Lt. Comdr. Steve Gimber, went over the side. He worked his way back to the unwelcome appendage and, using a hammer, drove a wooden wedge whittled from the ship's shoring lumber into the impeller so the torpedo could not arm itself. If the ship had to dive, only the massive bronze inner doors on Tubes Nine and Ten would keep back the sea.

Luckily, the torpedo from Tube Nine did not make a circular run back toward the boat—which it could have easily done had it damaged its rudder vanes on the sprung outer door.

The incident was certainly another learning experience. The trip to Australia continued at reduced speed.

◆ ◆ ◆

On 18 September, the *Rasher* arrived in windy Moreton Bay on the east coast of Australia. A pilot boat and escort greeted her off Bishop Island with fresh milk and ice cream, an amenity that few sailors other than submariners enjoyed when entering port. The pilot boat carefully nosed alongside the submarine's bow, being mindful of her fragile diving planes, and the pilot awkwardly jumped the seesawing gap between the two ships. Then he headed straight for the bridge to greet Commander Hutchinson. With a cup of strong submarine coffee in hand, he guided the *Rasher* the sixty-odd miles up the Brisbane River to the city of Brisbane and the sub base at New Farm Wharf. The *Rasher* had steamed 9,600 nautical miles from New Orleans.

When Hutchinson made his last position report the night before arriving, he requested the *Rasher* be berthed starboard side out, so the protruding torpedo would not come in contact with the pilings. When he warped her in, the line handlers on the pier looked the *Rasher* over as though she might blow up any minute. But more than one submarine had put in with a similar problem.

As was his custom, Capt. James Fife, commander of Task Force Forty-two, and his staff were waiting on the dock to welcome the *Rasher* and her commanding officer to Australia. Like a broken record, a Navy band assembled behind his entourage played "Waltzing Matilda" over and over.

Fife was as fine a submarine officer as there was. He had a reputation, however, for professional aloofness and personal austerity that bordered on the ascetic. He had formerly skippered the *Nautilus* and commanded the submarine school at New London. Presently he was boss of the largest concentration of submarines in the Pacific. Fife went aboard the *Rasher* for a tour and to size her up. Then he and Hutchinson repaired to his headquarters ashore to discuss the current situation in SoWesPac and review the *Rasher*'s operation orders.

Australia was unknown to nearly all hands except for Commander Hutchinson, and every sailor was eager to see real kangaroos. Aside from the United States, it was considered the greatest place in the world to rest up and refit during the war.

Because the layover in Brisbane was so brief, the *Rasher*'s crew was split in half and rotated on three-day leaves to the submarine rest camps. The camps were located on the east coast at the Sea Breeze Hotel, fifty-five miles south of Brisbane in Coolangatta, and Toowoomba, in the mountains northwest of the city. A new one was under construction at Redcliffe, a resort town to the north on Moreton Bay. Captain Fife wisely wanted to keep the submariners out of trouble by keeping them out of Brisbane. It was a brawling, hard-drinking town populated by U.S. Marines, feisty New Zealand kiwis, and Australian soldiers recently returned from North Africa who were fiercely protective of their women. Add to that combustible mix U.S.

submarine sailors, and the Navy discovered it was not unusual to have a murder or near-riot every day.

The Sea Breeze proved less than ideal. It was too cold to swim, since it was now late in the Australian winter. With little else to do, most of the bluejackets drank beer all day. The rest camps got their minds off the war and grueling twelve- to fourteen-hour days of work and training. But it did not take their minds off girls—or, rather the lack of them, the major problem with rest camps situated in the outback. Still, Fife believed that his brand of austerity, if carried over to matters of the flesh, would keep his submariners healthy and in one piece to fight the Japanese.

Meanwhile, a quick refit and repair job by the submarine base and the tender *Fulton* got under way. Brisbane had complete overhaul facilities for diesel engines, torpedoes, periscopes, and anything imaginable.

Dry docking was required to pull the dangling torpedo and to fix the damaged outer doors and tube shutters. The *Rasher*'s refit included, among other things, the installation of a much-needed conning tower air conditioning unit, which had not been ready in time for her departure from Manitowoc. A serious leak in the radar mast antenna trunk for the air search radar—called the "SD"—was also repaired.

More debugging was also necessary. In a blunt report to BuShips on 11 September 1943, Commander Hutchinson complained about training and azimuth troubles that plagued the periscopes. Both scopes were hard to rotate. He diagnosed the problem as improper bearing installation in Manitowoc, made worse during removal and reinstallation in New Orleans. As evidence, he noted that the barrels were fretted where they contacted the bearing collars. After the *Fulton*'s periscope shop worked on them, he reported that scope Number One, the search scope, was noticeably better, and that scope Number Two, the attack scope, though still balky, was "usable." While they were at it, the Submarine Repair Unit acid-etched both tubes to reduce their reflectivity. Properly tuned periscopes were absolutely vital to the *Rasher*'s combat effectiveness, even to her very survival. Knowing the schedule he had to keep, Hutchinson hovered impatiently over the refit crews.

After repairs were completed, the *Rasher* began three days of intensive combat indoctrination with a Royal Australian Navy corvette. Firing practice torpedoes in Moreton Bay afforded the control party an opportunity to further refine approach and attack techniques. The training officer assigned to the ship worked the men hard day and night. While the *Rasher* trained, underwater static sound tests were conducted with decibel meters to determine if any of her machinery was excessively noisy and might give her away to the enemy's sonar. The exercises also included depth charge orientation to acquaint the men with their effects. With a fully raised periscope showing a nice feather so the patrol craft could keep track of her, depth charges were dropped at a safe distance. *Ba-whoomp! Ba-whoomp!* At that distance, one man confessed, the explosions sounded more like someone was beating on a dusty carpet hanging from a clothesline than hull-busting depth charges.

After the exercises, the *Rasher*'s fuel tanks were topped off and provisions loaded. Into every nook and cranny were crammed canned goods of every description, while two tons of frozen stores were packed into the freezer spaces. At sea, fresh produce would be consumed first, since it would last only two weeks.

Hutchinson was extremely pleased with the crew's performance and the overall condition of the boat as they prepared to leave Brisbane. He called both "outstanding" in his final report to the commander of Submarine Squadron Sixteen, to which the *Rasher* had been assigned. So did her training officer. After his own inspection, Captain Fife declared that the *Rasher* had one of the best-trained crews he'd ever seen, and he especially praised their high morale and state of readiness. This was not just idle talk. Many submarines passed through Brisbane from both Pearl Harbor and the States. A lot of them were veteran boats, and Fife knew what traits to look for in a successful submarine crew. He saw them aboard the *Rasher*.

It was standard procedure to send new boats first into a patrol area that was less active, to give them a chance to get acquainted with the war, so to speak. But when an outstanding ship and crew came along, they got a hot area for their first assignment. The *Rasher* got the Makassar-Celebes area, one of the hottest.

Ambon-Bound

For the Japanese High Command's war plans to succeed, it was imperative that Japan capture Borneo, Celebes, Malaya, Java, Sumatra—the Dutch East Indies. With the U.S. Pacific Fleet crippled, the Japanese believed the United States would be too weak to crack the defensive perimeter they planned to erect around their expanded Empire. After the raid on Pearl Harbor, the rapid Japanese advance had pushed the Asiatic submarine fleet south, forcing it to abandon Cavite when the Philippines fell in the spring of 1942, then Surabaya, Java, when it too was overrun. Australia, with the sub bases at Brisbane and Fremantle, was the last refuge.

For the Allies in the southwestern Pacific, the battle was essentially to regain control of the Dutch East Indies and the Malay Barrier. Lose the Barrier, and Australia was in danger of falling. If it did, the Americans, the Dutch, and the Aussies would find themselves at the South Pole; there would be no place left to run. By mid-1942, the Japanese had conquered an area so vast—approximately 8 million square miles—it seemed to the Allies an impossible task ever to retake it. But the unique geographic nature of the region turned out to be a blessing in disguise.

While the Japanese controlled a huge area, little of it was actually land; most of it was water. To maintain their far-flung military garrisons they required a huge web of supply lines and fleets of merchant vessels to carry cargos. It fell to U.S. submarines to sink this merchant fleet by waging all-out, unrestricted warfare. That in turn necessitated deep penetration into Japanese-held waters throughout the South China Sea, the Philippine Sea, and the Flores, Java, Banda, Timor, Arafura, Celebes, Sulu, and a dozen other seas. It was essential that submarines penetrate the hundreds of straits and archipelagos scattered throughout Malaya, the Philippines, Borneo, and Java. And that was just for starters.

So it was that the *Rasher*'s first war patrol would be conducted in the Makassar Strait and southern Celebes and Molucca Seas. She had orders to sail from Brisbane on the east coast of Australia, attack Japanese shipping, and at the end of her patrol return to the big submarine base at Fremantle on the west coast.

The Makassar Strait lies between Borneo and Celebes, two of the largest land masses in the region. It extends about 450 miles from Cape Lojar in the southern part of Borneo to Mangkalihat in the north. The Celebes Sea lies between the northern Celebes and Mindanao in the Philippines. East of the Celebes lies the Molucca Sea. Because the Japanese convoyed thousands of troops and hundreds of thousands of tons of materiel throughout the region, these three bodies of water were rich hunting grounds for U.S. submarines.

◆ ◆ ◆

Freshly briefed on his patrol orders, Hutchinson went aboard the *Fulton* to draw charts of the patrol area from her stacks. Back aboard the *Rasher*, he spread them out on the wardroom table and with his officers had a good, close look at the area as he planned their first patrol.

The pale blue and dun-colored charts showed the area was dominated by Borneo and Celebes, the latter's peninsulas and capes reaching out into the Molucca Sea like the tentacles of an octopus. The officers noted the position of the 100-fathom curve and the wildly varying depths of water near hostile coastlines. There was a myriad of small islands to make patrolling hazardous and navigation difficult. Harbors and inlets were known to be infested with Japanese patrol boats of varying capabilities and armaments. Numerous enemy airfields had been hacked out of the jungle terrain; often their specific whereabouts were not known. There also were minefields to avoid. The captain stepped off distances with navigator's dividers: the patrol area itself could easily encompass a half-million square miles. And it held a lot of Japanese shipping.

◆ ◆ ◆

The directive to conduct unrestricted warfare issued by the chief of naval operations, Adm. Harold R. Stark, on 7 December 1941, meant that a lot of planning had to go into each war patrol.

Every submarine skipper hoped he would draw a "hot" area, one that would present the opportunity to attack plenty of Japanese convoys en route to or from the home islands and the conquered territories. Since the hottest areas had lots of targets, they allowed for a quick depletion of torpedoes and early return for refit. "Dead" areas offered fewer targets and sometimes required patrols of seventy or more days with less satisfactory results. But while the dead areas offered fewer opportunities to sink enemy shipping, it was demonstrated time and again that the skipper who combined imagination and skill with an aggressive style could, with luck, create success even there.

Setting out on patrol was as fraught with danger as was the patrol itself. On the run from Australia to the Dutch East Indies, a submarine might encounter enemy minefields, enemy submarines, air attack, and

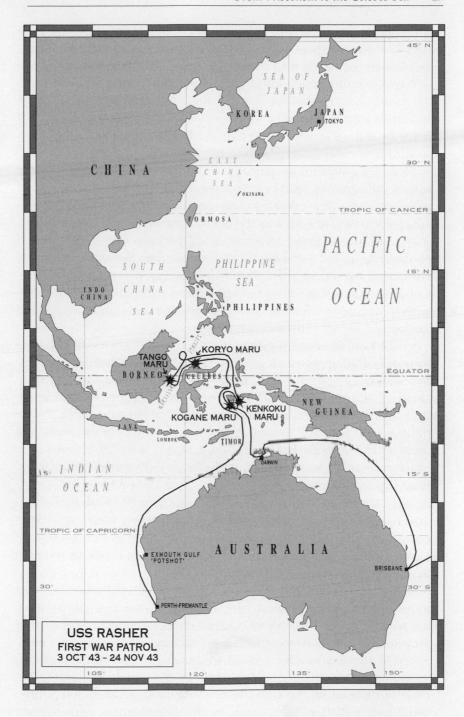

USS RASHER
FIRST WAR PATROL
3 OCT 43 – 24 NOV 43

anti-submarine surface patrols. Except in confined waters where anti-submarine activity was expected, transits to and from the patrol areas were always made on the surface at a speed that took into consideration fuel consumption, weather conditions, navigational hazards, and the scheduled arrival in the area. On the way, daily training exercises and drills were conducted and last-minute repairs were made so that the ship and crew would arrive in the highest possible condition of readiness.

Overall strategy for the patrol was planned well in advance by the commanding officer, usually in concert with his officers. Patrol reports from other boats that operated in the area were studied, and any pertinent information provided by the operations officer and his staff at the refit bases was reviewed carefully. The Operation Order itself, which contained specific instructions and sometimes certain restrictions, would be reviewed with the staff officers prior to departure. Commanding officers always hoped for a carte blanche "Op-Ord" with few or no restrictions, thus permitting maximum initiative and flexibility to adapt to the unexpected.

There were too many variables involved to develop a standard doctrine or operating procedure once submarines reached their patrol stations. Each area was different. Its traffic might be dominated by merchant vessels rather than naval units, or it might be close to, or far from, Empire waters. Among the variables the skipper evaluated were the extent of previous (or anticipated) anti-submarine measures, the depth of water where ship traffic was expected to be found (especially in coastal waters), locations of minefields, and the routes convoys had used in previous weeks.

With all these considerations and limitations in mind, each commander tried to place his submarine at the location where maximum contact could be expected. Setting aside the factor of luck, those captains who conceived the best coverage plan, and then pursued it aggressively, were usually the most successful.

Good patrol area coverage entailed operations within one or two miles of the coastline, usually the area where enemy ships traveled. Invariably, ships of all types hugged the shoreline to avoid being attacked. Patrol boats were stationed to seaward to act as a screen. Close to shore, ships were hard to detect because of background return on radar (called "grass" because of the jumble of green spikes that it produced on the cathode ray tube) and because poor sound conditions in shallow water made it difficult to hear the ships' screws.

To complicate matters, charts were often misleading or inaccurate, and navigational aids were nonexistent because the Japanese had removed them.

In areas of open ocean, plans for coverage usually began with a determination of which parts of the patrol area enemy convoys had crossed most frequently in the past. In some cases—say, Nagasaki to Shanghai, or Tokyo to Singapore—the route was obvious. But most areas required systematic effort to efficiently cover the most likely locations as early as possible before the Japanese realized a submarine was on the prowl.

In any case, it was absolutely essential to radio the earliest contact reports to headquarters for transmittal to other submarines so that they could also attack targets passing within their striking range. These basic tactics were the precursor to the formation of "wolf packs" later in the war.

In addition to meticulous planning and preparation, submarine skippers had another strategic advantage over the enemy: Ultra.

By May 1943, the United States had cracked both the Japanese naval and merchant marine codes. This code-breaking enterprise, known as Ultra (for ultra secret), enabled American submarines to be routinely deployed with very accurate information about Japanese convoys. Often, detailed descriptions of convoy movements were extracted from decoded radio traffic and passed on to submarines within minutes. Ultra even permitted headquarters to direct submarines to individual ships with great precision. In fact, many times submarines arrived at the precise locations given them only to miss their intended targets because of Japanese navigational errors. By estimating the location of the submarines and correlating the information with Japanese attack reports gleaned from their coded radio transmissions, it was even possible for ComSubPac to estimate the number of torpedoes left on board for use in future attacks.

The role Ultra played in the *Rasher's* overall success is impossible to gauge. While she was directed to specific targets from time to time, her commanding officers' skill in using the information they received when they engaged remained crucial. No matter how effective Ultra was as a strategic weapon, it had little or no influence on the actual attacks themselves.

The submarine attacks developed with the help of Ultra were later reviewed to evaluate strategic coordination (or lack thereof) between codebreakers and naval units on the scene. This evaluation was performed by the Submarine Operations Research Group (SORG) whose job it was to study intelligence and tactics, including enemy anti-submarine measures, to determine which ones were the most dangerous and which evasive tactics were best employed.

Until Ultra was declassified in the 1970s, there was still widespread belief in the romantic myth of the lone submarine sent to patrol enemy waters, searching for targets, trusting only to her wily skipper and plucky crew. Even the crewmen were ignorant of Ultra, though they suspected that sometimes something more than luck was at work. Ken Tate, torpedoman second class aboard the *Rasher*, recalled:

> I often wondered why we sometimes were in the right place at the right time. It's a big ocean. We never knew the U.S. had broken the Japanese codes. We knew of coast watchers, but weren't sure how the information came to us. Although, as soon as a radioman brought a message to the captain, things began to happen!

Without Ultra, the submarine war against the Japanese merchant fleet would have become a long, tedious process of hunting for *marus* (*maru* being Japanese for merchant ship) over an immense expanse of water, guided by planning, luck, and the hope that by criss-crossing enough square miles of ocean *something* would show up sooner or later. Nonetheless, Ultra was never a substitute for superior submarining, thorough preparation, and excellent search techniques.

◆ ◆ ◆

"All hands are aboard and the *Rasher* is ready in all respects to get under way, Captain."

The *Rasher* lay in the submarine nest, three boats outboard of the *Fulton*. Final preparations for departure were complete, and her diesels were idling. Hutchinson ordered the special sea detail stationed. He and Captain Fife were enjoying a final cup of coffee together in the wardroom prior to the traditional midafternoon departure for patrol when he got the report that the *Rasher* was ready to go. The two men finished, then went topside, where the lines had been singled up. Fife wished Hutchinson good luck and Godspeed, then saluted the colors and crossed the brow to the neighboring submarine. The lines were taken in, and the submarines, taking a strain on their capstans, breasted out to allow the *Rasher* to back clear of the nest into the channel. She squared away smartly and headed to sea for the long run to Darwin on the northern coast. Aboard was a civilian pilot who knew the vicissitudes of the Great Barrier Reef and the treacherous currents and shoals of the Torres Strait. The date was 24 September 1943.

Darwin, Australia, peacetime population 600, home of the kookaburra bird, was hot, dusty, and seemingly a ghost town of boarded-up stores. Stray dogs wandered the streets. Everything had a patched together, temporary look about it. On 19 February 1942, Japanese Vice Adm. Chuichi Nagumo—the same Nagumo who had directed the attack on Pearl Harbor—attacked Darwin with carrier-based planes from the Java Sea, sinking nearly a dozen ships in the harbor and destroying most of the shore installations. Thereafter, Darwin served principally as a forward supply base where submarines operating out of Brisbane could top off and take on torpedoes before shoving off on their patrols. It was not a place high on the Navy's list of favorite duty stations.

The *Rasher* tied up at the fuel dock in the wreck-strewn harbor, and her crew readied for their first war patrol in Japanese-controlled waters. Provisions were restocked; a full load of twenty-four torpedoes equipped with the troublesome Mark-6 magnetic exploders went aboard; big hoses were coupled to the deck connections and diesel fuel flowed to the transfer mains to top off tanks; spare parts were rechecked and reinventoried.

Some of the sailors who were not needed in work parties or were not standing watches were permitted to go ashore for a few hours, with the admonition to return in plenty of time prior to departure. When they did, Dean Brooks, radioman third class, found a surprise waiting for him and his buddies.

> When we got back to where we left the boat, we couldn't find it, and we thought they had shoved off without us until we found out they had a twenty-four foot tide in Darwin and the boat had dropped out of sight at the dock. What a relief!

Such extreme tidal oscillation was due to Australia's location in the Southern Hemisphere where the gravitational effects of the Earth, Moon, and Sun, the Southeast Trade Winds curling up over the equator, and the Southern Ocean Current that swept around the continent all exaggerated the tidal forces. The effect was especially pronounced in Darwin because of its narrow harbor. Though the deep water was ideal for anti-submarine netting, the Navy did not permanently base tenders, auxiliaries, or submarines in Darwin for fear that if sunk they would be impossible to salvage.

On 3 October 1943, the *Rasher* stood out on a slack tide, finally under way for the real thing. Bill Norrington put it succinctly in his diary:

"Departed Darwin for Japs."

◆ ◆ ◆

The *Rasher*'s Operation Order, Number 33-43, directed her to arrive off Ambon Island on 6 October 1943, after which she was to patrol throughout the Molucca Sea, southern Celebes Sea, and Makassar Strait. Her track was laid out parallel to longitude 130° E, running due north through the Malay Barrier between Babar Island and the Tanimbar Island group east of Timor. Once in the Banda Sea, a cut northwest would take her to Ambon, whose captured port was being used as a staging area for Japanese convoys passing through the Manipa Strait into the Ceram and Banda Seas on their way to the Philippines and New Guinea. After patrolling off Ambon, the *Rasher* was to track northward again to her primary patrol areas above the Celebes.

In Beagle Gulf, Hutchinson conducted brief training exercises with two Australian Navy motor launches. At precisely 1630, he released them, saying goodbye via blinker tube. With her escorts astern, the *Rasher* was on her own.

Bob Mathewson's feelings at that moment were typical of many young submarine sailors setting out on their first war patrols.

It was with a sense of anticipation on my part that the boat departed on her first patrol. I had turned 17 in November of 1941 and enlisted in the Navy shortly after Pearl Harbor with the feeling that I had to go soon or the war would be over before I would see action. So after being in the Navy for a year and and nine months, this was it!

The *Rasher* entered the Timor Sea and turned north to follow the rhumb line on the navigation chart in the conning tower. When Hutchinson was satisfied with the feel of his ship and the posture of his crew, he turned the conn over to the officer of the deck, signed his Night Orders book, and lay below to the wardroom for an early supper. The book was left on the control room worktable in plain sight for all watchstanders to read as needed to clarify the patrol parameters set by the skipper. In it he had specified course, speed, engine combination, explicit orders about what to do in emergencies or in case of contact with the enemy, and under what circumstances he should be called to the bridge. He reminded all hands to be extra alert, since they were now patrolling in enemy waters. Pete Sasgen described standard submarine patrol procedure:

> When on patrol runs, we generally cruised on the surface on two engines at 15 1/2 knots. The officer of the deck, quartermaster, and four lookouts were topside, with the lookouts stationed up on a platform in the periscope shears. Each lookout covered a sector of 110 degrees so there was an overlap of their areas. Many times we spotted the masts of ships over the horizon without seeing the enemy vessel. We also searched for enemy ships with radar and with a raised periscope. These three methods gave us full coverage.

Sharp-eyed lookouts with 7 x 50 binoculars were essential for submarine surface patrolling. They often sighted enemy ships before radar contacted them. Experienced lookouts could tell the difference between a dark cloud and a subtle smudge of smoke on the horizon from a hull-down *maru* stack. An alert lookout could spot floating mines and other hazards that were impossible for radar to detect. And lookouts frequently spotted enemy aircraft before they appeared on SD radar.

SD was an aircraft warning radar, its dipole antenna mounted on a extendable mast aft of the periscope shears. Because it was omnidirectional, the Japanese could easily home in on it; therefore, it was used sparingly. As a result, sometimes submarines were surprised by enemy planes no matter how good their lookouts were. While SD provided accurate ranges, it could not provide a visual display of an aircraft flying toward the submarine, or away from it. SD could only tell the radarman there was a plane out there somewhere.

The *Rasher*'s SJ radar was a surface search type first introduced to the fleet in August of 1942. SJ's rotating, solid parabolic antenna was mounted on an extendable mast that stood forward of the shears. SJ furnished accurate ranges and bearings on enemy ships and visually showed their size by the relative height of the "spike" struck on the unit's small A-scope in the conning tower. But it did not provide a complete picture of target disposition. (That feature would come later when submarines were fitted with a Plan Position Indicator, or PPI scope. Rather than just a jumble of electronic spikes, the PPI accurately displayed the target's position and size relative to the submarine.) SJ was also useful for navigation, especially near land at night.

In late 1944, ST periscope radar was added to the boats as they were refitted. It ran off the SJ's power supply and combined a miniature ultrahigh-frequency radar unit with the periscope's optics, providing very accurate target ranges and bearings.

Submarine radar was riddled with problems. War patrol reports abounded with descriptions of SD and SJ radar malfunctions and outright failures. In time, this engendered a healthy mistrust of the equipment among submariners. It made many a skipper rely instead on good, old-fashioned visual sightings to guide him, with only an occasional glance over the shoulder at the radar screen. Such misgivings were certainly justified. In the *Rasher's* case, the SD unit failed two days out of Darwin: a leaking antenna mast had grounded out the unit.

SJ radar was no more reliable than SD, perhaps even less so. It was designed to pick up targets at over 20,000 yards, or ten miles. Sometimes under ideal conditions it could even pick up land fifteen miles away. But frequent and damaging water leaks, range unit failure, blown vacuum tubes, electrical shorts, and the like prevented it from operating at full strength—if it operated at all. Consequently, targets were often difficult, if not impossible, to contact.

Part of the problem with SJ radar was heat. Sometimes the small fans designed to dissipate heat from the equipment would fail, and heat buildup would quickly prove fatal to other vitals. The radar gear itself was crammed inside long, rectangular metal boxes designed expressly to fit through submarine hatches and be mounted against the curved pressure hull of the conning tower. To repair the components, the radarmen had to draw the gear out of the boxes and go to work with circuit diagrams, load testers, flashlights, soldering irons, and other tools scattered on the deck, while keeping out from under the feet of whomever was conducting periscope sweeps. Sometimes the machinist's mates were called upon to manufacture whole new parts. Malfunctioning radar would prove to be a serious problem on all of the *Rasher's* patrols.

Using a high periscope to search for enemy ships during surface patrolling involved nothing more than keeping one of them raised. When fully extended, the head of the scope was nearly forty-five feet above the surface of the water, which enabled the periscope watch to see farther over the horizon than the lookouts could.

When an enemy ship was sighted by one of the three search methods—lookouts, radar, or periscope—the skipper commenced the approach phase. First he stationed the tracking party to plot the target's speed and course from the ranges and bearings as they were developed while the submarine closed in on the zigzagging target.

Next came the attack phase, during which the submarine reached her firing position and launched torpedoes. Pete Sasgen described the whole business in its most elementary form, including an exacting tactical maneuver and a vital shipboard problem-solver:

> Optimum attack position was ahead of the target, so we usually tried an end around and submerged to await the target's arrival. Meantime, we had our attack plan all figured out by the TDC.

While the submarine was "ending around"—getting ahead of its target—the Mark-3 Torpedo Data Computer was hard at work. The TDC was a mechanical, analog, fire-control computer installed in the conning tower. (There was so much equipment crammed into the conning tower that any space parceled out for humans to work in was a decidedly secondary consideration.) The TDC solved the complex trigonometry involved in tracking and attacking. And, unlike radar, it was extremely reliable. Older submarine officers such as Hutchinson were familiar with it from the days when they trained on the ARMA Corporation's Mark-1 models, installed, rather inconveniently, in the old P-class submarines' control rooms. This unwieldy arrangement forced the plotting party to shout back and forth between the control room and conning tower or climb up and down the ladder to relay vital information. In the *Rasher*, everything was in one place.

The TDC had two main components: the position keeper, which provided a continuous display of the relative positions of the target and submarine, and the angle solver, which generated the torpedo gyro angle. The gyro angle was the angle between the fore and aft axis of the submarine and the actual course the torpedo would take when fired. It was automatically transmitted to whichever torpedo room was doing the firing.

As the chase unfolded, the submarine's course and speed were fed into the TDC automatically from the gyro compass and the pitometer log, which displayed the ship's speed through the water. While the commanding officer observed the target, its relative position was determined from the bearing and range marked from the periscope by the assistant approach officer or, in surface attacks, by the Target Bearing Transmitters (TBTs) on the bridge. This information was fed to the TDC. The target's speed was calculated by intermittent observations as the submarine closed to her predetermined firing position. The target's course was obtained from the captain's determination of its angle on the bow, port or starboard. Even if the target was zigzagging, its base course could be figured out by Plot from all the bits of accumulated information. Nothing was left to chance. The skipper made vital decisions based on the information provided by his team in Plot and Fire Control. If everything went as planned, the torpedoes ran hot, straight, and normal. (Torpedo and exploder problems were another matter.)

Tactics for night attacks were similar to daytime, except that every effort was made to remain on the surface for better maneuverability and speed and to take advantage of the confusion that always erupted when a convoy was under attack.

Nevertheless, it was astoundingly difficult to bring together all the disparate and dynamic parts of the equation so the torpedoes—launched from a moving platform—would reach their intended target—also a moving platform—at the appropriate moment, detonate under her keel when influenced by her magnetic field, and blow the ship out of the water. When everything worked, it was a thing of beauty to behold.

In the Realm of the Enemy

The *Rasher* entered the Banda Sea, skirting the Tanimbar Islands. At dawn on 4 October, when she was just west of Banda Island and 130 miles from Ambon, SD radar (working once again) reported an aircraft contact, seventeen miles and closing fast. At approximately 200 miles per hour, the plane would be there in about five minutes. It had to be Japanese; there could be no other aircraft in the area. Hutchinson pulled the plug.

"Clear the bridge!"

Two blasts of the diving alarm resounded through the boat.

"Dive! Dive!"

The *Rasher* made her first dive in Empire waters.

Every man flew into action; no one had to tell them the enemy was boring in and that there was no time to waste getting the ship under.

The chief of the boat, his hands a blur, yanked open the vent valves. Topside, fore and aft, geysers of spray shot up through the slotted deck as the vents popped open on each ballast tank group. Since the *Rasher* had been "riding the vents," once the air pressure inside the ballast tanks was released, water quickly filled the tanks through the flood ports without the need to open flood valves.

The lookouts scrambled below. The officer of the deck, the last man down the hatch, held it shut with his weight by the braided copper lanyard while the wheel was spun to dog it.

"Hatch secured, Sir!"

"Flood negative!"

Pressure rose quickly as negative tank was vented inboard and air was bled into the boat from the air manifold. Negative tank's thirty-one tons of sea water started the *Rasher* down in a hurry. Already the bow was settling as water spouted through the bull nose.

The conning tower engine annunciators clinked over to "All Ahead Full." In the control room, a man stood by to operate the bow planes with the big chrome plated wheel the instant the "rigged out" indicator light came on. Another man took over the stern planes and immediately put them on full dive. As the ship tilted down, the planes begin to take effect .

In the engine rooms, all four engines were shut down by snapping closed the fuel shut-off valves. The sounds of the hammering diesels ceased abruptly. In the maneuvering room, the propulsion control levers were rearranged to put the battery on the screws.

The chief of the watch, stationed in the control room, waited for the engine indicator lights to go green, confirming that they were no longer pumping exhaust overboard. When they did, he pulled a lever to shut the thirty-six-inch main induction valve; it closed with a solid "ka-thunk." Then he reported, "Main induction shut! Green board, Sir! Pressure in the boat!"

"Eight-degree down bubble!" from the diving officer. The planesmen leaned into their wheels. An increasing dive angle was registered in degrees on the curved inclinometer.

Hutchinson asked what the airplane's range was before the SD antenna went under. "Fourteen miles and closing, Sir!"

"Very well. All ahead two-thirds!"

The *Rasher* had submerged in less than a minute. Her speedy disappearance allowed at least four minutes for her bubble track to dissipate and smooth out before the airplane reached her diving position. Good work!

Hutchinson ordered her down to ninety feet. The diving officer's litany continued until she reached it. "Easy on the bow planes! Blow negative to the mark! Shut negative flood valve! Passing six-oh feet! Ease your bubble!" He leveled her off at the ordered depth. "Nine-oh feet, Conn!"

The skipper acknowledged the report and kept the ship at that depth and on her present course until he was sure the plane had had time to pass clear.

An hour later he ordered the boat back up to periscope depth for a look around. Caution was in order. Not knowing what might be on the surface—or in the air—waiting for the submarine to show herself, the boat was carefully planed up, then held for a moment at eighty feet to check her trim so she would not broach when she came up to periscope depth. A 360-degree sound sweep indicated it was quiet all around; no enemy screws were in the area.

When the diving officer announced the boat was at sixty-five feet, Hutchinson motioned for the periscope to be raised. He grabbed its folded handles as soon as they cleared the well and snapped them down. When the scope popped above the waves, sea water streamed off the viewing lens, momentarily distorting the skipper's view. He focused, then draped himself over the handles and rapidly swept the sky for the plane and the sea for ships; he shortly announced it was all clear topside.

"Down periscope!"

Hutchinson decided to remain submerged during daylight hours for the next two days as they approached Ambon. If the Japanese were alerted to the *Rasher*'s presence, air patrols would be out from Ceram and Buru searching for her. Each night they would surface to shoot stars and accurately fix their position, charge batteries, and ventilate the boat. At dawn they would submerge again.

As they drew closer, the captain studied the charts spread out on the conning tower worktable in order to form a clear mental picture of the area into which he was taking his submarine. Mountainous Ambon was formed by the Hitu and the Timor Peninsulas, which were connected by a narrow isthmus. Between the two jutting fingers lay Ambon Bay, a deep natural harbor. On its southern shore was Ambon City, from which in peacetime were shipped the island's riches of mangos, cloves, and hardwoods, the last favored by cabinetmakers around the world. Hutchinson double-checked the depth tables in *The Coast Pilot* to see whether they were in feet or fathoms—an easy mistake to make, but one that could be fatal, since there would be no way to kedge off a reef or bar in those waters.

◆ ◆ ◆

"Control, prepare to surface!"

It was 1900. A periscope and sound sweep showed all clear. The control room watch stood by for the order to surface. The conning tower was rigged for red, with the captain, the officer of the deck, the quartermaster, and lookouts all wearing red night vision goggles. They had binoculars slung around their necks as they waited at the foot of the ladder leading to the bridge.

"Surface the boat!"

Three blasts of the klaxon, and high-pressure air roared into the ballast tanks. The *Rasher* shuddered and lurched up. As the depth gauges unwound, the diving officer shouted the readings up from the control room. "Four-oh feet, three-five feet, three-oh feet!"

Black and sinister-looking, the *Rasher* boiled out from under the Banda Sea. Water cascaded from her glistening decks and conning tower and poured from the limber holes in her superstructure.

Hutchinson ordered the hatch cracked; the quartermaster spun the wheel, undogging it. High-pressure air whistled out past the knife edge. When depth to the keel registered twenty-five feet, the conning tower was above the surface. The hatch clanged open, releasing a blast of air that blew back some of the water pouring in over the coaming, though most of it landed on the captain, darkening his khaki shirt. In seconds, he and the quartermaster were topside scanning the surface with binoculars.

"All clear forward! All clear aft! Lookouts to the bridge! Open the main induction! Start a low-pressure blow!"

On the surface, the *Rasher* wallowed in the gentle chop, her decks awash. From deep below decks came the howl of the turbos expelling water from her ballast tanks to put her in a higher, more seaworthy attitude for cruising.

Aft, first one, then two, then two more diesels rolled over, charged with high-pressure air from the starting bottles. The engines exploded to life, spewing exhaust smoke and cooling water into the sea from each muffler with the force of a fire hydrant. Three engines were shunted to a battery charge to make sure the boat had a "full can" for the next day's submerged patrol. Fresh air swooped through the ship, displacing the stale, sweaty, diesel fume-laden air from the long submergence. The annunciators clinked over to "Ahead One Third," and slowly the *Rasher* began to make way in the direction of Ambon.

On her bridge, the officer of the deck, quartermaster of the watch, and the lookouts searched for enemy ships. In the conning tower, the radar watch studied the spikes on the screen. Some were return from small islands eastward toward New Guinea; others were swift-moving rain squalls to the south. In the control room, the chief of the watch kept an experienced eye on things, as he received reports from various parts of the ship. Meanwhile, the navigator noted the *Rasher*'s speed and course, taking into account the local current drift; the engineers adjusted their machinery; the electrician's mates monitored the battery charge. Every man paid close attention to his duties; this was the real thing.

Meanwhile, Commander Hutchinson, still wearing red night vision goggles, toured his ship. In the forward torpedo room he found the sailors had painted eyes, teeth, and snappy messages on the torpedoes that awaited a Japanese target. In the booming engine rooms, the sailors communicated by shrugs and facial expressions that they were ready for action. Hutchinson nodded his approval and moved on. In the maneuvering room he conferred with the electrician's mates in the control cubicle, and farther aft, he talked with his torpedomen, who patted the tin fish affectionately.

Throughout the ship he found the men cocky and full of enthusiasm for whatever was to come. He noticed how the newer men hovered near their battle stations in anticipation of imminent contact with the enemy. The veterans were more blase; they knew better. It might be days before the *Rasher* encountered anything. The skipper told them all to relax: they had a long patrol ahead.

Satisfied with what he saw stem to stern, Hutchinson returned to the control room and climbed the ladders to the bridge, where he took up his binoculars and joined in the search for enemy ships.

The *Rasher* drove a little east of due north. But for the hiss and slap of water on either side of her bow, the submarine seemed suspended in a black void south of Ambon.

As planned, at dawn on 6 October, the diving alarm sounded two blasts and the *Rasher* submerged on station. Ten-mile-long Ambon was just visible in the haze off the port bow. The navigator's morning star fix confirmed their position at latitude 04° 42′ N, longitude 128° 15′ E. Hutchinson noted the time on the conning tower clock—they were right on schedule. Over the 1MC, he announced that they had arrived.

By day, periscope sweep-around revealed all manner of small craft—sampans, fishing trawlers, sailboats. They darted to and fro like water bugs. It was almost impossible to keep out of their way, and harder still to poke up the periscope without putting it through the bottom of a spitkit. From time to time a snooping sampan would drift near the *Rasher*'s submerged position and drop anchor. There was no way to know whether the natives suspected a submarine was there. Wary of them nevertheless, and afraid of being entangled in their fishing nets, Hutchinson maneuvered away, and that night the *Rasher* changed position to an area closer to the approaches to the Manipa and Kelang Straits.

For the next two days and nights, the *Rasher* patiently patrolled near the southern approaches to the straits, five miles offshore in deep water, assiduously avoiding contact with anti-submarine patrols that occasionally would appear without warning out of the surface haze. It was evident from the enemy's search techniques that they did not know the *Rasher* was in the area. The native sailors must not have known either, or by now one of them would have alerted the local panjandrums.

The Japanese patrolled in a completely haphazard manner, it was noted, stopping, speeding up, sometimes echo-ranging, sometimes not, and lying to for long periods for no apparent reason. Near Cape Hapale, the periscope watch spotted Japanese sailors swimming off the side of a patrol boat in their underwear, while their skipper relaxed on the bridge with his cap pushed back on his forehead, feet propped up on the bulwark, drinking tea and taking the sun. A shallow-running torpedo up against his hull would be one hell of a surprise, someone in the conning tower cracked.

While the *Rasher* patrolled submerged, the bathythermograph, or BT, was used to record underwater temperature gradient layers. Since the layers deflected sonar, it was essential for a submarine to know at what depths they could be found; a submarine could slip under them like a protective blanket, hidden from the enemy.

The effects of temperature on the transmission of sound through water were well known by the 1920s. But the equipment for measuring temperature gradients at that time was crude, complicated, and wholly unsuited for submarine use. Spurred by wartime research, the Woods Hole Oceanographic Institute in Woods Hole, Massachusetts, developed an easy-to-use temperature measuring device to protect submarines from enemy sonar. It utilized a stylus that traced a vertical wiggling line on a lampblackened card as it visually recorded every temperature change encountered during deep dives. The equipment saved many boats from destruction during the war.

At night, the bright equatorial moonlight in the Southwest Pacific made surface patrolling near land risky. SJ sweeps located many small islands scattered along the serpentine Buru and Ceram coastline, and strong electronic interference dancing on the radar scope indicated the presence of a powerful shore-based radar on Ambon. Also, Japanese coast watchers looking for submarines were known to be stationed on the beaches. Cautiously, the *Rasher* made her way north. But no ships worthy of a torpedo were to be found.

Hutchinson counseled patience as the *Rasher* passed through the Manipa and Kelang Straits at night.

At 0030 on 9 October, in bright moonlight and on a sea that looked like glass, a ship and her heavy smoke were sighted heading south. Hutchinson, notified, bolted to the bridge. With binoculars he could see her easily enough. She appeared to be unescorted. The skipper asked for the target's range and true bearing—the clockwise angle between the north-south line and the line of sight. "Range twelve thousand yards! Bearing three-five-zero degrees True!"

"Station the tracking party! All ahead full! Left full rudder! Come to course three-five-zero!"

The *Rasher* immediately responded to the rudder and engine orders by yawing around to her new heading.

The call to battle stations torpedo chimed mellifluously throughout the ship.

Excitement and anticipation were palpable; this *was* the real thing. In record time, one by one, each compartment reported it was manned and ready. (The swiftness of the response was not coincidental; as word of the contact had spread through the ship, the men had anticipated the call and were standing easy at their battle stations when it came.)

Charles Reuff, electrician's mate second class, was at his battle station in the maneuvering room.

> My battle station was on the port side of the control panel. Since our attack was on the surface, we were using four main engines. Once the machinist's mates gave the "ready light" for the engines, the electricians took control of the loading and the speeds. During a surface run like this there can be many speed changes, and it's important that the engines be loaded properly so as not to give off too much smoke that might disclose our position. Underload the engines and you get white smoke. Overload them and you get black smoke. Being in the maneuvering room we were in contact with the bridge at all times. Although we didn't know how many ships were out there, we knew what was going on.

Four main engines were rung up on propulsion. Their exhaust smoke unrolled astern as the *Rasher* headed for an attack position marked by a prominent "X" on the conning tower chart: this was where the Japanese vessel would be in about twenty minutes if she maintained her present course. With air howling through the main induction outlets in the engine rooms' overhead, thundering diesels deafening, the machinist's mates tending the engines communicated by hand signals.

The electricians at the control cubicle in the maneuvering room adjusted the control levers to bring the generators up to full voltage, paralleling them to increase their loading to the maximum. A turbo blow added half a knot to the *Rasher*'s speed. A roiling phosphorescent wake hissed out behind her.

To the sailors below decks, the roar of diesels at full song announced that the chase was in earnest.

Now Hutchinson's tactical skills came into play.

Since the target was steaming at nine knots, and with the range just under six miles, Hutchinson decided on a surface approach to overtake her as quickly as possible. However, with the sea placid and a bright yellow moon hanging near the horizon, the *Rasher* ran the risk of being sighted by the target's lookouts. Nonetheless, a high-speed surface approach afforded the skipper more maneuverability as he closed in. When the submarine was in position, he would submerge and attack.

Along with radar, the forward Target Bearing Transmitter on the bridge was employed during the approach. The TBT was essentially a pair of large, waterproof and pressure-proof binoculars permanently mounted in a set of gimbals attached to a stand that allowed training in any direction. When the user pressed a button with his thumb, a target's relative bearing was sent directly to the TDC.

The *Rasher* lunged ahead. When the range to the target had decreased to 10,000 yards, or roughly five miles, Hutchinson spotted another ship on the target's port beam. He identified her as an escort, type unknown. It was time to dive for the attack.

The klaxon sounded, the upper conning tower hatch thumped shut, and the *Rasher* submerged just off Manipa Light, the only navigational aid the Japanese permitted in the dangerous and cramped passage.

The diving officer brought the ship to periscope depth smartly, and Hutchinson poked up three feet of scope for a look. The conning tower was rigged for red, and to the captain's night-adapted eyes the moonlit surface of the sea was like daylight. The two darkened ships were heading directly for the *Rasher*.

"Range—mark! Bearing—mark!"

The periscope's built-in stadimeter gave a close approximation of the distance to the target by using her masthead height as a guide. "Six-zero-five-zero," answered the exec, reading from the periscope's range dial. Three and a quarter miles. The target's bearing was read from the periscope's azimuth collar on the overhead packing gland. "Three-five-oh, Captain."

"Down periscope! Make ready all stern tubes!"

At last the question of which torpedo room would fire the first war shots had been settled.

Hutchinson was reminded it was time for another look.

"Up periscope! Range—mark! Bearing—mark! Down periscope. What's his course and speed now?"

"Course one-six-five. Speed nine-and-a-half."

"Right full rudder, come to course one-six-five!

Well ahead of the oncoming ships, and on a normal approach course, Hutchinson maneuvered the *Rasher* to parallel the targets. Then he swung the boat to bring the stern tubes to bear on a 90-degree track.

"Up periscope!" The sheaves and hoist cables droned as the tube started up.

While Hutchinson gave a running description of the target, Plot studied ONI 208-J, the Japanese merchant ship recognition manual, looking for a ship that matched. A quick glance through the Identification Index, with its different stack and superstructure configurations, led to the right one. Another peek through the scope to confirm, and Hutchinson marked two pages that showed a 1,000-to-2,500-ton passenger-cargo ship with one funnel, high masts, and a composite superstructure. That looked like their target. The other vessel could not be identified. As Hutchinson watched, the target *maru*'s angle slowly changed, becoming more broadside to the *Rasher*'s stern. Unwittingly, she was setting herself up to be torpedoed.

"Down scope! Distance to the track?"

"Eight-double-oh."

To prevent the periscope and its feather from being spotted by the target's lookouts, Hutchinson made frequent, brief observations—five seconds and the scope was on its way down.

"Up periscope! Range—mark! Bearing—mark! Down periscope! Set depth ten feet!" Three stern torpedoes were set to run ten feet beneath the surface; their warheads would contact the *maru*'s hull just above the turn of the bilges.

Now the attack procedure gathered speed.

"Track angle?"

"Zero-one-zero."

"Gyro angles?"

"Three-two-three, three-three-one, three-one-zero."

"Match gyros aft!"

Knowing the track angle—the angle between the fore and aft axis of the target and the torpedoes' track to it measured from the target's bow—the TDC operator cut in the gyro regulator for the after torpedo room and checked to be sure it was indeed matched at the tubes and set into the torpedoes.

"Open outer doors! Standby aft! Standby Seven! Distance to the track?"

"Seven hundred."

"Up scope! This is a final shooting observation!"

The tube hummed out of the well as the captain squatted on the deck waiting to grasp the folded periscope handles when they cleared the opening. When they did, he rose with the scope, right arm now crooked over a down-folded handle. The atmosphere in the conning tower and throughout the ship was tense. The moment they had all trained so hard for had finally arrived. Every man held his breath as they waited to hear torpedoes scream out of the tubes.

Instead: "Target's zigged left! Damn it!"

The two ships had abruptly and inexplicably altered course to the east, ruining the carefully plotted setup. Had they spotted the periscope? Or had they merely executed a pre-planned change of course?

No matter. "Right full rudder! All ahead full! Make ready tubes forward!"

Hutchinson quickly swung the *Rasher* for a bow shot, but by the time she got around, the target vessel was too far away. The range was now 3,600 yards—more than a mile and a half.

Hutchinson was frustrated but not angry; he was too good a skipper for that. Instead, he ordered the *Rasher* to the surface to start an end around, the classic submarine attack maneuver.

Because the target's speed was slower than the *Rasher*'s surface speed (and if the enemy ships were also zigzagging off a straight baseline course they would take even longer to travel a given distance), the submarine could easily run around them to a position seven or eight miles ahead where she could lay in wait for their arrival. The run would require her to travel twice as fast and twice as far as her targets, but with speed on her side she could work around before daylight.

The engine room crews and electricians sprang into action. Within minutes they had four main engines on the line, the auxiliary on a battery charge, and 5 million watts of electricity from the generators ramming power to the screws. The wailing turbos had the *Rasher* high out of the water as she swung around hard to give chase at full speed.

Hutchinson kept the tracking party and sound-powered telephone talkers at their stations and had the rest of the crew stand down from battle stations. The cooks, anticipating the action to come, and realizing that meals would have to be grabbed on the run, had prepared huge platters of sandwiches and urns of hot, fresh coffee. But most of the men were too keyed up to eat.

Though radar constantly confirmed the target's presence out there, plodding along seven miles away on the *Rasher*'s port beam, the submarine ranged well to the south of the target, out of visual sight, and then ran southeast, parallel to the enemy's course. Working ahead of a target sight unseen required a sharp sixth sense and close concentration on the mechanics of the approach. As new data were passed to them, the tracking party adjusted their plot ever so slightly, marking and remarking the *Rasher*'s curving route on a navigation chart. The two tracks, the *Rasher*'s and the target's, converged at about latitude 03° 36′ S, longitude 127° 44′ E.

It was all business in the conning tower. The radar screen and TDC face glowed with green, orange, and red lights. The conning tower itself was bathed in spectral red from the night vision lights. It was warm, the atmosphere close. From topside through the open hatch came the thunder of diesel exhaust and the hiss of seas sweeping up the submarine's sides as she raced at twenty knots. Time stood still until the sky in the east brightened perceptibly. Then at morning twilight the convoy was located by its smoke.

"Battle stations torpedo!"

When the range to the targets had narrowed to 13,000 yards, the *Rasher* dove to start her run-in.

In the pale light of dawn, Hutchinson could see the ships clearly through the periscope. He got quite a surprise. What he had originally thought to be an escort was in reality a large freighter with black and gray dazzle camouflage paint. He asked for a look at ONI 208-J and, yes, she was identified as a 3,000-to-5,000-ton coal-burning freighter with high masts and a junky composite bridge: most likely a *Kogane Maru*-class freighter. Here was a golden opportunity to sink *two* ships.

"Bearing—mark!"

The assistant approach officer placed his hands next to the captain's on the periscope handles, guiding the engraved bearing mark around the azimuth ring, jockeying the periscope onto the enemy ships' position.

"Bearing zero-three-zero degrees."

"Range—mark!" The captain's hand fell to the range knob on the scope.

"Ten thousand yards."

"Down periscope!"

The *Rasher's* soundman reported he had picked up the slow beat of the enemy's screws. Hutchinson nodded, then consulted the target's plotted track relative to the *Rasher's*. He kept all of the information in his mind in order to form an accurate mental picture as the two Japanese vessels lumbered into torpedo range again.

The problem, as always, was to outguess the enemy and keep them in sight without being detected—no easy task. Not studying the situation carefully enough might prevent the skipper from catching some dodge they were employing to ruin the setup or, worse, endanger the submarine and her crew. If, for instance, he failed to detect a zig that put the submarine bow-to-bow with her quarry, there might not be time to go deep to avoid a deadly depth-charging. (*Marus* were known to be equipped with depth charges.) Conversely, a sudden zig away could put the targets out of reach again. The possibilities for disaster or failure were endless.

"Captain, enemy course is one-three-six, speed nine."

When Hutchinson was advised of the time that had elapsed between his periscope observations—about a minute—he acknowledged by motioning for another look. "Make ready bow tubes! Distance to the track?"

"Four-five-double-oh."

"Track angle?"

"Port one-twenty."

"Down periscope!"

Hutchinson planned this time to divide six bow shots between the two ships. Cheers broke out in the forward torpedo room, while in the after torpedo room, the men swallowed their disappointment.

When the moment arrived for the final shooting observation, Hutchinson squatted by the well as the oily tube whizzed up. The whirr of the hoists and the soft hiss of ventilation were the only sounds in the conning tower save for the quiet hum of the TDC's selsyn motors and cooling fans. Anticipation was palpable as the skipper made a quick sweep-around, looking for intruding enemy aircraft and ships. All was clear topside except for the unsuspecting merchantmen.

"Range—mark!" The skipper twisted the periscope range knob.

"Two-seven-double-oh."

The TDC operator cranked in the range and confirmed it was set into the TDC. "Set."

"Bearing—mark!"

"Zero-three-zero."

"Set!"

"Open outer doors! Standby forward! Standby One!"

When all the information was in agreement, the TDC's "Correct Solution Light" came on, indicating it was time to fire torpedoes.

"Shoot any time, Captain!"

Hutchinson laid the periscope's cross hairs on the first target's stack.

"Fire One!"

In the forward part of the conning tower, the firing key operator heard the captain's order to fire torpedoes. Six red lights, one for each of the forward tubes, glowed through their glass windows. Below them was a brace of six arming switches and a brass firing plunger. The sailor repeated the firing order into his sound-powered phones and whacked the firing plunger with the palm of his hand.

In the forward torpedo room, the tube captain standing between the two banks in the tube nest watched the firing panel, ready to launch the torpedo manually if the electric firing solenoid failed to work.

A rumble of water, a hiss of compressed air, and the 3,000-pound torpedo was ejected from the tube. Its turbine lit off with a whine like a buzz saw. The *Rasher's* first war shot was on its way to the Japanese.

Once clear of the submarine's bow and under its own power, the tin fish sought out its preset depth and course. The boat shuddered from the force of the ejection and the sudden loss of a ton and a half of weight forward. Interior air pressure rose sharply as the poppet valve opened, swallowing the air bubble inboard to prevent it from rising to the surface and giving away the *Rasher's* position. Sea water rushing back into the empty tube and through the open poppet valve was diverted into the drain tank in the torpedo room bilges. In the control room, the busy diving officer had to flood from sea to compensate for the loss of weight as each tube was fired so the boat would not suddenly rise uncontrollably and broach.

Back in the conning tower, the firing key operator got the report from the forward torpedo room: "Number One tube fired electrically!" Then he released the plunger and readied the next tube for firing. At ten-second intervals, two more torpedoes were fired.

"Shifting targets!" Hutchinson laid the cross hairs on the second ship, checked her range with a single sonar ping, then gave the order to shoot again.

"Fire Four. . . Fire Five. . . Fire Six!" Three more times the *Rasher* shuddered; three more times the deadly whine of high-speed screws, the momentary increase in air pressure.

"All torpedoes running hot, straight and normal," Hutchinson was advised by the sonarman. Stopwatch stems were thumbed to time the runs: a click under two minutes—a lifetime.

Every man in the boat urged the fish on to their targets. As they waited and listened, the torpedoes' piercing Doppler whine faded away, merging with the familiar sounds of the submarine's ventilators and machinery. In the conning tower, all eyes were on the stopwatches' sweeping hands: the wait seemed interminable. Impatient as anyone, Hutchinson motioned thumbs up for the periscope to be raised. When it broke the surface, he saw traces of blue exhaust smoke wafting from the six torpedo wakes as they fanned out toward the two *maru*s at more than forty-eight knots.

Precisely at the end of the first timed run, two geysers of water shot skyward from the camouflaged ship's hull. An instant later came two rolling thunderclaps that rocked the submarine and rattled china in the galley. The veterans confirmed that, yes, those were the *Rasher's* torpedoes exploding on the hull of Hirohito's ship! One torpedo broached, throwing off a splendid rooster tail, and then dove under the target; the other three also missed.

While the terror and destruction of the *Rasher's* attack were not recorded by the Japanese, it's possible to imagine what it must have been like aboard the *Kogane Maru*.

Perhaps the captain was studying a report from his chief engineer, about to turn his attention to his navigator's recommended course adjustment for a slant south-southeast to the Manipa-Kelang Straits. Suddenly, from the lookout on the starboard bridge wing, he would hear the panicked scream of *"TORPEDOES! TORPEDOES!"*

The captain bolts from the wheelhouse in time to see three frothy wakes heading straight for his ship. One of the torpedoes broaches the surface and throws up a trail of spray. Rigid with fear and disbelief, the captain watches the torpedoes run right up to the side of his ship. The first one tears open the *maru*'s hull under the captain's feet, the blast ripping off the bridge wing where he's standing, and part of the wheelhouse too. The torpedo that broached dives under the ship's keel. The third one blows up under the engine room. Debris rains down on the doomed ship and the sea around her.

Men working below decks are killed instantly by the concussions and by super-heated steam roaring from ruptured lines in the machinery spaces. Razor-edged shards of wrenched bulkheads and hull plating tear through compartments and upper decks. Watertight doors are blown from their hinges. Interior framing collapses. Instantly, the ship is filled with toxic fumes and thick smoke. Sea water bursts through the gaping wounds in the hull with such force it shatters bulkheads and drowns sailors before they can scramble topside. Only a few survive. Those that do, abandon ship by clambering down hastily unfurled cargo nets, or by sliding down lines, or by just falling or jumping into the sea. The men are covered with oily coal soot. Destruction is everywhere. They struggle to grab floating wreckage and hatch bails to save themselves. They get no help from their convoy mate, who opens fire wildly with a deck gun mounted on her fantail. The frightened *maru* skipper recklessly drops depth charges in an attempt to ward off further attack as he maneuvers frantically to escape. The depth charges explode under the *Kogane Maru*'s helpless sailors.

Through the periscope, Hutchinson watched the 3,132-ton passenger-cargo ship settle and sink under a huge cloud of black coal dust and boiling smoke. He felt no remorse. Where the enemy was concerned, in undersea warfare there was no place for pity. Instead, everybody on the *Rasher* was slapping each other on the back for a job well done. Some of the unseasoned submariners boisterously asserted that there was nothing to the stories they had heard about Japanese depth charges; their eruptions sounded like somebody was beating on that old carpet again. The *Rasher*'s own torpedo explosions had been much more impressive, they boasted. Those hands who knew better kept their opinions to themselves.

Hutchinson wistfully watched the other ship steam off at full speed unscathed. By the time the *Rasher* could maneuver for a new setup and stern tube attack, the *maru* would be in shallow water off Harta Wanu. When he was satisfied that the torpedoed ship would sink, he withdrew to deep water. A search by patrol craft alerted to the attack could be expected.

The sinking of the *Rasher*'s first Japanese ship was summed up in three terse sentences in Hutchinson's patrol report:

Just prior to firing, observed there were two ships and no escorts so used divided fire. Missed first ship. Sank second.

To Bob Mathewson, before this attack the *Rasher* was just a ship. Afterwards, his feelings about her, and no doubt those of his shipmates, changed.

From reading and watching movies I was aware that old-time sailors regarded their ship as "she" and as having a soul. After this attack, Rasher was no longer just a mass of steel and other materials, but seemed to gather a life of her own which I could now think of as "she" and refer to proudly as MY BOAT with a feeling of pride and accomplishment in myself and my shipmates.

Over the 1MC, Commander Hutchinson congratulated every man for his outstanding work and reminded them that they were now eligible to wear the submarine combat pin. The award was authorized whenever a submarine sank an enemy ship—naval vessel or merchantman—displacing more than 1,000 tons. It was a coveted decoration that veteran submariners wore with pride along with their twin dolphins. In just three and a half months from Manitowoc to Buru, the *Rasher* and her men were now combat-tested veterans.

Late that night Hutchinson radioed a contact report to ComSubSoWesPac detailing the attack on the *Kogane Maru*. Then he set a course for the shipping lanes north of Buru.

◆ ◆ ◆

"Captain to the conning tower!"

Four days later, on 13 October, the *Rasher*'s track had brought her south again near Ambon. She was patrolling submerged off the mouth of Ambon Harbor, the officer of the deck maneuvering carefully to avoid being set by the treacherous currents. At 1310, smoke was sighted coming out of the harbor. Shortly, four ships rounded the point: two tramp merchantmen with an escort on either beam. A float plane hovered over them protectively.

Hutchinson left behind the remains of his meal and took the conn. He ordered the boat planed up a couple of feet so he could see better, then examined ONI 208-J. Two profiles resembled the ships. Both appeared to be heavily loaded 3,000-to-5,000-ton freighters, each with a bulky stack aft. The two escorts could not be positively identified.

"Battle stations! Battle stations!" sounded over the 1MC. The convoy's track was quickly laid out, and the *Rasher* speeded up to begin her approach.

As soon as the convoy cleared the harbor and began zigzagging, the tracking party had the targets' speed, bearing, and other essentials worked out. Sound reported echo-ranging from the escorts. It could be heard faintly through the *Rasher*'s hull; it sounded just like the pinging from friendly destroyers so familiar from training exercises. But this pinging was anything but friendly. Six tubes were made ready forward.

"Enemy course?"

"Two six five."

"Using divided fire! Track angle to the first target?"

"Port one-zero-six, one-one-zero, one-one-three."

"Gyro angles?"

"Three-two eight, three-two-nine, three-three-oh." The torpedoes were spread to allow for variations in target speed and range.

"Match gyros forward!"

In short order, Hutchinson worked the *Rasher* into an attack position and fired three torpedoes at each of the merchantmen. There was the familiar shudder, the whine of turbines and props, and the momentary rise in air pressure as six fish blasted from the tubes.

Thirty seconds into the timed runs, Hutchinson motioned for the scope to be raised. No sooner had he oriented himself to the situation topside than he saw an explosion dead ahead of the *Rasher*'s bow. Either a torpedo had prematured, he reported, or the float plane had spotted the torpedo wakes and swooped in to attack, dropping a bomb. Whichever it was, the detonation shook the submarine violently from stem to stern and blasted water into the air, obscuring the targets.

Alerted that the convoy was under assault from the port flank, the near escort peeled off and charged the *Rasher*. She meant business. Black smoke belched from her stack, and a fierce-looking bow wave erupted below her anchors.

Knowing the Japanese skipper hoped to catch the *Rasher* near the surface and ram her, Hutchinson went deep and rigged for depth charge and silent running. Air howled into the control room as negative tank was vented inboard and the flood valve opened. Watertight doors were slammed shut and dogged; air conditioning compressers stopped abruptly; ventilation flappers snapped closed; the rudder and bow and stern planes were shifted from hydraulic to hand control;

every piece of unessential machinery was shut down to reduce noise.

The skipper ordered ahead full and the rudder hard right to twist away from the torpedo firing position. The bow and stern planes were cranked on full dive, clawing for deep water and the safety of a thermal layer to hide from the escort's pulsing sonar.

As the *Rasher* passed ninety feet, four sharp reports reverberated underwater—American torpedo warheads blowing holes in another *maru*. Next came the eerie crunching, shrieking sounds of collapsing bulkheads and buckling decks, and the crash of heavy cargo tearing loose as His Imperial Majesty's ship headed for the bottom. Inside the *Rasher* the *maru*'s death rattle was so loud and distinct it sounded as though the vessel was breaking up directly overhead. To the uninitiated it sounded for sure that the sinking ship would drag the submarine down with her to the sea floor two miles below.

There was no time to celebrate. Both escorts were now roaring in at full speed; short-scale pinging, thrashing propellers, and exploding depth charges obliterated the horrific screeching and popping of rending steel.

The depth-charge blasts were wide of the mark; still, the boat shuddered and rattled. Twenty-four of them were chalked up on the blackboard Pete Sasgen had installed in the forward engine room to keep count. The ashen-faced sailors would no longer joke about beating on carpets.

The *Rasher* was hiding under a temperature gradient, running silent, barely making steerage way. With the ventilation system shut down, heat from the motors, batteries, and electrical gear sent temperatures soaring throughout the boat. The air was close. Condensation dripped from cold sea water fittings. The conning tower, jammed with men, was especially hot and uncomfortable. Silence reigned. Time stood still.

The escorts churned overhead hunting for the *Rasher*, listening for a return sonar bounce from her hull that would divulge her whereabouts and invite a deadly rain of depth charges. But after twenty minutes the pinging slowly drifted off to the west and disappeared. The escorts had lost the scent.

An hour later a thorough periscope sweep disclosed a desolate seascape. The escorts were gone. There was not a trace of wreckage from the torpedoed 3,127-ton *Kenkoku Maru*, now on the bottom. Hutchinson waited another hour, then brought the ship to the surface to try and regain contact with the remnants of the convoy:

At 1818 surfaced and commenced working ahead for daylight position of target. Have strong suspicion convoy returned to Ambon, as
was only at deep submergence two hours, and I believe we would
have seen smoke from ships on our first look at 1718.

The search continued into the next day.

Underway, working ahead for estimated position of target.
Submerged at 0500. . . . Nothing sighted. . . . Gave up prospects of
relocating convoy so surfaced at 1759.

That night the *Rasher* received a radio message with her call sign,
N5GW, flagged with the Ultra prefix.

Surfaced, a submarine always monitored or "guarded" radio traffic
called Fox schedules, a system of serialized messages that were transmitted by ComSubPac from submarine headquarters. The submarine
maintained radio silence and acknowledged the messages only when
ordered to do so. Foxes were broadcast at varying times on different
frequencies from a network of relay stations in Australia, Hawaii, the
United States, and other locations to permit the boats to receive messages directed to them that they might have otherwise missed during
a prolonged submergence. This method thwarted Japanese radio jamming and ensured that the messages were received over the more than
64 million square miles of Pacific Ocean despite the unpredictable
nature of the ionosphere and its effect on shortwave.

Aboard the *Rasher*, special decoding wheels with a bewildering
labyrinth of cogs were fitted into the special ECM decoding machine.
The broken message, now in submarine English and on a long paper
strip, was immediately passed to the captain.

Hutchinson was ordered to proceed north to the Talaud Island traffic lanes, where a convoy was expected to pass south on or about 17
October. The Talaud group was 550 miles north of the *Rasher*'s present
position in the Philippine Sea. While the message was intended only
for the eyes of the commanding officer and communications officer,
scuttlebutt soon had its salient points racing through the ship.

No sooner had the *Rasher* come about to head for her new station
than two diesel engines faltered and lost power. Hutchinson took the
report in stride. He ordered the two good engines put on propulsion
and instructed his engineers to find and fix the problem as soon as
possible. They had a two-day run to the Talauds; then, if the convoy
was found, they would need all the power four engines could provide.

The breakdown was quickly traced to burned and cracked exhaust valves and seats in several cylinder heads that had overheated during the full-power end run on the morning of 9 October. Norval Wilson attributed the failure mainly to a design flaw in the General Motors diesels.

> The design failure started in Manitowoc but didn't get serious until we reached the combat zone. On older engines we had always set our exhaust valve clearances by hand. This system had been working well for many years. But GM had a "better" idea. They installed lash adjusters which were designed to keep the tappets at zero degrees clearance at all times. This system had never been properly tested. As a result we were busy around the clock changing burned-out exhaust valves.

The automatic lash adjusters did not allow sufficient clearance between the rocker arms and valve stems, which kept the valves from fully closing onto their seats. When the valve gear got hot and expanded, the condition was aggravated. In any internal combustion engine, gasoline or diesel, when the exhaust valves are held off their seats during the combustion cycle, the edges of the valves are burned away, actually losing material in the process. The valve seats, unprotected by the valves, then cracked from the heat of combustion. This in turn led to cracked cylinder heads and reduced power as the hot combustion gases escaped into the exhaust manifolds, and, if the cracking was severe enough, into the water passages in the head.

The difficulty of tearing down and repairing a big diesel engine aboard a submarine at sea was mind-boggling. To begin with, unless the repair was effected submerged, there were pitching decks to contend with. And the work had to be done in close quarters. Nevertheless, Chief Sasgen relished the task of pulling cylinder heads and regrinding the valves and valve seats.

> There was room for only one man between the curvature of the hull and the outboard bank of cylinder heads. When it was necessary to replace a head, I would go back there and break loose all the hold-down nuts. Someone else would loosen and remove the water and exhaust manifold bolts, the fuel lines, etc., until the cylinder head was clear for removal. I'd then go back by myself, raise the head up and over the exhaust manifold to someone in the center of the engine room. They would hand me a new cylinder head, and I

would lower it in place. Reversing the procedure, we'd get the head back in service.

Bob Mathewson wrenched his share of bolts, too:

> We had to do this one engine at a time, pulling the heads, performing the necessary repairs and having the engine ready to go on line by the next morning in case it was needed for a chase. [I] forget how many nights we worked on this, but the whole engineering gang was plenty tired by the time the work was completed. This was in addition to standing our regular watches!

While repairs were made the *Rasher* headed north through Molucca Passage to be in position to intercept the convoy.

She arrived on 16 October as scheduled and found nothing but sampans and sailboats. Hutchinson patrolled the traffic lanes from the Talauds to Djailolo Passage, and from Siaoe Passage to Halmahera. Then he moved on to a new position off the North Loloda Islands, and from there to the traffic lanes near Siaoe Passage and Manado, Celebes, all the while searching in vain. If there had ever been a convoy, it was gone.

The *Rasher* moved into the Celebes Sea and northern Makassar Strait with all four engines back on line. If Hutchinson hoped to find *marus* steaming for the home islands loaded to the gunwales with iron, tin, copper, and other vital materials dug from mines deep in the mountains of Celebes, he was disappointed. For ten days the lookouts saw nothing but a motley collection of converted yachts, sailboats, and assorted small craft. Some mounted large antenna arrays typical of anti-submarine pickets posing as fishing vessels. The *Rasher* assiduously avoided contact with them while she trolled the shipping lanes from Mangkalihat Point on the coast of Borneo to Balikpapan. Sometimes she even patrolled boldly on the surface in daylight in order to cover more territory. Sea birds, mistaken for flights of Japanese planes, occasionally sent the *Rasher* deep, but there was no trace of enemy merchantmen.

The men grew impatient. Now that they had had a taste of action, they were anxious for more. They used the slack time for routine shipboard maintenance, housekeeping, training, catching up on laundry, and studying their qualifications manuals and submarine course books. Pete Sasgen challenged all comers on his cribbage board. Morale was high; the *Rasher* was a happy ship.

That is, until one of the cooks, Dave Brown, seaman second class, made a revolting discovery. After rummaging around in the refrigerator for cold cuts, a chief petty officer came to Brown holding his nose. To Brown's dismay, 600 pounds of beef stowed in the freezer compartment was putrid. He had put a ration of the meat in the refrigerator to thaw so it would be ready for the weekly steak fry.

Shipping out with frozen spoiled beef was not an uncommon occurrence. When frozen stores were transshipped to Australia from the United States, they often underwent ruinous cycles of freezing and thawing between ship, rail car, truck, warehouse, and submarine. Sometimes the commissary and supply officers did not notice.

Brown and his mates had to unload the entire freezer and put the beef in weighted gunny sacks, fifty pounds at a time. The burned diesel engine exhaust valves came in handy for this ballast; broken cylinder head hold-down studs, tin cans, and other junk were thrown in, too. Then, while the *Rasher* lay to on the surface at night in enemy waters, all the sacks had to be lugged to the after torpedo room. The escape trunk—which also served as a convenient storage locker for potatoes—had to be cleared out so the rotting meat could be hauled topside and tossed to the sharks. As Brown pointed out,

> What did I know? It was on-the-job-training, cooking and provisioning for a submarine crew.

Nobody blamed the cooks, but chicken was chicken, not steak.

Days passed. The patrol area once so hot had cooled off.

Finally, on 26 October, the *Rasher* made contact with the enemy while she scoured the main traffic routes between Balikpapan and Truk and Palau. Hutchinson reported:

> At 2212 sighted ship position Lat. 0° 25' N., Long. 119° 23' E. Commenced approach. Sighted at 5400 yards by radar. Estimated course 230° T.—speed 14—angle on bow 50 P. Lost target while working ahead. Target was again picked up 20 degrees ahead of bearing showing a speed of 18–19 knots. Trailed until possibilities of intercepting target were exhausted.

> Then reversed course on a retiring search curve.

In his diary, Bill Norrington described the frustration of searching for an elusive enemy:

Finally picked up a target on radar, after ten days of inactivity. Target was very fast and couldn't be caught. Never saw it. Own sub, or very fast single tanker. Crossed equator headed south on submerged patrol. October 30 crossed equator going north. Seas very smooth with very little rain. Saw small patrol boat. Getting restless for some action.

Then, on 31 October at 1429, stick masts were sighted off the Celebes coast near Watcher Island. Hutchinson was summoned to the conning tower and battle stations were sounded. The TDC was already warmed up.

As the target hove into view, the captain described the ship as an old-style tanker with one stack aft. From the look of her, with her bow plowing low in the water, she was heavily loaded. ONI 208-J was no help when it came to identification; the tracking party could not find a profile that fit. Nevertheless, Hutchinson estimated her to be a 6,000-to-8,000-tonner, a true prize. She was heading north, most likely having set out from the port city of Palu, Celebes. To avoid submarine attack, the ship steamed inside the small islands that dotted the coast. She hugged the shoreline so tightly she ran the risk of running aground or fouling her water intakes in the shallows.

Like the approach on the *Kenkoku Maru*, this approach was complicated by a float biplane air escort that looked like a Nakajima E8N. From time to time the pilot set his craft down close to the tanker, then taxied and took off again to circle overhead. Hutchinson doubted the *Rasher* could get in closer than six miles for an attack without being seen from the air. So he decided to tail the target until dark, then surface and go in after it.

Five and a half hours later, it was time. The float plane had returned to its base at dusk; the target, now near Simatang Island off Dondo Bay, was unprotected. Three blasts of the klaxon; the *Rasher* surfaced and stood in.

Chester M. Kenrich, radar technician first class, was on the SJ radar. Something did not look right to him. He reported to Hutchinson that the target's radar pip was so weak that the ship either must be made of wood or was not as big as the captain estimated. Regardless, Hutchinson worked the *Rasher* into position to fire the stern tubes at her.

The target was tracking northeast around the hump in the Minahassa Peninsula, probably heading for the port at Manado. Before she drew abeam of the old Dutch coastal fort at Salumpaga, Hutchinson attacked. At 2204, three torpedoes streaked out of the after tubes straight for the target, which was just a dark smudge on the horizon. The fish ran hot, straight, and normal. As usual, the timed runs seemed interminable.

In his patrol report Hutchinson said,

> Two minutes and twenty-nine seconds after firing, a flash and explosion were seen from the bridge, and another about ten seconds later. Pulled out to a safe distance and was going over the approach, and had decided we had missed because time of explosion did not check with torpedo run. Commenced tracking for another approach on target.

Hutchinson dropped down into the conning tower to check things over. The explosions he described looked more like gunfire than torpedo warheads.

Suddenly:

> At 2215 O.O.D. passed the word that target had exploded and was in flames. We were about nine miles from the firing position, and the glare from fire illuminated the entire area. Fire with intermittent explosions continued until 2345 when target evidently sank.

Burning petroleum lit up the sea and sky. There were no longer any doubts about the torpedoes.

After the attack, Ken Tate, who had been up in the periscope shears as a lookout during the surface run-in, made this notation in the diary he kept stashed in his locker:

> Oct. 31, 1943: Battle stations. Made after tubes ready. Fired 3 fish, 2 hits. He fired his deck gun at us but none came close. Half an hour later heard a loud explosion and tanker we hit. . . burst into flames. About 500 feet in the air. First ship I saw sunk.

The ship he watched sink was the *Koryo Maru,* a 589-ton tanker whose small size explained the weak radar pip that confounded radarman Kenrich. The disparity between the *Koryo Maru*'s 589 tons and Hutchinson's 6,000-to-8,000-ton estimate demonstrated just how difficult it was to accurately identify ships and estimate their tonnage. It was a problem that bedeviled the submarine force until the end of the war. Many years later it would bedevil former submariners and historians alike.

◆ ◆ ◆

The *Rasher* moved about a hundred miles north, just above the equator, to continue her search for *maru*s in the Balikpapan-Truk-Palau shipping lanes.

At 0700 on 8 November, the *Rasher*, patrolling submerged, sighted the masts of a ship. Like so many of the vessels encountered in the coastal waters of the Makassar Strait, this one, a dilapidated tuna boat, proved upon close inspection to be too small to engage. So the *Rasher* sheered away to avoid revealing her presence.

At 1440, while Hutchinson was in the conning tower making a routine periscope walk-around, he sighted something. "Heavy smoke on the horizon! Range 20,000 yards! I can see her mast!" The target was bearing 194° True, with a sharp angle on the bow.

The gongs chimed battle stations, and the *Rasher* came to the heading that Plot quickly worked out for an interception. When the range closed to 15,000 yards, a conference convened over ONI 208-J.

On page 273 was a profile of an old-style tanker equipped with a high stack aft not unlike the *Koryo Maru*. ONI identified her as the *Tango Maru*, a worthy target indeed. Unlike the *Koryo Maru*, however, the *Tango Maru* rode high in the water, suggesting her cargo holds were empty. A solitary patrol boat was stationed about 2,000 yards off her port beam.

"Make ready stern tubes!"

The plotting and attack parties were by now a finely meshed team, and Hutchinson made a deft approach.

"Up periscope! Final shooting observation!"

Hutchinson flipped the periscope into high-power magnification and was catapulted onto the *Tango Maru*'s deck. He was face-to-face with a Japanese lookout wearing a yellow polo shirt and matching cap. The sailor raised his binoculars and seemed to look right at the American submarine skipper. But somehow the man did not see the *Rasher*'s periscope.

Without a moment's hesitation, Hutchinson fired a spread of three torpedoes from the stern tubes. The unmistakable whine of high-speed props resonated through the hull like musical notes as he watched their wakes streak for the target. The colorfully dressed lookout was still at the rail with his binoculars; he never even saw them.

Hutchinson was rewarded by two sharp explosions that blew the tanker's old-fashioned counter stern right off. The lookout had vanished—along with a sizable portion of the deck on which he was standing. The *Tango Maru* lurched around 90 degrees and stopped abruptly, steam whistle hooting frantically. Hunks of iron, splintered wood planking, twisted sheet metal, and sea water blown sky-high rained down, pelting the ship. The smoking, amputated stern bobbed oafishly alongside the mortally wounded vessel.

Hutchinson turned his attention to the startled escort, now less than a thousand yards away. She cut toward the *Rasher's* periscope at flank speed, bow wave growing larger by the second. The patrol boat was already dropping depth charges.

As the *Rasher* went deep, the sea erupted with thunder.

The submarine's deck plates jumped and rattled. Chunks of cork insulation popped from the hull. Dust motes and paint chips danced in the air. Pipes and gauges buzzed. Air manifold wrenches flew off their fittings and clattered to the deck. The entire fabric of the ship was under assault—every hull plate and frame, every bolt and weld. Less than an inch of tough Manitowoc steel protected the men from violent death.

However, the feisty escort's attack and search pattern proved to be uncoordinated and ineffective. After dropping fourteen depth charges (all duly noted on Sasgen's chalkboard) and pinging for the better part of an hour, the Japanese skipper gave up the hunt, and the *Rasher* crept away undamaged. The only noises the sound watch reported hearing were the snapping and popping of sea life. When Hutchinson surfaced the boat at 1839, not a thing was in sight.

To the bottom of Makassar Strait had gone the 2,046-ton tanker, *Tango Maru.*

The depth-charge attacks following the *Rasher's* torpedoing of the *Kogane Maru, Kenkoko Maru,* and *Tango Maru* were typical of Japanese anti-submarine warfare in late 1943: certainly hair-raising, but perfunctory.

Most convoy escort vessels were inadequately deployed for maximum effectiveness against submarine attack, and their crews were poorly trained in the techniques of anti-submarine warfare. Moreover, Japanese escort commanders had a propensity to give up on the attack too soon. Many submarines that were nearing the end of their endurance after a prolonged depth-charging managed to survive because the escort commander erroneously assumed the submarine had been sunk, even in the absence of proof in the form of wreckage or a telltale oil slick.

Other factors contributed to the amazing ability of American submarines to survive. One was the skills of the submariners themselves.

Another factor was the great strength of their ships' hulls and the high quality of their construction. Yet another was the use of bathythermographic recorders to locate sonar-deflecting underwater thermal layers.

Perhaps most important of all was the fact that the Japanese grossly underestimated how deep the boats could dive. Consequently, it was not until late 1944 that they set their depth charges for detonation below 200 feet.

Despite the tactical weaknesses of the Japanese anti-submarine forces, they sank at least half of the 52 U.S. submarines lost during the war. So they were not to be taken lightly.

Japanese depth charges, like their American counterparts, resembled twenty-five- or fifty-five-gallon oil drums and were packed with an explosive charge of 300 to 440 pounds of TNT. The detonator was set manually and activated by hydrostatic pressure. The depth charges, or "ash cans," as they were affectionately known, were dropped from racks on a ship's fantail. Some vessels were also equipped with single side throwers and Y-guns that used an explosive charge to launch depth charges to port or starboard, or to both sides simultaneously. These devices allowed an anti-submarine vessel to lay a huge saturation pattern of depth charges over a submarine.

The depth charge did not have to score a direct hit to mortally wound a submarine. If the underwater explosion was close enough— within fifty feet or so—the blast wave in an uncompressible medium like water exerted enormous force, enough to rupture the submarine's hull or damage her internal machinery. Unstemmed leaks from ruptured valves and pipes, sprung hatches, or packing glands could overwhelm the submarine's pumps and sink her. Damage like this, or a prolonged submergence during which the batteries and air were exhausted, would force the submarine to surface and slug it out with waiting escorts with her deck guns.

No matter how moderate or how heavy the assault, depth-charging was always frightening and perilous for submariners.

Pete Sasgen described what it was like:

> They were the one thing most feared by submariners. Our test depth was 312 feet, although many times we went deeper to escape the depth charges and sub chasers.
>
> Many times the depth charges were so close to us you could hear the detonator explode before the charge exploded. That is a close escape. A depth charge going off above the ship would cause it to descend twenty to thirty feet and, conversely, if it went off below the

ship, it would raise it twenty to thirty feet. Under these circumstances it was difficult to control the submarine, since it would be moving at a speed of only two or three knots to avoid making any noise.

While under attack you avoided all noise, sometimes rigging for silent running with all machinery shut down. When the depth charges went off, the noise was used to hide the noise of the sub, which would use evasive action. During silent running, no air conditioning was used, and temperatures in the boat would rise to 110 to 120 degrees.

At battle stations, Dean Brooks manned the underwater sound gear.

I could always tell the skipper when depth charges were coming as I could hear them arming themselves just before they exploded and could get the earphones off before they detonated.

Bob Mathewson sweated out the attacks.

Due to lack of ventilation and heat from the machinery, the temperature in the boat would become quite hot, and with nervous tension added in, everyone would be sweating profusely. I can remember times when our clothing was so soaked with perspiration that we were sopping wet—humidity would get so high that a dark, wet slime would condense on the decks.

We could hear the thrum and swish of the attacking vessel's screws as the noise carried through the water and the hull. I often observed that at this time, everyone's eyes would be following the sound of the attacking ship.

After each attack there would be a momentary feeling of relief that one had survived, but [it] would almost immediately be followed by the gut-wrenching tension of the next one.

When the enemy was evaded and the word was passed to secure from depth-charging and silent running, you had a feeling of being born again.

The *Rasher* moved to the middle of the Makassar Straits to resume patrolling. At 2230, in extremely bright moonlight that permitted almost unlimited visibility, two ships were sighted at a range of about nine miles.

Hutchinson turned the submarine toward the ships and stopped in order to determine their bearing and speed. They were on a base course of 225 degrees, making fourteen knots. If they were using a zigzag plan, it was too soon to tell how radical it was. SJ radar, which earlier had been working perfectly, was now inexplicably unable to pick up the targets. While the radarmen worked frantically to repeak it, Hutchinson stationed the tracking party, began an approach, and called the crew to battle stations.

At 2300, the officer of the deck sighted a third ship, hull down; from the size of her stick mast, it might be an escort. Hutchinson saw her, too. Because the moonlight was so bright—it seemed like daylight on the bridge—he knew it would be impossible to approach within two miles of the targets to take accurate radar bearings without being sighted. He decided to work ahead of the ships, submerge on their track at dawn, and go in. He ordered the crew to secure from battle stations and gave chase.

Two hours later, just as the *Rasher* was pulling ahead of her targets at a range of eight miles, another ship, not part of the convoy being stalked, was sighted bearing approximately 235° T. It was obvious that if the *Rasher* maintained her present course she would be sighted by the interloper as the two vessels drew abeam of each other on nearly parallel tracks. This newcomer called for a reappraisal of the situation.

Hutchinson clambered down into the conning tower to study the chart marked with the *Rasher*'s and the convoy's track. He stepped off the distances to the targets. He pondered the SJ's questionable reliability. He mulled over the unidentified ship and the convoy's relatively high speed.

To continue on the present course meant discovery; that was clear. If the *Rasher* dived, the targets would surely escape. To attack the interloper first meant losing the two primary targets; they would flee as soon as they spotted the flash of exploding torpedoes. Hutchinson decided there was no choice but to abandon the end around, reverse course back to the two targets and their escort, make a dangerous high-speed approach on the surface to get as close to them as the moonlight would allow without being seen, then dive for a quick attack.

The musical chimes and 1MC announced battle stations. It was hardly necessary; most of the men had never left their stations.

The *Rasher* pressed in on the targets' starboard quarter as close as Hutchinson dared—10,000 yards. With two blasts of the diving alarm he took her to radar depth—forty feet—a tactic that kept the SJ mast extended above the surface to take ranges and bearings while the boat was submerged. Any lingering doubt about the radar's reliability had to be pushed aside. One of the radarmen gave the set a loving pat as the submarine bored in.

"Up periscope! Control, make your depth four-oh feet!"

The periscope and SJ antenna slicing through the glassy Celebes Sea made a big feather, perfect for some alert Japanese lookout to spot in the moonlight.

As the attack party flipped through the recognition manual, Hutchinson described the two ships as large, unladen tankers of approximately 10,000 tons each. They were extraordinarily beautiful targets, but nothing in the manual quite resembled them. So be it. Plot had their course, speed, and tracks worked out. To everyone's relief, the SJ was working just fine; the radarman bent over the scope called out the ranges and bearings, while the captain ordered the *Rasher*'s last six torpedoes made ready—four bow and two stern.

As for the convoy escort, the moonlight revealed a graceful but menacing prow, laid-back stack, two armored gun mounts forward, and busy top hamper. The darkened ship appeared to be an Imperial Japanese Navy destroyer, not some second-rate patrol boat. Once her tubes were empty the *Rasher* would be defenseless, so a careful setup and escape plan were imperative.

As the range ticked down to 4,500 yards, Hutchinson dunked the radar mast; he continued boring in at periscope depth. At 4,000 yards the trio conveniently zigged 45 degrees to their left, putting the *Rasher* right between the two tankers for easy simultaneous bow *and* stern shots. The convoy gave no sign of having sighted the submarine's periscope in its midst.

"This is a shooting observation! Standby forward! Up periscope!"

Hutchinson laid the cross hairs on the left-hand target's stack. "Bearing—mark!"

"Zero-two-three! Set!"

"Range—mark!"

"Fifteen-hundred! Set!"

The Correct Solution Light came on. "Shoot any time, Captain."

At 0122 Hutchinson fired four bow tubes at the left-hand target, then the two stern tubes at the right-hand target. The periscope zoomed down, but Hutchinson ran it right back up to see the results. All other eyes were on the stopwatches.

Calmly the captain announced that the right-hand target had fired a signal rocket to alert the destroyer. Either the *Rasher*'s periscope had been spotted, or a lookout had seen torpedo wakes and sounded a warning; the four bow torpedoes missed astern of their intended target. With that, the skipper clanged the periscope handles up, ordered the scope down, and sent the boat deep.

Rigged for depth charge, the *Rasher* took evasive action. With the destroyer heeling around for a counterattack, there was no time to hang around to see the results from the stern tubes. The gush of flooding tanks, the roar of venting, and the shouted tangle of orders to the helm and diving planes drowned out everything else. Every man expected a terrific working over from the destroyer. But to their relief the Japanese dropped only a few distant, random depth charges; the destroyer's screws and echo-ranging rapidly faded away. An hour later, when it was all clear topside, the *Rasher* surfaced into a heavy rain squall. Nothing could be seen; no oil, no wreckage, no bodies, no survivors. Nothing.

Torpedoes expended, it was time to head for home.

Perth-Fremantle

Captain Hutchinson radioed a departure report to Fremantle, then turned the *Rasher* south toward Cape William for a high-speed run through the Makassar Strait. It would be tricky transiting the strait. The Japanese normally patrolled its great length and breadth carefully, hunting for submarines; and since the *Rasher* had put four ships on the bottom within the last thirty days, the Japanese Malayan command more than likely had redoubled the efforts to find her.

As was his habit, Hutchinson displayed practiced caution to avoid detection. Even so, on the night of 9 November, just south of Sabang Point, Celebes, the *Rasher* was spotted by a Japanese patrol boat that immediately came about and flashed the three dot, five dot command: "Identify yourself!"

Hutchinson instantly changed course to evade at high speed. To confuse the enemy, he ordered the quartermaster to return fake blinker signals. But the patrol craft's skipper was not taken in. Instead, he fired white illumination flares. When they burst, there off the starboard bow was a swift black submarine, hunkered low in the water. The loom of a searchlight reached out to finger her; 40-millimeter Japanese guns blazed away. The chase was on!

Hutchinson bellowed orders to his engineers. "All ahead flank! Give me everything you've got! To hell with burned exhaust valves!"

The motor macs massaged the governors to squeeze as much

horsepower from the thundering engines as they safely could. The electricians readjusted the load to coax an extra amp or two from the howling generators. A turbo blow was good for an extra half-knot. The *Rasher* was giving it everything she had—and then some. A look at the whirring propeller shaft tachometers revealed 342 turns, while in the conning tower the Bendix pitometer speed log stood proudly at 20.5 knots. But with the enemy on her tail, it seemed like she was standing still.

The patrol boat steadfastly held her position four miles astern, bearing two points off the starboard quarter. Persistent she was, matching every twist and turn and radical course change Hutchinson devised. For two hours she refused to give ground. But as the *Rasher* drew closer and closer to the treacherous waters of the mangrove-dense coast of Cape Laga, Celebes, the Japanese broke off the chase and disappeared into the dark. The *Rasher* had escaped.

Free of the patrol boat, Hutchinson took stock of the situation as they worked south again. Even though the *Rasher* was running at flank speed, it would be impossible to make Cape William and slip through the deep-water navigation channel on the surface before daylight. A daytime submerged transit meant the submariners needed to be extra alert for prowling patrol boats. But the bone-weary skipper and crew had had no sleep for almost twenty-four hours. So shortly after midnight, Hutchinson took the *Rasher* down to a hundred feet so all hands could have a good night's rest. Men not standing watches turned in for some sorely needed shut-eye. Exhausted as any man aboard, Hutchinson flopped into his bunk for a nap fully clothed.

For the next ten hours, as the *Rasher* crept south, echo-ranging antisubmarine patrols scoured the area. At 1035 the next morning, a routine periscope sweep sighted an elderly four-stack destroyer patrolling southward on a lazy east-west course across the *Rasher*'s track. With a destroyer in the area, Hutchinson quickly changed plans. He knew a revealing moon would be up when they surfaced that night. Rather than risk a confrontation with the tin can in the confined waters of Cape William, he decided to reverse course and go north around the Celebes mainland, then south through the Molucca Strait, more or less retracing their route from Darwin.

The *Rasher* surfaced onto a moonlit sea, the crew rested and in good spirits. A patrol boat was sighted at 2006; it took nearly two and a half hours to work around her. She disappeared at 2230, and the *Rasher* came back to a northerly heading.

Then at 0132 another patrol boat was sighted off the port bow.

Hutchinson's pithy comments about the encounter hardly convey how perilous it was.

> Reversed course, but he had sighted RASHER. Our only course to evade would take us south, so at 0215 made quick dive, rigged for depth charge, and silent running. From 0215 until surfacing at 2158, we furnished services to one "Nip" P.C. boat, who made excellent use of his sound equipment.

Immediately after the *Rasher* dove, the patrol boat found her. She circled overhead, firing single sonar pings, listening for a telltale return echo. Three hundred and fifty feet below, the *Rasher* crept along at her slowest possible speed—about a knot and a half, enough speed to maintain depth control under a convenient temperature gradient without making excessive noise. As usual, every nonessential piece of machinery was shut down to quiet the ship. The only noise the *Rasher* gave up came from a vibrating topside antenna or a belch from a stray air bubble trapped in the superstructure.

The men settled down to sweat and wait out the enemy, hoping that this guy, like so many of his counterparts, would prove to be impatient. If so, he would soon enough tire of the game and go away.

But this particular Japanese was in no hurry to leave. Instead, he employed a nerve-wracking waiting game. He knew the cardinal rule of anti-submarine warfare: Stay with the enemy.

An hour passed, then two, then three. From time to time the patrol boat chugged by overhead, as if to announce her presence. When she did, Hutchinson speeded up and changed course to put her astern and slip away. To his consternation, the Japanese would stop pinging, reverse course and take up his position again. Every time the *Rasher* seemed about to break away, the patrol boat was somehow able to find her and hem her in again. It was uncanny. The hours dragged by. This hold-down was unlike anything the sub's crew had ever experienced.

By 1400 the *Rasher* had been down for twelve hours. Carbon dioxide began a slow, insidious build-up, and the men labored for breath in the hot, foul atmosphere. The Higgins and Marriott test equipment revealed that carbon dioxide levels in the boat were rising inexorably toward the danger level of 4 percent. Two percent CO_2 would cause a man some discomfort if he undertook strenuous labor, but it was not generally noticeable under normal conditions. However, at 3 percent it was difficult for a man to breathe even when at rest.

Carbon dioxide absorbent, which soaked up the deadly gas on contact, was spread out on mattress covers slit open and stretched taut over bunks in the living spaces. Oxygen was bled into the boat from flasks in each compartment. But oxygen and CO_2 absorbent would not halt the deleterious effects of a poisoned atmosphere and approaching heat exhaustion; only fresh air on the surface would do that. The situation was tense.

As if the bad air and heat were not enough, another problem was developing aft.

Sea water was weeping by the stern tube packing into the after torpedo room bilges. If not stemmed, the added weight would require an ever-sharper up-angle on the diving planes and greater speed on the props to keep the boat from sinking deeper. More speed meant more noise from the motors and reduction gears—just what the alert patrol boat above needed. It would also increase the drain on the already partially depleted battery.

Normally, when submerged, excess water in the bilge sumps was sucked through the after drain line by the drain pump and discharged into the expansion tank, or pumped through the trim system into the variable ballast tanks. It was kept there so that any oil in the water would be held rather than discharged overboard and allowed to rise to the surface to give away the submarine's position.

In the *Rasher*'s present situation, pulling a suction on the line and moving the water from one location to another via the electric drain pump was out of the question; the enemy's sonar would hear the noise. In addition, it would deplete the battery. If the water level continued to rise, a bucket brigade would have to transfer the water to the forward torpedo room bilges to keep it from overflowing into the motor room bilges, where it could cause even more serious trouble.

When apprised of the situation, Hutchinson calmly ordered the leading chief in the after torpedo room to keep an eye on it and to keep him informed. He brought the boat up to 180 feet to reduce the sea pressure on the tube packings. But the submarine was getting heavy aft and slowly but surely becoming harder to control. Trouble loomed. The bedeviled and bewildered crew cursed the Japanese patrol boat's ability to locate the submerged *Rasher* so easily.

The mystery of the enemy's success was soon to be solved.

Late in the afternoon the sonar operator reported he could no longer hear the patrol boat's screws. Exhausted from the heat and drawing short, hard breaths, Hutchinson slipped on a pair of headphones as the sonarman slowly worked around the compass, listening for telltale noises from the enemy. The captain knew well the vagaries of underwater sound transmission in the Southwest Pacific and the dangers it often masked, so he listened carefully. Except for an occasional snap and whistle from albacore and grouper, there was only silence.

Wary of a trap, Hutchinson nevertheless ordered the boat up cautiously for a look around. At ninety feet he motioned for the periscope to be fully raised and for the boat to be planed up very slowly so that just a few inches of the scope would break the surface. At sixty feet the boat could easily broach, especially when the men at the diving station were enervated. They had to control the diving planes with sheer muscle power, a task that required great strength even under the best conditions. The diving officer, as fatigued as anyone, had to be alert and prepared to order the planes on full dive and the motors on "All Ahead Emergency" should the enemy, his machinery silenced, be laying in wait for the submarine to show herself. Hutchinson was set for a very quick observation—no more than a second or two to walk the scope around and look for their friend.

The diving officer croaked out the depth as the submarine rose. Hutchinson, his khakis soaked, his face glistening with sweat, grasped the training handles as the periscope cleared the well, unfolded them, and rose upright, his eye to the lens.

The periscope was oriented aft, so he was looking through it underwater toward the *Rasher*'s stern while waiting for the scope to break the surface as the ship swam upward. It afforded him an opportunity to observe the sea from an unusual perspective. An eerie, greenish light penetrated the limpid water just far enough to illuminate the minute sea organisms that floated in front of the periscope lens, and it gave some substance to the otherwise amorphous underwater shape that was the submarine's long, dark body.

The light was bright enough at seventy-five feet to reveal something shocking: a stream of bubbles rising from the main deck to the surface! Air under high pressure was leaking from an air bank in Number 6 Main Ballast Tank, leaving a perfect trail for the enemy to follow. The *Rasher* might as well have had a float tied to her with a sign that said, "Here I am, come get me!" At night the bubbles could easily be followed on the surface with a searchlight.

Hutchinson was momentarily stunned as he described what he saw. Then he turned his attention to the situation topside as the periscope broke the surface. Sure enough, off in the late afternoon haze, the patrol boat was laying to.

"Take her down! Two hundred feet! That bastard's still there!"

Down the *Rasher* went, trailing her bridal train of bubbles.

An inspection of the high-pressure air system that passed through the forward engine room uncovered a leak in four bottles of the Number 5 Air Bank, where air for blowing ballast was stored under 3,000 pounds of pressure. Repairs were impossible until the boat was back on the surface.

Inside the *Rasher*, conditions worsened until 2100. Then the sound watch reported that the patrol boat lay dead astern of the submarine; it appeared the enemy had lost the scent. Seizing the opportunity, Hutchinson ordered "ahead two-thirds" and adroitly slipped out of the noose before the Japanese skipper realized what had happened.

Bill Norrington completed the harrowing story:

> Finally lost him temporarily at 2100, and surfaced at 2200 in bright moonlight after being down 20 1/2 hours. If the moon hadn't been so bright it wouldn't have been so tough. But he saw us as soon as we surfaced and chased us again. By this time we were ready to shoot it out with him with our deck gun, but we gradually outdistanced him as we eased our course to the north. Were we tired!

A normal surface routine commenced as soon as the boat was ventilated by using the engines to suck fresh air through the foul compartments. The traitorous air bottles were bled down and secured at the hull stop. Bilges were pumped, batteries charged, and from the galley came the sounds and delicious aromas of a hot meal being prepared. Submariners were a resilient lot; their usual playful and profane banter returned in no time at all.

Over chow in the crew's mess and wardroom, the main topic of conversation centered on why they were not depth-charged during the long hold-down, and why the Japanese skipper had not put out a call for help. If he had, it was observed with cool objectivity, the *Rasher* would have been in serious trouble—maybe even sunk. For that matter, the sailors asked, why didn't the patrol boat that chased them down the Celebes coastline the night of 9 November radio for assistance? Working as a team, two patrol boats could have boxed them in, possibly with disastrous consequences.

As always, these imponderables were ascribed to the impossibility of fathoming the Japanese mind. Certainly at this middle stage of the war no one underestimated their fighting abilities, least of all a crew of submariners who were nearing completion of a successful but arduous first patrol. But to American naval officers and enlisted men used to meticulous planning and a strong central command structure, Japanese tactics seemed wretchedly uncoordinated and unsupervised by higher authority. It was a weakness the submarine force would exploit with spectacular success in the coming years.

The next morning, when the *Rasher* dove to avoid another patrol boat, the conning tower was soaked as sea water sluiced through an open hatch. The deluge grounded out a periscope hoist motor panel and electrical switches that controlled the air conditioning compressors down in the pump room. The gear was returned to service after a dry-out in the ship's oven. The mishap did not slow things down one bit, and the *Rasher* cleared the Makassar Strait on the evening of 12 November and stood eastward from Mangkalihat Point toward the Minahassa Peninsula of Celebes.

Off Mangkalihat Point, a ship resembling a submarine—Japanese or friendly unknown, range 10,000 yards—was sighted by a lookout. Her position was duly noted by the officer of the deck, who put the rudder over hard and sounded the diving alarm. The sonar watch could not pick up screws but did report what sounded like a submarine blowing its tanks. Hutchinson cleared out at high speed and continued south, avoiding several more patrol boats.

Eight days later the *Rasher* entered a submarine safety zone off the coast of western Australia.

West of Rowley Shoals, SD radar picked up a plane contact at a range of ten miles and closing. Dead astern, a Navy Black Cat PBY-4 Catalina lumbered into view on the horizon and headed for the submarine. On the bridge, the quartermaster checked the daily recognition signals chalked on the periscope shears and, using an Aldis lamp, flashed them to the plane. For good measure he fired a green flare, indicating the *Rasher* was a friendly.

There was no response from the flying boat.

"Six miles and closing!"

Hutchinson did not hesitate another second.

"Clear the bridge! Dive! Dive!"

Emergency speed was rung up.

"Full dive on the planes! Right full rudder!"

The *Rasher*'s deck tilted down precipitously. Loose gear crashed to the deck. She heeled sharply to port while turning right to get out of the PBY's glide path.

"Passing twenty-five feet!" It was the fastest dive the *Rasher* had ever made. "Passing forty-five feet—mark!"

Of all the things that could befall a submarine, being bombed by a friendly plane was the worst. The men prayed the ship would get under in time.

"Passing fifty-five feet! Take the angle off!"

Four 500-pound bombs missed their mark but exploded so close aboard that they sent heavy shock waves through the boat. The impact was like depth charges.

Hutchinson was furious. Allied forces were prohibited from attacking any submarine found in the safety zones. Yet despite this prohibition and the issuance of daily submarine position reports, attacks on friendly submarines continued. In part it was due to navigational errors, improper briefings, and failure on the part of air crews to read or understand the governing directives. But mostly attacks happened because the flyers were young and overzealous. Every air crew wanted a submarine silhouette or two stenciled on their plane's nose. Submariners soon learned that no one was their friend.

The Black Cat PBYs—painted a sinister-looking flat black—were part of Patrol Wing Ten, based at Pelican Point on the Swan River, near the southern edge of Perth. The base, a former yacht club, was now dubbed "The Swan River Flying Club." Hutchinson vowed that some club members would have their asses kicked but good.

Bill Norrington noted succinctly: "I hate aviators!"

After the attack, Hutchinson cautiously brought the *Rasher* to periscope depth and, satisfied it was safe, surfaced and continued on to Cockburn Sound.

Fifteen miles from port the *Rasher* was met by a destroyer and pilot boat that guided her safely up the Swan River into Fremantle, the port city of Perth, Australia. Prior to her arrival, the ship was squared away and prepared for the reception committee that would be waiting to greet her. At 1300 on 24 November 1943, the *Rasher* put in with her off-duty sections at quarters topside, tied up at the dock, and officially ended her first war patrol.

Rear Adm. Ralph Christie, Commander Task Force Seventy-one, and his staff were waiting on the pier that fronted the big wheat storage sheds that served as the Navy's shore-based submarine repair facilities. Christie made it his business to greet his returning boats. The brow was barely in place before he was aboard the *Rasher*, pumping hands and passing out congratulations for a very successful first patrol. After a brief tour of the ship, he and Hutchinson retired to the wardroom for a cup of coffee and a review of the highlights of the patrol report the captain and his department heads had prepared en route to Fremantle.

While the two officers chatted, the mess room was cleared for pay-
day. When the disbursing officer arrived with his satchel of Australian
pounds (in 1943, three Australian pounds equaled one U.S. dollar), the
impatient crew lined up in alphabetical order, eager to get off the ship
and aboard the buses waiting to take them to the delights of Perth.

◆ ◆ ◆

Following standard procedure, twenty members of the *Rasher's*
crew were detached and sent to the repair facility, to other submarines, or back to new construction in the States. To begin the refit,
the leading petty officers stood by with their department heads to
meet with the submarine repair officer and his assistants and review
the work lists.

All in all, the *Rasher's* material condition was excellent, considering
she had spent two months at sea. Nonetheless, dozens of items needed
repair. Three important ones topped the list: the air system, diesels,
and radar. Repairing the four leaky air bottles in Number 6 Main
Ballast Tank required dry-docking in Fremantle's makeshift slipway;
the bottles could be reached only by cutting a manhole in the tank on
the starboard side. In the engineering department, Number 2 and
Number 3 main engines needed an overhaul, including new cylinder
heads and valves. As for radar, both the SD and SJ needed waterproofing and retuning. The *Rasher* was also scheduled to receive a camouflage paint job, a measure being applied to all refitting SoWesPac
boats.

As repairs got under way, the enlisted rates were billeted at the
Ocean Beach Hotel, while chiefs and first class petty officers were billeted at the King Edward Hotel in Perth. There, a sailor could sleep in
a real bed, and for two pence, heat water and bathe in a real tub. After
nearly two months of breathing diesel fumes and the piquant aromas
engendered by eighty-some humans living in a sealed-up submarine,
it was enough to make a man feel like, well, King Edward.

Perth, with a population of 60,000, had the look of a lovely English
town, complete with snug homes, quaint churches, and a turn-of-the-
century tram that rattled through the business district. But it was also
a town where, if one frequented the right places, "one's wildest
dreams come true," as a Navy flyer put it. At night there were pubs,
Swan beer, and beautiful Australian women. But as in Brisbane,
Aussie soldiers, New Zealand kiwis, U.S. Marines, and submarine
sailors proved a combustible mixture. Too often brawls turned deadly.

◆ ◆ ◆

The *Rasher*'s first war patrol lasted sixty-two days. That included the time en route to and from her assigned area. Amazingly, forty-two days were spent submerged. The patrol combined daring tactics with undaunted persistence, most notably in the end run to track down and sink her first enemy ship, the *Kogane Maru*, and the aborted end run leading to the unsuccessful attack on the 10,000-ton tanker. The *Rasher* recorded forty-five ship contacts of various types and launched eight torpedo attacks, firing all twenty-four of her torpedoes and scoring eleven hits. There were eight contacts with aircraft. She steamed 11,433 miles, 5,672 of which were logged in the patrol area itself, and burned 109,615 gallons of diesel fuel. She returned with 6,970 gallons left in her tanks, and the only limit to her ability to remain on station was a lack of torpedoes and the endurance of her crew. Hutchinson claimed four ships sunk for 21,260 tons.

Commander Hutchinson's patrol report exhaustively documented the *Rasher*'s eight attacks and her daily routine at sea. The report's information would be digested, sifted, and analyzed by submarine command and SORG, after which the relevant portions would be passed on to other boats soon to be operating in the same area. Such analysis permitted the Navy's operations officers to check their progress against the Japanese and adjust their tactics as needed. It also provided a means of evaluating the accuracy of Ultra intercepts and the effectiveness of the manner in which the boats employed the data. Were the targets where they were supposed to be, and were the subs able to intercept and sink them? (In the *Rasher*'s case, the Ultra information proved to be incorrect.) And finally, it gave other submarine skippers an opportunity to critique their own tactics and modify them as necessary.

Hutchinson reported on operational aspects as well. He praised the crew's training and preparedness for combat. As an experienced submarine skipper, he knew that the first patrol after commissioning and training was the acid test. He wrote that the performance of all personnel aboard the *Rasher* was everything he'd hoped for, considering that the number of war-seasoned officers and men was fewer than expected. And he strongly disagreed with critics who complained that the dilution of experienced personnel to round out crews for new construction had weakened the force. He also praised the excellent quality of food and noted the role good chow played in keeping morale high and the crew healthy.

On the purely strategic side, Hutchinson reported on weather and sea conditions; noted the location of shore-based radar installations; assessed merchant traffic routes; noted ocean thermal density layers and submerged sound conditions; and, last but by no means least, described Japanese anti-submarine tactics. He observed that even the troublesome Mark-6 magnetic exploders on the torpedoes worked when they were supposed to, notwithstanding the one shot he thought might have been a premature.

All of this information and record-keeping did not obscure the report's principal fact: skippered by Edward Hutchinson, the *Rasher* claimed as sunk four ships worth 21,206 tons. However, after the war, the Joint Army-Navy Assessment Committee (JANAC) officially credited the *Rasher* with four ships worth only 8,894 tons on her first patrol. Such discrepancies were to become the most controversial component of the assessment of the submarine war in the Pacific. Even today historians and former submariners debate the issue.

◆ ◆ ◆

After the war, ComSubPac asserted that 190 U.S. submarines sank about 4,000 enemy ships, both naval and merchant, totaling nearly 10 million tons. JANAC downgraded this to 1,314 ships and 5.6 million tons—eliciting shock and outrage in the postwar submarine navy. With access to Japanese records, JANAC changed many of the claimed sinkings to the categories of "probables" or "damaged." In some cases, verified sinkings were disallowed for lack of corroboration by Japanese records. Needless to say, the Japanese records were themselves frequently inaccurate or incomplete.

A number of factors conspired to thwart the authentication of ship sinkings by submarine skippers. Weather, faulty identification, and visibility played a role. So did malfunctioning torpedoes, which included duds and prematures. The physical impossibility of hanging around to witness a sinking in the face of a vigorous anti-submarine counterattack created problems. And there was the poor Japanese record-keeping, which some said was a deliberate attempt to save face.

In 1989, the Naval Institute Press published *U.S. Submarine Attacks During World War II,* by John D. Alden, a former World War II submariner. Commander Alden's book clearly sets out the discrepancies between the sinkings claimed by submarine commanding officers and those credited by SORG and JANAC. In great detail, it lists every known attack on Japanese naval and merchant shipping by U.S. submarines. Alden had complete access to Japanese records—including some not available to JANAC in 1947—and was able to undertake a more thorough job of research than any official entity heretofore. Alden concluded that some boats—including the *Rasher*—should be credited with more total tonnage than JANAC's tally.

According to Alden, the *Rasher* sank 20 ships worth 114,732 tons, not JANAC's 18 ships and 99,901 tons. (For a complete list of the *Rasher's* official JANAC score, see page 339.) But until Alden's work is accepted as the official word on the subject and JANAC's scoring disavowed or discredited, the *Rasher's* score will be 18 ships and 99,901 tons. An enviable record, nonetheless.

◆ ◆ ◆

The endorsements to the *Rasher's* first patrol report read in part:

The first war patrol of RASHER, covering a period of sixty-two days, including the time en route to and from area, 24 September to 24 November inclusive, was conducted in the Makassar Strait and the extreme southern portion of the Celebes Sea.

Area coverage was most thorough. All attacks were handicapped by the clear weather and bright moonlight during a portion of this patrol.

The Commanding Officer, officers and crew of the RASHER are congratulated for an effective, well conducted patrol.

J. M. Haines, Commander Submarine Squadron Sixteen

The thoroughness with which the patrol area was covered and the able exploitation of shipping routes bespeaks [sic] the seasoned judgement of an experienced combat submarine captain. The decision to return to base via the Molucca Passage rather than by the confined waters of Cape William under existing A/S and visibility conditions was sound. The damage inflicted on the enemy was considerable; however, it does not serve adequately as a measure of the patrol's excellence. A study of the report evidences the aggressive, indomitable will of the commanding officer to seek out the enemy and destroy him which, coupled with sound planning and skillful execution, makes this patrol outstanding.

This patrol is considered "successful" for purpose of awarding the Submarine Combat Insignia.

The Force Commander congratulates the Commanding Officer, officers, and crew of the RASHER on this excellent patrol. . . .

Ralph W. Christie, Commander Task Force Seventy-One

The crew of the *Rasher* had much to be proud of. They started out untested and inexperienced, yet acquitted themselves with exceptional confidence and professionalism. The *Rasher*'s first patrol was one of four that would later be cited in her Presidential Unit Citation award. She was also named flagship of Submarine Squadron Sixteen, a rare honor for a new boat—but in this case, one that had proved her mettle. Edward Hutchinson was detached from the *Rasher* and promoted to the command of Submarine Squadron Twenty-two. His experience would be invaluable in preparing new boats and crews for the rigors of combat when they arrived in Fremantle. Admiral Christie made the announcement when the two met for cocktails and supper at his luxurious residence, "Bend of the Road," outside of Perth.

After his meeting with Christie, Hutchinson turned the *Rasher* over to thirty-two-year-old Lt. Comdr. Willard R. Laughon. Like all submarine skippers at that time, Laughon was an Annapolis graduate. He was a slender young man with a high forehead, chiseled features, and an aloof bearing that was all business. (After a few weeks on patrol, however, he would allow himself the radical luxury of growing a beard.)

Laughon had arrived in SoWesPac from SubLant, where he'd made eight anti-submarine war patrols out of Bermuda, the last four as commanding officer of the ancient *R 1*. He despaired of R-boat sailors ever seeing the Pacific, but in the spring of 1943 he was ordered to Prospective Commanding Officers School in New London, Connecticut. Now, after completing a two-week stint in the Task Force Seventy-one Submarine Operation Office acquainting himself with the complexities of undersea warfare against the Japanese, he was anxious to go to sea in a combat-tested boat.

Part 2

Laughon's Luck

A Veteran Ship

The *Rasher*'s crew returned to Fremantle rested, anxious to go to sea, and happy—although more than one man was nursing a black eye or adjusting to missing teeth.

Besides a new commanding officer, they discovered their ship had a new look. Her weathered jet-black Measure 9 camouflage had been repainted with the new Measure 32/3SSB camouflage scheme. Instead of overall solid black, her horizontal surfaces and decks were gloss black, and all vertical surfaces were light, medium, and dark gray. The color scheme was designed to visually break up the submarine's mass and length and make her blend into the background of tropical ocean and sky. After much debate and endless experimentation with a variety of colors—including both sky blue and desert tan—the Navy settled, not too surprisingly, on gray and black.

The question of submarine camouflage had been a sticky one for the Navy. Many die-hards from the prewar school believed that the only proper color for a submarine was black. (Never mind that in the thirties the old S-boats and V-boats had been light gray and black.) They asserted that for combat operations, especially at night, black was best. But it was learned soon enough that an all-black submarine was easy to see at night because the surrounding envelope of sea and sky was never as totally black as the submarine itself. The new color combination proved very effective. Skippers returning from patrols with newly painted boats described how they had been able to approach targets on the surface to very close range—sometimes less than 800 yards—without being seen. Their camouflage got the credit.

Following the formal change of command on 9 December 1943, the Watch, Quarter, and Station Bill was reorganized and a training schedule worked up. With a new commanding officer aboard and nearly a quarter of the men replacements, some of them fresh from sub school, plenty of work was needed to whip things into shape.

As the *Rasher*'s refit drew to a close, the two Winton diesels were tested dockside and the last items of repair were ticked off the list. Tools, manuals, and diagrams were stowed, electrical gear packed away, and spare parts reinventoried. Then the ship was cleaned up and given a final inspection by Laughon and the senior repair officer from Submarine Repair Unit 137 on the tender *Pelias*. After the inspection, the *Rasher* put to sea in deteriorating weather for post-repair trials, degaussing, and sound tests. Laughon approved the refit work and brought the ship back to Fremantle, where she was provisioned and refueled in preparation for five days of intensive exercises and training with Dutch and Australian naval units.

Then tragedy struck.

On 13 December, during a routine dive seventy-five miles west of Cockburn Sound, a young lookout, Louis J. Westerhuis, seaman second class, was accidentally left topside. Despite the fact it was late spring in Australia, the weather was ugly. Seas were very rough; temperatures were in the forties. Westerhuis heard neither the order to clear the bridge nor the twin blasts of the diving alarm; heavy waves crashing over the decks and raw wind whipping through the periscope shears drowned them out. The other three lookouts scrambled below, and the quartermaster dogged the hatch. Pete Sasgen described what happened next:

> Normally the first two lookouts down the hatch manned the bow and stern planes and were relieved after thirty minutes. When it came time for the planesman to be relieved by the other two lookouts, Westerhuis was missing.

Precious time elapsed while the ship was searched from stem to stern, including the battery wells and ammunition magazine. Pandemonium and anxiety erupted as the realization Westerhuis was gone struck home. Ships and aircraft raced to the scene.

> We surfaced and reversed course. Two hours later we found him.

Both periscopes were manned and extra lookouts were stationed topside during the search. Westerhuis was found, alive, near the spot where the *Rasher* had submerged. He had taken off his clothes and made flotation gear from his dungarees. Rescue was difficult; they were fighting a Force 4 sea and could have easily run him down. Several minutes were spent devising a method of recovery. Laughon ordered the *Rasher* to lay to, and the bow planes were rigged out as a rescue platform. Gunner's mates Ferdinand Galli and Dick Baun used a line-throwing gun to get a line to the struggling man.

Sasgen continued:

> He was still swimming and grabbed the life preserver as we came alongside. (A swimmer went over the side to rescue Westerhuis.) Once he was aboard we immediately wrapped him in heavy blankets, but the ordeal was too much for him, and he died.

When he heard the cheering in the control room, cook Dave Brown knew they'd found Westerhuis. And when the ship hove to and the pharmacist's mate called for some hot soup on the double, he knew they'd recovered him. He heated some as fast as he could and took it straight to the conning tower ladder and passed it up. But it was too late to help.

It was a grim arrival in Fremantle, where Westerhuis's shipmates carried his body to a waiting ambulance while curious sailors lined the wharf to watch. Ken Tate was a close friend of Westerhuis's:

> We were both the same age, had the same time in the Navy, and [were] both from New York; me from Long Island, Joe from upstate. I went home with him on leave, met his family and his girlfriend. I was very saddened by his death. I was permitted to write a letter to his mother regarding his death in addition to the official telegram. About a dozen shipmates attended the funeral in a beautiful, well-kept cemetery in Perth. It was a short but nice service.

After the funeral, the *Rasher* was put through an extensive and exhausting training period of torpedo runs and attack problems with the Dutch and Australians. Helium balloons were sent aloft as targets for the 20-millimeters and .30-caliber Brownings. Being a very thorough skipper, Willard Laughon drilled his crew over and over again until he was satisfied. All the while the loss of Joe Westerhuis loomed large.

Lieutenant Bill Norrington described those days in his usual terse fashion:

> Ship needed plenty of training with new skipper. This training period plenty rugged. Runs all day and evening, and then early morning watches to stand. Never have been so worn out before.

Laughon seemed impressed by his crew's high level of proficiency and how quickly the new men assumed their duties like veterans. He approved of the way the senior chiefs took charge and the smart fashion in which they ran their departments. With only a few minor adjustments, the officers and men quickly meshed with their new commanding officer.

Back in Fremantle, Admiral Christie reviewed the *Rasher*'s pending patrol and her combat readiness. Laughon's reports must have pleased the admiral. With a fine ship and crew, the young R-boater was being given an exceptional opportunity in his first fleet submarine command.

◆ ◆ ◆

As 1943 came to an end, the war in the Pacific was taking a new and optimistic turn for the Allies. The invasion of the Marshall Islands was planned for January, and offensive carrier strikes on Truk and the Palaus were set for March. By late spring, the balance of power would be shifting inexorably to the Allies. But the Japanese remained a formidable presence in the Southwest Pacific, although they were feeling the effects of the attacks on their supplies of raw materials and food and the decimation of their merchant fleet.

The *Rasher*'s Operation Order No. 49-43 sent her to the South China Sea. The primary objective of her second war patrol, according to Annex "Dog," a secret supplement to the op-ord, was to lay a minefield off the coast of Indochina, between Puolo Condore and Cape St. Jacques, an area known as the Mouths of the Mekong. After completing this, she was to resume a normal offensive patrol. Her track north from Australia would take her through the Lombok and Makassar Straits, the Balabac Strait between Borneo and Palawan, then into the South China Sea. When he returned from his meeting with Christie, Laughon pored over charts of the patrol area.

In their 1942 drive on the Dutch East Indies and Philippines, Japanese troops attacked from staging bases in China, Indochina, Hainan, and Formosa. To supply those bases, the enemy had to run convoys south from the home islands and across the East China Sea. Submarines could not possibly cover every shipping route, but mines laid in coastal waters would in effect be on station all the time. Moreover, minefields close to shore had the effect of driving shipping out to deeper water, where submarines could maneuver safely while attacking. But there were limits to how close to the coast a boat could work to lay them. Knowing this, the Japanese installed beacon lights along the shorelines to guide shipping through narrow but safe channels. Inevitably, more ships than not escaped destruction from submarine-laid mines.

Adding to the difficulties associated with laying mines and interdicting *marus* along the coast of Indochina was the fact that the region was a filigree of inlets and tidal flats fanning into the South China Sea. The shallow coastal water south of Bong Son was a potential death trap for a submarine fleeing from enemy patrol boats. Navigation charts revealed that where the *Rasher* would lay her mines off Cape St. Jacques, the water in many spots was less than ten fathoms deep.

Mining operations were greatly disliked by submarine sailors. Besides taking up too much of their time and labor, they restricted the submarine's effectiveness by reducing the number of torpedoes she could carry. The result almost always was an unproductive patrol, in terms of shipping sunk. And minelaying was dangerous business. Sometimes unruly mines exploded while the minelayer was still in the field completing her work. So even though laying a minefield might serve the *Rasher's* own cause at some future date, her orders were met with groans of displeasure.

The patrol area was a big one. Stepped off, it was more than 4,000 miles to Indochina from Fremantle. The Lombok and Makassar Straits would be the two nastiest choke points; veterans of the *Rasher's* first patrol could vouch for the latter. There was no reason to think Japanese anti-submarine activity had abated there, unless, of course, as it was jokingly pointed out, they finally got tired of looking for the *Rasher*. The Balabac Strait north of Borneo, though mined, was a relatively short run that could be executed on the surface at night. Under the right conditions of moon and sea, the closely patrolled Lombok could be run after dark, too.

On 19 December 1943, the *Rasher* was ready to commence her second war patrol. She was topped off with diesel fuel and loaded with fresh stores. Eleven Mark-12 mines with their heavy anchors attached were winched aboard and struck below to the after torpedo room. Each mine was equipped with M-3-N detonators. Their sensitivity was set to compensate for the Earth's relatively weak magnetic field in tropical latitudes. Thus, when influenced by the passage of a undegaussed ship, the mines would explode.

Like torpedoes, submarine mines were a precious commodity.

USS RASHER
SECOND WAR PATROL
19 DEC 43 – 24 JAN 44

They arrived in Fremantle from Melbourne by ship rather than rail due to the peculiarities of Australian railroads, which were notorious for having incompatible track gauges between states. Since each mine was only half the length of a torpedo, twenty-one tin fish could still be stowed. But in every man's mind was the thought that, short loaded, they would be at a disadvantage if they encountered enemy shipping. Worst of all, they would be operating in an area too far north for a quick run back to Australia for more torpedoes. Looking on the bright side, there was the distinct possibility that the patrol would be short, which meant they could be back in a few weeks.

Admiral Christie was present to see the *Rasher* off. She lay alongside the dock ready for sea, her diesels loping, steam and engine cooling water spewing from the exhaust ports. The special sea detail had already been stationed and the lines singled up. When it was time to get under way, Christie exchanged salutes with his skipper and wished him good hunting. Then the admiral went ashore over the brow. The lines were cast off, and, with a blast of her horn and boiling prop wash, Laughon backed the submarine into the stream smartly while the pilot helped out with some body English. At 1550 the *Rasher* stood out from Fremantle for her second patrol.

The water was rough in Cockburn Sound when they transferred the pilot to a boat; it was even rougher when the *Rasher* reached the Indian Ocean, where her course was set for the exercise zone. The helmsmen had a hard time keeping the lubbers line on course as they fought heavy seas and high winds.

It was nearly dark when the *Rasher* rendezvoused for torpedo runs and drills with the frigate HMAS *Horsham.* Sea conditions vibrated the periscopes and made depth control so difficult to maintain that it discouraged any protracted workout. So after two grueling hours Laughon released the frigate and set a course via the submarine safety zone for the fueling station and PBY base at Exmouth Gulf, code-named "Potshot," on the western coast of Australia 750 miles away. Topping off at Exmouth would add two days to the *Rasher's* cruising range. Over the 1MC the captain announced their destination and described minelaying as the primary objective of the patrol, but he added that he fully intended to sink as many Japanese ships as possible after that was done.

Two nasty problems cropped up as soon as the *Rasher* was under way on her new heading: the SJ radar quit working, and a valve to provide sea water for flushing a head in the crew's compartment sprang a prodigious leak. Laughon was advised of the situation shortly after he had retired to his stateroom. He had to hope it was not an omen of things to come. Since Fremantle was long over the horizon, the radar would have to be tinkered with while under way; the valve would have to be repaired at Exmouth.

The next day the weather took a turn for the better. The wind abated, the barometer rose, and warmer, more seasonal weather returned. Just after the noon meal, a patrolling Black Cat PBY-4 was sighted. Unlike the episode off Rowley Shoals, this time the day's recognition signals were successfully exchanged by Aldis lamp. But radar gremlins struck again. Even though the PBY was only four miles away when the signals were flashed, SD radar failed to pick up the plane. Instead of showing the proper sharp spike, the scope jumped and quivered with meaningless electronic jibberish. The cursing radarman shut down the unit and yanked it from its case in the control room to diagnose the problem. Meanwhile, in the conning tower, another radarman was scratching his head as he sorted through the SJ's parts that lay scattered over the deck plates.

Later in the day, while the *Rasher* zigzagged along on the surface in the safety zone at fifteen knots, came a chilling encounter. During a routine periscope observation just south of Dirk Hartog Island, the chief of the boat, Tom Herrmann—who happened to have the watch—sighted what he claimed was a torpedo wake broad on the port quarter. He instantly notified the officer of the deck, who ordered the rudder over hard right to parallel the torpedo's track. The chief swore he saw it pass abeam to port about seventy-five yards away. Disaster, it seemed, was narrowly averted.

Mysteriously, the sound watch did not hear high-speed screws, and the torpedo's source—if indeed it was a torpedo—remained a mystery. The chief was the only one who saw the wake, but he was too experienced a submariner (and a torpedoman at that) to have his word dismissed lightly. Laughon himself was skeptical, saying it had to have been a porpoise. Nevertheless, he sharply altered course away from the spot of the sighting and radioed a contact report to Fremantle describing the incident. Ken Tate wrote in his diary: "Dec. 20, 1943: Torpedo fired at us by Jap sub. Missed."

The *Rasher* pulled into Exmouth Gulf three days before Christmas. Potshot was situated inside the protective hook formed by North West Cape, the westernmost outcropping of the Australian coast. It was a desolate, forbidding place populated by a few hearty outbackers who lived in small pearl fishing villages. Enormously high tides racked the narrow gulf, and ferocious winds known as willy-willies howled out of the northwest, piling up water in the anchorage. Ashore, the sharp, pointed spinafex grass sprouting from sand dunes and alongside every road and trail could cut human flesh like a razor. In hot weather clouds of ravenous flies swarmed over everything. Submariners who dropped in on their way north departed feeling mighty sorry for the lonely PBY crews who lived aboard a tender, the old, converted four-piper destroyer *Childs*. She was moored with her brood of black "Dumbos" in the choppy roadstead. It was tough duty without much to look forward to when the flyers returned from their missions.

At Potshot, a Royal Netherlands Navy tanker, the *Oneida*, was providing fuel service for the submarines in place of the unmotorized "dumb" lighter that was usually moored in the harbor for that purpose. The gulf's wind-whipped water and swift tidal current sorely tested Laughon's seamanship when he came alongside the tanker to tie up. Nonetheless, he warped the *Rasher* in nicely. As soon as her lines were over Lt. G. J. Quesada, Potshot's commanding officer, came aboard to offer his services.

Laughon explained his needs and also asked permission to use one of the small, uninhabited islands off the mouth of Exmouth Gulf for some gunnery exercises on the way back to sea. Lieutenant Quesada, the perfect host, gave Laughon what he required and insisted on providing his guests with ice cream and local fresh vegetables as well. He even presented them with a coveted delicacy: his personal Christmas fruitcake.

While these luxuries were laid below and fueling got under way, the engineering department tackled the leaky sea valve. First, shallow-water diving gear was broken out on the *Rasher*'s deck. It consisted of a mask, rubber air hose, and woolen long johns. Next, someone had to volunteer to go over the side and plug the hull so the leaking valve could be removed and repaired. The volunteer was Mike Pontillo, motor machinist's mate second class. Tom Herrmann found some bricks and tied them around Pontillo's waist to furnish negative buoyancy, then helped him over the side. Since a number of sharks had been spotted cruising the harbor, three men with small arms were posted for protection. Pontillo drove a wooden plug into the hull fitting with a mallet. Then Pete Sasgen removed the sea and stop valves and fixed them. Sasgen gave a couple of raps on the hull with a wrench to signal him, and Pontillo worked the plug back out. In short order the repair was finished. As Pontillo was getting ready to haul himself up:

Out of the corner of my eye I saw this fish. My mind said, "SHARK!!" I was really scared. When I turned my head to get a better look I discovered that the "shark" was a six-inch fish only a few inches from my face plate.

Meanwhile, the radarmen had disassembled the SD masthead and recoated it with Glyptal waterproofing. They also fabricated and installed a new dipole connection for the SJ. By the time Pontillo was on deck, both units were back in operation at full strength. With everything squared away, the crew exchanged holiday sentiments one last time with the crew of the *Oneida* and Lieutenant Quesada, and cast off to make for the gunnery range.

Laughon wanted to conduct some long-range spotting practice, so he nosed the *Rasher* in about a mile off the southern end of tiny Murion Island in the mouth of the gulf. The gun crews anxiously stood by on deck to fire the 3-inch gun at 50-gallon oil drums lined up above the island's high-tide line. After thirteen rounds, the gun's breech block refused to close. The block had to be disassembled and fixed while the submarine lay to, diesels idling. But when the reassembled mechanism was tested, a projectile separated from its shell casing. Gunner's mate Galli carefully extracted it by hand from the breech and tossed it overboard. Laughon had had enough; with darkness descending, he ordered all ammunition struck below, the gun secured, and the *Rasher*'s course set for Lombok Strait. It was time to get on with the real war.

Indochina Intrusion

Drills, drills, drills. Man overboard drills. Chlorine gas drills. Damage control drills. Collision drills. Willard Laughon proved to be the quintessential drillmaster. And since the *Rasher*'s operation order also directed her to collect bathythermographic data throughout the patrol area, he ordered frequent deep dives to work out on the BT. The deep dives revealed several small but infuriating air leaks similar to the one that proved so dangerous on the *Rasher*'s first patrol. One was coming from a pinhole in the high-pressure distribution manifold, the other from an air bank in Number 2 Main Ballast Tank—deja vu. The manifold was easily fixed, but the repair party could not get to the air bank, which was inside the ballast tank.

As the *Rasher* worked her way north toward the patrol area, sailors spent their time routing torpedoes—pulling them from the tubes to inspect the gyros, turbines, and other parts—and performing normal shipboard maintenance and procedures. Off duty and with free time on their hands, the men studied their qualification manuals and text-books under the guidance and prodding of the senior petty officers.

Knowing a hard-working submarine crew expects culinary excellence, the cooks had been planning a full-course Christmas dinner extravaganza ever since leaving Fremantle. The menu called for roast turkey and stuffing along with candied sweet potatoes, mashed white potatoes and gravy, green beans garnished with toasted bread crumbs, cranberry sauce laced with delicious little chunks of orange rind, freshly baked rolls, pumpkin pie, and Lieutenant Quesada's fruitcake divvied up into eighty-one pieces. As the *Rasher* neared Bali, flavorful aromas began to waft from the galley. Gradually they overpowered the pungent, pervasive smell of diesel fuel. Visitors began to drop by the bustling galley to get hourly progress reports. With a fine meal in preparation and a few simple Christmas decorations hung here and there, thoughts inevitably turned to home and family.

Christmas Eve 1943 found the *Rasher* fifty-six nautical miles south of Lombok Strait. From information supplied by Task Force Seventy-one's operations office, Laughon expected to encounter Japanese air and surface patrols from Bali at dawn. He studied the chart that detailed the pinched area between Nusa Penida to the east and Point Lombok to the west, the latter jutting into the mouth of the strait. The strait itself was ten to twelve miles wide, but minefields on either side of the passage and shore batteries on Cape Abah and Cape Ibus made it seem much, much narrower. Instead of waiting to make contact with the enemy and perhaps being forced to evade by reversing course or, worse, being trapped in the strait's narrow approach, Laughon decided to pull the plug well south of it and stand in submerged.

But when Japanese patrols failed to materialize by mid-morning Christmas Day, Laughon ordered the *Rasher* back to the surface to make landfall at three-engine speed. The radar watch and lookouts were cautioned to be doubly alert. Sure enough, at 1029, long-range contact was made with a patrol boat. Laughon ordered the *Rasher* down and decided this time to stay down so all hands could enjoy an undisturbed Christmas dinner. Ken Tate noted in his diary:

Dec. 25, 1943: Had a nice Christmas dinner and a shot of Scotch [most likely, some of the ship's medicinal brandy]. First Christmas I had underwater.

It was dark when the *Rasher* surfaced. The holidays over, it was back to business.

To be clear of Lombok Strait by dawn, the *Rasher* stood in at full speed. A muggy tropical night and lowering sky enveloped the ship as she drummed along on four engines. Her passage stirred up the phosphorescent marine plankton that abounded in those latitudes, leaving a glowing wake astern. Twenty miles off the port beam lay Nusa Besar. At the summit of its main promontory a mysterious fire burned like a bright red navigation beacon. The forty-mile run through the strait was uneventful, and by first light Lombok lay far to the south.

Near the equator very little time exists between dawn twilight and full daylight. Hence, morning star sights had to be taken in a hurry in order to accurately fix the *Rasher*'s position prior to diving for the day's patrol. While the navigator was shooting stars, a ship was sighted at a range of 5,000 yards. She appeared to be a small motorized fishing vessel. The SJ radar, which had been working beautifully up till then, showed nary a pip. Laughon was convinced that she simply was too small a target to be picked up by radar. If that was so, she did not warrant working into position for an approach. Instead, he dove to avoid detection.

Thirty minutes later the periscope watch sighted a small, engines-aft, cargo-type vessel. She was bigger than a trawler but smaller than a typical coastal steamer; her identifying details were obscured by dense surface haze. The ship was making ten knots, and to intercept would require a daylight end around. After a thorough periscope examination, Laughon concluded she was the same vessel sighted a half-hour earlier, though he admitted she looked different in the advancing daylight. He decided to stick to his original plan and let the ship proceed unmolested. When she was out of sight the order was passed to secure from battle stations. The *Rasher* surfaced and resumed her track toward the Paternoster group of islands north of Soembawa.

Shortly after 0800, a plane drove the *Rasher* down. When she returned to periscope depth an hour later for a look around, the plane was waiting for her and dropped a depth charge. The *Rasher* went deep again, and this time she stayed deep.

At 1300, the sound watch reported faint pinging on a bearing just east of due north. As soon as Laughon put the *Rasher*'s bow on an approach course of 010° T., the men jumped to their battle stations in anticipation of the developing situation. Forty minutes later the tops of two masts were sighted twelve miles away, hull down, steaming south. With a mirage effect playing visual tricks, the masts, one from a cargo ship, the other from an escort, shimmered in and out of view like tantalizing ghosts. Laughon ordered the boat planed up to fifty-five feet for a better look through the fully raised high periscope.

From this high vantage point he saw a Japanese bomber buzz low over the targets, which were just out of sight over the horizon. He turned the *Rasher* parallel to their track and for the next hour ran south with them, hoping they would turn toward her. But they refused to cooperate. Laughon monitored the situation, biding his time.

The plane disappeared late in the day, and Laughon decided it was time to surface and work ahead of the targets. He made a quick periscope sweep-around and was about to give the order to surface, but the plane suddenly reappeared—then, as if by magic, disappeared again. Patience was needed, the captain advised those around him in the conning tower. But his own frustration was mounting, making it difficult to heed his own words. He put his eye back to the scope. Again, no sooner did he open his mouth to give the order to surface than the plane reappeared over the target. It was a hopeless situation. The plane would see her if the *Rasher* surfaced; if she remained submerged, the targets would be long gone. Sure enough, when she finally surfaced at 1922, the targets had disappeared. Laughon abandoned the search for them near Sakala Island at 2200. Half a day had been wasted, and every man was tired and discouraged. A course was set for the Makassar Strait.

By midnight rugged Sakala was in sight. Since the SJ radar was acting up, a quick detour was made to retune the unit by taking ranges and bearings from the island. It was a wasted effort; whether sweeping across the island or out to sea, the scope displayed a flat green line. The SJ was stone dead. As the *Rasher* stood out and headed north toward the Lima Islands, the skipper hoped that the radar would be fixed and ready for another try at retuning against the Limas. At dawn, the boat dove for an SD aircraft contact, and Laughon elected to stay down to investigate thermal layers and have an undisturbed breakfast while the radarmen tinkered. The patrol was off to a discouraging start.

The SJ was still out of commission when, just south of Kalukalukuang, an extra-alert lookout spotted the tips of masts off the port bow, range nearly twenty miles. But just as quickly as they appeared, they vanished. Mirage effects were playing their nasty tricks again. Wardroom theorists explained that the phenomena were caused by a light-bending atmospheric inversion layer near the East Sibbalds Bank that lay to the west. Whatever the reason, the effect was enough to make a submarine sailor think he was hallucinating.

By early afternoon the technicians had the SJ back in commission. The *Rasher* cautiously stood in to Kalukalukuang so the radar could be tuned from ranges and bearings called out by the OOD and quartermaster from landmarks on a navigation chart. Laughon dropped down into the conning tower to see what miracle had been brought to bear on the pesky thing. The radarmen proudly displayed the homemade insulating sleeve installed over the dipole casting and smugly pointed out the rubber bands that in classic Navy jury-rigging tradition had been used to replace a broken spring in the tank of the range unit.

◆ ◆ ◆

"Smoke on the horizon, bearing one-three-zero degrees True!"

Late in the afternoon of 27 December, south of Laut Island, a lookout sighted a fast ship, range 24,000 yards, barely visible in surface haze. The tracking party was assembled, battle stations torpedo chimed, and four main engines were bent on in hot pursuit. But after studying the charts in the conning tower, Laughon pointed out that it would be impossible to make an end around; the target was just too fast—estimated speed nearly seventeen knots. Complicating matters was the fact that the tide and current tables in the ship's copy of the *Coast Pilot* warned of dangerous shoal water in and around Cape Lojar. In the process of chasing the target, those waters would have to be navigated at night. As it was, the latest navigational fix showed that currents had set the boat nine miles south already, so the *Rasher* was operating in treacherous waters. Laughon broke off contact and set a course for Cape William to the north. It was a prudent move, of course, but among men used to the strong hand of an aggressive skipper, Laughon's decision touched off a bit of skepticism about his qualifications for the job of boss of the *Rasher*. He would soon enough enlighten them.

Shortly after midnight of 28 December, the *Rasher* negotiated the tricky deep-water channel at Cape William. From there all the way north through the Sulu Archipelago, and across the Sulu Sea to Balabac Island off the tip of Palawan, target sweeps proved fruitless. The only thing encountered were scores of sailing vessels and trawlers, none of them worth a torpedo or surface gun engagement. A few of the larger vessels mounted complex antenna arrays, a dead giveaway that they were part of the extensive Japanese coastal anti-submarine network. Now and then false radar contacts from a passing ionized cloud or rain squall sent everyone scurrying to battle stations and gave the tracking party a good workout. As the *Rasher* passed adjacent patrol areas, anomalies indicative of a friendly submarine's SJ wobbled across the radar screen.

On New Year's Eve, Laughon conned the *Rasher* through the heavily mined and dangerous Balabac Strait. Sweeping north, the *Rasher* had passed exotic locales with colorful names such as Doc Can Island (or Dog Can Island, as the submariners called it), Pearl Bank (a famous torch singer, quipped Pete Sasgen), and Dangerous Ground. To everyone's great surprise and relief, the Japanese for some reason (could it be a shortage of oil, mused the wardroom strategists?) had curtailed their saturation patrolling in the Makassar Strait. Good weather held as the *Rasher* raced west toward Indochina to lay her mines.

To usher in 1944, the cooks laid on another splendid meal—Australian roast mutton, fresh baked goods, and, for dessert, Lieutenant Quesada's ice cream. All hands agreed it was a feast fit for a king—even a Japanese Emperor.

At 2225 on 3 January, the radar watch reported contact with Poulo Condore. The *Rasher* slipped by the tiny islands and, using a big white cliff northeast of Poulo Condore as a navigational aid, stood in on the surface, moon-set providing perfect cover. Fourteen and a half miles from the island, where she was to lay her mines, the fathometer showed only sixty feet of water under the keel—not much of a safety margin if she had to dive. After laying the eleven mines at intervals of 1,200 yards, the *Rasher* had two hours and fifty minutes to exit the field before they self-armed. Marked on a chart overlay, her track approximated a sine curve on a base course of 115° T. Operations commenced promptly at 0115. There was, however, one small problem. Bob Mathewson vividly recalled:

> I was still a member of the after torpedo room reload crew, and as we set up to lay the mines it was discovered we lacked an impor-

tant piece of equipment: a jointed pole with which to push the mine down the torpedo tube against the tube stop, where it had to be positioned in order to be fired out the tube.

Everything was at a standstill until I suggested I could slide into the tube, place my feet against the mine, and then someone else could place his feet on my shoulders and they could push us, using us as a "double ramrod" to seat the mine in the tube. Marshall Reb Partin, seaman second class, was the other part of this human ramrod, and we completed laying our mines in this manner.

As the mines had to be laid in a timed pattern, the tubes were not completely drained between firings, and Reb and I spent a considerable amount of time half submerged during the operation.

Whether the mines sank any ships is not recorded.

As soon as the last mine was ejected at 0159, Laughon got the *Rasher* back into deep water. As she retired to the southeast in the early morning hours, the radio shack snatched a message with the Ultra designation. It directed her to rendezvous with the submarine *Bluefish* to intercept a convoy of tankers heading north from Singapore. It was due to arrive in their patrol area about 1800 on 4 January.

Adm. Chester W. Nimitz, Commander in Chief, Pacific Fleet, had assigned a top priority to the destruction of Japan's oil tanker fleet. Without oil, Japanese troops and naval units in the conquered territories of the western Pacific, as well as those in the home islands, would be crippled. By January 1944, tanker losses from all causes—but especially submarines—were approaching a million tons. And here was the perfect opportunity for the *Rasher* to add a few thousand more to that total.

On the afternoon of 4 January, the *Rasher* was hunting for the *Bluefish* in the rendezvous box when a small ship sighted in the haze turned out to be her. *Bluefish*'s CO was Comdr. George Porter, a bearded veteran with six enemy ships to his credit. The two submarines hove to alongside each other so the skippers could talk things over via megaphone. Porter confirmed the *Bluefish* had received the same message as had the *Rasher*. He had formulated plans for a two-pronged attack on the convoy. If they could find it, they would launch a staggered strike on either flank. Laughon concurred, and they set off on the hunt.

◆ ◆ ◆

True to Ultra's word, twenty-eight miles to the north the *Rasher*'s lookouts sighted masts. Laughon advised Porter of the contact via

Aldis lamp, avoiding a plain-language radio transmission that might reveal their presence. Even though Porter was senior to Laughon, he generously offered him the first shot, which Laughon accepted.

Battle stations torpedo, and the *Rasher* made her approach. Three big ships—possibly more—were heading northward on a course of 325 degrees at nine knots. The targets were steaming in a loose procession, 2,000-yard intervals between them. Incredibly, they were unescorted. A bright quarter moon rising in the west silhouetted the targets and provided excellent visibility for a night surface attack.

As the *Rasher* closed in, two of the ships were identified as the 7,000-to-10,000-ton tankers *Hakko Maru* and *Kiyo Maru*. Both had engines aft and boxy superstructures in the style of Japanese wartime construction. For his primary target, Laughon selected the third ship, an unidentified tanker. He attacked from the starboard quarter at full speed and fired a spread of four torpedoes at the *maru*'s midsection. Stop watches were thumbed and—*goddamn!* One of the fish prematured dead ahead 400 yards away! Alerted that she was under attack, the tanker opened fire with tracers and wild shots from a deck gun.

Laughon ordered left full rudder to swing the *Rasher* around and bring her stern tubes to bear, but the tanker swung left, too, paralleling the *Rasher*'s track. Laughon had to pull away and head for a new firing position at flank speed.

It was hard to assess damage amid the confusion caused by enemy muzzle flashes and the prematuring torpedo, but the *maru* appeared to have taken at least one hit. She lost way. Her cargo and running lights flashed on and off and more gunfire erupted every which way from her decks.

As the *Rasher* stood in again to finish her off, the thump of distant explosions signaled the attack on the convoy's opposite flank by the *Bluefish*. With this, the crippled *maru* got under way again. Her maneuver forced Laughon to swing wide and run up on her port side for the follow-up attack. All the while he kept a sharp eye on the *Bluefish*'s position with radar so as to not confuse her with the enemy.

As the *Rasher* charged ahead, explosions flashed and rumbled to starboard. Suddenly, a ship burst into flame, turning night into day. It was an awesome sight. Dense black smoke billowed out over a sea turned red and yellow from fire; ships scattered in all directions, their steam whistles screeching in distress; terrified enemy gun crews fired tracers into the sky and at each other. Utter chaos reigned.

Ken Tate, on duty as a lookout this night, described the action he witnessed from up in the periscope shears:

We fired 6 torpedoes forward. Got 2 hits on 1 tanker, 2 premature torpedoes. Set it afire. Made reload and fired 6 more on another tanker. Three hits and set it afire. Both damaged but not sunk. BLUEFISH sunk one. We were fired on by a gun . . . they scared the hell out of me. Our torpedoes were blowing up, 2 ships were ablaze . . . gunfire from the targets was pretty damn close.

Radar advised Laughon that a ship on the opposite flank had managed to break away from the *Bluefish*'s attack and was attempting to join up with the *Rasher*'s target. Via radio, Laughon made sure Porter's boat was clear of the attack area and at the same time confirmed the location of the targets. Then, because it was too bright on the surface to attack without being seen, he ordered the *Rasher* to radar depth to finish off the damaged ship.

As the *Rasher* bore in, the *Kiyo Maru*—as yet unscathed—suddenly materialized out of the melee and interposed herself between the *Rasher* and the crippled tanker. Seizing the opportunity, Laughon decided to hit the *Kiyo Maru* first, then finish off the cripple. After a quick radar setup, six torpedoes from the bow tubes zinged on their way.

Twenty-seven seconds after firing, the *Rasher* was rocked by a second torpedo premature; a third one detonated prematurely twenty-eight seconds later. Laughon was furious. But two minutes, seventeen seconds after firing the fish, a single explosion ripped the *Kiyo Maru*, sending sparks and red-hot debris flying over her stack. Laughon reacted to the hit by instinctively pulling his eye away from the periscope buffer; his face was bathed in the red glow of fire mirrored down the periscope tube. The *Rasher* hauled out for another bow tube reload as explosions thundered from the *Kiyo Maru*.

Tate, a torpedoman, described what it was like to rush a reload under such difficult conditions:

A submerged reload was easier than a surface one because rough water could cause problems. The deck plates were removed easily enough so we could reach the lower tubes, numbers 3 and 6. After firing and draining the water from the tube, the door was opened and the reserve torpedo was loaded. This could be done in minutes.

We had a chain fall so torpedoes could be brought up to skids which were lined up with all the tubes. There was a pulley-type arrangement hooked to the tubes and the tail of the torpedo. Two guys pulled the lines while others pushed the torpedo into the tube.

Reload completed, Laughon ordered the *Rasher* back to the surface. Radar had contact with a target fleeing south, range 11,500 yards. Laughon rang up a full-speed end around. Far to starboard lay the blazing *Hakko Maru*, hit earlier by the *Bluefish*.

The ship the *Rasher* was chasing appeared larger than either of the two ships she had already attacked. She looked like yet another 10,000-tonner, a prominent stack aft, superstructure forward. Was this the *Kiyo Maru*, or the unidentified *maru* torpedoed in the initial attack? She resembled neither ship and appeared undamaged to boot. But as four bellowing engines brought the *Rasher* into position to attack again, it was not the time to worry about who was who.

Turning in, the *Rasher* cut hard to port and brought her stern tubes to bear as the *maru* bore down at full speed, black smoke pouring from her stack. Since the *Rasher*'s diesel exhaust discharge was stirring up phosphorescent plankton in the water, Laughon killed the engines and shifted to battery propulsion to reduce the chance of being spotted. Barely making steerageway, he waited for the tanker to cross astern, broad on the beam. Even from a mile and a half away, the target looked mighty big to the men on the submarine's bridge.

Laughon's patrol report described the action:

0403 The solution appeared good using course 225° T., speed 9 knots.

04-05-54 Commenced firing spread of four torpedoes from stern tubes, torpedo run 3,300 yards, tracks 79° to 76° port, gyro angles 172° to 175°, spread 1°, depths 18 feet and ten feet, and using an 8 second firing interval. I took special care to arrange the firing order and spread so that the torpedoes set at 18 feet would be fired first because I then believed that the shallower ones would be more likely to premature. I was wrong, however, because at 04-06-10 and 04-06-19 the first and second shots prematured. Three attacks[,] five prematures—were we unhappy!

04-08-04 Two explosions were heard below, hits by the third and fourth torpedoes.

0409 The target exploded and smoke and flame shot high into the sky. The explosions continued and the flames spread all over the target, and several ship lengths on either side. We watched him burn and settle for about twenty minutes and then drew away, since I expected planes out as a result of the earlier attacks.

0555   When we were about twenty miles away the flames[,] which had almost disappeared, shot up into the air again[,] then the flames and glow disappeared completely. I believe that he sank at this time.

Ken Tate's diary recounted what he saw:

Jan. 5, 1944: Just after midnight we chased last target in convoy. We laid still in the water and waited for him. It was pretty dark out. Fired 4 torpedoes aft, 2 prematures, 2 hits. Blew her sky high. Flames shot 1000 feet in the air. We could see Japs jumping over the side and swimming all around in the burning water. She was a 17,000 ton oil tanker. She exploded several times. We watched all this as we made the attack on the surface. We doubt if there were any survivors.

Bill Norrington described the final scene:

Target blew up immediately, and set on fire. Probably sunk 1 hour later when flames disappeared. What a sight! Glad I'm not on an AO [tanker]. Glad I'm not on any of these merchant ships. I've never heard so much dynamite go off in one night in all my life. We sank one tanker, and damaged a freighter. We evidently later sank the same ship we damaged earlier. Everything is sort of confused.

Everything was indeed confused. Ships were fleeing, torpedoes were going off, ships were blowing up, men were in the water, wreckage and flames were everywhere as the two submarines seemed to attack from all points of the compass.

The *Rasher* and *Bluefish*, anticipating the arrival of planes from Borneo and Malaya, quit the scene at flank speed. The Japanese would surely be hunting for the submarines that had devastated an Imperial convoy.

Later the two rendezvoused for a review of the attack by radio. Porter confirmed what Laughon surmised from reviewing his own tactics: the *Rasher* had damaged two tankers—the *Kiyo Maru* and an unidentified *maru*—and sunk a third. Porter added that he'd seen an explosion on the *Rasher*'s second target after she was hit, and he thought she may have gone down. For his part, Porter claimed credit for sinking the 6,046-ton *Hakko Maru*. Much to their consternation, one of the ships had escaped. Both skippers agreed it had been an extremely confusing, but profitable, attack. When they returned to

Fremantle, they would discover just how confusing and unreliable their "eyewitness" accounts of this battle could be. The *Bluefish*'s captain signed off with a "well-done." Dawn was breaking as the boats parted company to submerge for the day's patrol.

◆ ◆ ◆

In a little over twenty-six hours the *Rasher* had laid eleven mines, fired sixteen torpedoes (six, possibly seven, were prematures), sunk a high-priority target, and damaged two others. Willard Laughon's aggressive attack had laid to rest any doubts about his abilities and his courage under fire. The men, though tired, were proud of their work and especially of their new skipper. All the maneuvering, diving, and surfacing, the strain of being alert at battle stations for hours on end, the manhandling of torpedoes and work in hot machinery spaces, was physically exhausting. But a hot meal and a well-deserved rest had all hands in good spirits again.

To thwart Japanese radio direction finding stations, a southerly course was set while an attack report was radioed to Fremantle. After the message was sent, Laughon turned onto a northerly course and headed for the Tokyo-Singapore traffic route. He planned to intercept Japanese convoys making their way down the Indochina coast, the very convoys it was hoped would run afoul of the *Rasher*'s mines.

A day later, near Poulo Sapate, the weather turned dull, overcast, and chilly. Winds from the northwest were accompanied by rising seas. For the next six days rough, rainy weather made patrolling miserable. The drenched lookouts shivered in their foul-weather gear; below decks it was clammy. All the same, Laughon continued to dutifully investigate density layers and conduct drills. A general malaise descended on the ship.

Since departing Perth, about half the crew had at various times complained of sore muscles, headaches, fever, and nausea. The condition usually passed within twenty-four hours, helped along by the pharmacist's mate's ministrations. However, Laughon was concerned enough to order a sample of the drinking water taken aboard at Fremantle bottled up and set aside for analysis upon their return. In case the Australian canned goods were contaminated, he had the commissary officer withdraw them from the menu.

Drinking water laced with bacteria was a serious matter on a submarine. Several boats had had bacterial epidemics sweep through them. The source might be ashore; sometimes it was their own Kleinschmidt fresh-water distillers, which could harbor mold and bacteria growths in their filtration system. Despite the crew's lowered efficiency, Laughon kept the *Rasher* at a high level of readiness as the submarine worked her way north.

Starting at Phan Rang on the coast of Indochina, the shipping lanes were clogged with a nearly impenetrable thicket of sampans, junks, luggers, and craft of all descriptions. They navigated helter-skelter, as if participating in some mysterious water ballet. How they managed to avoid colliding or becoming fouled in the acres of fishing nets and glass buoys they towed was a mystery.

Early on the morning of 11 January, the *Rasher* submerged near Cape Varella Light to patrol. At 0915, the sound watch reported faint echo-ranging. The OOD immediately notified the captain, who was having breakfast, then ordered the helmsman to turn toward the source of the pinging, which was bearing 240 degrees. Laughon, a napkin in his hip pocket, arrived and took over the scope to survey the sector. It was shrouded in fast-moving rain squalls. After ten minutes of diligent searching, he sighted a Japanese patrol craft. It was five miles away, and heading northeast. Laughon speculated that the craft was on her way to meet a ship or convoy coming their way. So, he decided, the *Rasher* should idle in the area awhile and see what developed.

Just before 1500, Sound reported pinging north of the *Rasher*'s position. Something was coming. A medium-sized transport hove into view, barely visible in the gray curtain of a squall. Laughon stationed the tracking party and started an approach but did not yet order battle stations. As visibility improved an escort was located off the target's port beam. She was steaming this way and that on a random search pattern. She appeared to be the same ship Laughon had sighted earlier, although it was difficult to be certain. Unless they had very distinctive hulls or other features, escorts were hard to tell apart. Fifteen hundred yards behind the first transport, another one materialized out of the squall, which was passing astern of the convoy. Plot advised that the targets were on 220 degrees, and that it would take a fair-sized zig to bring them into firing range even though the submarine was closing in at high submerged speed. No sooner said than done: in lock step, the convoy conveniently zigged left to 160 degrees and put itself in an excellent position to be torpedoed. Now it was time for battle stations.

The *Rasher* headed for the second ship in line. The escort was 500 yards ahead of the convoy off the leading ship's port quarter. If alerted, she would have to come about hard to port, which would allow ample time for evasion. Now Laughon was sure she was the same escort he had spotted earlier off Cape Varella, and he congratulated himself for being right about her meeting a southbound convoy. The tracking party identified the *marus* as *Heito-* and *Paloa*-class APs.

The formation conveniently zigged to port again. Laughon marked the range at 3,000 yards; the hard-working trackers deftly revised the approach. Fast-moving squalls veiled the targets, complicating the task of ascertaining accurate final ranges and bearings, but Laughon confidently changed course for a 90-degree port track to adjust to the target's new heading. The bow tubes were ready.

He motioned "up" to make his final periscope observation before shooting. He anticipated a nice setup; instead he saw that all three ships had zigged to starboard, spoiling everything. Plot had their speed at nine knots going away. Nonplussed, Laughon watched them steam into a squall. Then he brusquely ordered the boat to the surface for a full-speed end around. He intended to work ahead of the convoy, then make a surface attack off its starboard bow. This would put the darkness of the Indochina coast behind the submarine and moonlight behind the targets. Surfaced, a high-pressure air-start on the diesels got the *Rasher* under way.

The end run took an hour and a half, and it seemed interminable. Smoke was finally sighted at 1812 right where Plot had calculated the convoy would be. The targets hugged the shoreline, using the outlying islands of Hon Lon and Iles De Pecheurs for protection. Steaming here was dangerous for convoy and pursuer alike, but the Japanese knew the grass from land return would confuse a submarine's radar. Their skippers were obviously old pros at this. They figured the threat of sucking mud into condensers and cooling systems was worth it if it lessened the chance of being torpedoed.

Laughon was anxious to attack before the targets reached Cam Ranh Bay, where Japanese convoys usually put in for the night to avoid marauding submarines. Dawn would force the *Rasher* to retreat to deep water offshore. The convoy could up anchor and be on its way in the morning, once again hugging the shallows.

At 1919, the moon rose full and bright as the *Rasher* headed in to cross the targets' projected track from port to starboard. Her shooting position brought her so close to the beach that the tops of palm trees could be seen from the bridge. But as she approached the spot where Laughon planned to launch the attack, two trawler-type patrol boats materialized out of the coastal haze 3,000 yards away. The patrols were laying to at the very spot to which the *Rasher* was heading.

Rather than risk detection, Laughon turned seaward. He would have to delay the attack until the convoy passed Cam Ranh Bay—if it did.

Once again, the crew accomplished the monotonous end run. The *Rasher* was waiting off Phan Rang when the convoy steamed into view. Just before it did, the radio room had picked up high-frequency transmissions that Laughon feared were warnings to the convoy that a submarine had been sighted by coast watchers. But rather than putting into Cam Ranh Bay, the *maru*s blithely continued south. Most likely they were loaded with cargos judged important enough to risk a nighttime submarine attack.

In his patrol report, Laughon said it was "a case of now or never," considering the shallow water (thirty fathoms and decreasing), the range to the beach (less than 5,000 yards), and the offshore currents setting the *Rasher* from astern. He pulled the plug and went to radar depth, wagering that, despite the bright moonlight, her parabola and periscope would not be seen in the moderate swell running down the coast.

He picked the leading ship for his first target. His strategy was simple: shoot three bow tubes, then shift targets and shoot three more at the trailing ship. He tried to anticipate prematures, allowing only a one-degree spread between the tin fish to concentrate the torpedo spread in the Middle of The Target (MOT). Thus, if a torpedo were to detonate before reaching the target, the gap between the remaining torpedoes would not be too wide when they struck. Said the captain in his patrol report,

> It's difficult to plan your spread when prematures must be taken into consideration.

The targets maintained a loose column formation, the pinging escort stationed off the leader's port quarter. With the first target a scant 750 yards away, Laughon gave the order to fire at eight-second intervals.

Away the tin fish whined, the boat shuddering each time the firing plunger was punched. As soon as the last fish was out of the tube, Laughon shifted his attention to the trailing target to check the setup. Suddenly—*Ba-Wham!* The first torpedo detonated on a thirty-second timed run with a deafening explosion. The concussion was so powerful it shattered light bulbs and popped paint chips off the *Rasher*'s bulkheads. It even knocked out the lights on the TDC for an instant. Water boomed in and out of the superstructure with such force some men thought a depth charge had gone off on deck. It was the loudest explosion they'd ever heard.

Laughon was so intent on getting off three shots at the trailing target before she zigged away that he didn't realize until after firing that the setup was faulty. The conning tower was abuzz with confusion from the unexpectedly powerful explosion, and information shouted to the TDC operator was misunderstood. Compounding the error, the attack team had miscalculated the target's range—it was almost twice as great as what had been cranked into the TDC. Laughon could only watch as the three fish missed astern. Both *marus* continued on their way south, neither one showing signs of having been hit.

Topside, three confused escorts milled around, signaling to each other. To Laughon's surprise, the two trawlers sighted north of Cam Ranh Bay had joined up with the convoy. Not only was he upset with his shooting errors, he was also aggravated that he had not been aware of the two additional escorts, a serious lapse.

The trawlers made a half-hearted search while the *Rasher* easily evaded at periscope depth. After twenty minutes the trawlers took off after the convoy. As a parting shot, five moderately loud depth-charge explosions rumbled from the south. After a sound and periscope sweep reported all clear, the *Rasher* surfaced. With only one torpedo left (damn the mines!) and the targets already in shallow water near Padaran, Laughon elected not to go after them.

The attack was an utter, demoralizing failure. There was not a thing to show for it but a bunch of broken light bulbs and paint chips littering the decks. Laughon's contact report concluded with the fact that he had but one torpedo left. As expected, the *Rasher* was ordered back to Fremantle.

Early in the morning of 12 January, near the western entrance to Dangerous Ground, Number 4 Main Engine had to be taken off line and secured. Because the weather was rough, Laughon submerged to facilitate repairs to two cylinder heads. It was a familiar problem: burned exhaust valves. For the better part of the day the machinist's mates laboriously relapped valves and seats, working furiously to get the engine bolted together and running again. A day later it was, and with all four engines back on line the *Rasher* worked her way southeast toward the Tizard Banks, through North Balabac Strait, then Sibutu Passage. The patrol had indeed been a short one—twenty-four days so far—and Laughon felt there had not been nearly enough time at sea to properly train the men. The men, on the other hand, felt they had been at sea long enough; Fremantle beckoned.

On the fifteenth, the *Rasher* stood into Siaoe Passage with the master gyro compass out of commission. Out came the tools and parts to repair a grounded motor connection. Steering by magnetic compass, the submarine entered the Molucca Sea and turned south. Good weather stayed with her all the way.

Two days later, at 0437, the radar watch picked up two ships at a range of seven miles. From the size and strength of the contact, one of them was mighty big. The tracking party was called away while the officer of the deck put the *Rasher*'s stern to the contacts and rang up "All Stop" to determine their bearing.

In the spreading light of dawn a large merchantman with escort lumbered over the horizon 14,000 yards away. Laughon got under way at flank speed, then dove to avoid sure detection as the targets zigged right and closed rapidly. He came to a normal approach course and headed for the targets at full speed, slowing only for periscope observations every few minutes as the two ships grew larger and more distinct. Laughon studied the targets through the attack scope, then huddled with the plotting party as more information was developed.

The AK was an *Aikoku Maru*-class cargo ship, a beauty of about 10,500 tons. She had a tall, boxy bridge structure festooned with small platforms and ladders aft of the forward well deck. She was accompanied by an escort that looked like a menacing *Terutsuki*-class destroyer. *Terutsuki*s were identifed by their tripod masts and a black, falling-back, single stack. The destroyer's shrill, monotonous echo-ranging was piped to the conning tower over the 1MC. If it was a *Terutsuki*, perhaps, she was guarding an exceptionally valuable cargo; first-line destroyers were not assigned escort duty unless a cargo warranted their protection.

Plot determined that the pair were zigzagging at six- to ten-minute intervals between 225 degrees and 280 degrees. On a typical zig leg their closest approach to the *Rasher*'s periscope was 4,500 yards. Speed estimates were revised every few minutes until Plot finally settled on eleven knots. At that range and speed, Laughon observed, by the time he swung around to fire the last torpedo from Number Eight Tube the range would be a whopping 5,000 yards—two and a half miles. A low power setting would have to be cranked into the torpedo for it to reach the target; the probability of a hit was nil. He ordered the boat to the surface to work ahead in order to have a chance at a more promising shot.

For the rest of the day, the *Rasher* raced full speed through the

Banda Basin, keeping out of sight, paralleling the targets as they steamed southward.

As the *Rasher* approached Padea Besar off the Celebes coast, Laughon was forced to work around a weather-ravaged three-masted schooner that approached from the northeast and tacked onto a converging course. Laughon sheered away, but the schooner forced the submarine off track. In the process the target was lost in squalls rolling along the horizon. Exasperated, Laughon seriously considered shooting up the schooner to teach the captain and crew a lesson. He suspected they were part of the extensive offshore Japanese anti-submarine network; a few pans of 20-millimeter through her hull and sails would send them limping home. But the *maru* was the important target, so Laughon ordered full speed, maneuvered around the old hulk, and resumed headlong pursuit. He kept up the frantic, driving pace, refusing to dive even when SD radar reported a rapidly closing plane contact. He gambled his ship would not be sighted, and he was right—the plane obligingly veered east toward Buru and disappeared from the scope. Not being the gambler Laughon was, the officer of the deck kept his hand near the diving alarm.

As the *Rasher* drove east of Manui Island, a flotilla of sailboats gave chase. They tacked from both quarters in a coordinated effort to get in the way and slow her down. A Japanese controller aboard one of the sailboats was undoubtedly orchestrating things; the radio room reported strong transmissions from a low-frequency transmitter in the immediate area. But Laughon handily worked around and left them pitching in the *Rasher*'s wake like so much flotsam.

At 1400 the *maru* was sighted again off the port beam, ten miles away. She had shed her escort and was proceeding alone at sixteen knots toward the northern entrance to Buton Strait. Once she entered the strait the chase would be over: it was barely two miles across at its widest point, very shallow, and prohibitively dangerous for a submarine. But luck was with the *Rasher*, for at 1520 the target turned southeast for Buton Passage, which lay in open water between Buton and Wangiwangi, thus giving her pursuers another chance. Still, this passage was only twenty miles wide between Cape Kassolanatumbi and the islands to the east. With such scant room for maneuvering, Laughon could not hope to work ahead of the target until she cleared the passage. So he decided to trail the enemy until after dark.

Shortly after sunset at 1800, Laughon closed in on the *maru* to re-establish radar contact and work into position. At Wangiwangi, the target exchanged blinker signals with a destroyer, which moved slowly from the lee of the island and fell in obediently on the target's port beam. Laughon worked around them to reach a firing position ahead and to port, all the while keeping a seaman's eye on the reefs surrounding the small island groups they were passing.

Now it was time for the final act.

With the *Rasher* ahead and to the left of the target's track, Laughon ordered "right full rudder" and "all ahead flank" to bore in. When the range was marked at 3,200 yards he slowed to fifteen knots and turned left to set up for a stern shot. At that very moment the big ship turned left too, but the *Rasher* kept her stern tubes pointed right at her.

"Standby aft, standby Eight! Track one-eighty! Gyro angle one-eighty! Here she comes! Fire!"

At 1952, fifteen long hours after making contact with the enemy, the *Rasher*'s last torpedo was fired—only to premature twenty seconds after leaving the tube!

Disgusted and as exhausted as any man aboard, Laughon retired at full speed for Ombai Passage.

That night Ken Tate made a diary entry.

> Jan. 17, 1944: Sighted a Jap transport with Jap destroyer as escort. Made a surface attack at nite with our 1 torpedo. A perfect shot and the damn thing was a premature. We were close to land with about 40 ft. of water. We started to go like hell on 4 engines. When the Japs heard the fish blow up they probably thought it was a plane so they went like hell the other way. Lucky for us.

The *Rasher* arrived in Fremantle on 24 January 1944.

The Damnable Tin Fish

Willard Laughon prepared the *Rasher's* second patrol report with care. His festering anger over the wretched torpedo performance was masked by the lively narration of the operational and technical facts of the patrol.

To be sure, the anger was shared by the entire submarine force. Virtually from the day the war started submariners encountered two main problems with their torpedoes: deep running and faulty exploders. The two difficulties were separate but related.

Submarine skippers told the same stories over and over again: they had a perfect setup; the torpedoes were fired; they reached their targets—and nothing happened. Duds! A variation on this theme involved reports of torpedoes slamming against the hull of a ship and, rather than the warheads blowing up, the air flasks exploded. In the *Rasher's* case it was torpedoes prematuring on their way to the target, warning the enemy they were under attack, and revealing the submarine's position. The sub commanders were mad as hell—they were risking their lives to shoot faulty torpedoes. As one of ComSubPac's staff officers said, the only reliable feature of the torpedoes was their unreliability.

To the submariners' astonishment, Submarine Command's response was to blame the skippers for poor marksmanship. An ossified, stubborn, and arrogant Navy bureaucracy refused to admit there was a problem, or to concede that the mighty technological resources at its disposal were not infallible. To the submariners, the handling of the torpedo problem by the Bureau of Ordnance during World War II bordered on the criminal.

When the war broke out, the Mark-14 torpedo was the latest model in quantity production. It weighed approximately 1 1/2 tons and had an effective range of more than 9,000 yards. It was a complex weapon comprised of five major sections: warhead and exploder; air flask with fuel and air tanks; midship section, where combustion took place; an afterbody with oil tank, turbines, and control devices; and the tail, with counter-rotating props and exhaust port. After the torpedo was ejected from the tube by compressed air, an internal hydrostatic mechanism sought out a preset depth, and with gyroscopic control the tin fish would settle onto a predetermined course and streak toward the target. Power was generated by spraying atomized water through burning alcohol to create steam to spin the turbine.

The Mark-14 carried an explosive charge of 668 pounds of torpex—a mixture of TNT, RDX, and aluminum powder, the last added as an accelerator to generate more punch. As the torpedo rushed through the water, it set in motion a spinner attached to a mechanical linkage that inserted the detonator into the fulminate caps after a minimum run of 450 yards. The detonator was the new, top-secret Mark-6 magnetic. This complicated, 98-pound influence mechanism was designed to explode when passing through the magnetic field of a steel-hulled ship. Because the exploder had been developed in such great secrecy, very little was known about it in the submarine force. What information did exist was locked in a safe at the Bureau of Ordnance (BuOrd).

The Navy started work on the Mark-6 in 1922, when BuOrd allocated $25,000 for development work. It was this exploder, not the Mark-14 torpedo itself, that would prove to be the nexus of the problem. And because of the way BuOrd developed its torpedoes and the way submarine torpedo practice was conducted in the prewar Navy, the exploder's defects remained hidden.

Unbelievable as it may seem, to economize on torpedoes (they cost $10,000 apiece) and prevent damage to the expensive mechanisms, no live tests were ever conducted with the Mark-14-Mark-6 combination. In practice firings, torpedoes were set to run under their targets so as not to damage either the torpedo or the target. While this proved adequate to test a submarine skipper's ability to conduct an approach and attack, it was wholly inadequate as a test of the exploders and torpedoes themselves. Even after the outbreak of hostilities with Japan, no live test of the exploder, contact or magnetic, was conducted. Assurances of perfect performance were expected to be accepted on faith alone.

The German Navy abandoned its magnetic exploders because they were too erratic for submarine use and too complicated to build, much less maintain at sea. Had the U.S. Navy done some rudimentary testing of its own, the same conclusion would have been reached. Similarly, problems with the Mark-14's faulty depth-controlling hydrostatic mechanism would have been identified and corrected. But even as evidence of deep running and deficient exploders inexorably piled up, the Navy ascribed all torpedo failures to poor maintenance or faulty fire control, choosing to believe that American know-how was infallible. By mid-1942, however, the evidence could no longer be ignored.

Charles Lockwood, who had replaced Capt. John Wilkes as ComSubSoWesPac in April 1942, approved a simple test to demonstrate the deep-running problem to a stubborn BuOrd. A fishing net was moored outside the harbor in King George Sound, Australia, and torpedoes with deactivated exploders were fired at it. An examination disclosed that where the Mark-14s had pierced the net they had run an average of eleven feet deeper than set. Lockwood promptly reported his findings to BuOrd. Even with his evidence staring it in the face, BuOrd questioned the accuracy of the data. Nevertheless, the bureau was forced to conduct its own tests at the torpedo station at Newport, Rhode Island, in August of 1942. Reluctantly, the bureau admitted that indeed the Mark-14s were prone to roughly a ten-foot depth error.

While this solved the deep-running problem—shots were simply set shallower to compensate—it only exacerbated the nightmarish problems inherent in the Mark-6 exploder. During the torpedo's run to the target, the exploder employed a complex countermining device that disabled the firing pin so the warhead could not be detonated by a nearby explosion or by the magnetic field of another torpedo. Once the deep-running problem was solved, the torpedo ran closer to the surface, where turbulence and pressure differentials caused the countermining device to fail. The result was prematures. Another complication was the discovery that the magnetic fields of ships (and torpedoes) were significantly altered by the Earth's own magnetic field, especially near the equator. Rather than being perfectly symmetrical, as had been assumed, a ship's magnetic field in reality was squeezed into a flat, elliptical shape radiating far out to the ship's sides, leaving only a very small magnetic field under her keel. Warheads often exploded when torpedoes entered the outer edge of the compressed field, too far from the ship to be effective.

BuOrd tried to pretend the problem lay elsewhere, anywhere but in the exploder mechanism itself. It blamed maintenance personnel, faulty target data, or just plain incompetence on the part of submarine fire-control parties. To the bitter end, BuOrd vociferously maintained that there was nothing wrong with the Mark-6.

Notwithstanding BuOrd's assurances, there was a lot of discussion in submarine command about the advisability of deactivating the magnetic portion of the exploder. Many officers, including Admiral Lockwood and Admiral Christie (who had played a major role in the development of the Mark-6, and thus had an abiding interest in seeing that it not be scrapped), were reluctant to deactivate it because of the proven devastating effect of a torpedo explosion under a ship's keel. That kind of hit could only be obtained using the magnetic influence feature. But it was obvious that somewhere in Christie's device lay a serious, hidden flaw. Evidence came not only from the boats returning from patrols, but from the Japanese themselves. From decoded Ultra intercepts, Lockwood knew that many of the hits his submarine skippers claimed were in fact nothing more than prematures or air flasks exploding when they were crushed on impact with a ship's hull. Most damning of all were the Japanese messages noting how fortunate it was that American torpedoes so frequently passed under Imperial keels without exploding. For Lockwood it was humiliating. And it was the final blow.

After reviewing Lockwood's reports, Admiral Nimitz ordered ComSubPac to deactivate the magnetic exploders. Admiral Christie, however, directed SoWesPac subs not to deactivate them. He contended that his headquarters in Fremantle was not subject to Nimitz's orders because Christie reported not to Nimitz but to Vice Adm. Arthur S. Carpender, commander of naval forces in Australia. As Christie pointed out, Carpender's chain of command ended with Gen. Douglas MacArthur himself. Such were the Byzantine workings of command Down Under. But his order would not stand. In January 1943, Admiral Carpender was relieved by Rear Adm. Thomas Kinkaid, who, after a review of the torpedo situation, ordered Christie to deactivate the Mark-6 exploders. Christie had to admit defeat at last.

The deactivation of the magnetic exploder and the fix of the Mark-14's deep running, however, did not put the torpedo problem to rest. Instead, a new problem was revealed: there was a serious flaw in the contact exploder as well. Renewed gloom descended on the sub force.

A test was devised to isolate the problem. The Navy's chief technical innovator, Capt. C. B. "Swede" Momsen, inventor of the Momsen Lung breathing device for submarine escape, convinced the dispirited Lockwood (by now ComSubPac) to fire some war shots against the sheer cliffs on the Hawaiian island of Kahoolawe. He argued that any duds could be easily recovered, dismantled, and inspected to see what had gone wrong. Lockwood liked the idea—though he fretted that tinkering with unexploded torpedoes would have them shortly, as he put it, "shaking hands with St. Peter."

Three torpedoes were fired, resulting in two explosions and a dud. When the dud was examined, it was discovered that the firing pin guides were bent. While the pin itself had traveled the length of the guide into the fulminate caps, it had lacked sufficient force to set them off. With the exploder problem traced to the firing and guide pins, another series of tests were conducted. Dummy warheads were dropped onto a steel plate. When the torpedoes hit at a right angle, the majority were duds; dropped at an oblique angle, half or fewer were duds—hardly an improvement. The evidence was there for all to see: when the warhead hit a solid object, more often than not, the firing pin mechanism was crushed.

The Pearl Harbor submarine base went to work on a new contact exploder designed around a strong, lightweight firing pin. It worked beautifully. At long last the despised Mark-6 exploder was fixed and the worst aspects of the torpedo problem solved. It was then October 1943; the war had been raging for nearly two years. There would continue to be sporadic difficulties with the Mark-14s, but once they were used up they disappeared for good, replaced with new Mark-18 electric torpedoes. Although the Mark-18 had its own problems, it was generally a reliable torpedo.

It has been said that the war of attrition against Japan did not actually start until the Navy had a dependable torpedo. If so, the war finally got under way in early 1944.

The effect that duds, prematures, and misses had on morale was harder to fix, however. A submarine's crew is a tight-knit group, the captain their leader. He relies on his men to perform to the best of their ability. The men must trust the captain's judgment and skill. Failure can cause trust and respect to erode quickly in both directions. Questions and doubts arise. Who is to blame? Is it the skipper? The torpedomen? The attack party? With continued failure the most important element in a submarine's combat success—unity—is destroyed, perhaps forever.

Being familiar with the history of the Mark-14s, Laughon left it to his superiors to draw whatever conclusions they wished about the *Rasher's* torpedo performance. The ship's yeoman typed up a smooth draft and prepared the stencil sheets necessary for mimeographing the report for distribution.

Australian Respite

A brass band, mail, ice cream, fresh milk, and other pleasures awaited the *Rasher's* arrival in Fremantle. Sailors on other boats were
eager to find out how many ships the *Rasher* had sunk, since fierce
competition had developed among the submarines for the honor of
having the top score. More and more boats returned from their
patrols with coxcombs of miniature Japanese flags flying from the
periscopes or with a broom lashed to the shears, indicative of a
"clean sweep."

Admiral Christie was at the pier to greet the *Rasher*. He caught
one of her heaving lines and worked its eye-spliced end over a cleat
on the pier. Once aboard, he shook hands, passed out congratulations, took a quick tour of the boat, and settled into the traditional
wardroom coffee klatch over the patrol report.

When the pleasantries were concluded, Laughon described the
problems they'd had with torpedo prematures. The admiral reiterat-
ed that henceforth SoWesPac submarines would go to sea with their
magnetic exploders deactivated. He listened to Laughon relate the
gripping tale of the chaotic attack on the tanker convoy. The story
about the human ramrod used to load mines on the night of 4
January got a lot of laughs. Christie joked that he'd personally recommend that it become standard operating procedure. When the
disbursing officer arrived it was time to clear the messroom and
passageways for a restless crew waiting to be paid and then to
board the buses for Perth. By 1600, the ship, save for the relief crew,
was deserted.

The patrol report Lieutenant Commander Laughon submitted to
the CO of Submarine Squadron Sixteen was extremely detailed. He
described what he had seen of the makeup of Japanese convoys and
their tactics, aircraft contacts, and weather. Shipboard material
defects covered everything from the 3-inch gun breech to leaky sea
valves and air banks to the grounded gyro compass. From his singular experience with makeshift wolf pack communications, he recommended a more secure code for the TBL 7 voice transmitter. The SJ
and SD radar malfunctions were covered in detail, as were the
Winton diesels' cylinder head woes. (The same problems were crop-
ping up in other boats whose engines were equipped with automatic
lash adjusters.) Laughon praised the *Rasher's* new camouflage for its
effectiveness on the surface both day and night. He submitted the

water sample suspected of being contaminated and alluded to the withdrawal of Australian canned goods from the menu. At the end of the report the skipper praised Lieutenant Quesada for his cooperation at Exmouth, and even made mention of his donated fruitcake.

The statistical side of the report had the *Rasher* on patrol for thirty-seven days, twenty-four of them spent north of the Malay Barrier, a short run by any measure. She had steamed a total of 4,384 miles and burned 49,990 gallons of fuel. Twenty-two copies of the report were prepared for distribution to fifteen commands, and another fifty copies were run off for distribution to other submarines for their skippers to review.

After a more detailed study, Christie attached his personal endorsement and sent it, like all war patrol reports, on its way to Admiral Nimitz, a former sub sailor who kept a sharp eye on current operations. Christie's endorsement, dated 11 February 1944, was particularly fulsome in its praise of Laughon's aggressiveness and persistence. No mention was made of the minelaying operation in the confidential portion of the report. The attack on the tanker convoy was the highlight of the patrol.

◆ ◆ ◆

After a close analysis of Laughon's and Porter's patrol reports, Admiral Christie's staff, contrary to the skippers' view of the engagement, concluded that in all likelihood the *Rasher* had attacked the same ship—the *Kiyo Maru*—three times, damaging her twice and finally sinking her on the third try. Comdr J. M. Haines, CO of Submarine Squadron Sixteen, described it this way:

> The first attack was a night surface attack made on the flank ship of a three ship convoy. A premature gave warning of the attack but it is probable that one hit was made. The second was a submerged night periscope attack made on what, from analysis and comparison with the BLUEFISH report, appears to have been the same target. Two torpedoes of six fired prematured; one hit was made. The second hit reported by the BLUEFISH, which was in company, must have been an internal explosion as it occurred twenty-four minutes later as the RASHER was surfacing. The target at this time took a heavy list. The third attack was a night surface radar attack made on what was possibly this same target. Although there were two prematures out of four torpedoes, two hits were made from a range of 3100 yards and the target, a tanker, burst into flame.

Paragraph three of Christie's endorsement set out his view of the battle, essentially agreeing with Haines's.

The possibility exists that the tanker sunk on the morning of 5 January, 1944, was a different target than the damaged KIYO MARU, but the evidence is not conclusive enough to justify credit for sinking an additional vessel of another type.

The *Rasher* was credited only with the 7,250-ton *Kiyo Maru*. JANAC's postwar analysis proved this correct. It was a perfect example of how an expert like Laughon could be fooled into thinking he had sunk and damaged more ships than he actually had. Even though there were only three ships in the convoy and the *Bluefish*'s target, the *Hakko Maru*, was in flames and visible from the *Rasher*'s bridge, Laughon believed he had damaged two ships and sunk a third. (He also mistakenly claimed damaging one of the ships attacked on 11 January off the coast of Indochina.) Laughon's confusion is understandable, given the fluid nature of the situation. The episode underscores the difficulties of assessing the highly controversial postwar JANAC scores and the inflated claims of sinkings that were to follow many years later.

Although not all her claims were validated, Christie awarded the Submarine Combat Insignia and congratulated the *Rasher*'s commander, officers, and crew for a well-conducted and aggressive patrol. Willard Laughon was Christie's type of captain, the *Rasher* his kind of submarine.

◆ ◆ ◆

Fresh from the Submarine Operation Office where he'd attended briefings and studied intelligence reports, the *Rasher*'s skipper drew charts from the submarine tender *Pelias* so he could study the area he and his men would patrol next.

Her Operation Order, number 20-44, stated that after topping off at Exmouth, the *Rasher* was to patrol the Surabaya-Ambon traffic route north of Bali. She was to arrive on station about 25 February. On 1 March, she would shift her position to patrol the Celebes as far north as the Talaud Islands. Once again her track would take her through the Lombok and Makassar Straits. Return to Fremantle was plotted through the Molucca, Ceram, and Banda Seas.

Using fresh Ultra intercepts from Japanese convoys to position themselves, Fremantle boats had found good hunting in the Celebes

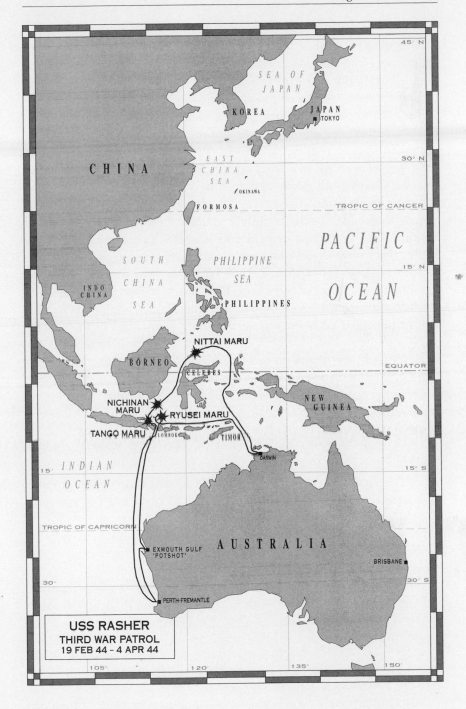

SEA OF JAPAN

KOREA

JAPAN
TOKYO

CHINA

EAST CHINA SEA

OKINAWA

FORMOSA

TROPIC OF CANCER

PACIFIC

OCEAN

SOUTH CHINA SEA

PHILIPPINE SEA

INDO CHINA

PHILIPPINES

NITTAI MARU

BORNEO

CELEBES

EQUATOR

NEW GUINEA

NICHINAN MARU

RYUSEI MARU

TANGO MARU

LOMBOK

TIMOR

DARWIN

INDIAN

OCEAN

TROPIC OF CAPRICORN

AUSTRALIA

EXMOUTH GULF 'POTSHOT'

BRISBANE

PERTH-FREMANTLE

USS RASHER
THIRD WAR PATROL
19 FEB 44 – 4 APR 44

Sea. Their reports indicated that anti-submarine activity was heavy once again throughout the Lombok and Makassar straits. Skippers returning from patrols north of the Malay Barrier revealed that unescorted enemy shipping was a rarity, and they warned that Japanese escorts were becoming more adroit in their tactics and use of sonar. The reports also noted a marked increase in air patrols. Laughon integrated all of this information into his planning.

In addition to regular patrolling, the *Rasher* was nominated by Task Force Seventy-one to conduct periscope photography. This entailed shooting photos of enemy convoys and escorts and, if feasible, coastal installations and other features of interest to Navy intelligence. The tender's optical shop installed a camera bracket on the Number One Periscope designed to accept a Primaflex single-lens reflex 2 1/4" x 2 1/4" roll-film camera. The periscope itself was altered by fully enclosing its well in the control room with a sleeve that confined its use to the conning tower, like Number Two Periscope. This modification would allow for the installation of updated radar and radio equipment between and around both periscopes in the control room at a future date.

Meanwhile, the attack party was schooled in the proper use of the camera. Members needed a thorough understanding of the basic principles of the reduced transmission of light resulting from the technical peculiarities of periscope optical systems: only about 35 percent of the light would actually reach the film plane through the exit lens. In addition, they were shown how to overcome gross vibration of the periscope tube by utilizing high shutter speeds to obtain sharp pictures. The Kodak roll film the Navy used for periscope photography, Plus-X and Super XX, had ASA ratings of 125 and 400, respectively. They were particularly unforgiving when underexposed. Accurate exposures were essential to success. For personnel who were not professional photographers, it was no easy task—especially in a cramped, hot conning tower in enemy waters.

While the *Rasher*'s crew spent two weeks at the somewhat Spartan rest camps, the submarine herself lay alongside the *Pelias* undergoing a refit. This time, along with overhauling and rebuilding two main diesel engines and the auxiliary, the machinist's mates installed General Motors' second-generation lash adjusters. The manufacturer promised they would end once and for all the problem of burned valves and damaged seats.

When the *Rasher*'s full complement returned on 7 February, the Watch, Quarter, and Station Bill had to be reworked as a contingent of new men reported to replace those detached to other boats. By now only about half the *Rasher*'s original crew was still aboard. Prior to departing for trials and exercises, the ship was cleaned up, fumigated, and loaded.

Into the Maelstrom I

On 9 February 1944, the *Rasher* stood out of Fremantle in company with the converted yacht *Isabel* and the submarine rescue vessel *Chanticleer* for five days of sea trials, training, deep dives, and sound tests. The weather was beautiful, with temperatures in the eighties. The *Chanticleer* provided target services for the *Rasher*'s yellow-nosed practice torpedoes and dropped the requisite indoctrination depth charges. The only casualty this time out was the freshly overhauled auxiliary diesel engine's timing gear, which self-destructed and sheared off most of its teeth.

Back at Fremantle, final loading for departure went ahead with noticeable enthusiasm while the auxiliary engine was repaired. A damaged flexible coupling between the auxiliary and its generator delayed departure until the nineteenth. While repairs were made, Laughon conducted more training exercises as the boat lay tied up alongside the *Pelias*.

On 19 February, with her pilot aboard and an impatient crew at quarters, the *Rasher* backed out of the nest and came about in the Swan River. Christie and his group, aboard one of the nested boats, flashed Laughon a final salute as they watched his submarine head for sea.

◆ ◆ ◆

The *Rasher*'s passage through the submarine safety lanes was uneventful. Laughon held drills for all three sections, including day and night gun drills with the 3-incher and 20-millimeters. At Exmouth Gulf, which was all white caps and hot, whipping wind, the *Rasher* moored to the fuel lighter and took on 11,590 gallons of diesel. Laughon signaled his regards to Lieutenant Quesada. When the conning tower clock stood at 1339, the *Rasher* slipped her moorings and was under way for Lombok Strait.

The two-day passage north through the Indian Ocean was routine, punctuated only by more drills and training as the chiefs rotated the watch to indoctrinate the new men and acquaint them with the realities of war patrolling. The weather was balmy and skies were blue. A steady fifteen-knot northwest wind kicked up six-foot seas. Frolicsome flying fish landed on deck like uninvited passengers. Not liking the accommodations, most departed immediately; others, their long pectoral fins trapped between the teak deck slats, struggled to free themselves.

The *Rasher*'s call sign had not been included in the nightly Fox schedules guarded by the radio watch since her departure from Fremantle. But on 24 February, it appeared with the added import of an Ultra designation. The communications officer rushed the decoded paper strip to Laughon. It directed him to rendezvous with the submarine *Raton* for a sweep of Raas Strait. Their quarry was a two-ship convoy due to arrive on 25 February between 1800 and 2000.

The *Rasher*'s Manitowoc-built sister ship, the *Raton*, was likewise on her third patrol. Her skipper was Lt. Comdr. James W. Davis. The coordinates for the *Raton*'s position provided by Ultra and the approximate position and track of the convoy were quickly transferred to the navigation chart on the conning tower worktable. There was no time to waste. No sooner had the captain read the message than word of its contents spread through the boat.

Cautiously, but with four engines on the line to make landfall as early as possible on the twenty-fifth, Laughon approached Lombok Strait from the south at full speed. As always, there was a good chance Japanese patrol boats would be lurking near the mouth of the strait, perhaps hidden by rain squalls or concealed against dark headlands. He might have a date with a convoy, but Laughon could not be careless getting to it. The SJ radar, working stronger than ever, picked up Nusa Penida from more than 70,000 yards. Laughon hoped to take photographs of the coastline, but it was too dark by the time they arrived. All hands were at battle stations as the *Rasher* slipped into the strait. By 0200, they were through and heading for the Raas Strait west of the Kangean Islands.

Twenty miles north of Bali, the *Rasher* collided with heavy squalls as she closed in on the *Raton*'s position. As the miles clicked off, the men relaxed by listening to radio broadcasts by the infamous Iva Ikuko Toguri d'Aquino—"Tokyo Rose." Between tinny renditions of popular tunes by Tommy Dorsey and his orchestra, singers like Rosemary Clooney, and others, Tokyo Rose gloated about ominous, but false, Japanese advances all along the Asian front, bolstering her claims with bogus Allied casualty figures. The sailors welcomed her as a comic distraction from the serious business that lay ahead.

By the first dogwatch the *Rasher* received a voice transmission from the *Raton*. She was ten miles south of the *Rasher*. She shortly materialized out of a squall—a perfect twin of the *Rasher*, right down to the gray-black camouflage and 3-inch deck gun forward. Both boats lay to while Davis and Laughon talked over their search plan. Davis suggested that he search south of a line bearing 120 degrees from Raas Strait, while the *Rasher* searched north of the line. Laughon agreed, and the two made last-minute additions to the radio voice code they would use. At 1650, as they were overtaken by a squall line, the boats parted company.

◆ ◆ ◆

Ugly gray-green seas erupted over the *Rasher*'s bow and sent a shiver through her stout hull. At twenty knots she skirted a phalanx of heavy, dark squalls that hindered the search for the targets. Then, at 1730, the superstructures and masts of two cargo vessels and two escorts were sighted simultaneously from the drenched bridge and through the high periscope. Once again, Ultra was as good as its word.

Even though the enemy ships were shrouded by fast-moving squalls, to avoid being seen, Laughon put them astern and started working ahead for an attack. He contacted the *Raton* by voice radio to inform Davis that the *Rasher* would be in position to attack after sun set at 1842. By 1900, the *Rasher* was seven miles ahead of the convoy's projected track. With darkness coming down rapidly, conditions were perfect for a high-speed surface attack. The plotting party had the targets zigzagging at roughly six-minute intervals. They were offset, the larger of the two *marus* leading the way, the smaller one 1,500 yards distant on the other's starboard quarter. The two escorts were outboard of the formation, port and starboard.

ONI 208-J did not offer an adequate identification of the larger ship, which had two decks, a single deep well, and composite superstructure. Through his 7 x 50s, Laughon estimated her to be a 6,500-tonner. The smaller one resembled a *Panama Maru*-class AK of about 5,270 tons displacement. She was so heavily laden that her Plimsoll line—the waterline for a ship with a full, safe load—was below water. The two escorts were small, shallow-draft vessels, their superstructures protected with thatched bamboo shrapnel mats. Both badly needed paint and most likely had not seen the inside of a dry dock in years. Laughon wanted to get pictures of them, but it was too dark.

"Make ready all tubes!"

The *Rasher* headed in. Since visibility was poor, she could pass astern of the escort stationed on the large AK's port bow without being seen. The Mark-6 exploders were set to actuate on contact. Depth set for eight feet, the torpedoes would pass under the escort, which would be unaware of the attack until explosions erupted on the target.

Over the roar of wind and diesels, the bridge speaker crackled that the setup checked perfectly. "Shoot any time, Captain," Laughon was advised.

Without once looking away from the forward TBT, Laughon gave the order to fire. Four torpedo wakes disappeared into the blackness beyond the *Rasher*'s bow. No sooner was the last one on its way than Laughon bellowed the order for flank speed and hard right rudder to come about and set up on the second target. As if anticipating the order, the controllermen in the maneuvering room immediately responded with more power. Her screws energized by 6,400 horsepower, diesel roar swelling to a frantic pitch, the *Rasher* dug in hard and heeled to starboard, spewing black smoke from her exhaust pipes.

To port, exploding torpedoes ripped open the 6,200-ton *Tango Maru*.

As the *Rasher* hauled out for a torpedo reload, Laughon scuttled down the ladder into the conning tower to confirm the disposition of the targets. He watched the busy radar screen; the plotting party had its hands full tracking four spikes on SJ. Two of the spikes, the smaller AK and her escort, were fleeing, while the *Tango Maru* lay in flames 1,500 yards away, about to roll under. Her escort had charged off looking for the *Rasher*; not finding her, the Japanese skipper made a wide return sweep to assist the torpedoed ship. But three heavy underwater explosions from the *maru*'s boilers signaled that it was too late. From initial hit to the moment the *Tango Maru*'s stack disappeared, only four minutes had elapsed.

The second target and her escort were 30 degrees off the port bow, 6,200 yards away, steaming southeast as fast as they could. Laughon returned to the bridge and prepared to attack.

The second target's escort was conveniently positioned off her port bow. Laughon's strategy called for the *Rasher* to barrel astern of the *maru* on the surface 3,500 yards away and work up her starboard side. An approaching rain squall complicated things, but Laughon swung the *Rasher* hard left and made his cut.

A voice message from the *Raton* confirmed her position 9,000 yards off the *maru*'s port bow, ready to come to the *Rasher*'s assistance if needed. Laughon replied that he was going in on the attack. Fourteen hundred yards from his target, he fired four torpedoes.

The setup was perfect. The first torpedo hit smack between the bow and the MOT. *Ka-boom!* The second one hit directly under the stack. *Ka-boom!* For an encore, the third torpedo hit the ship's stern. *Ka-boom!*

Sheets of white-hot flame burst from the *maru*'s innards. Debris pinwheeled hundreds of feet into the air in every direction. The heavily loaded ship collapsed like a pricked balloon and settled by the stern. Her bow pointed to the sky, the dying ship hesitated a moment, then slid backwards and plunged to the bottom, the eerie shriek of collapsing bulkheads and whistle of escaping air from crushed compartments issuing from her hulk. All that was left to mark her grave was a swirling dome of bubbles and steam. Elapsed time from the first torpedo hit: six minutes. Barely into her third war patrol, the *Rasher* had already sunk her seventh ship, the 4,797-ton passenger-cargo vessel *Ryusi Maru*. Ken Tate was sure the *Rasher* had set a record, "sinking 2 ships just 6 days from Perth."

The sweating men below decks could not see the action firsthand, but the telephone talkers relayed information throughout the boat as fast and as accurately as they could. Their blow-by-blow description was almost as good as being on the bridge with the captain. Every man aboard savored the stop and start of diesels, the lurch and roll of the ship's wild maneuvers. They heard the sharp detonation of torpedoes and felt the deep rumble of superheated *maru* boilers exploding in cold sea water.

As the *Rasher* hauled away at fifteen knots, Laughon radioed the *Raton*, apologized for "hogging the show," and confirmed there were no targets left—save for the confused escorts. Two small, fast, pips appeared on radar, but contact was quickly broken off. (One of them may have been the *Raton*. In his patrol report, Laughon said he was "unsure whether he was the tracker or trackee.") Then word was passed to secure from battle stations. Over thick sandwiches and fresh coffee in the crew's mess and wardroom, the men, keyed up from the battle, tried to relax while they reviewed the action in minute detail. As the *Rasher* headed northeast at full speed, thirty miles astern the loom of a searchlight was visible carving across the horizon as the escorts searched for survivors.

After a dawn star shoot fixed the submarine's position, a course was laid out for the enemy's shipping lanes near the Lima and Kalukalukuang Islands off the southern Celebes coast. The action in Raas Strait had been merely a warmup for Laughon and the *Rasher*.

◆ ◆ ◆

The reports of increased air activity proved to be correct. SD radar picked up numerous aircraft as the *Rasher* drew close to the Celebes. Though the planes were never actually sighted, their presence was a constant threat that slowed forward progress by forcing the submarine to dive. However, none of the planes approached closer than twelve miles. Most of them crossed the *Rasher's* track heading west toward Borneo. As she approached Laurel Reef under the cover of darkness, the SJ scope showed indications of another radar in the vicinity—an aircraft unit at the limit of its range, from the looks of it. It produced a wobbling, shimmering interference that flickered across the scope. SD reported no contacts, however. Since the Japanese had few radar-equipped planes capable of flying at night, Laughon believed the plane—if it was one—might be covering an important ship movement between Pulo Laut and Makassar City, the latter but thirty miles away. Spreading out the charts, he examined the southern Celebes-Borneo traffic route. It was worth an investigation. A course was shaped and four-engine speed rung up.

On paper it looked promising. Tanker traffic ran south along the coast of Borneo from Balikpapan to the island of Sebuku. When ships reached Cape Mangkok, they usually doubled the shallows off the island, then turned southeast and made a high-speed run to Makassar City. A submarine waiting patiently offshore might be rewarded as they arrived. A convoy leaving Makassar City bound for Balikpapan was exposed to the sea the moment it got under way; there was no protective harbor to speak of, just a crumbling breakwater along the corniche. Were it not for the abrupt coastal shelving and shallow water, a submarine could sneak right up to the beach and torpedo ships at its leisure.

The *Rasher* reached a position off Makassar City in a little more than two hours. She found the area deserted: even the ubiquitous native fishing boats were nowhere to be seen. Normally their lanterns created a colorful display on the water. This night, however, the sea was pitch black. The mysterious radar emanations had vanished, too. After only an hour on station, Laughon's patience deserted him. Hoping to find better hunting, he headed north toward Cape William and Mankhalihat.

By morning the *Rasher* was twenty miles west of Cape Mandar, headed through the Makassar Strait. At 0958, ship masts were sighted. With four engines bent on, they were pursued until the vessel was identified through the high periscope as a whale-hunting ship, more than likely doubling as an anti-submarine patrol. Laughon broke off contact.

Before the noon meal was served, another contact was made. It developed into a cat and mouse routine, one in which the cat lays in wait around a corner for a mouse it expects to appear at any minute. But in this case, the mouse had other ideas. Laughon's patrol report described what happened:

1110 Sighted two masts of a ship just to the left of CAPE WILLIAM. We headed towards him, and determined by his change of bearing that he was on a southerly course. We could see that he was a MFM [small coastal patrol boat] type, but could not judge his size. We came to the normal approach course at 18 knots, heading for the southern part of LIBANI BAY which was an excellent spot to catch anything proceeding in close down the coast.

1149 We were in a good position and submerged to wait for him to come into view again. We had been unable to see him after he had come into the land background after he came south of CAPE WILLIAM.

The *Rasher* crouched like a cat, waiting patiently.

1530 The target had not been sighted, so we pulled out from the beach at six knots for one hour and at

1645 surfaced and headed up the eastern side of MAKASSAR STRAIT towards SOUTH WATCHER at 15 knots, patrolling ten miles off the coast. My only conclusion in regard to the vessel that disappeared is that he was a high-masted patrol vessel similar to one that we saw in the same general vicinity on the last patrol, and that he patrolled part of the way down the coast and then turned around and went back before he came into our field of vision while submerged.

The search for worthwhile targets continued, complicated by strong currents sweeping south through the strait. They bore navigational hazards in the form of hatch covers, oil drums, logs, and spars—all of it wreckage from ships that had been torpedoed weeks earlier. The spars, a foot in diameter and fifteen to twenty feet in length, could hole a ballast tank or wreck a prop shaft. Luckily, radar picked them up from a safe distance.

The *Rasher* swept across the Basilan Strait traffic routes looking to intercept ships steaming south from the Philippines for ports in the Celebes and Halmahera region. But for five days not a single target was sighted. From South Watcher Island to the pass below Sangihe Island, the Celebes Sea was deserted except for a group of small fishing trawlers tending trot-lines across the main traffic lanes off Sangihe. Near Karakitang Island, the *Rasher* passed through a line of netted glass buoys topped with staffs and streamers. From a distance they looked like floating mines, a deadly hazard since the Japanese could not be trusted to abide by the Geneva Convention that required mines to self-disarm if they tore loose from their underwater moorings.

As the *Rasher* stood into the pass south of Sangihe Island after sunset on 2 March, she encountered more than a hundred small, lantern-bearing fishing *banca*s. They were impossible to avoid. They parted like the Red Sea for Moses as the *Rasher* passed through, her bow wave making the little outriggers rise and fall like corks in a bathtub. Laughon assumed the fishermen would report the submarine to the local Japanese commander.

At 0750 the next morning, an SD radar contact drove the *Rasher* down. And again at 0954. "Plane contact! Seven miles and closing!"

A speck on the horizon swiftly materialized into a 300 mile-per-hour twin-engined Mitsubishi Type 96 "Nell." It came in literally skimming the waves.

The *Rasher* was a blur of action as vents popped, watertight doors were slammed shut, and hatches were dogged. She nosed down and was safely under in thirty seconds. Three minutes after the initial contact, two bombs exploded harmlessly as the *Rasher* passed one hundred and twenty feet.

Laughon mulled things over.

> . . . decided that the plane might be covering a ship movement, and that the only way to find out was to surface and look around. Of course if it was only a plane out to look for us as a result of having possibly been sighted the previous night, the best place for us was at 200 feet.

Laughon's intuition would prove to be correct.

The day started out with a high, thin overcast. Visibility was very good. Only a few wind slicks disturbed the light following sea. At 1150, an exceptionally alert lookout, Seaman 1st Class Robert Cashel, sighted smoke on the horizon eighteen miles away. The target's position was due west of the Sangihe Islands and 150 miles south of Mindanao. Plot worked out the essentials as Laughon started an approach.

"Bridge, target bearing two-eight-zero. Target course one-four-five. Speed seven knots."

She was heading southeast, likely making for Manado, Celebes, to deliver a badly needed cargo of war materiel or rice to Japanese troops on the Minhassa Peninsula.

"Come to course two-three-zero! All ahead full!" Laughon ordered.

The assistant approach officer reported he could see through the attack periscope the tops of not one but two ships. "Angle on the bow port zero-eight-zero! Recommend course two-seven-three! Range sixteen miles!" he advised.

Laughon gave orders to the helmsman and the *Rasher*'s bow swung left as she came to her new heading. In another ten minutes more masts and smoke were sighted. It was shaping up into a fair-sized convoy; a lot more than rice was being lugged south.

Other submarines returning from patrols in the *Rasher*'s area had reported that southbound convoys were often accompanied by aircraft escorts from bases on the Zamboanga Peninsula of the Philippines. Therefore, Laughon was certain this one too had air cover. While it would complicate matters, he was supremely confident they could still get ahead of the convoy submerged. After all, the ships were only sixteen miles away. And if the plane's pilot neglected to patrol aggressively, he'd never spot the *Rasher*. So Laughon took her down, mindful of the currents from abeam that would set her toward the targets' track and make submerged navigation tricky.

"Up periscope!"

What a sight! Laughon counted six cargo ships and three escorts, all zigzagging together off their base course. By Japanese standards it was an unusually large convoy; they generally favored smaller ones, which were easier to protect. This was a real prize.

Just as Laughon suspected, the convoy did have air cover. A twin-engined "Sally" bomber, with its characteristic high, center-mounted radio mast, was cruising back and forth over the ships at a low altitude, sticking close to its charges. From a distance the Sallys looked a lot like U.S. B-26s, so it was easy to be fooled into thinking they were friendlies.

The convoy was steaming in two three-ship columns, one escort on the starboard bow of the left-hand column leader, another escort on the port side of the right-hand column leader. An escort was trailing the formation. There was nothing in the identification manuals resembling these particular *marus*. They were stubby passenger-transports of 5,000- to 7,000-tons displacement, with blocky deckhouses typical of Japanese wartime construction that rushed merchant ships down the ways as fast as they could be built to replace ever-increasing losses. Most likely, Laughon speculated, these vessels carried troops as well as cargo. When the range closed sufficiently for a closer look in high magnification, he expected to see Japanese soldiers lining the rails ten deep.

Easier to identify were the pinging escorts. With their undulating forecastles and falling-back stacks, they had the characteristic look of *Chidori*-class torpedo boats whose profiles were prominently displayed in ONI 41-42. *Chidori*s mounted three shielded 4.7-inch guns, various anti-aircraft weapons, and three 21-inch torpedo tubes. The vessels were also equipped with depth charges and depth-charge throwers. Dual Kampon boilers and Parsons geared turbines producing 8,000 horsepower gave the 268-foot ships a maximum speed of 28 knots. They were real submarine killers, exceptionally maneuverable at high speed.

"Bearing—mark!" Laughon rotated the periscope slightly left and right, steadying for a moment on each of the two ship columns.

The exec read the bearings from the azimuth collar. "Two-six-four and two-seven-niner."

The captain adjusted the stadimeter knob. "Range—mark!"

"Seventeen thousand yards."

"Angles on the bow from fifteen port to ten port! Down periscope!"

The setup looked good as the submarine settled on a normal approach course at seven knots. To document the convoy for Navy intelligence, the Primaflex was attached to the periscope fixture when the near column was 8,000 yards away, and several frames of film were exposed, using various shutter speeds and f-stops.

At 1400, as Laughon was busy snapping more pictures, the situation changed abruptly: the targets veered away, altering their base course from southeast to south. Laughon concluded that the *Rasher* had been detected:

> I believe that at about this time the convoy commodore received information that we had been sighted in the morning, and that he changed course from about 145° to 180° to run around our possible position.

For the Japanese, it was not difficult to plot the probable track of a patrolling American submarine. All they needed were a few reported sightings from their network of fishing vessels, coast watchers, and aircraft. With this information, convoys could be warned to steer clear. Assuming this was the case, Laughon turned south and shadowed the convoy until dark. At 1626, when he could no longer see their smoke through the periscope, he surfaced the boat and headed for them at seventeen knots. Not being equipped for night operations, the bomber had returned to its base, leaving the *Rasher* free to make her move without fear of detection from the air.

In the light of a half moon, the targets' smoke was sighted again at a range of fifteen miles. To reduce her silhouette as much as possible and conceal her approach as she drew abeam of the targets, the submarine was flooded down until her decks were awash.

To Laughon's surprise, one of the ships in the rear of the convoy opened up rapid fire with her deck guns and poured in twenty rounds. Despite exposing only the conning tower, the *Rasher* had been sighted in the purple of late twilight. Shells ripped overhead. Water spouts erupted. The escort on the port bow of the formation opened fire and peeled off to attack, her stack erupting in a cloud of black smoke as her fire rooms answered bells for full power.

Warned, the convoy abruptly turned southwest to put the submarine astern. The *Rasher* had no choice but to put her own stern to the fast-approaching *Chidori* and pull away at flank speed before the Japanese got the range and put a round into the periscope shears. The escort pressed the chase for ten miles before finally breaking off to return to her consorts. The *Rasher* turned onto 270°T. to work around and come back in for another try.

At 2147, as she was pulling ahead of the convoy, SJ radar suffered a power failure. Since the lower antenna trunk had to be dropped to find the problem and fix it, there was no way to tell when, or if, it would be back on line. Without radar, Plot would have to rely solely on visual contact and a tricky bit of paper navigation to set up the attack. Laughon had hoped to position the *Rasher* for an attack after moonset at 0100. But rather than risk a protracted end around without radar, Laughon boldly decided to submerge and get in at least one attack straight away. By dawn he could be in position for another.

Laughon hoped the SJ could be repaired in time, so he first submerged to radar depth. But when the radarmen shook their heads, he took her to sixty feet and rigged for depth charge as a precautionary measure. Up ahead, the targets stood out sharply in the moonlight 12,000 yards away, plodding along at 7 1/2 knots. Though the hour was late, the convoy commodore was more than likely just sitting down to his evening meal after a long trick on the bridge trying to foil a submarine attack.

Aboard the *Rasher*, all tubes were ready. With the targets looming up in the periscope, all Laughon had to do was avoid being run down by them, make a snap setup, and, when they closed to 1,500 yards, shoot. He picked out the nearest ship, swung the boat left for a zero gyro angle, got a single sonar ping range, and fired three bow tubes. Then he ordered right full rudder for a zero gyro angle on the next target, gave the setup to the TDC operator, and got the green light at 1,700 yards. Three more fish shrieked on their way.

One right after the other, three torpedoes slammed into the first target and blew up, lifting the ship out of the water. Laughon ran the scope back up just in time to catch the third fish hitting the target's stern. Bedlam erupted. Finding himself virtually in the middle of the convoy, Laughon quickly maneuvered to bring the stern tubes to bear on a third target, a large transport in the near column that was rapidly bearing down on the *Rasher*'s periscope. She was only 600 yards away, angle on the bow five starboard, closing way too fast to get off a down-the-throat shot, since the *Rasher* still had another 90 degrees to swing in order to use her stern tubes.

In an instant the skipper assessed the situation. Sweeping around with the scope, he saw that the ship he'd hit was covered for its entire length by black smoke; hundreds, if not thousands, of enemy troops were being disgorged into the Celebes Sea. To port, he saw that the second salvo of three fish had missed their target. Dead ahead, angle on the bow zero, a *Chidori* was charging in, high bow wave giving her the classic bone-in-the-teeth look, searchlight playing on the water to find the telltale periscope. If Laughon did not dunk the scope and go deep immediately, the transport bearing down would ram the very periscope the *Chidori* was looking for!

"Take her deep! Three hundred feet! Flood Negative!"

At full speed the big transport roared overhead, dropping depth charges, while the *Rasher* angled down under her, heading deep and in the opposite direction. The first salvo went off as the boat was passing 180 feet. Debris, dust, and pieces of cork hull insulation jumped to life. Pipes and fittings vibrated until they were a blur. As the *maru* swept astern, two more depth charges went off a half-minute apart. The charging *Chidori*, meanwhile, passed astern of the *maru* and joined up with a second *Chidori*. Together, they swept over the spot where the *Rasher* had dived.

While the submarine ran silent 325 feet deep under a sonar-deflecting thermocline, the two escorts made random depth-charge runs. Their high-speed screw cavitation resounded through the *Rasher's* hull with the characteristic SWISH-A, SWISH-A, SWISH-A, making the boat's interior vibrate ominously. While the *Chidoris* caused some tense moments (earlier in the patrol a stalwart had deposited a roll of toilet paper in each compartment, marked "For Depth Charge Use Only"), their search pattern and widely dispersed depth charges revealed that the Japanese had no idea where their prey was. Nevertheless, while the *Rasher* was held down, the remnants of the convoy made good their escape.

While the hunting *Chidoris* churned up the surface, conditions below were typically unpleasant. Without air conditioning or ventilation, heat from the submarine's machinery, electrical equipment, and a hundred other sources made the temperature soar. Moisture dripped from pipes and valves filled with cold sea water. Sheets of condensation formed on the hull and trickled into the bilges. In the hot confines of the conning tower, the radarmen calmly worked on the SJ's lower antenna connection, the fragile parts spread out on the clammy deck plates, protected by rags from concussion and dripping sweat.

Just before midnight the depth-charging ceased. The escorts drifted off to the southeast; the sound of their screws grew fainter and disappeared. On the stroke of midnight the *Rasher* surfaced into the cool, fresh, salt air of the Celebes Sea. The yellow orb of the moon lay on the horizon. Three miles away, barely visible in the haze, was a circling *Chidori*. Pinpoints of twinkling lantern light showed where oil-soaked swimmers and rafters bobbed, praying for rescue. Stealthily the *Rasher* slipped away to search for the remains of the convoy, now missing the 6,484-ton cargo ship *Nittai Maru*.

The submarine swept by an oil-stained motor lifeboat filled to the gunwales with shivering, water-logged Japanese soldiers. Surrounded by floating wreckage and robbed of their equipment and arms, they were a pitiful lot. Laughon sped on.

At dawn, when the *Rasher* neared the Balikpapan-Palau traffic route, she dove. A normal submerged routine was set, and Laughon gave the men a rest while he planned his next move.

After a hearty breakfast of powdered scrambled eggs, french fries, ham, and fresh rolls washed down with cups of steaming coffee, Laughon and the plotting party broke out the patrol area charts on the wardroom table. With dividers and navigator's protractor, they shaped a course to track down the convoy. Most likely it was heading east-southeast, making for the Morotai Strait in northern Halmahera. To find it and finish it off, Laughon decided to patrol the 120-mile-long Sangihe Island chain strung out above the northwest tip of the Celebes. For a convoy to cross the Molucca Sea and reach the Morotai Strait, it had to first make its way through one of five narrow passes between the islands making up the Sangihe group. Estimating the convoy's optimum speed at about ten knots, Laughon figured it would be possible to be in position to cover its track through any of the five passes. If they did not make contact with the convoy before daylight, they would retire to a position ten miles northwest of North Loloda Island, a position virtually in the mouth of the Morotai Strait and wait for the convoy to arrive. Unless a plane forced the *Rasher* down, it could hardly be missed. With agreement all around, Laughon ordered the *Rasher* to the surface to start the chase.

All day on 4 March, she drummed along on three engines, steering a little north of due east, headed for the islands. By early afternoon the SJ was back in business after a machinist's mate made a new bushing for the wave guide casing to prevent metal chips from working their way between the rotating surfaces of the dipole and antenna trunk and shorting out the unit.

The *Rasher* went through the main pass south of Sangihe Island at twilight, then turned southeast onto the first leg of the search plan. Once again, Laughon's submarine instinct paid off. At 2117, in an awesome display of visual acuity, a lookout sighted a puff of smoke in the moonlight fifteen miles away. It was the convoy. The officer of the deck turned the boat toward it. At 13,350 yards, radar made contact with five large ships, course 080, speed 8 1/2 knots. Their position was fifty miles west of North Loloda Island. It looked to be a replay of the attack twenty-four hours earlier.

Sure enough, as the *Rasher* headed in, a flanking escort turned toward her and fired. Laughon pulled away until the escort dropped back to rejoin the convoy. Undaunted, he circled around to re-establish contact with the main body of ships. Again, Laughon's plan was to get ahead of them and attack after moonset at 0145.

By 0219, the targets were neatly arrayed to starboard as the *Rasher* drove up their flank. Laughon reported,

> We were ahead of them at a range of about 12,000 yards and there appeared to be five large ships and two or three escorts . . . they had

just made a radical change of course from 140 to 040°T., apparently to shake us off in the reduced visibility. We began to get into attack position on their starboard bow, distant 8,000 yards. We flooded down and made all tubes, two forward and four aft, ready. Our plan was to shoot the bow tubes at the leading target and the stern tubes at the one behind him. We kept the bow on the first target and went in at 17 knots.

Two torpedoes were away at 0302.

I watched these two torpedo tracks as we swung right for a zero gyro angle with the stern tubes on the second target, and saw them both run [harmlessly] under the target.

"Goddamn the torpedoes!"

There was no time to hesitate. "Right full rudder! All ahead full!"

Up on the bridge, the gyro compass repeater unwound crazily as the boat swung around to bring the stern to bear on another large *maru* in the van. Four torpedoes whined out of the after tubes. Next, a quick maneuver put an escort on the starboard quarter where she could be watched; she had not yet seen the submarine or the torpedo wakes, but soon would.

Looking astern through his binoculars, Laughon saw a hit geyser on the second target's bow. The report reached his ears a split second later. Ships' lights flashed on and off. Steam whistles screeched in the blackness. More explosions thundered across the water. The surprised escort wheeled and headed at full speed toward the torpedoed ship, which was already covered by a shroud of thick smoke. The convoy commodore, no doubt rousted from his sea cabin by the explosions, must have watched in disbelief.

The *Rasher* pulled away to load her last four torpedoes. That accomplished, she went in for an attack on the two trailing ships. They were the largest vessels in the convoy and close enough to allow for a quick setup. Dawn would break in an hour; anything more complicated and the attacking submarine would be revealed and lose the initiative.

As two escorts closed in from starboard, Laughon shouted rudder and engine orders down the hatch to the conning tower, fired the remaining torpedoes, then ordered flank speed to put the escorts and their guns astern. Four minutes after the torpedoes left the tubes, the distinct sounds of three exploding warheads reached the *Rasher*'s bridge over the roar of her diesels. At high speed she cleared the area, heading westward, the escorts in hot pursuit. As they dropped off the radar screen, Laughon ordered the submarine about on a long lazy curve to watch the fiery red glow on the horizon. A shower of sparks and cloud of smoke signaled that a flaming ship had gone under.

Laughon got as close to what remained of the convoy as he dared and took pictures through the periscope. At 0505, with dawn breaking, he saw four undamaged AKs making for Morotai Strait at full speed.

At 0629, the *Rasher* submerged for the day's patrol, to rest her crew, and to await instructions via the nightly Fox schedules. It would be a bitter revelation to discover later that despite what they saw with their own eyes, the *Rasher* was not given credit for sinking a ship during her second attack on the convoy.

On 5 March, she was recalled to Darwin to re-provision, refuel, and take on more torpedoes. There would be no major repairs or shore leave; as quickly as possible, she'd head back to her station, making what was known as a double-barreled patrol.

Into the Maelstrom II

In early March, while the *Rasher* was torpedoing ships in the Celebes Sea, Navy code breakers in Hawaii developed information pointing to the possibility that Japanese Fleet Adm. Mineichi Koga was preparing to move a fleet of aircraft carriers, battleships, heavy cruisers, and destroyers from Singapore to Surabaya, Java. Admiral Christie saw this as ominous, for Surabaya was but a thousand miles from Australia, and he feared the Japanese were preparing to attack Fremantle. Aware that the information was not fully developed, Christie nevertheless ordered the *Haddo*, already on station in the area, to patrol the northern approaches to the Lombok Strait, on the lookout for an enemy foray south. The *Haddo* was commanded by Lt. Comdr. Chester Nimitz Jr., son of the commander in chief of the Pacific Fleet.

On 6 March, the *Haddo*'s radar picked up several large ships at long range. Nimitz tried to make visual contact but lost them. Though unsure of their significance, he duly reported the contacts, remembering, he said, the lessons of Pearl Harbor. His message convinced Christie that the Japanese were on the move and might soon be in position to launch an attack from the Indian Ocean. Australian and U.S. forces prepared for a possible raid by carrier planes, and every submarine, refitted or not, was made ready for sea to engage the enemy.

In the Submarine Operations Office, Christie likely pondered the *Rasher*'s name on the deployment board. She had picked up torpedoes and was now one day out of Darwin, heading north for the Banda Sea. If instead she turned west, in two days she could be in position above the Lombok Strait to intercept the anticipated task force. Christie knew she was a first-rate boat with an experienced skipper and fine crew; he had complete confidence she would stand tough and do her best to deflect the Japanese thrust, if and when it came. That night the call went out to her.

The *Rasher* had arrived in Darwin on 8 March to take on stores and torpedoes in order to resume her war patrol north of the Barrier. At the time, Laughon and his men were unaware of Christie's concerns about Admiral Koga's intentions. Provisions and other consumables were hastily loaded to get the boat back out as fast as possible. To play it safe, a spare bushing for the SJ radar's wave guide casing was rounded up and put aboard. Darwin's operations officer was on hand to collect the *Rasher*'s exposed periscope film and deliver it to Task Force Seventy-one's intelligence group for processing and evaluation.

There was a major problem with the torpedoes, however. Of the twenty-four Mark-14s that were loaded, eleven did not have speed rings installed in their control valves. Several hours were lost while the valves were adjusted by the *Rasher*'s torpedomen. Laughon was furious; the torpedoes had passed inspection after being overhauled by Darwin's torpedo shop days earlier. After the work was completed, the *Rasher* got under way just before noon on 9 March, ran the degaussing range, and dove to check trim and look for water and oil leaks. By 1830 she was well on her way.

The *Rasher* was just past the barrier islands near Timor when she received Christie's coded message ordering her to take a position north of Lombok as soon as possible to intercept the enemy force. She headed west at full speed.

From Timor, it was nearly 635 nautical miles to the Lombok Strait, a two-day run with good weather conditions. So a taut radar watch was set and the lookouts were cautioned to be extra alert as the *Rasher* ran on the surface at eighteen knots on four engines against a stout easterly current.

Mile after mile, her wake stretched out in a straight line and disappeared over the eastern horizon. Her diesels beat out a steady, unbroken tune. Flying fish gamboled along her bow wave as though urging her on. Sailors relaxed, read, studied, routined torpedoes, slept, and of course played cribbage. At day's end the swollen sun set off the starboard bow with such a riotous display of violets and magentas it would have inspired the painter John Singer Sargent.

After a five-month gestation period that began in Brisbane, the first issue of the ship's newspaper, *The Bilge Pump*, appeared on this leg of the voyage. It was published by the radiomen using the ship's office as a makeshift city desk. Intrepid diarist Bill Norrington served as editor-in-chief; the machinist's mates, the only sailors on board whose business it was to stick their noses into every nook and cranny on the ship, served as beat reporters.

The Bilge Pump was chock full of tidbits of interdepartmental gossip, facts about the latest mustache-growing contest, baseball scores, news from the Pacific and European theaters, the names of those men who had passed tests for advancement in rating, and much more. The paper was a great morale booster and source of entertainment. And for those who had their foibles exposed to public scrutiny, officer and enlisted man alike, it was the source of plenty of good-natured ribbing.

As the *Rasher* drove west, a plane contact came and went; so did the Maria Reigersbergen and Zandbuis Banks. The Paternoster group of islands north of Soembawa disappeared astern. In late afternoon of 12 March, the highest peak on Lombok, 3,726-foot Mount Rinjani, was in sight from thirty miles out, poking above the haze line on the horizon; the strait was just around the corner. As the *Rasher* got down to business, every man knew what to expect. For Ken Tate, it was one small ship versus the Imperial Navy:

> March 12, 1944: Arrived at our area. Northern Lombok Strait. Expecting Jap task force to come through headed for Australia.

As the evening meal was being served, Laughon was called to the bridge. A smudge of smoke on the horizon developed into a chuffing tug with a barge in tow, moving close to shore along the northern coast of Lombok at Desaanyr. Steaming in the opposite direction ahead of the tow, almost hidden against the island's dark slopes and tree line, was an old, sixteen-knot, coal-burning gunboat. Laughon maneuvered to avoid making contact with her, but still the *Rasher* was sighted. It took a moment for the ungainly two-stacker to get up full steam from its antique boilers and come about, just enough time for Laughon to sheer away and give her the slip. But the Japanese knew a submarine was in the area.

Laughon set a course to take up their patrol station near the Trawangan Islands guarding the northern mouth of the strait. As the *Rasher* rounded the coast off Tanjung at 2001, both radar and sound picked up a pinging PC-1 submarine chaser. She was dead ahead, 6,400 yards away, closing in from the south at twenty knots. No doubt she had been alerted to the *Rasher's* presence by the skipper of the gunboat.

The PC was as long as a submarine and very agile and well-armed. She was put astern and tracked by radar as the *Rasher* came around to a northerly heading. When the full moon rose in the south, spilling light over the Bali Sea, the submarine stood out on the surface. The sub chaser spotted her and, bow surging up out of the water, went to full speed.

The *Rasher* was lightened by blowing safety, negative and the rest of her ballast. But even at flank speed with the tanks blown dry, the enemy patrol boat started overhauling her. When bursts of 40-millimeter tracers straddled his ship, Laughon knew it was time to dive and shoot some fish down the enemy's throat.

The vents popped open, the ship tilted down, and the planesmen leaned into their wheels, urging the *Rasher* under for all they were worth. The sub chaser stayed right with her, dropping depth charges to drive her deep so she could be pinned down and worked over.

Instead, Laughon held the boat at periscope depth and placed the cross hairs on the PC. In the moonlight he saw a curling bow wave break to either side of the sub chaser's stem as she bore down at high speed. The Japanese dodged and weaved slightly, wary perhaps of what might be in store for him.

It was difficult and dangerous to try to hit such a narrow target at night with torpedoes from a thousand yards away. If the enemy skipper was lucky enough to see the fish, he might be able to turn away in time to avoid being hit. If not, a torpedo might catch the vessel under the forefoot, or hit her broadside as she turned left or right into the spread. If neither of those things happened and the torpedoes missed, the *Rasher* would be in for a hell of a depth-charging.

Laughon tersely described what he saw through the scope while the setup was cranked into the TDC. The range counter next to the "own ship" and "target" dials on the TDC's face unwound at an alarming rate. But Laughon did not flinch.

"Standby to shoot! Set depth—zero! Range—mark!"

"One-one-double-oh!"

"Set!"

"Shoot!"

Laughon's patrol report described what happened next:

> 2100   Commenced firing a spread of four torpedoes from the stern tubes. . . . The target must have seen the impulse bubble or wake of the first torpedo as he started changing course to his right very soon after I started firing. He seemed to spin on a dime. I kept putting in check bearings and changing his angle on the bow, but I probably wasn't keeping up with him. All missed, and the last two that were fired broached several times. But they discouraged him for the time being and he drew off and at
>
> 2113   started signalling to two other ships that had arrived on the scene. We opened out until we thought we were well clear. We could see them signalling, but were beyond radar contact at 45 feet.
>
> 2146   Surfaced and started working around the patrol boats to the north and west at full speed on four engines.

Laughon thought these patrol boats might be screening an important ship movement near the Lombok Strait, maybe even the Japanese task force the *Rasher* was looking for. So he decided to see what was going on.

Just beyond the mouth of the strait, the *Rasher* blundered into two Class 13 AM 7-12 coastal minesweepers. These were slim, dual-purpose ships armed with 4.7-inch guns and heavy anti-aircraft machine guns. Though equipped with coal-fired boilers, they were capable of twenty knots.

The first indication that the *Rasher* had been seen came when the minesweepers' stacks belched black smoke. The pair rushed her from the starboard bow, while a third minesweeper materialized and bore down off the starboard quarter from Sepanjang Island. The *Rasher* was about to be trapped in a pincer. Laughon sent the lookouts below, put the rudder over hard to port, and turned away. Muzzle flashes flickered astern.

At flank speed, Laughon headed north. Slowly he eased westward toward Bali, betting the Japanese would just keep tearing north. By the time they realized their mistake, Laughon hoped to be in the Strait of Madura. Unfortunately, one of the pursuers caught on and broke from the pack to head the *Rasher* off. Laughon rolled northeast toward the Kangean Archipelago so the Japanese would think he was heading for the Makassar Strait. They weren't fooled by this move either, and when Laughon made his cut, two minesweepers turned inside the *Rasher*'s track onto her starboard quarter and closed in.

With her tanks bone dry, the *Rasher* was making a tick under twenty knots. Laughon demanded more speed. The motor macs trimmed the engine governors a notch; the electricians increased the loading on the generators and fine-tuned the rheostats. That was all they could do. The pit log stood stubbornly at 19.8 knots. Slowly but surely, the minesweepers gained ground, their gunfire growing more accurate as the range decreased. Rounds whistled overhead and splashed alongside the ship, tossing spray over the bridge. One landed just twenty yards off the port beam.

At one point during the chase, the skipper and OOD dropped down into the conning tower to scrutinize the radar screen and navigation charts. A junior officer stationed aft on the cigarette deck to keep a sharp eye on the pursuing minesweepers with his famous night vision was shocked to find he was the only man topside as the *Rasher* careened through the Bali Sea.

At 0104, near Sepanjang Island, a fourth minesweeper joined in the chase. The safety of sixty fathoms was less than an hour away, Laughon noted. It would be a close shave getting to deep water—4.7-inch shells were straddling the ship. At 0150, with the minesweepers only 1,000 yards astern, the skipper hit the diving alarm and headed for 300 feet, rigged for depth charge and silent running.

The Japanese were on her like a cat on a mouse. As the *Rasher* passed 180 feet, eleven depth charges went off close aboard, forcing the boat sideways, down, and up, generally causing havoc inside the ship. Topside, something carried away, making a terrible racket on the hull over the crew's berthing compartment. The submarine leveled off at 350 feet under a 3-degree thermocline. Only fifteen fathoms remained under her keel as she ran silent and deep slowly off to the north, away from the knot of pinging minesweepers, toward deeper water. Overhead, screws stopped and started. In his patrol report, Laughon noted how persistent the patrol boats were.

During the remainder of the night we had sound contact on echo ranging and/or screws from one to three vessels at all times. They seemed to be patrolling the area very thoroughly to prevent us from surfacing and making off before daylight.

The minesweepers were tenacious, alternately pinging and listening, dropping depth charges, waiting patiently for the sound of a pump, a motor, the ring of a metal object on a deck, or the noise of uncontrollable flooding that meant disaster for their adversary. But at length the rolling thunder of depth charges ceased, and the screws faded to the south.

A hush came over the *Rasher*. There was only an occasional hull creak or soft moan from the hydraulic system. At 0550, a sound sweep indicated topside was sufficiently quiet for a look. Laughon ordered the ship eased to periscope depth, then motioned with his thumbs for the scope. As it took up, the noise of the periscope hoist motors and cable sheaves seemed unnaturally loud in the silent conning tower. Sea water trickled from the periscope's flax packing in the overhead, corkscrewed down the barrel, and puddled on deck; the packing would need attention next refit. Laughon didn't notice; he had his eye to the scope even before it bounced to a stop. Was it okay to surface? Every man awaited his verdict. The captain walked the scope around twice, then snapped the handles up, a signal it should be lowered. "Our friends are still up there."

Twenty-five hundred yards away, gray ships milled around in the morning haze. Laughon took the *Rasher* deep to wait them out. Four hours later, at 0950, the enemy gave up and departed. Nevertheless, Laughon elected to stay down the remainder of the day; he anticipated aircraft patrols.

The run-in with the minesweepers was a mere hint of what was to come.

◆ ◆ ◆

"Surface the boat!"

It was 1707. The familiar roar of high-pressure air blowing water out of the ballast tanks resounded through the ship. It was dark when the *Rasher* surfaced into a freshening sea and cool air braced with the tang of the Southwest Pacific. The ship was ventilated with the engines, a battery charge started, and a southerly course set for the Lombok patrol station.

The racket heard over the crew's compartment during the depth-charging needed investigation. Mike Pontillo was convinced the fueling hose stored in the superstructure had been jolted loose and carried away. He volunteered to go topside. It was an extremely dangerous job, since the boat might have to submerge at any moment, leaving him trapped in the superstructure. Machinist's Mate Pontillo recalled:

> It was pitch black topside. I went on deck with a flashlight with a blue lens which permitted me to see a foot ahead of me. I dropped down to the pressure hull and then proceeded aft to the port side where the fuel hoses were clamped to the inside of the superstructure. After crawling over angle iron and other impediments, I located a brass fitting of the fuel hose which was hanging loose because the bracket had broken. I tied the loose fitting to the bracket as best I could with the water sloshing around my feet. The Japs were looking for us, and I had thoughts of Joe Westerhuis in the back of my mind.

But the job was finished without incident. At dawn, the *Rasher* dove.

The sea was as smooth as oil, making submerged periscope work dangerous. But with its judicious use, the watch in the conning tower sighted smoke just after breakfast. It was coming from two minesweepers—most likely part of the gang that had worked the *Rasher* over the day before. Their smoke was so heavy it almost obscured the Nakajima E8N float plane lolling overhead. Pretty soon the upper works of a small transport hove into view. She was followed by another, which took station off the starboard quarter of the first. They were joined by the two minesweepers and the float plane.

Laughon took the conn and started an approach. Quickly he worked into position for a 90-degree starboard track on the larger of the two targets. But as the submarine rose for a final periscope observation, a bomb from the float plane detonated several hundred yards away, a tremendous explosion. Laughon had been keeping the boat at ninety feet between periscope observations because he knew her dark shape could easily be seen moving under the extraordinarily smooth, clear sea. He went deep, then came back up for another try, but a second bomb went off. This one was very close and just as powerful; it smashed light bulbs and spun open sea valves. Men lost their footing and were thrown to the deck. Laughon broke off the attack and went deep again. Both blasts came as a complete surprise. Several men were badly shaken.

The minesweepers delivered a flurry of depth charges over the spot where the plane had dropped its bombs. Using a temperature gradient at 290 feet for protection, the *Rasher* drifted northward away from their bombardment. After four hours of futile searching and random depth-charge runs, the angry minesweepers rejoined their convoy.

When the *Rasher* reached periscope depth for a look around at 1400, the surface was deserted save for passing squalls and sea birds. To Laughon's consternation, the bombing and depth-charging had claimed a casualty. Debris inside Number 2 Periscope had shaken loose and deposited itself on the mirrors and lenses, rendering the scope useless.

After dark the boat surfaced, and a course was set for the north-western coast of Bali. Cruising lazily on one engine, charging batteries and resting the crew, Laughon decided to stay close to their station rather than go hunting for the two *marus*.

That evening, 14 March, Ken Tate made a diary entry describing the aborted attack:

> Battle stations. Just as we were getting ready to fire, a plane spotted our periscope and dropped 2 bombs that nearly knocked us out of the water. Then the escorts came over and really gave us hell. They came so close and so fast we had a job counting them. We got 46 close ones and 22 that were a distance away. They knocked half our lights out and the cork was flying off the bulkheads. By the afternoon they finally laid off and our nerves began to calm down.

As if the damaged periscope was not trouble enough, the SJ radar needed work again. Ugly grinding noises and blue sparks were coming from around the dipole and wave guide casings. Tiny bits of metal had somehow managed to work their way between the rotating surfaces again. The antenna trunk had to be dropped so the spare antenna bushing could be installed. After reassembly, the ship stood in toward the coast of Cape Bungkulan for the radarmen to tune the set by taking ranges from volcanic Mount Batukau, twenty miles away in the interior. Their effort was wasted. The technicians dropped the trunk again, but even their saintly patience was wearing thin. By dawn they had the SJ working intermittently, but it failed to pick up a patrol boat just 4,500 yards away. The *Rasher* dove before she was spotted.

◆ ◆ ◆

Searching for Admiral Koga's task force, the *Rasher* worked back west along the coast of Bali, then north to a position midway between the Kangean Archipelago and Cape Ibus. The cape protruded into the northern entrance of Lombok Strait. To stand into the strait, ships had to pass the cape. Patrolling east and west for a half hour in each direction off a north-south base course would cover the area.

Right before the noon meal, Sound picked up the menacing report of a pinging patrol boat. No sooner were the masts of a minesweeper sighted than it made sonar contact and headed for the *Rasher* at high speed. She went deep. Another minesweeper joined in, and for two hours they swept the area and dropped depth charges. After they departed the *Rasher* surfaced and continued north. Intermittent, distant echo-ranging was heard throughout the day. Clearly, the Japanese knew an American submarine was stationed in the area and were mounting an extraordinary effort to find her. To carry out Admiral Christie's orders, the *Rasher* had placed herself in great danger and was facing formidable odds. Her log was filled with enemy contacts, each one requiring evasive action.

0645   Sighted Class 13 AM [minesweepers] patrolling to the northwest.
0953   Heard echo ranging and sighted Class 13 AM six miles off the coast of BALI. At a range of 8000 yards he picked us up and headed for us. We went deep and ran silently until he passed clear. During the remainder of the day two AMs remained in the vicinity searching for us.
2204   Echo ranging from patrol vessel on course 120°T.
0820   Two AMs conducted an intensive A/S search in our general vicinity.
0230   Over a period of several minutes about 25 depth charges were heard at an estimated range of two miles.
0813   Sighted reconnaissance Float Plane over escorts.
1640   We sighted an AM with a small angle on the bow. Eventually we went deep to avoid him as he obtained contact on us and speeded up. He kept us down until 1823.

Depth charges seemed to thunder twenty-four hours a day. It was exhausting for everyone, especially the men who guarded the radar screen and sound gear. The lookouts, too, had to be alert every second they were topside. At any moment, a patrol boat could materialize out of the surface haze. Bill Norrington described the situation as the days wore on:

Patrolling off Lombok. About three times a day have to go deep to escape detection from patrols. They are persistent—at least two of them, sometimes three. Guess they figure we are around, or something important is up. Held down an hour after dark on night of the 16th. On the 17th heard 16 D/C in distance. Could see smoke of patrol. Don't know what they are after. Also saw plane during morning. This place is hot, and the crew have had their fill.

Ken Tate certainly had:

March 15, 1944: Forced down again by patrol boats all day. Rigged for depth charge and silent running.

March 16, 1944: Picked up again by patrol boats, forced deep. They dropped 38 depth charges. Further away than usual. (Thank goodness.) Later in the day they dropped about 16 about 6 miles away.

March 17, 1944: Same area, forced deep again. 8 close ones this time.

In his patrol report, Willard Laughon related the effect it had on everyone's nerves.

Sound reported weak echo-ranging dead ahead. This contact was not developed due to two other sound and radar contacts close aboard during the next two hours, apparently on porpoises as nothing could be seen at the reporting ranges of 1000 and 1500 yards. The sound and radar operators are getting quite jumpy by this time.

The *Rasher* continued patrolling around the Kangean and Sunda Islands, the coasts of Bali and Lombok, and the approaches to the Lombok Strait. Weather was beautiful, the days hot and sunny with high, scattered overcast, the Bali Sea so smooth it was like steaming through warm oil. At night, a billion stars appeared in the vault of the heavens around a bright, revealing moon.

The *Rasher* spent the better part of 18 March avoiding sailboats as she patrolled off Bali's Cape Bungkulan. Though they varied greatly in size, from small sloops to large yawls, most of them failed to appear on the radar screen. A minesweeper kept her down with depth charges from late afternoon until 1914. While she was evading, the radarmen broke down the SJ antenna assembly for the sixth time to repair the sleeve around the wave guide casing. Their maledictions had no effect whatsoever on the parts strewn over the conning tower deck. Though they would have preferred to smash the thing to bits with a scuttling sledgehammer, they dutifully slipped a new bushing over the guide and reassembled the trunk. Once back on the surface, the radar hummed to life again.

Then on the nineteenth, at 1138, ship contact No. 34 was entered in the log.

"Captain to the conning tower! We've got a Nip sub up here!"

Laughon was up the ladder and into the conning tower in a flash. The men were electrified. This was submarine versus submarine—the ultimate confrontation.

It was indeed a Japanese submarine the officer of the deck had spotted. She had just surfaced 4,000 yards away, wet and glistening black in the sunlight. Visibility was excellent, and the sub stood out clearly against hazy Cape Bungkulan ten miles distant. Because of its flat conning tower and low freeboard, at first the OOD thought it was a sailboat. ONI 220-J, the *Japanese Submarine Identification Manual*, identified her as an *RO-51* type. She sported, of all things, a Japanese merchant flag painted on the conning tower. The tall radio masts characteristic of RO-boats were erected fore and aft.

Laughon knew as well as any man that a submariner's biggest fear was being in the position this Japanese was in: wallowing on the surface under the tubes of a submerged adversary and not knowing it. Since a submarine has but 30 percent reserve buoyancy and a relatively fragile hull, all it would take would be one torpedo to send her to the bottom. Whether her crew drowned when the hull collapsed or were killed by the blast of high explosive, it would be over in the blink of an eye. Nothing would be left but a few pieces of debris, some foam, a diesel oil slick.

If there is a brotherhood of those who serve under the sea, this was no time to reflect on it. Willard Laughon acted quickly:

1149 Commenced firing spread of four torpedoes from the stern tubes.
1150 The target sighted the torpedo tracks and changed course rapidly to the left and presented a track angle of about 180° before we could bring the bow tubes to bear.

For the Japanese submariners, it was their lucky day. Because of a TDC firing solution error and a communication mix-up in fire control, the torpedoes missed ahead. The RO-boat immediately put her stern to the *Rasher*, turning the tables. The *Rasher* pulled away at flank speed lest she become a victim herself.

After this failure, Bill Norrington observed:

Back to the old grind. Knowing the patrols are there, and they knowing we are here, make the situation tough. It is a constant game. Sound school for them and evasion for us.

Two hours later, a pair of echo-ranging minesweepers thoroughly searched the area where the *Rasher* had fired at the submarine. Throughout the afternoon they dropped random depth charges. Then they hauled off to the northwest mysteriously, only to reappear at 2100 for another search that lasted all night.

Starting again on the morning of 20 March, and continuing for six days, the *Rasher* was hunted by Japanese anti-submarine patrols. She was harassed by echo-ranging, depth charges, and aircraft. It was exhausting; and there was no sign of an enemy task force. Tate kept track.

March 20, 1944: Forced deep again but no depth charges (unusual).

March 21, 1944: Forced deep again. 7 fairly close.

March 22, 1944: Forced deep and to silent running 3 times during day.

March 23, 1944: Forced deep. Patrol boat still pinging on us. Silent running.

March 24 to 26, 1944: Same thing every day, forced deep and silent running.

Early in the day on 27 March, the *Rasher* was cruising off Sepanjang Island, submerged for the day's patrol, heading north-northwest. The men were resting, waiting for the day's bombardment to begin. A dull, aching fatigue was now routine. At 0639, Sound reported weak pinging, and the boat was planed up for a look. Several columns of smoke were sighted about eighteen miles away. The weather was exceptionally clear, and behind the smoke Laughon could see the low shape of Pagerungan Besar Island. He ordered the rudder over, and the annunciators clinked to full speed to intercept. The musical chimes of battle stations torpedo reverberated through the boat. Perhaps, the skipper speculated, this was the phantom Japanese task force at last.

At 0830, plans for an attack on a huge naval target had to be altered when the masts developed into four zigzagging transports with three minesweeper escorts arrayed on the port and starboard flanks. A fourth minesweeper was positioned between the two columns of transports.

Laughon inspected the convoy through the periscope. ONI 208-J identified one of the ships as the *Chile Maru*, 5,900 tons. She was covered with scabby patches of rust at the waterline and painted an unusually light shade of tropical gray. Another ship he identified as the *Heito Maru*, 4,467 tons. She had a less cluttered topside than her ONI portrait depicted, perhaps because of a recent overhaul; the hull looked freshly painted. The other two *marus* had no equivalent in the identification manual, though they both looked like 3,000- to 4,000-ton cargo vessels.

As the *Rasher* came to a normal approach course, Laughon described the setup to the fire-control party. There was a bow-stern overlap of the *Chile* and *Heito Marus*, perfect for nailing both with one salvo. The approach and attack were quickly worked out. When the submarine arrived at the firing point, Laughon launched four torpedoes from the bow tubes at the first target, followed by two more at the second target. He left the periscope up and watched the smoking torpedo wakes fan out hot, straight, and normal.

The whine of torpedo turbines faded away. Except for the familiar sounds of ventilation blowers and hydraulics, dead silence descended on the conning tower. All eyes focused beyond its curved pressure hull, on torpedo junction.

"Should be there, Captain."

Yes, indeed! A loud, resounding explosion, and Laughon saw a hit blossom just aft of the first target's stack. In quick succession, three more explosions were heard and felt. Debris splattered around the ships. A huge pillar of orange-red flame burst out of the second target and shot 500 feet into the air. The huge explosion and underwater pressure wave made the submarine shudder. Twisted deck plates, broken cargo booms, crushed ventilation stacks, and other bits of topside trash rained down on the convoy. The *maru* settled deep, her cargo hold gutted and burning.

Laughon swung the scope back to the first target. She was wallowing, down at the head, steam venting from her stack. Japanese sailors frantically abandoned ship like ants pouring from a stove-in nest. As he swung the scope to port, something caught his eye. Sure enough, the escorts and the trailing *marus* were bows-on; they'd seen the *Rasher's* periscope and were trying to ram.

"Take her deep! Flood Negative! Three hundred feet! Rig for depth charge!"

The *Rasher* went deep as the enemy screws swept overhead. For more than an hour the escorts hammered away at her. Between depth-charge salvos, Sound reported hearing the unmistakable noises of a ship breaking up.

Laughon's patrol report described the aftermath of the attack:

> We had opened out from the scene of the attack about 4000 yards when we heard two tremendous explosions 13 seconds apart. I believe that ammunition or oil on the first ship attacked blew up at this time. After this we heard renewed sounds of a ship breaking up. The escorts also began to work back in our direction so we continued to open out to the west before coming to periscope depth.

Not finding the *Rasher*, the escorts headed back toward the remnants of the convoy. Laughon brought the boat to periscope depth for a look. Along the horizon a pall of dark smoke was spreading eastward.

Laughon headed for the convoy while torpedoes were reloaded. From a position four miles away he stopped to watch while the two remaining *marus* hunted for survivors and the escorts continued their anti-submarine search. One of the *marus* had a boom over the side to pick up a lifeboat. When they finished their work and got under way, Laughon headed in to finish them off. But then an aircraft appeared on the scene, a "Pete." It was followed by a twin-engined "Betty," then a "Jake." They zoomed in over the wrecked convoy. With three planes searching the area, Laughon broke off the approach and turned south toward the Lombok Strait to let things cool off.

Ken Tate made note of the attack :

> March 27, 1944: Hit one ship and blew it to bits. Got hits on the other one which didn't sink for about an hour later. Escorts were right on us and dropped 39 depth charges. . . . Broke light bulbs, knocked around loose gear, and cork started flying off the bulkheads again.

Despite clear visual evidence (which included periscope photography) that the four-ship convoy had been reduced to a two-ship convoy, the *Rasher* was credited by JANAC at the end of the war only with sinking a 2,750-ton transport, the *Nichinan Maru*. JANAC based its conclusions on Ultra intercepts, disregarding Laughon's detailed report that he had sunk a second ship. He wrote:

> It is believed that this ship sank a little over two hours after the attack. It was definitely absent from the convoy three hours after the attack. It could have been easily recognized if it had been present

because it was painted a lighter shade of gray than the other three ships, and it was quite rusty in spots, particularly near the waterline. It is not at all likely that one ship would have been permitted to leave the convoy without escorts when two others were kept in the vicinity of the attack picking up survivors. Also if only the second ship attacked had sunk there would have been no reason for it taking three hours to pick up survivors because it went down in a hurry.

The other three ships in the convoy were the *Kuniyama Maru, Heian Maru*, and an unknown *maru*. According to Ultra, none of the three was officially listed as damaged or sunk. Laughon's description, like those of other sub skippers, would fuel postwar controversies over the accuracy of JANAC and Ultra reports.

◆ ◆ ◆

On 29 March, a long-awaited radio message arrived recalling the *Rasher* to Fremantle. The crisis had passed. In fact, there never was an Imperial plan to attack Australia. After the Allied invasion of the Marshall Islands, Admiral Koga had simply ordered his major fleet units, which included the battleships *Yamato* and *Musashi*, to abandon their bases in Truk and move west.

With time to reflect on the patrol on the way back to Fremantle, Bill Norrington tallied up the depth charges:

> 208 depth charges to date since March 12. At 300 pounds per— about 31 tons of explosive.

Ken Tate spoke for the whole crew when he wrote:

> March 29, 1944: Our last 2 days patrolling Lombok Strait. The whole crew is relieved after the tension of those 18 days of hell.

> April 1, 1944: We're finally on our way home. "Oh happy day."

When the *Rasher* exchanged recognition signals with a Black Cat PBY on 3 April, she was home safe at last.

Calm Seas

With her off-duty sections at quarters, the *Rasher* moored alongside the submarine tender *Orion* in Fremantle. The sailors on other boats recognized her when she approached the nest and stopped their work to look her over. Her reputation as a hard-hitting ship-killer was well-established by now, and they viewed her with respect and admiration. Admiral Christie was on hand to greet her. With his entourage, he crossed the gangplank from the tender to deliver approbations to Laughon and his weary crew for an excellent patrol. They surely deserved it.

Considering what she'd been through, the *Rasher*'s overall material condition was excellent. Rust showed through weathered paint, but scraping, priming, and repainting would have her looking new again.

Lieutenant Commander Laughon's report detailed the forty-five day patrol, which included eighteen days of reconnaissance north of Lombok Strait. He had fired thirty-eight torpedoes at nine targets and gotten thirteen hits—about average shooting. He claimed five ships sunk. Engineering, torpedo, and radar casualties were itemized—especially radar—as well as the measures used to rectify them. A normal refit was scheduled. In addition, Number 4 Main Ballast Tank would be converted to a fuel ballast tank.

Laughon described the crew's state of training as excellent and their performance in combat eminently satisfactory. Several men were singled out and recommended for awards for extraordinary performance and skill under conditions that often had demanded more than men could reasonably be expected to endure. Christie again awarded the Submarine Combat Insignia for this patrol. Typically, his endorsement was effusive in its praise:

> RASHER's Third War Patrol is outstanding both in infliction of severe damage on the enemy and in unflinching determination to effectively patrol a station in which the enemy was exerting every possible effort in opposition. In spite of the arduous and exhausting anti S/M measures, the Commanding Officer and a stout crew carried on and aggressively and courageously inflicted all possible damage to the enemy and effectively fulfilled their reconnaissance mission. The RASHER truly wrote another glorious page in our Submarine History.

Christie concurred with Laughon's sinking and damage claims once they were confirmed by Ultra intercepts, though apparently not the same ones used by JANAC in 1947.

SUNK

1—AP (TANGO MARU)*	6,893 TONS
1—AP-AK (RYUSEI MARU)	4,797 TONS
1—AP-AK (NITTAI MARU)	6,484 TONS
1—AK (CHILE MARU)	5,860 TONS
1—AP-AK (HEITO MARU TYPE)	4,468 TONS
TOTAL	28,502 TONS

DAMAGED

1—AK (TATUKAMI MARU TYPE)	7,604 TONS
GRAND TOTAL	36,106 TONS

Ultra's code breakers used their routine eavesdropping on Japanese merchant marine radio traffic to judge the accuracy of action reports from submarines. It was easy enough to do, since the Japanese convoy commanders religiously informed stations ashore of their estimated noontime positions for several days in advance so their own forces could keep track of them. As described earlier, by utilizing this information, ComSubPac vectored submarines right to the hapless convoys. But almost as important as the news of convoy locations were the reports of recent submarine attacks. This information, detailing sinkings and damage, was passed from Ultra in Pearl Harbor to Capt. Richard Voge, Admiral Lockwood's operations officer, who then sent it to the various submarine commands and, when appropriate, to the submarines at sea. Thus, Admiral Christie was able to correlate fresh intelligence with submarine patrol reports to verify which enemy ships had been sunk, damaged, or otherwise put out of commission.

Ultra information was not perfect, however. Far too often the identities of ships sunk or damaged were inaccurate. Transmissions were sometimes garbled or misunderstood by those ashore, including Ultra's code breakers. Worse yet, the descriptions of attacks were often wildly overblown or underestimated by the Japanese themselves. Such may have been the case with the attacks launched during the *Rasher*'s third patrol. JANAC's postwar evaluation, influenced by Ultra's intercepts, gave this patrol credit for:

---

* *Second vessel of that name sunk by the* Rasher.

```
SUNK
1—AK  (TANGO MARU)...................................................................6,200 TONS
1—AK-AP  (RYUSEI MARU)...........................................................4,797 TONS
1—AK  (NITTAI MARU)................................................................6,484 TONS
1—AK  (NICHINAN MARU).........................................................2,750 TONS
                           GRAND TOTAL              20,231 TONS
```

Thus, according to JANAC's tally, the *Rasher*'s total score for three war patrols was:

SUNK
9 VESSELS FOR 36,379 TONS THROUGH 27 MARCH 1944

By comparison, Task Force Seventy-one's totals were:

SUNK
10 VESSELS FOR 57,012 TONS THROUGH 27 MARCH 1944

DAMAGED
4 VESSELS FOR 25,581 TONS THROUGH 27 MARCH 1944

Although the difference in the number of targets sunk was only one, Task Force Seventy-one's tonnage total was nearly 21,000 tons higher. Regardless of the precise tally, the *Rasher* had amassed an impressive record in only seven months of combat.

Treacherous Waters

The *Rasher*'s officers and men returned from the rest camps on 18 April. There were many new faces. Less than half her original crew was left as new submarines gobbled up her experienced men. Ken Tate, among others, was transferred to the relief crew and would sit out the next run. As usual, intense training was necessary to prepare the newcomers for combat and get the ship ready for patrol. With hard work, post-repair inspection and loading were finished in two days. Then the *Rasher* put to sea for sound tests, trials, training, and deep dives to check for air and water leaks. The *Isabel* and *Chanticleer* provided target services for approach exercises.

On 30 April 1944, the *Rasher* stood out of Fremantle for her fourth war patrol. With her were the *Isabel*, the Australian frigate *Horsham*, and two submarines, the *Puffer* and *Angler*. The *Puffer*, another Manitowoc boat, was commanded by Lt. Comdr. Gordon F. Selby. The *Angler*, skippered by Lt. Comdr. Robert I. Olsen, had on a previous patrol rescued fifty-eight men, women, and children from Panay, the Philippines, right from under the nose of the Japanese. As a result, Olsen was something of a swashbuckling hero to the sub force Down Under.

The submarines spent a day conducting attack training and torpedo runs. Then the *Rasher* and *Puffer* were escorted to the bombing restriction lane, where together they set course for Darwin. The *Angler* returned to Fremantle.

During the run north, Laughon and Selby conducted day and night submerged approaches and trained their lookouts, radar operators, soundmen, and control parties. The extended training was beneficial to both boats. It prepared their new crewmen for the rigors of the days ahead.

There were several casualties, however. The most serious one came on the *Rasher* when a sailor suffered a fractured and lacerated hand when an unsecured hatch fell on it. In addition, a sight on the 3-inch/50 gun flooded out during a deep dive, the forward TBT was out of commission with a broken electrical contact, and gremlins attacked the SJ.

As if that was not bad enough, halfway to Darwin the cooks discovered a perilous shortage of frozen chicken. The commissary officer hung his head while the crew grumbled. How could the new cooks try out their long-awaited southern fried chicken recipe? Laughon radioed ahead to request a replacement for the injured sailor, spare parts for the SJ's range unit, a new gun sight, and, most importantly, more chicken.

Exceptional weather allowed the submarines to cruise at seventeen knots on just two engines. It put them a day ahead of schedule. Selby elected to hang back and use a day for training, thus maintaining his original schedule. Since Laughon preferred to pick up the extra day, the *Rasher* and *Puffer* parted company.

On the fifth, 150 miles west of Adele Island, a submarine was sighted off the starboard bow on an opposite and parallel course. Through the periscope it looked like a Japanese *RO-60* type, and Laughon started an end around. It turned out to be the Dutch *K-XV*. When the Dutchman sighted the *Rasher*, he dove, and the boats cautiously maneuvered around each other.

At Darwin, the replacement for the injured man was waiting on the pier, along with the gun sight and range unit that had been flown up from Perth. But no chicken. Submariners being stoic souls, they ruefully accepted the chicken shortage as part of the cruelties of war.

The *Rasher* refueled and took on fresh water. On 8 May 1944, she got under way for her station in accordance with Operation Order Number 49-44. Locked in the safe in Laughon's stateroom were sealed orders he was to open only upon receipt of a special radio message from Commander Task Force Seventy-one.

◆ ◆ ◆

The *Rasher*'s fourth patrol encompassed a large area. It stretched north from Wetar, Buru, and Ceram all the way to Davao Gulf in the Philippines; west to Cape Arus on the Minahassa Peninsula of the northern Celebes; and east toward the coast of New Guinea in the vicinity of 132° east longitude. From Darwin, a course was set to transit the Malay Barrier between Sermata and the Babar islands. On the way, Laughon slowed only long enough to try out the new gun sight by firing some practice rounds from the 3-incher and 20-millimeters at an improvised target made from empty five-gallon milk tins.

As was his style, Willard Laughon prepared himself and his ship for what would be one of the most aggressive submarine patrols of the war. Typically, he had incorporated into his planning the latest information available, especially the reports from other SoWesPac boats that had recently been where the *Rasher* was going.

During the course of her patrol she would cover the major Japanese traffic routes connecting Ambon, Manado, and Mindanao to the Palaus and Halmahera. These routes were clearly marked on the charts. Proving the war of attrition was wearing down the Japanese merchant marine, patrol reports from other submarines described how the Japanese had recently begun using aircraft as freight carriers between the Philippines, Halmahera, and New Guinea. The result was that less and less cargo was reaching its destination. There were also reports of diminished anti-submarine air activity in the southeastern Barrier. This indicated that the Japanese were pulling air units from the Dutch East Indies to bolster their dwindling air forces in the north. Along with airplanes, aviation fuel was also in short supply due to Nimitz's war within a war—the destruction of Japan's oil tanker fleet. The upshot was that fast daylight surface running to the patrol area was now safer. It was noted, however, that air coverage had increased north of the Barrier both day and night, and that more

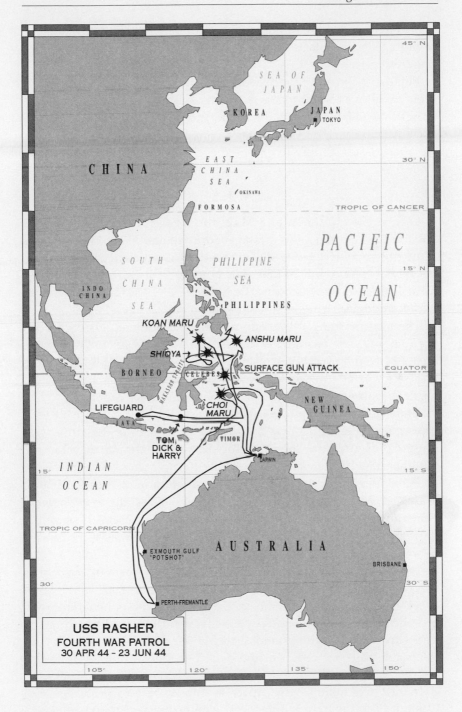

USS RASHER
FOURTH WAR PATROL
30 APR 44 – 23 JUN 44

planes than ever were radar-equipped. Some boats had reported 150 or more aircraft contacts during a patrol. Therefore, vigilance was still imperative.

Finally, the patrol reports described how convoys systematically used circuitous coastal routes to thwart submarine attacks. Of course Laughon was familiar with this tactic and knew from his own experience that it was rare to encounter a convoy in open water. Given the situation, a sub skipper had to be more resourceful and bolder than ever.

◆ ◆ ◆

Late in the afternoon of 8 May, the *Rasher* was passing east of Babar Island when a radio message from Fremantle detoured her to a position twenty-five miles off the coast of Ceram near Cape Samal to rescue the crew of a B-24 Liberator bomber downed while returning from a strike on New Guinea. The location was 420 miles away; even with four engines bent on, it would take a day to reach.

The next morning, Fremantle revised the downed aviators' position, giving new coordinates farther east. The *Rasher* arrived in the area that evening and began a slow, careful search along the most logical track, considering currents and sea conditions. Laughon hoped to locate the airmen before they reached land and were captured.

Under a full moon and partly overcast sky, visibility was at least three miles in any direction. But there was no sign of the airmen. At daybreak, with extra lookouts topside and a periscope manned, Laughon searched to the northwest until a plane contact drove the *Rasher* down. After surfacing, the search continued westward until midnight, when Laughon decided it was hopeless; the aviators were either dead or captured. He broke off the search and set course for the northern approaches to Manipa Strait. A radio message to Fremantle detailed their efforts.

The *Rasher* was soon in the Sula Island group north of Buru, submerged about fifteen miles south of Sanana Island. On navigation charts the island bore a resemblance to the head of a salamander with a truncated, flattened body. Just after the noon meal, the high periscope watch sighted smoke ten miles away. The captain was informed while the officer of the deck put the ship on an approach course.

In forty-five minutes, five Japanese ships hove into view. One ship was the *Cheribon Maru*, a transport. Another appeared to be a 4,000-ton transport; a third seemed to be a naval auxiliary or minelayer of about 3,000 tons. Accompanying them were two small anti-submarine vessels similar in appearance to *Toshima*-class CMc 1-10 coastal minelayers. These were 430-ton ships good for twelve knots, and armed with two 3-inch guns. One escort was broad on the leading transport's bow, the other out front on point. All five ships were zigzagging 30 to 60 degrees to either side of their base course.

The *Rasher* worked into position until the starboard escort was only 500 yards away. She steamed past without seeing the periscope poking up between the waves. Laughon fired four of the Navy's new Mark-23 torpedoes (updated Mark-14s) straight across the escort's wake, aiming for the transport in the van. He fired two more at the trailing ship. As the last fish screamed out of the tube, he went ahead two-thirds with right full rudder to get off the firing point.

A sharp-eyed Japanese lookout saw six white streaks in the water and sounded the alarm. Rudder hard over, the escort two-blocked her signal flags to warn her companions and heeled around to find the submarine. Alerted they were under attack, the *marus* sheered south. The torpedoes missed, shrieking harmlessly into the expanse of the western Ceram Sea.

Both escorts rushed in, dropping depth charges, while the *Rasher* evaded. She came to periscope depth two and a half miles away, and Laughon watched while they hunted for her. Just before sunset, one escort departed to rejoin the convoy; the other kept searching. As soon as the sun dipped below the horizon, Laughon surfaced the boat and went after the targets.

Smoke was spotted on the horizon near Buru. Laughon followed until it was lost in darkness at 1800. Ending around to attack again, he studied the situation with the plotting party. There were several possibilities to weigh. The convoy was tracking south-southeast, making for Manipa Strait. Laughon was convinced they would decide to anchor for the night in the roadstead off Bara Bay, nothing more than a bight on the northeast hook of Buru. Kayeli Bay to the east offered a better anchorage, but it was much farther away. So the *Rasher* headed for Bara Bay at eighteen knots.

It was the right decision. At 1820 radar had contact with the convoy as it steamed toward Cape Palpetu, the western edge of Bara Bay. But instead of putting in, the convoy turned southwest around the cape, then south, hugging the coast of Buru. Laughon maneuvered to be in position for an attack off Waflia before moonrise.

The tricky part came after the *Rasher* caught up with the ships. Despite the fact they were only 2,500 yards off the coast, Laughon deftly maneuvered to get between the targets and the beach. It was tight quarters, and the coastal shelving was not accurately marked on the charts. Still, it was worth the risk. The darkness of land would hide the submarine and help her strike with complete surprise.

The *Rasher* crossed ahead of the enemy's track unseen, closed to within a mile of the surf line—lights could be seen twinkling picturesquely in Waflia's tiny fishing harbor—then turned seaward to attack.

The two transports were steaming in column, a small escort ahead, the large auxiliary astern. The setup looked good until the other escort was discovered hiding on the near beam of the trailing *maru*. It was too late to pull away without being seen. Laughon ordered, "All engines stop and secure! Shift to battery!" Silent, with no frothing diesel exhaust wake to give her away, the *Rasher* glided toward the targets. The escort slid by only 600 yards from her bow. Incredibly, the submarine wasn't sighted. The escort clear, Laughon lit off the diesels and attacked the trailing ship. If the *Rasher* was not sighted, he would fire a spread at the leading ship, too.

Laughon fired three bow tubes at the trailer and watched two fish run under the target without exploding. The third missed astern. Shifting targets, he fired the other three bow tubes at the leading ship. Incredulous, he watched them run harmlessly under the target too! Frustration and anger boiled over; he was absolutely certain he'd get hits from the second salvo.

His patrol report tells what happened next.

> It looked as if we would have to dive at this stage; the ship that we had just fired at started blinking a red light, the port escort which we had passed close aboard a few minutes previously had turned towards us, and the ship first fired at was abeam and headed towards us with a zero angle on the bow, range 550 yards by SJ.

Then came a daring maneuver.

> We went ahead flank and since they had not started firing at us yet, I decided to pass between the two ships and fire the after tubes at the transport as he passed astern. But shortly before we were ready to shoot, this target turned right rapidly, the angle on the bow changing from 30° starboard to about 40° port. This necessitated swinging left and almost paralleling the leading ship which was about 1000 yards away a little abaft the port beam, in order to fire

zero gyro angles at the AP-AK. As we swung left we changed the depth setting on the after tubes to six feet, and at 1943-35, commenced firing a spread of four torpedoes at the transport.

Bill Norrington called it the "Battle of Buru." In his diary he sketched a diagram of the *Rasher's* daring run through the middle of the convoy.

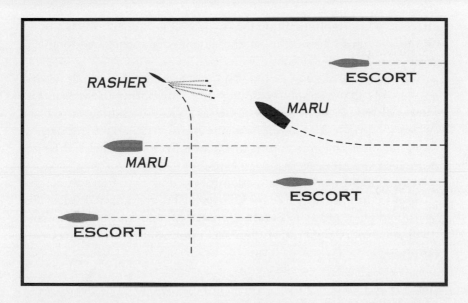

Two torpedoes exploded against the hull of the transport, flinging water spouts higher than her king posts. By chance, the auxiliary pulled out from behind the target just in time to catch a torpedo that had missed astern. It hit smack under her bridge; the blast lifted her out of the water. Badly damaged, she staggered out of the convoy.

The two *marus* and escorts fled southeast. The vessel that took two hits showed no sign of slowing, or even that she had been hit. As they fled, both the *marus* and escorts dropped depth charges and fired guns helter-skelter. They did not realize the *Rasher* was actually on the surface some distance away reloading torpedoes and racing to get ahead for a follow-up attack.

Working into position, fighting heavy rain squalls all the way, took two hours. Laughon tracked his quarry, submerged, and fired four torpedoes from the stern tubes. This time he had success.

One blew up under the target's spoon stern with such force it ripped open the poop deck like a tin can; flame and debris roared from her stack. In an instant her topsides flashed afire; fearsome explosions wrenched open her hull. Laughon tried to bring the bow tubes to bear on another target, but she was too close and the trailing escort had the *Rasher* in her sights.

The submarine went to 300 feet and slipped away from the thrashing screws and booming depth charges. When she came back up for a look, a burning ship lay dead in the water in the distance, escort standing by. A mile and a half away, another escort searched for the attacker. When lightning lit up the sky, the other transport was visible on the horizon to the northeast. The damaged auxiliary had long ago disappeared into the gloom.

The *Rasher* surfaced and started an end around on four engines for a follow-up attack on the remaining ship. The burning *maru* was left astern, decks awash in a pool of flaming gasoline a quarter-mile in diameter. Under way, Laughon transmitted an attack report; he requested permission to return to Darwin for another load of torpedoes, since only four were left forward.

It again took two hours to work into position. Laughon submerged to head in, but the target's radical zigzag and gusting rain foiled the approach. He decided to break off, go deep, end around, and make another try in daylight rather than waste torpedoes on a ship he could hardly see.

◆ ◆ ◆

Laughon started around in driving rain punctuated by lightning. The situation was complicated because during the long, running battle, both target and submarine had worked their way around Buru to its southernmost point and were now heading east toward Ambelau Island. Getting ahead of the target meant tracking well south around Ambelau while the *maru* and her escort navigated the narrow channel between the island's leeward side and the southern coast of Buru. Like many a sailor before him, Laughon had misgivings about the waters in that area; he knew the Navy's charts, derived from old Dutch and Portuguese maps, were notoriously inaccurate with respect to soundings and the location of reefs. The ship's copy of *The Coast Pilot* had no information whatsoever on Ambelau Island. The only option was to be alert for shoal water and to keep a sharp eye on the fathometer. On the plus side was the probability that morning air patrols would be grounded by the heavy rain and thick overcast, thus allowing for an unimpeded attack and withdrawal.

The end around would take nearly four hours. Knowing all hands needed rest, Laughon ordered them to secure from battle stations so those not on duty could turn in. Before he rolled into his own bunk for some shut-eye, he left word to be called the moment contact was made with the enemy.

◆ ◆ ◆

Battle stations torpedo chimed through the ship at 0815. The target was in sight. SJ radar had contact at 20,000 yards. Another 20,000 yards beyond lay the coast of Buru. To the east, the weather was clearing. Laughon was worried planes would respond to the *maru*'s frantic calls for help before the attack could commence.

The *Rasher* passed south of Ambelau Island, then cut northeast for several minutes to be in position ahead of the target as she cleared the channel. Then the submarine submerged. The target and escort, having made nearly a complete circuit of Buru, were striking for Manipa Strait, Laughon guessed.

He rigged for depth charge and silent running, then planed down to 150 feet and continued the approach at high speed on the *maru*'s sound bearings. At that depth, there was little chance the *Rasher*'s dark shape would be sighted if planes were searching for her. As she bore in, sound reported a confusing shuffle of screws and the distant thunder of depth charges rolling in from the target's bearing. The escort was sending a warning.

When Laughon brought the *Rasher* to periscope depth for a final look before shooting, he discovered that two PC 40-44 submarine chasers, probably from Kayeli Bay, had rendezvoused with the target. They were heavily armed, serious-looking ships with sensuous, undulating lines and streamlined bridges.

But the escorts didn't faze Laughon. Ignoring them, he bored in on the *maru*. She was helming frantically—nearly reversing her course on a radical zigzag. When she was perpendicular to the bow tubes he fired four fish at her proffered broadside. As number four left its tube, the *maru* swung sharply, bows on, turning the attack into a classic down-the-throat shot. Laughon watched the fish streak through the Banda Sea. One of them should get her, he knew, unless. . . . The spread fanned out, three going wide, one porpoising, kicking up a rooster tail, and veering crazily 30 degrees to starboard. The ship steamed untouched right down the track the erratic torpedo would have traveled. Laughon watched in utter disbelief.

"Goddamn the torpedoes!"

He recovered in time to order right full rudder and 350 feet to find a thermocline. The escorts wheeled and charged. Depth charges thundered fore and aft.

Laughon's patrol report described the most frightening moment as escorts converged over the spot where the *Rasher* had gone deep, planes on full dive:

> One of the escorts gradually overhauled us from astern and passed directly over us at a very slow speed; we could hear the beat of screws through the hull for *four minutes*. I thought that he had us for sure since there was no density layer down at 350 feet, but nothing happened. Apparently he just happened to pass over us.

The counterattack proved half-hearted and uncoordinated. The escorts dropped a final warning shot, rejoined their consort, turned northeast, and sped off for Manipa Strait, leaving a pall of black coal smoke. The *Rasher* surfaced and headed south before planes from Ambon arrived. She was out of torpedoes and out of torpedo luck.

Despite the danger posed by Japanese radio direction-finders on Buru and Ambon, a flurry of priority radio messages flew back and forth over the 4155 kilocycle submarine frequency between the *Rasher* and Task Force Seventy-one.

Laughon sent a serial message describing the ship sunk, an unidentified transport of about 4,000 tons displacement. He claimed damage to a *Cheribon Maru*-type passenger-transport, also 4,000 tons, and a naval auxiliary of 2,500 tons. In fact, JANAC would credit her only with a ship named *Choi Maru*, a 1,074-ton cargo vessel.

Fremantle acknowledged the message and instructed the *Rasher* to relieve the *Pargo*, presently on duty in the Java Sea off Surabaya. Planes launched from the USS *Saratoga* and HMS *Illustrious*, stationed in the Indian Ocean, were scheduled to attack Surabaya on 17 April. The *Rasher* was to join submarines assigned to rescue downed aviators and guard against attacks on the strike force by Japanese naval units that might attempt a sortie from the Java Sea. Laughon was directed to open his sealed orders, which contained the coordinates and radio voice codes for use during the air strikes. Again he advised Fremantle that the *Rasher* had no torpedoes. Regardless, he was directed to get under way for Surabaya.

But first, Number 4 Fuel Ballast Tank, its fuel load consumed, had to be converted to a water ballast tank. Conversion was a hazardous job, all the more so because it had to be carried out on the surface at night.

The job fell to members of the engineering department. Plans of the tank and hull were broken out and scrutinized while the necessary tools were rounded up. After dark the ship lay to with extra lookouts topside. Dressed in long johns, wrenches tied to their wrists, Motor Machinist's Mate 3rd Class Roland Soucy and another man went out on the main deck, opened the access grate, and climbed down inside the superstructure. As Mike Pontillo had done when he secured the fueling hose, they crawled twenty feet over and through a forest of structural cross members as the ship rolled and pitched. When they reached the tank, they removed the blanking pads bolted to the vent riser openings. Sea water poured in through the deck and limber holes, filling the work space and swirling around their armpits. After reconnecting the hydraulic actuating linkage and lubricating the mechanism, the men banged on the pressure hull, the signal for a test of the apparatus. Job completed, they crawled out, thankful the submarine had not had to submerge while they were at work under the deck. Under way again, even though it was dark, Laughon changed direction before flushing the tanks so any oil trail discovered on the surface would not reveal their true course.

At three-engine speed, the *Rasher* headed west for her new assignment. Every man aboard wished a fresh load of torpedoes was in the tubes, but orders were orders.

◆ ◆ ◆

The *Rasher* was just west of the Sabalana Islands, slicing along at full speed, rolling in long swells from the south. Cumulus clouds built on the horizon. All day she had been diving for plane contacts and maneuvering to avoid the ubiquitous spitkits that plied the Flores Sea. The weather was hot and sultry; strong winds hummed through the topside antennas. Laughon was in the wardroom finishing a sandwich when the 1MC summoned him to the bridge.

"Captain, we've got something in sight off the port bow. Looks like a raft."

It was about a mile away, rising and falling abruptly in six-foot seas. Through binoculars the lookouts could see it was a boat flying a tattered cloth for a flag; three men were aboard. Laughon ordered small arms brought topside, then coached the helmsman to bring the *Rasher* close aboard to inspect it.

They discovered a small, overturned outrigger with three young

Malays perched on it. The men wore only loincloths. As the submarine approached, they signaled that they were thirsty and hungry. Despite the ever-present danger of enemy planes, Laughon flooded down and called away a rescue party to help the natives aboard. He cautioned his sailors not to let anyone get trapped between the outrigger's hull and the submarine's swagging superstructure when the quartering seas brought the two in contact.

The Malays were so weak and dehydrated that they could hardly walk. They were hoisted to the conning tower and gently lowered down ladders to the control room, where the pharmacist's mate took charge.

Using pidgin English, sign language, and a Malay phrase book, the crew learned the castaways' story. They were from the island of Salayar, off the southernmost tip of the western Celebes. Ten had set out seven days before, hoping to reach Australia to escape the Japanese. After their outrigger capsized, seven had succumbed to exposure. The three men said the Japanese would kill them if they returned to Salayar, or to any other Japanese-occupied island. They begged to be taken to Australia and offered to work to earn their passage. The oldest man said he had once visited Surabaya and had traveled throughout the neighboring islands. He confirmed that all of them were occupied by Japanese troops.

Laughon assured the natives he would keep them aboard until they were stronger, then transfer them to a passing sailboat heading in the direction of Australia. He told the stewards that when the men regained their strength they were to be trained for mess duty. The trio were issued clean dungarees and, after a bit of debate, named Tom, Dick, and Harry. They in turn dubbed the submarine the *"Sea Dragon."*

Under way again, the *Sea Dragon* entered the Java Sea, crossing the 100-fathom curve on 15 May. She darted through the traffic routes northeast of Surabaya, avoiding swarms of sailboats, luggers, and spitkits. On the sixteenth, she encountered nearly sixty small craft along her track. Early on the morning of 17 May, a radar fix was taken from Bawean Island to accurately locate the submarine's position in the air corridor. Then she headed for her assigned lifeguard position forty miles north of Surabaya. The city lay inside the Strait of Madura, not far from where the *Rasher* had outrun the three minesweepers on her last patrol.

Submarine lifeguard operations were rather primitive, hastily organized affairs, complicated by inadequate communications between rescuers and airmen. The submarines off Surabaya—the

Angler, Bluefish, Cabrilla, Flasher, Gunnel, Puffer, Raton, and now the *Rasher*—were assigned fifty-mile-wide slots along the approach and retirement corridor used by the bombers. The pilots were well briefed. Should they have to ditch, they were to find a submarine before going in—if they could. The submarines were ordered to stay on the surface to receive "Maydays" and be visible to the airmen. The boats had no air cover of their own for protection or to act as guides to locate downed aircrews. To complicate matters, Japanese signal jamming interrupted radar reception and created a rough, buzzy signal on voice radio. It sounded like interference from a gasoline engine magneto. Rescue work was dangerous duty that left the boats exposed to hostile planes and submarines.

Her position in the strait gave the *Rasher* a ring-side seat for the air raid. Starting at 0730 on 17 May, a towering column of black smoke rose over Surabaya as planes hit the Bratte Engineering Works, the Wanikroma Oil Refineries, and the navy yard and harbor in the city's Semampir District. The sky was spotted with flak, but the opposition to the American and British planes was weak. Dive bombers could be seen through binoculars from the bridge as they made their runs. Both periscopes were raised, and all hands were given an opportunity to see the spectacle. When told what was happening, Tom, Dick, and Harry broke into big smiles.

The *Rasher* received two Maydays giving coordinates for a plane ditched in the harbor six miles from the city. She could do nothing to help; the harbor was too shallow for a submerged submarine to enter and too well protected. By noon the raid was over. Dense smoke spread to the east on prevailing winds. At 1244, the planes retired from the target, and the *Rasher* was ordered back to Darwin for fuel and torpedoes.

The Bilge Pump put out a special edition:

MAY 18, 1944

EXTRA!   EXTRA!   EXTRA!   EXTRA!   EXTRA!   EXTRA!

SURABAYA BOMBED

Leaving huge billowing clouds of dense smoke behind, aviators early today strongly attacked the enemy stronghold of Surabaya.

Sweeping down from the clouds, bombers quickly struck at the enemy's port, and soon put all opposition out of commission. So great was the destruction that not a single enemy ship was able to get under way. Thus our own undersea raiders were inactive on the daring raid. It is believed that some of the fleet could have sailed, but they preferred to take the air bombing rather than face a fate worse than death—our subs.

Famine has already started in the city proper, due to destruction of all warehouses. A large fleet of fishing vessels, thirty-one altogether, is at this moment madly racing to the stricken city with fish to relieve the starving natives. Surabaya will never forget May 17, 1944.

This paper wishes to point out the fact that the above release is probably the greatest scoop in the history of the press! This is the first release of the bombing in any paper in the world. The story was obtained after many days of privation and hardships by a reporter on board a United States submarine.

Lurking underwater and stealthily sneaking around the waters of Surabaya, the submarine finally surfaced practically in Surabaya Harbor and allowed this reporter to have a first-hand view of the action using a little imagination. Literally thousands of planes could be seen milling around in the sky. Frequent trails of smoke and flame bore witness to another enemy pilot going to the great beyond. A dense smoke covered the city, rising from the ruins of a once-great city. Or was it a haze? Anyway, it seems it was another job well done.

◆ ◆ ◆

Heading east, the *Rasher* encountered scores of sailboats. Remembering the one they nearly tangled with on the second run, Laughon decided to investigate what these boats were up to.

The craft he chose was old and badly weathered by years at sea in the hot Malaysian sun. Her frayed lines and halyards were wiry hemp. Reed mats draped the gunwales, and piles of fish nets and glass buoys lay tangled on deck. She was under full sail as the *Rasher* cautiously approached from the starboard quarter.

The four-man crew didn't know they were being overhauled until they heard and felt throbbing diesels. When they saw the submarine draw abeam, they scurried around on deck like madmen, pointing to the *Rasher*'s menacing gray bow, mouths agape.

On the submarine, gunner's mates stood ready as the sailboat was overhauled. The 20-millimeters were trained out; the bridge bristled with .30-caliber machine guns, Browning Automatic Rifles, and Thompson submachine guns.

The Malay crew doused the mainsail and jib and, in exaggerated gestures, begged not to be killed. Laughon carefully maneuvered close aboard. Both vessels rolled heavily, water sucking and surging between them, pushing off the frail craft. At first Laughon intended to bring Tom, Dick, or Harry topside to question the sailors, but thought better of it. They were obviously fishermen and nothing more. No radio antennas or guns were in sight; nothing but nets, dried, smelly fish, and a charcoal cookstove amidships. The submariners tossed over some canned goods and cigarettes as a gesture of goodwill, and the *Rasher* continued on her way to Darwin.

Laughon had planned to pass Tom, Dick, and Harry to a civilian boat, but he changed his mind and decided to take them to Darwin. Besides being terrific mess stewards, he believed they would be excellent sources of intelligence. When the captain announced his decision, they were ecstatic. In just a few days the men had gained weight and learned some rudimentary submarine English. They seemed happy as they worked in the scullery, mess, and wardroom under the watchful eyes of the cooks and stewards. The Malays were practically members of the crew already. Soon the chiefs would have them studying qualification manuals.

On 21 May 1944, the *Rasher* rounded Cape Fourcroy, Bathurst Island, entered Beagle Gulf, and hove to outside the gate of the antisubmarine net boom at Darwin. Tom, Dick, and Harry were turned over to a Royal Australian Navy motor launch crew that met the ship. The Malays stood forlornly in the launch's stern sheets, waving goodbye to their rescuers. Each of the castaways held a bag filled with cigarettes, candy, fruit juice, Australian pounds, and extra skivvy shorts to help start him on a new life. The submarine sailors who so often boasted of their tough, unsentimental nature were genuinely sad to see them go.

Then it was back to work.

In twelve hours the *Rasher* loaded 24 Mark-14-3A and Mark-23 torpedoes, fresh water, diesel fuel, food, and was back out through the channel heading for the Romang Strait east of Timor. When she reached Leti Island, her course was set for Manipa Strait. The next day, after investigating the northern approaches to Kelang Strait, where only a few shallow-draft coasters were sighted, she bypassed Buru and Ceram and bore for Molucca Passage.

On 24 May, midway between the Lifamatola and Obi Islands, the radar watch had a contact that developed into a thirty-five-foot sloop. The sloop had a low deckhouse athwartships with a rowboat lashed on top. Because she was much larger than the boats usually found in the area and had new sails billowing from her yards, she was suspect; she had the look of an anti-submarine picket. Since her crew had already spotted the *Rasher* approaching out of a rain squall, Laughon decided to investigate.

The approach was from abaft the starboard beam. The 20-millimeter guns were loaded, arming levers stroked, barrels trained out; machine guns were mounted in pipe stanchions; Laughon himself was on the bridge and armed with a Colt .45 pistol. As they drew alongside, he cautioned all hands to be alert.

The sloop tacked hard to port, her six-man crew giving no sign they were about to heave to. Laughon ordered bursts of 20-millimeter fired across her bow. With tracers lashing the water six inches from her forefoot, her crew tightened the sheets and maneuvered to evade. That was all Laughon needed to see. He ordered the gunners to shred her sails. The mates did a thorough job; when they stopped firing, only the jib on the bowsprit was still up, and it was in tatters. Frayed reefing lines and broken spreaders hung from the masts and dangled over the sloop's gunwhales.

The sailboat's crew had dove for cover below decks and, with her helm unmanned, she drifted in the swell. As the *Rasher* closed, the unmistakable radio antenna of a submarine spotter was seen rigged between the masts. Still, Laughon considered leaving well enough alone and heading for the patrol area. But when the radio shack reported high-frequency transmissions—undoubtedly a call for help—emanating from the sloop, that did it. He ordered the deck riddled to flush out the crew. Guns stuttered, hot slugs ripping through planking, gunwales, and hatches.

Still, there was no sign of the crew. Very well.

"Sink her! Commence firing!"

Methodically, the sailboat's hull was smashed to kindling at the waterline.

"Cease fire! She's going under!"

The *Rasher* backed off as the wrecked sailboat rolled over, exposing her barnacled planks. Three sailors appeared, floundering and frantically trying to unlash the rowboat as it went down with the wreckage. They were a long way from shore.

Here was the enemy made real—human beings, not just a band of diabolical Oriental fanatics. Though the submariners had sent hundreds of Japanese to their deaths, the nature of undersea warfare inhibited direct contact with them; sailors rarely saw their victims up close. This time they did.

Norrington noted in his diary: ". . . bloody job."

The *Rasher* shoved off for her patrol area.

Maru Hunt

Willard Laughon sat at the wardroom table fingering his beard, a half-eaten meal by his elbow, his attention focused on the charts spread out in front of him. Where, he pondered, was the best spot to find enemy ships?

He knew there were three major convoy traffic routes in the northern part of the patrol area: 1. From Tarakan and Balikpapan in eastern Borneo to the Palaus and Truk in the Carolines (the last known as Japan's "Gibraltar of the Pacific"); 2. From Davao, the Philippines, to Morotai Strait, and hence to Halmahera, Waigeo, Misool, New Guinea, and Ceram; 3. From Japan's home islands and Manila down the eastern littorals of Mindanao to Moratai Strait and the islands to the south—Bacan, Obi, Buru, and Ambon. The routes crisscrossed the Talaud and Sangihe Islands like a busy traffic intersection.

Laughon stepped off the distances in twenty-mile legs and marked a position on the chart 130 miles south of Davao Gulf. He weighed the advantages of this location. The Talauds and Sangihes were loosely strung out along a line running northeast to southwest, providing plenty of open ocean to develop ship contacts without the targets being able to made a quick run for the protection of a coastline. At the intersection, *maru* traffic would be far greater than along just one route. More importantly, it was an area where a submarine was likely to encounter Imperial Navy units on their way to the Palaus, Truk, and New Guinea.

There were, however, two distinct disadvantages to this region. One was the impossibility of adequately patrolling such a huge area—it was 300 miles a side, nearly 90,000 square miles in all. To effect decent coverage would require running on the surface in daylight. Narrow straits and passages funneled traffic to a waiting submarine; but in this area enemy ships were free to range all over the sea and could easily be missed. The other problem was enemy air patrols from the Philippines, the Talauds, and Halmahera. As noted in the patrol reports Laughon had studied before leaving Fremantle, increased anti-submarine air activity in the region was badly hampering daytime surface patrolling, the very tactic essential for effective area coverage. Those radar-equipped planes would be particularly troublesome, especially if they were able to home in on SD radar. But, Laughon reasoned, they had dealt with the problem in the past by being extra alert.

He studied the chart again.

The next best location to hunt for ships was the northern entrance to Morotai Strait in northern Halmahera. Ship traffic could not possibly enter the strait without being sighted—the funnel effect. But there were distinct disadvantages associated with this location, too. Like the southern Philippine area, air and surface patrols meant submerged daylight patrolling, again severely limiting area coverage and maneuverability. And, in a narrow passage, only one attack on southbound traffic could be mounted before convoys were diverted west to other ports between Halmahera and the Celebes.

Despite its drawbacks, Laughon decided the region north of Morotai Strait was an excellent place to get started. He circled its position on the chart and laid in a rough course to get there.

The patrol reports were absolutely correct. Beginning on 25 May, as the *Rasher* patrolled northward in the Molucca Sea along the coast of Halmahera, pesky Japanese air patrols had her going up and down all day. Bettys, Petes, Lilys, and Jakes were all over the place. Bill Norrington kept score in his diary:

> May 25–28. Patrolling south of Talaud Islands. Plenty of planes. Very hard on the nerves. You have to see them first. (Japs homing on SD.) Made plenty of quick dives to avoid being sighted. Generally, after being forced down three or four times, would stay down for the day. Bright moon at night.

> On the 25th, dove 3 times for planes. Saw 1 other.

> On the 26th, dove 2 times for planes. Saw 2 others.

> On the 27th, saw 6 planes in periscope near Morotai Island.

> On the 28th, saw 2 planes.

Laughon hoped all the activity presaged ship movements into the area. He approached Morotai Strait, submerged the boat two miles from Rau Island—a hump of black volcanic rock and palm trees off the mouth of the strait—and patrolled. Nothing was sighted except more planes and fishing boats. A radio message from Fremantle advised the *Rasher* the submarine *Cero* would be passing through her area. The *Cero* was contacted on radar and identified late in the day. (Aboard was Charles Nace, an officer destined to command the *Rasher* in the not-too-distant future.) Laughon moved on to the northernmost portion of the patrol station.

On 29 May, the better part of the day was spent dodging airplanes. But at 1558, while the *Rasher* patrolled the traffic lanes south of Kaburuang Island, heavy black coal smoke was sighted through the periscope, range a whopping 48,000 yards. The klaxon sounded three times, the ballast tanks were blown, and the chase was on.

As the *Rasher* worked ahead at seventeen knots, the target was easy to track from her heavy smoke puffing north-northwest at nine knots. The smoke changed course at twilight to 330° T., toward Kaburuang. Rain squalls on the horizon spelled trouble.

"Bridge, Radar! We have contact at eight thousand yards! Sound has her too!" The *maru's* old single screw thump-thumped through the headphones. Time to dive.

The *Rasher* slid under, SJ reflector above the water. Laughon motioned for the periscope.

Squally conditions hid the target, though radar tracked it between 310 degrees and 350 degrees, making five-minute zigs, range 5,000 yards.

"Down periscope!"

Laughon secured the radar and ordered the boat to sixty-five feet.

"Make ready all tubes forward!"

Sound reported two escorts getting close.

"Up periscope!"

The near escort was on a course to cross 1,000 yards astern.

"Down periscope!"

Pinging grew louder as the escort approached, crossed, and passed without detecting anything.

"Up periscope!"

Squalls made periscope work impossible; Laughon was groping blind.

"All ahead full! What's the escort's bearing?"

"One-ten relative, sir."

"Range?"

"One thousand."

"Target bearing?"

"Single screw, three-two-zero."

"Range?"

"Two thousand."

"Steady as you go!"

Sheets of rain hissed on the surface.

"Can't see a damn thing!" Laughon complained. "Where the hell is she? Bring me up another foot! Got her!"

The skipper got a look at his target, a transport resembling the *Sinsyu Maru*. She had an old-fashioned, sweeping counterstern and was listed in ONI 208-J as displacing 4,160 tons. She was accompanied by two escorts, a PC 40-44 submarine chaser and a vessel resembling a trawler or coastal patrol boat.

"Shooting observation! Give me a ping range!"

"Twelve hundred. Set!"

"Bearing—mark!"

"Three-three-one. Set!"

"How's the TDC look?"

"Final bearing and shoot, Captain."

"Bearing—mark!"

"Three-three-seven! Set!"

"Fire!"

Ears popped from impulse air pressure as three torpedoes whined on their way. Laughon saw the escort astern come about, headed for the *Rasher*.

"He's seen us! Take her deep! Three hundred feet! Right full rudder! Rig for depth charge!"

Ba-whang! Exploding torpex rang through the *Rasher*'s hull. Sound reported the target's screw had stopped. There was only a split-second to savor the hit—already the escort thrummed overhead. The sonarman tore off his headphones. "He's dropping!"

A string of seven depth charges went off 400 yards away. Another escort swept overhead, circled, and dropped more—closer this time. The two thrashed back and forth, pinging, drifted south, separated, came back slowly, listened, and disappeared. They were satisfied the enemy submarine had fled—or was sunk.

At 2019, the *Rasher* was back at periscope depth. The rain had stopped, but visibility was poor. There was no sign of the target, but nor were there any lifeboats to confirm she had gone to Davey Jones's locker. Laughon surfaced the boat. As soon as she was up, search radar reported three ships lying to 10,000 yards away off the starboard bow. Tubes were reloaded while the hunter crept in for a look.

There the *maru* was, still afloat but dead in the water. The escorts milled around like worried hens. Laughon elected to wait until moonset before going in for the kill.

Just after midnight, the escorts worked around north of the damaged ship, leaving her southern side—the port—exposed. Seizing the opportunity, Laughon flooded down and arrowed in to finish the job. Realizing the *maru* was vulnerable, an escort reversed course to head back and cover her. It was a race to see who would get there first.

When the *Rasher* was 1,100 yards away, Laughon slowed and fired a single torpedo, zero gyro angle. He hoped one would be enough. But when it veered right before settling on course, streaking for the target's stern, a possible miss, he fired another, this time with a two-degree gyro left.

"Right full rudder! All ahead flank! Let's get the hell out of here!"

Too late: the escort saw the *Rasher* heel sharply to make her getaway amid diesel smoke and spray.

Nothing from the first torpedo. Then . . . the second one hit under the bridge, blowing the ship to pieces with an explosion so powerful it turned night into day. Debris rained on the sea for a quarter-mile around. No tin or bauxite in this *maru*'s hold; more likely barrels of gasoline. (Intelligence would later determine the *Rasher* had vaporized not the *Sinsyu Maru* but the *Anshu Maru*, a converted gunboat of 2,601 tons.)

The escort veered around the flaming pyre and opened up with a 3-inch gun. The shots were high but close enough for Laughon to send the lookouts below until the escort disappeared astern. The *Rasher* cleared out, headed east.

At daybreak on 30 May, forty-five miles east of the site of the *Anshu Maru* attack, the *Rasher* submerged for machinery repairs. Both air compressors were suffering from piston ring fractures; the bow plane hydraulic system's control cylinder seals had blown out; and one periscope's hoisting gear was out of commission, flooded with sea water, motor armatures burned up.

In the wardroom and crew's mess, men broke out cribbage and acey-deucy boards to pass the time while the engineering department went to work; others caught up on their sleep. At 1741, repairs complete, the *Rasher* was back on the surface and ready to go.

Before dark, the radio watch monitored a contact report broadcast by the *Cabrilla* and the *Bluefish*. They had seen a Japanese task force departing Tawitawi in the Sulu Archipelago, headed east. According to the report, the task force might reach the *Rasher*'s area between noon and 1600 on 31 May. Unknown to Laughon and the others, it consisted of the battleship *Fuso*, four or five heavy cruisers, and eight destroyers. It was on its way via Davao Gulf to Biak, a small but strategic island north of New Guinea where MacArthur's forces were engaged in heavy fighting.

The Japanese viewed the Allied assault on Biak as a serious threat to A-Go, their plan for a decisive battle to annihilate American forces in the Marianas. If Biak fell, the Japanese would be vulnerable on their southern flank to bombers based a mere 600 miles from the Palaus. To reinforce the island and destroy MacArthur's sea and land-based forces, they launched Operation Kon. Twenty-five hundred reinforcements from the amphibious brigade stationed on Mindanao were shipped to Biak, accompanied by the *Fuso* task force with its big guns.

Laughon and the plotting party huddled over charts in the ward-room and picked a position twenty miles south of Kaburuang Island in the Talaud group as the best place to intercept the task force. All day the *Rasher* patrolled the area at one-engine speed, waiting for something to show up. All that appeared were the ubiquitous air patrols of brownish-gray Bettys and Jakes. At night Laughon changed position to patrol the east-west traffic crossroads near the Nanusa Islands. He waited patiently.

◆ ◆ ◆

On 2 June, Task Force Seventy-one in Fremantle radioed new orders: proceed to the vicinity of Davao Gulf, relieve the *Gurnard* and the *Ray,* and reconnoiter until 6 June. Then the *Rasher* was to shift position to patrol an area between longitude 121° and 127° east and from the equator to 4° north. The region took in a large part of the eastern Celebes Sea and the Talaud and Sangihe Islands. On the thirteenth, she was to depart for Ambon, patrol there for a day, then return to Fremantle on 23 June. With no task force in sight, it appeared the Japanese had changed their plans.

By 1615, the *Rasher* was on her way north.

Just before midnight, below the Sarangani and Balut Islands off Mindanao, two phantom-like ships were sighted in the moonlight heading south-southeast at high speed. The *Rasher* was in the right place at the right time. These ships were part of the original *Fuso* attack group from Tawitawi, now split into two parts to avoid detection. Though they could be seen on the moonlit horizon, SJ radar could not make contact on them. The green spikes were just a tangle of electronic jibberish.

When first spotted, the ships were on a zigzag leg away and much too fast to overhaul. Still, Laughon moved to get ahead on four engines. The range slowly but surely opened, the ships pulling away. It was theoretically possible to run down a fast zigzagging warship with a slower one, but in reality it was virtually impossible. Nonetheless, Laughon gave it a try.

His persistence paid off fifty minutes later as the targets zigged right, closing the *Rasher*'s quartering position. From her wind-swept bridge ten miles astern, the ships were identified as large men-of-war, possibly heavy cruisers, screened by at least four destroyers, two on either flank—prize targets if ever there were any.

The *Rasher* pounded along full speed while Laughon hoped for another zig his way to put the ships in position for a submerged attack. At 0101, radar made contact at 13,000 yards. Plot reported they were making twenty-two knots, zigging every ten minutes, steaming for Karakelong Island. With a base course of 115 degrees, they would skirt its northeast coast.

Even at 10,000 yards, the ships could be seen clearly enough to identify them as *Atago*- and *Nachi*-class heavy cruisers. The *Atago* had the characteristic heavy tripod mast abaft her bridge, pylon foremast, and raked forward stack. The *Nachi* had a secondary battery mounted on old-fashioned sponsons port and starboard over stepped belt armor.

At 0128, a screening destroyer sighted the *Rasher* on the port quarter of the task force and peeled off, stacks boiling smoke. Laughon put the stern to her. The destroyer skipper, thinking she had submerged, turned back after dropping warning depth charges. But the Japanese task force commander knew they had been discovered—barely out of sight of the Philippines, 1,500 miles from their objective.

The *Rasher* swung back to parallel the enemy's track and resume the chase. With the cruisers' three- to four-knot speed advantage, it was futile. At 0320, Laughon reluctantly broke off contact, disappointed that such important targets had slipped away.

As soon as she reversed course for Davao Gulf, radar picked up a fast destroyer—the same one that had broken away from the task force to drop warning depth charges. She swept by at high speed, 6,200 yards away, hurrying to rejoin the cruisers after conducting an anti-sub search along their southern flank. She didn't know it, but the *Rasher* was virtually in her lap.

Forty minutes after Laughon transmitted a contact report giving the enemy's speed and base course, three more cruisers speeding north of the Nanusas spiked the SJ screen. It was the second part of the *Fuso* group heading for Biak.

Laughon was off at flank speed to try again. By 0434, with dawn coloring the east and threatening to reveal the *Rasher* to the destroyer screen, she worked up their flank inside 7,000 yards, but the big ships swept on by at more than twenty knots. ONI 41-42 identified the trio as two more *Atago*- and *Nachi*-class heavy cruisers and an old oil- and coal-burning *Natori*-class light cruiser.

Laughon surfaced to transmit another contact report, but planes providing air cover for the cruisers drove her down before the transmission could be completed. Laughon tried again, and this time the radiomen managed to key the entire message before the planes appeared. The *Rasher* and the other boats had done their job: the Japanese knew they had been sighted.

Lacking the element of surprise, the Japanese turned back to the Philippines, Operation Kon in ruins. A second attempt to reinforce Biak would be aborted when word of the Marianas invasion reached the headquarters of Vice Adm. Jisaburo Ozawa. Thus when he turned his fleet north to fight the long-planned decisive battle (what became known as the "Marianas Turkey Shoot") against Rear Adm. Raymond Spruance's carrier forces, Ozawa sealed Biak's fate. By the end of July the island was in American hands.

After her encounters with the cruisers, the *Rasher* headed for her new station in Davao Gulf. She arrived on the morning of 4 June and submerged in the mouth of the gulf twelve miles off Calian Point, the hook of lower Mindanao. Coastal currents were swift, setting her into the gulf. As she closed the beach, the periscope swept over impenetrable stands of hardwoods, lush palms, and dense bougainvillea. It was safe to assume coast watchers spotted the *Rasher*'s scope ranging offshore parallel to the surf line.

Under the bald promontory at Lawa, Laughon turned seaward to take up position five miles off the beach and keep an eye on air traffic flying in and out of Davao City, seventy miles away at the head of the gulf. By the time a third round of coffee was passed up to the conning tower, six planes had already been logged in. It was a busy place.

At 0818, an unescorted *Atago*-class cruiser steamed majestically into view off Talagutong, heading north. Three planes followed overhead. She was the *Takao*, a remnant of the *Fuso* task force and aborted Biak reinforcement, and was returning to Davao. A formidable target, she mounted five 8-inch/50 turrets, three forward and two aft. A massive bridge and funnel structure towered over her decks.

Submerged, all Laughon could do was photograph her as she went by at twenty-one knots just 6,000 yards away. Had he known how vital a role the *Rasher* had played in the Japanese decision to abandon their plans to reinforce Biak, he would not have felt so disappointed as he watched the prize target disappear in the haze.

Before the noon meal was served, a small, sonar-equipped tug, landing barge in tow, arrived on the scene and somehow managed to locate the submerged *Rasher*. The tug immediately turned north, back to Davao City, to report the contact; the *Rasher* headed east for the opposite shore. When a *Fubuki*-class destroyer showed up late in the afternoon to investigate, Laughon stationed the tracking party and started an approach. Upping the periscope for a final shooting bearing, he discovered the *Fubuki* heading right for the scope at twenty-seven stout knots. On her fantail frenzied sailors struggled to cast loose depth-charge racks secured for sea. Laughon reported:

> The periscope was sighted on this observation and the DD started swinging right and going to battle stations. I guess that they were going to battle stations—anyway they were running around the decks madly as he passed about 100 yards ahead.

The *Rasher* plunged to 300 feet before the *Fubuki*'s sailors managed to unlock the racks and roll a string of nine ashcans. Shortly a *Hatsuharu*-class destroyer joined in. It wasn't until after dark that the two gave up the hunt and returned to Davao City. The *Rasher* surfaced to make for Cape San Augustin, thirty miles across the gulf.

The next day, 5 June, a score of aircraft contacts kept the *Rasher* down for the day. Laughon patrolled the center of the gulf, hoping that ship traffic would be detoured that way by the reports of a submarine haunting the coastal waters. But not a single ship appeared.

As ordered, the *Rasher* quit Davao Gulf on 6 June and headed south under a full moon for Molucca Passage and Morotai Strait.

After lunch the next day, heavy smoke was sighted southwest of Morotai Strait: southbound ships lugging cargo were just over the horizon. An airplane patrolling off Mayu Island complicated things, but Laughon avoided it by heading south to work around to intercept the convoy.

In position at 1340, Laughon ran the scope up and beheld a glorious sight: eight medium-sized transports and six escorts 16,000 yards away from the *Rasher*'s torpedo tubes! A huge collection of ships had formed up, possibly from two separate convoys.

"Down periscope! Steady on course one-eight-zero!"

When the *Rasher* was 8,400 yards from the nearest ship, two transports were identified as 2,500-to-4,000-tonners, five others as 5,000-to-6,000-tonners, and one as an engines-aft 1,900-ton AK. Escorting the convoy was a PC 40-44 and two *Wakatake*-class destroyers—radar-equipped, from the look of their top hampers. Two other escorts could not be identified.

A sixth escort resembling an American flush-deck World War I destroyer turned out to be the legendary ex-USS *Stewart*. She was captured by the Japanese in 1942 at Surabaya after demolition charges planted by retreating U.S. forces failed to go off and destroy her in dry dock, where she was undergoing repairs. The Japanese converted her from a "four-stacker" to a "three-stacker," changed her main mast to a tripod mast, then sent her out to lead a charmed life as a convoy escort. Recovered after the war, she was recommissioned and sent back to the United States. The hairline in the *Rasher*'s periscope bisected the old girl as Laughon described her to Plot and took her picture for Naval Intelligence. Then he turned his attention to the targets.

The convoy was organized into three groups in following formation, each group 3,000 yards apart and zigzagging 30 to 60 degrees off their base course every ten minutes.

The *Rasher* closed in. A pinging sub chaser turned bows on. She was joined by a *Wakataki*. The pair made sonar contact on the submarine. Laughon went to 200 feet. The escorts searched for twenty minutes before rejoining the convoy.

Laughon swung back, resumed tracking until 1730, then surfaced the boat into a full moonrise to start a curving end around. As the *Rasher* ran up the convoy's port side, a small transport and escort were sighted on the port beam 11,600 yards away. Since they were not part of the larger convoy, Laughon ignored them.

Dodging another escort, he worked ahead again, only to have the convoy abruptly change course northeast. Undeterred, Laughon worked around and submerged on the convoy's track—only to see it change course again, this time east-southeast toward Morotai. The *Rasher* was out of position in left field. Things were not looking good.

2255   Sighted a Jap BETTY bombing plane over the convoy. A little later we sighted a float-type ZERO also.

0038   The ships could just be seen through the periscope. We surfaced and pulled out from the convoy to get clear of the planes. . . .

0048   Made an estimate of the situation and decided that we could neither get ahead of this convoy, [n]or get into a position for a submerged attack in MOROTAI Strait before daylight.

0109   Set course for SIAOE Pass at 17 knots (instead) . . . it would be necessary to go through this passage during daylight. If the planes weren't too thick we could make it.

Reluctantly, Laughon broke off contact. In the morning the hunt for ships developed westward into the vast waters of the Celebes Sea.

◆ ◆ ◆

In the afternoon on the eighth came the report: "Smoke on the horizon!"

Sure enough, a smudge could be seen fifteen miles away: two ships, both heavy smokers. One of them, the *Asame*, an ancient, former coal-burning cruiser dating from before the turn of the century, clipped along at sixteen knots. ONI listed her as a converted auxiliary of 9,240 tons. She was in terrible shape, all rusty and patched up. The Japanese obviously were desperate for anything that floated. The other smoker was an *Amatsukaze*-class destroyer that patrolled back and forth across the *Asame*'s bow two miles ahead.

The old cruiser was a sitting duck. Laughon came in submerged from starboard and fired a spread of six torpedoes from the bow tubes.

1641-25 . . . saw and heard the first torpedo hit under the bridge, throwing a column of water mast high. I saw two other hits in the vicinity of the after turret followed by what appeared to be a magazine explosion, since the entire after part of the ship up to the stacks was immediately obscured by flame.

1642 The target was obscured by flame up to the bridge and by smoke past the forward turret, and it had a starboard list of about 15°. Sailors on the forecastle were scrambling up to the port rail. We started down to 300 feet as we swung left off the firing point.

1644-47 Eight depth charges, fairly close.

1655 Loud breaking up noises . . . the loudest we have ever heard.

When the *Rasher* returned to periscope depth, Laughon saw three separate fires burning on the surface over an area a half-mile in diameter. Huge clouds of thick black smoke rolled skyward. The escort circled helplessly around a mast attached to a piece of floating wreckage jutting above the surface from a pool of fire. The sinking was an apt way to celebrate the *Rasher*'s commissioning anniversary. (Despite Laughon's certain identification, JANAC would conclude the victim was the *Shioya Maru*, a 4,000-ton tanker.)

Surfaced; all clear by SJ. . . . transmitted our serial twelve to CTG
71.1 reporting the sinking on the First Anniversary of the RASH-
ER's commissioning.

◆ ◆ ◆

Except for aircraft contacts, the next two days were quiet. On 11
June, Laughon decided to shift two of the six torpedoes in the after
torpedo room to the forward torpedo room, which had only one fish
left. Three forward and four aft would offer more flexibility. Since
submarine doctrine did not prescribe approved methods for this
highly unorthodox operation, the torpedomen improvised. To be
sure, it was risky. And back-breaking.

After moonrise at 2224, the *Rasher* surfaced. Extra lookouts were
sent topside. Using batteries for propulsion, the submarine glided
silently into the lee of a small island to make the transfer. The smell of
damp, musky jungle vegetation wafted out to the boat. There had
been scores of islands to choose from, some no more than hummocks
sprouting a palm tree or two. Laughon had carefully surveyed several
possibilities on the charts before selecting a small island off the
Celebes coast.

Making the transfer in moonlight, hatches open, men on deck, ship
sitting in shallow water, was extremely dangerous. Should a Japanese
patrol boat stumble upon her, the *Rasher* would be done for.

With judicious use of blue-filtered flashlights, torpedo handling
masts and booms were broken out and erected. Next, the torpedoes
were winched topside from the after room, swung outboard, and
lowered over the side with lines on their tails and noses. Then the fish
were walked forward, hauled out of the water, and struck below into
the forward torpedo room. Even in a flat sea, the job was far more difficult than Laughon had anticipated. It took nearly five exhausting
hours to complete the transfer.

◆ ◆ ◆

Twenty-four hours later the *Rasher* was working along the outlying
islands of the northeastern coast of the Celebes. She had had to carefully pick her way around boiling reefs and shoals, but now, near
midnight, she cruised on one engine over a silky, moonlit sea off the
village of Lolak. The OOD reported targets and Laughon bounded to
the bridge. Skirting the 100-fathom curve was another exceptionally
large convoy of eight ships and four escorts, steaming west-southwest
at nine knots.

Laughon and the plotting party studied the charts and the convoy's likely track. With present speed and course, in five and a half hours it would be near Huha Island, where the 100-fathom curve was only a mile from reefs encircling the island, a perfect spot for a submerged attack. Laughon ordered up full speed to get there before the convoy did, and before morning air patrols got off the ground.

At 0429, sharp lookouts sighted a darkened ship dead ahead. By her size and shape, she was a destroyer. She was steaming westward, the same direction as the *Rasher,* which was literally following in her wake. To work around with dawn breaking meant detection for sure. While Laughon and the plotting party were deciding what to do, convoy smoke appeared astern in the first rosy glow of morning. The convoy was right on schedule, passing outside the shoals north of Tanjung Dununglag and heading west-northwest. Brightening eastern skies scuttled Laughon's Huha Island plan. Always quick to revise his plans when necessary, Laughon submerged and sheered away from the destroyer to start an immediate approach. Ignorant of the drama unfolding astern, the destroyer continued west.

Laughon advanced at full speed, poking up the scope every fifteen minutes to check his progress. But at 1607, the targets turned away from the coast, forcing the skipper to convene another meeting over the charts.

The convoy's original base course was roughly 290° T. Now, swinging north, it steadied on 330° T. Laughon was unsure whether the Japanese commodore had merely executed a change of course planned for daybreak or a scouting escort had picked up the submarine on their heels and issued a warning. Plot confirmed the convoy's speed was still steady at nine knots, making a submerged approach all but impossible. Still, Laughon pursued, hoping for a favorable convoy course change or zig. But an hour and a half of high speed running rapidly depleted the battery. With the convoy still six miles away, he called it quits.

Planing up to fifty feet, he identified the targets. Among the eight ships were the 5,270-ton *Panama Maru*, the 5,652-ton *Havana Maru*, the 7,025-ton *Matunoto Maru*, and the 4,862-ton *Tarusima Maru*. Two others looked like *Yokahama Maru*-class ships. Two 4,500-to-7,000-tonners could not be positively identified from the ONI manuals. Of the four escorts, two were identified by their top hampers as destroyers.

The *Rasher* surfaced to charge batteries and end around. But air patrols from Kuandang Bay homed in on the SD and foiled the plan. The *Rasher* dove as the planes dropped bombs. When the sky finally cleared at 1800, Laughon brought the ship to the surface and

started searching for the convoy at 15 knots. We worked on the assumption that it would make a radical change of base course at dark to a course between 290 and 010° T. . . . We started searching along the westerly course first.

◆ ◆ ◆

Eleven hours later, at 0512, smoke was sighted on the horizon as the sky reddened in the east. The convoy was 240 miles north of the Celebes coast, two-thirds of the way to the Jolo Islands. Once again, Laughon's finely developed submarine instinct paid off. The annunciators in the conning tower clinked over to "Ahead Flank"; the diesels changed their tune from a low murmur to a deafening roar. At 0717, with a closing aircraft contact on SD, Laughon pulled the plug.

The masts of eight ships and several escorts were in sight. In addition to a *Chidori* torpedo boat and destroyer, there was the old *Stewart* again, chugging along on the convoy's port flank.

The skipper planned to work into position ahead of the formation, fire two torpedoes at each of two targets from the stern tubes, then swing around and fire three bow tubes at another. Because the ships were lightly loaded and riding high in the water, he ordered depth settings of six feet.

A convoy zig put the *Rasher* ahead of the two ships on the port side of the formation, thus placing the center column of ships in an ideal position for the attack. He had picked a ship in the van as the first target, but at the last minute Laughon set up on a better-looking target right behind her, identified as the big *Matumoto Maru*. Two torpedoes sped from the stern tubes. Shifting to an unidentified trailing *maru*, he fired two more.

"Down periscope!"

Minutes dragged by. *Ba-whang!* A hit!

"Up periscope!"

Ba-whang! Another hit. Already the large ship was settling by the stern, plumes of dark, ugly smoke billowing up around her.

The *Stewart* aimed for the *Rasher's* periscope feather, but at the last minute the destroyer sheered left, afraid of being a target herself.

Ba-whang! Ba-whang! Two more hits somewhere in the convoy!

The formation scattered in panic.

Laughon swung the periscope back to the first target. She was already belly up, showing off her big propeller, her sailors flailing in the water among the oily flotsam.

Laughon took aim at a ship that looked like the *Yokahama Maru*. A setup whirred into the TDC; he swung the *Rasher* around. No time to waste; a transport was bearing down, big riveted prow growing larger in the scope, angle on the bow zero. Time to shoot and get out!

> I ordered "300 feet—use Negative" and immediately thereafter, "Shoot the bow tubes." The firing circuits were pulled [a precaution that was part of rigging for depth charge], but put back in time to fire one torpedo. . . .

The fish left the tube as the *Rasher* nosed over and headed down. At 150 feet, the crew heard a ringing torpedo explosion. It was followed by a string of ten close depth charges.

In minutes the *Rasher* was back at periscope depth. The *Stewart* was picking up survivors. No other ships were in sight, only distant masts and smoke going over the hill toward the Jolo Islands.

Laughon headed for the *Stewart* to put the *Rasher*'s last two torpedoes into her. The old destroyer's three stacks belched smoke. Off she went after the convoy, escaping destruction again.

The ship that did not escape the *Rasher*'s torpedoes was the *Koan Maru*, a 3,183-ton transport that bore a striking resemblance to the old *Matumoto Maru*.

A course was set for Ambon.

◆ ◆ ◆

On the afternoon of 14 June, the *Rasher* recorded her 103rd aircraft contact on a plane that stood off several miles away, circled in, teased the SD, flew away, and came back, finally forcing her to dive.

After dark, with the weather deteriorating, the *Rasher* proceeded to Bangka Passage on the northern tip of the Celebes to investigate the anchorage at Talisei Roads. It was empty. With wind and rain lashing out of the northeast, Laughon wistfully noted in his patrol report that

> this would have been a wonderful night for a surface attack. It was one of the darkest nights I have ever seen, with lots of rain and wind.

Early in the morning the *Rasher* made contact with the *Paddle*, and Laughon paid his respects to her skipper, Lt. Comdr. Byron Nowell.

Nowell would later in the year sink the *Shiniyo Maru*, which, unknown to him, was transporting hundreds of Allied POWs from Mindanao to Japan. Only eighty prisoners would survive. Presently Nowell was on his way to patrol around Halmahera. The two captains swapped scuttlebutt briefly, then parted company.

The *Rasher* headed east to Ambon. She submerged twelve miles from the Ambon Bay entrance light to reconnoiter and wait for what might show up.

At dawn a few planes winged out of Ambon, heading west. Fishing vessels poked along the coast. Things were quiet, even boring. Conversation turned to hot times anticipated in Perth. At 0838, it was back to reality: a ship stood out of Ambon Bay. Laughon held his fire, however, when he saw what type of ship it was:

> The target was identified as a small inter-island passenger vessel of about 500 tons and about 175 feet long. It had a single stick mast just aft of a low bridge, and a narrow comparatively tall stack about half the height of the mast. There were four ventilators aft of the stack. It had two passenger decks extending about two-thirds of the length of the ship. Forward of the bridge the gunwales were cut away to form a well, and forward of the well the forecastle had a small decked over structure. It was making twelve knots and was unescorted. We took several pictures of the ship at 3500 yards range. It had one small gun mounted on top of the bridge and possibly another one of the same size aft. It would have made an ideal gun target had it been sighted any place else.

Laughon allowed the steamer to pass unmolested.

After the noon meal, a submarine chaser stood out from the western side of the bay. Was it coming out to meet a ship? the men asked. Sure enough, a few minutes later a medium-sized transport emerged out of an approaching rain squall two miles south of the Hitu Peninsula. She was identified as a split-superstructure AK resembling the *Kizan Maru*, 5,072 tons. With her were two sub chasers, one well ahead on the starboard quarter, the other far enough astern not to interfere with an attack.

Laughon fired the *Rasher*'s last two torpedoes at her, going deep before he could see the results. Both hit on timed runs. A prolonged, rumbling explosion echoed through the submarine's hull.

The depth-charging that followed was surprisingly close considering the escorts were at a disadvantage: heavy rain beating on the surface must have interfered with the escort's sonar search, and a negative thermocline hid the *Rasher*. When the thundering ceased, Laughon came up for a look around.

Sheets of rain gusted across the Banda Sea. Mysteriously, the target and escorts had vanished. On the horizon lay the hump of Ambon's Hitu Peninsula, partly in shadow, partly in bright, cloud-dappled sunlight. A yacht-type patrol boat tacked northward, seemingly unperturbed. No other ships were in sight. Using the heavy squalls as cover, a puzzled Laughon headed his ship for Ombai Passage and home.

◆ ◆ ◆

On 23 June 1944, the *Rasher* moored at North Wharf in Fremantle, ending an extraordinary patrol.

◆ ◆ ◆

The *Rasher* stood in from her fourth war patrol weather-beaten and salt-stained, but with an impressive coxcomb of Japanese flags flying from a periscope and a proud crew at quarters topside. Her exploits had been broadcast all over Fremantle, and she returned to a hero's welcome, complete with a band, dignitaries, and the trappings of victory. Christie skipped across the brow and passed out congratulations and well-dones as fast as he could find hands to pump.

The *Rasher* was credited by Task Force Seventy-one with sinking four *marus* and a sub spotter, a grand total of 24,410 tons, and damaging five other ships totaling 20,900 tons. (Her official JANAC totals were four ships sunk for 10,867 tons.)

She had steamed 15,300 miles on her double run and consumed a whopping 167,000 gallons of diesel fuel. Laughon fired forty-two torpedoes, seventeen hits and twenty-five misses. To sink the sloop on 24 May, the 20-millimeter guns used 348 rounds of ammunition. The most amazing statistic was the 110 aircraft contacts she'd recorded. Laughon praised the excellence of the lookouts, quartermaster, and officers of the deck who, he said, had of necessity developed into excellent plane spotters.

Laughon noted in the patrol report with some pride that despite logging 2,535 engine-hours, the *Rasher*'s propulsion machinery had not suffered a major breakdown of any sort. What made this all the more impressive was the fact that a large part of the time the ship ran at three- or four-engine speed. It may have been a record for submarine reliability. The skipper extolled the engineering department for a great job of upkeep while at sea and credited the excellent overhauls during the last two refits. He detailed the normal problems with radar, radio, and, of course, torpedoes—particularly the ones loaded at Darwin. No episode in the report was more impressive than the night torpedo transfer off the Celebes coast. Admiral Christie was incredulous. No submarine had ever before made this dangerous transfer in enemy waters.

Laughon also critiqued Japanese convoy protection:

> More and stronger surface escorts were used in all cases, but in general their efforts were ineffective in preventing an attack, and they showed their usual lack of persistence after an attack, although they used depth charges liberally in the vicinity of the firing point. On only one occasion was a surface escort left behind to hold us down.

Near the end of the report he added:

> The Commanding Officer notes with pleasure the growing pride and affection evidenced by members of the crew for their ship. This is made apparent by the general reluctance of personnel to being transferred to the relief crew and by the general tenor of their conversations.

Admiral Christie attached his endorsement to the patrol report:

Subject:
U.S.S. RASHER (SS 269)—Report of Fourth War Patrol—Comment on.

1. RASHER's Fourth Patrol, conducted in the MOLUCCA-CELEBES SEA area, was her second consecutive outstanding patrol.

2. Closing the enemy at every opportunity and attacking with aggressiveness, determination and skill, RASHER again inflicted heavy damage upon the enemy. In two patrols and in spite of intense anti-submarine measures, RASHER has sunk or damaged 80,900 tons of enemy shipping.

3. Although areas were well patrolled by enemy aircraft, RASHER judiciously employed surface running to effectively develop many ship contacts. Special assignments to both lifeguard and offensive reconnaissance duties were well planned and courageously executed.

4. This patrol is designated "successful" for purposes of award of the Submarine Combat Insignia.

5. The Force Commander takes great pleasure in congratulating the Commanding Officer, Officers and Crew for maintaining their record of outstandingly successful patrols. . . .

After three highly successful and aggressive patrols, Christie detached Laughon from the *Rasher* and assigned him to a staff position with Commander Submarines Seventh Fleet.

Under Laughon's command the *Rasher* had sunk nine enemy vessels and damaged many more. He was now a highly respected skipper, and he had helped make the *Rasher* one of the most famous submarines in the Pacific.

Part 3

Dead Eye and
"Great Eagle"

Dead Eye

The Battle of the Java Sea was fought on 28 February 1942 between the Japanese and the combined American-British-Dutch-Australian (ABDA) naval forces. It was a disaster for the Allies. ABDA lost six ships; the Japanese lost none. Overall command and strategy were virtually nonexistent, and communication between the battle groups was so poor that some Allied warships steamed aimlessly in circles looking for the enemy. The eight-hour battle deteriorated into a tactical shambles.

Among the ships that picked up survivors was the *S 38*, commanded by a coolly professional, self-effacing lieutenant commander named Henry Glass Munson. He found fifty-four oil-soaked men from the destroyer HMS *Electra*, got them aboard the old submarine, and took them back to Surabaya.

Hank Munson was heard from again on 8 August 1942, when he attacked a Japanese relief convoy bound for Guadalcanal and sank the 5,628-ton *Meiyo Maru*. Since it was difficult to torpedo anything with a "Sugar boat," the sinking earned him the nickname "Dead Eye." He simply said it was a lucky shot from deep submergence. Nevertheless, the *Meiyo Maru*'s loss northwest of Bougainville in St. George's Channel prompted the Japanese convoy to flee back to Rabaul.

By November 1943, Munson was in command of the *Crevalle*, operating out of Fremantle. His first patrol in that boat was a good one. Notwithstanding rumors that he had night blindness, Munson reported four ships sunk. Accordingly, Admiral Christie presented him the Navy Cross. His second patrol in the *Crevalle*, while not as successful in terms of the number of ships sunk, was nevertheless conducted in typical Munson style. He attacked a variety of ships, including a Japanese submarine and, off the Talauds, a nine-ship convoy. Munson was rewarded with a second Navy Cross and promoted to full commander. Christie was very impressed with the man and hon-

211

ored his request to be relieved of command for a rest. Munson was sent to the staff of Submarine Squadron Sixteen, where he was ostensibly in charge of submarine refits. But Munson was too good a skipper to be left on the beach, and Christie was determined to get him back to sea in the right boat.

The thirty-four-year-old Munson, who stood third in the Naval Academy class of 1932, was a Rhodes scholar and brilliant mathematician. He was lanky and intense and shared the patrician mien of his maternal grandfather, Adm. Henry Glass, a former commander of the Asiatic Fleet. He had other illustrious forebears of high achievement, including a signer of the Declaration of Independence. Perhaps it was in his breeding to know what it took to succeed. At squadron headquarters, he gained a reputation for driving his repair crews hard to get the boats refitted and back at sea as quickly as possible. Christie no doubt quietly observed all of this from his headquarters and bided his time.

Meanwhile, the *Rasher* was due for an overhaul in California upon completion of her next war patrol—her fifth. But first, she needed a skipper. Seizing the opportunity to utilize one of the Navy's top submarine officers, Christie tapped Hank Munson. It was an excellent choice and was to prove a perfect match.

From the moment Hank Munson strode aboard the *Rasher* in his overseas cap and crisp khakis, he commanded respect and loyalty. To this day, former crew members speak of him with awe and reverence. His forty-four-day command so inextricably linked Munson with the *Rasher* that the two would be forever synonymous.

The skipper set out his own feelings about his crew and ship years later in a letter to Pete Sasgen:

> Altho' I had commanded two other boats, both with wonderful crews and a record that I don't have to apologize for, there was always something special about RASHER. Perhaps it was the instant way the whole crew accepted me as shown by the wonderful cooperation they gave me and I have the clearest memories of this and very precious ones they are too! Things just seem[ed] to work the way one wanted them on the RASHER and I could only wish I had been with you longer.

Munson's first order of business was to see to his new command's refit. Assisting him was a new executive officer, Bill Norrington.

Major items of work included the complete overhaul of two main engines and the installation of an SJA radar unit and Plan Position Indicator (PPI) scope, a new trim pump, and updated sound gear. The hydraulic plant was rebuilt, and three days were spent in dry dock for hull cleaning and painting.

New-style Gould trim pumps were being installed in submarines as fast as they could be delivered from the factory. The *Rasher's* original pump was noisy and, like all older units, had severely limited capacity below 300 feet. The Gould was a six-stage unit capable of delivering 35 gallons per minute against a 600-foot pressure head of sea water.

The boats were also being fitted with JP sound gear newly developed by the Navy's Underwater Sound Laboratory in New London. This equipment, which was designed only for listening and not for echo-ranging, had a T-shaped hydrophone that protruded from the main deck on the starboard side over the forward torpedo room. The forward location isolated the sound gear from the ship's relatively noisy machinery spaces aft. The JP was sonic and manually trained, whereas the old-style retractable JK-QC sound heads, which could listen or echo-range, were supersonic and were trained using hydraulic motors. When not in use the heads were retracted into protective trunks in the forward torpedo room to prevent them from being wiped off should a submarine bottom accidentally, as often happened when hiding from Japanese patrol boats. In combination with the JK-QC, the JP gear offered greater flexibility when tracking and ranging on enemy ships.

After refitting came days of training, night approaches, and convoy attack exercises. Many new officers and enlisted men had come aboard at the end of the fourth patrol. Now only eleven men from the Manitowoc days who had been on every patrol were still present, though some others were rotated back aboard after sitting out a patrol or two as part of the relief crews stationed on sub tenders.

A final detail—change of command—took place on 17 July.

But before the *Rasher* was due to get under way for her fifth patrol, tragedy struck.

Motor Machinist's Mate 1st class Maurice Smith and his pal Roland Soucy were joint owners of a motorcycle they'd purchased in Fremantle. When they learned the *Rasher* was heading back to the States for an overhaul after the next run, they decided to sell their wheels. Five days before departure, the two were on their way to show the bike to a potential buyer when they slammed into the back of an Aussie command car. Soucy was thrown seventy feet and suffered a fractured skull and two broken arms. Smith went through the vehicle's rear window. He died a week later from massive internal injuries. Word of his death reached his shipmates while the *Rasher* was at sea.

Wolf Pack

The Pacific submarine force was in a formidable position in the summer of 1944. There were about 140 submarines operating out of Pearl Harbor and Australia. The basic torpedo problem had been solved. Ultra was able to locate and track enemy ships at will. As a result, shipping, the lifeblood of the far-flung Japanese forces, was hemorrhaging at a fearsome rate. In 1944 alone, U.S. submarines sank 2,480,000 tons. The Japanese merchant marine had lost more than 100,000 officers and men. As the Allies began to move west decisively and recapture enemy-held territory, submarines were increasingly being called upon to provide lifeguard and reconnaissance duty in support of fleet operations. However, SubPac's main objective was still the destruction of the enemy's merchant fleet.

One of the ways to more rapidly and efficiently send ships to the bottom was by use of wolf packs. Wolf packs were not a new idea; they had been introduced to U.S. submarine operations as early as September 1943, but with limited success compared to the wolf packs of German U-boats in the North Atlantic. One reason was the smaller size of Japanese convoys and the littoral environment in which they operated. Another was the very nature of undersea warfare, which is characterized by individual initiative. Aggressive, independent-minded submarine skippers were loath to give up their freedom of action in favor of the closely orchestrated tactics required for wolf packing. It was tough enough to master the difficulties of conventional submarine warfare without adding to it the complicating and dangerous dimension (communications, collision, friendly torpedoes) of several submarines operating in the same waters. So training, practical experience, and, above all, belief in the basic concept were essential.

The wolf pack training entity was named "Convoy College," and its campus was, of all things, the big dance floor of the Submarine Officers' Mess at Pearl Harbor. The floor had a checkerboard pattern of foot-square black and white tiles. This became the game board on which submarine skippers learned the business and earned their degrees.

The "college faculty" moved convoy models over the board. From behind screens at each corner of the board, the fire-control parties approached and attacked blind, relying solely on information—coordinates, ranges, and bearings—received from other participants in the exercise. Once they established "contact" with the enemy, the trainees were permitted a brief look at the convoy, as they would if using a periscope. These gaming exercises then moved to sea, where the boats practiced "attacking" U.S. convoys approaching Hawaii from the West Coast.

The tactical principle employed in wolf packing was relatively straightforward. Once a convoy was located—by Ultra or other means—the submarines maintained a column formation (more or less) in the direction of the convoy's track with a prearranged distance between them to permit wide-ranging searches. When a submarine made contact with the enemy, the location was transmitted to her pack-mates. The initial attack was then launched on the convoy's flank. The attacking submarine would then withdraw and reload torpedoes while her pack-mates launched a second or third attack. The submarines would make repeated attacks in this fashion until the convoy was sunk. Cripples would be finished off by trailing submarines. Since Japanese anti-submarine efforts were relatively ineffective, small groups of boats—no more than two or three—were adequate, unlike U-boat wolf packs that needed many submarines to crack the formidable defensive perimeter thrown up around Allied convoys.

In theory, this tactic worked very nicely. In practice, however, it was difficult to predict with certainty where one's pack-mate might be at any given moment, and, when the shooting started, how best to talk to her and direct her to where she would do the most good. As in lifeguarding, communications were the weak link in wolf packs. In both the *Rasher*'s previous encounters with coordinated attacks—with the *Bluefish* in January 1944, and with the *Raton* the following month—those two boats were essentially relegated to the role of bystanders, while the *Rasher* did most of the shooting and worrying about where her pack-mates were. Nevertheless, more and more wolf packs were being deployed to speed up the destruction of the Japanese merchant marine.

By the end of the summer of 1944, Japanese shipping in the Pacific was almost entirely confined to the South China Sea, East China Sea, Yellow Sea, and Empire waters. Essentially, the *marus* were hiding behind a formidable wall of mines sown along the coast from Kyushu to the Formosa Straits. The once-busy convoy route from Formosa to Palau was abandoned in July. Routes from Singapore to Borneo were next to go. Others were terminated in August and September, more in October and November. By December, the principal materiel support for the Imperial Army's withering garrisons throughout the Southwest Pacific came only from Japan and Formosa. With the impending Allied invasion of Leyte, the war of attrition shifted to the interdiction of enemy shipping in and around Luzon, Formosa, and the mainland of China.

Accordingly, for her fifth patrol the *Rasher* was dispatched to the South China Sea off Luzon, the Philippines. It would be one of the most famous war patrols ever conducted.

Her Op-Order, Number 95-44, directed that she form a wolf pack with the *Bluefish* (now skippered by Comdr. Charles Henderson). Munson would be in overall command. The two submarines were to proceed together to the bombing restriction lane off the west coast of Australia, conduct wolf pack attack exercises, and then split up. The *Rasher* would sail to Exmouth Gulf for fuel. She would reach her patrol area via the Lombok and Makassar Straits, Sibitu Passage, and Mindoro Strait. The *Bluefish* was detailed to Darwin, then the Molucca Sea and through the Molucca and Sibitu passages and Mindoro Strait to a rendezvous with the *Rasher* off the Philippine coast.

The patrol area itself was code-named "Whitewash." It was an immense area of more than 105,000 square miles. Whitewash's southern boundary was latitude 14° 15' north; the northern one was 18° 30'. The eastern boundary was the coast of Luzon; the western was Scarborough Shoals at longitude 115° east. On 30 August, Munson was to terminate the patrol, transit Balintang Channel north of Luzon, and proceed to Midway Island for fuel. From Midway, the *Rasher* would sail for Pearl Harbor, then California.

Munson's plan for conducting the wolf pack was quite simple. A search plan would be developed day-to-day on the basis of contacts, intelligence, and whatever could be picked up from submarines operating in adjacent areas. Each night the *Rasher* and the *Bluefish* would rendezvous at a prearranged spot and relay instructions for the next day's search by Aldis lamp. Voice radio would be used only when contact was made with the enemy. Munson believed that the simpler things were, the better chance of success they had.

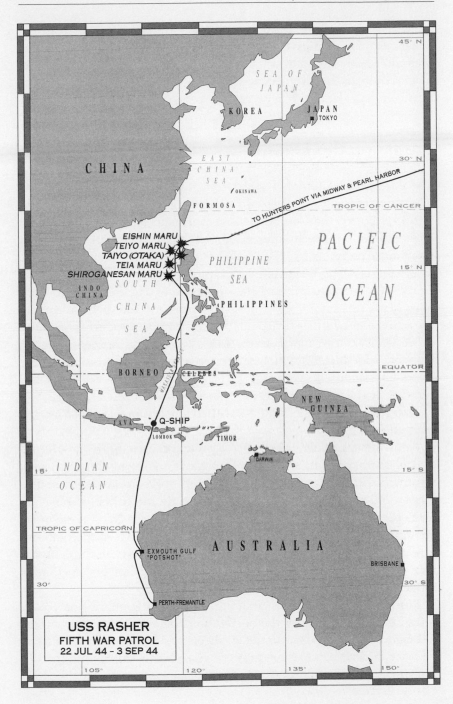

45° N

SEA OF JAPAN

KOREA

JAPAN
TOKYO

CHINA

EAST CHINA SEA

30° N

OKINAWA

FORMOSA

TO HUNTERS POINT VIA MIDWAY & PEARL HARBOR

TROPIC OF CANCER

PACIFIC

EISHIN MARU
TEIYO MARU
TAIYO (OTAKA)
TEIA MARU
SHIROGANESAN MARU

PHILIPPINE SEA

15° N

OCEAN

INDO CHINA

SOUTH

CHINA

SEA

PHILIPPINES

BORNEO

CELEBES

EQUATOR

NEW GUINEA

JAVA

Q-SHIP

LOMBOK

TIMOR

DARWIN

15° S

INDIAN

OCEAN

15° S

TROPIC OF CAPRICORN

AUSTRALIA

EXMOUTH GULF "POTSHOT"

BRISBANE

30°

30° S

PERTH-FREMANTLE

USS RASHER
FIFTH WAR PATROL
22 JUL 44 - 3 SEP 44

105°   120°   135°   150°

At 1315 on 22 July, Munson saluted Admiral Christie from the bridge as he maneuvered his submarine away from North Wharf in Fremantle and headed to sea. The USS *Rasher* departed the great submarine base for the last time.

Rasher vs. the Empire

The pack-mates alternated with each other in playing target in the bombing restriction lane while practicing day and night torpedo attacks. Munson was an excellent skipper and tactician. His smooth and accomplished technique, combined with the *Rasher*'s seasoned fire-control party, "sank" the *Bluefish* every time.

While the *Rasher* was acting as a target for the *Bluefish* northwest of Shark Bay, a lookout sighted the periscope of a third and uninvited party. This was no porpoise; the sonar operator had an echo contact on a sub 2,000 yards off the port beam. Munson ordered up flank speed, warned the *Bluefish*, and cleared out. He was certain it was a Japanese submarine, but he hesitated to attack because there was the remote possibility it was a friendly. Munson speculated that the reason the Japanese skipper did not attack was because he thought the *Rasher*, which was echo-ranging at the time, was an anti-submarine patrol vessel.

After the encounter, the *Rasher* parted company with the *Bluefish* and headed for Exmouth Gulf. The anchorage was its usual self: windy and ragged with whitecaps from northwesterly gales. The *Rasher* tied up at the fueling dock alongside the British submarine HMS *Clyde*. While she awaited her turn to fuel, the base commander asked the *Rasher* to retrieve a loose barge at the head of the gulf and tow it back to its moorings. Munson readily agreed, nicknaming his ship "Tugboat *Rasher*." With the tow job finished and the fuel tanks topped off, she got under way for Lombok Strait.

Munson conducted drills, training dives, and gunnery practice en route. A very satisfactory gunnery target was cobbled together from old fruit boxes, swab handles, and sheets and tossed overboard. The *Rasher* submerged while the gun crews and ammunition train were organized and positioned. Then the order was passed over the 1MC: "Battle surface!"

The submarine plowed out from under the sea, a turbo blow already in progress to get her decks out of the water as fast as possible. In a flash the gunner's mates were on deck and the 3-incher cast loose and trained out.

"Commence firing!" Munson ordered.

As the ship rolled, the pointer cranked down toward the target; the trainer cranked left, then a smidgen right, and the rounds kicked off. *Bam! Bam! Bam!*

From the bridge, a cheering Munson watched a very impressive performance: after two misses, the shooting was right on the mark. The submarine closed with the target remnants so the 20s and machine guns could finish them off. Then Munson called a halt and ordered the guns secured. Unused ammunition and 3-inch shell casings were struck below, spent casings kicked over the side, and the *Rasher* was back on course again.

Munson elected to approach Lombok Strait submerged to avoid detection by planes, then to make a dash through the narrow passage on the surface. A half-hour before midnight he brought the boat to the surface under a three-quarter moon, made landfall, and stood in at eighteen knots on four engines. The new PPI scope was a superb aid to navigation. Its clockwise sweep displayed Nusa Besar Island and both sides of the strait on the twelve-inch diameter scope as clearly and as precisely as if on a chart. Just before clearing the strait, radar made contact on two patrol boats. The PPI showed their range markers and blips in relation to the *Rasher* herself. The Japanese vessels were sleepily patrolling, one in the middle of the strait, the other off its northern approaches; neither noticed the *Rasher* as she went by at full speed.

◆ ◆ ◆

Dawn broke clear and bright on 29 July 1944. Since the *Rasher* would be sprinting across the air transport lanes from Java to the southern Celebes (the Japanese had stepped up their use of aircraft to move cargo), Munson planned to dive east of Sakala Island and make a submerged run north to avoid being seen by Japanese air patrols from Kangean Island.

At 0745, just before Munson was going to pull the plug, a large, nondescript trawler was sighted plodding along north of Sakala. Dead Eye made a cautious approach to look her over.

She had a radio antenna strung between her masts, and her erratic maneuvers suggested to Munson she was a Q-ship—a decoy disguised as a fishing vessel to lure submarines into gun range. Since Navy intelligence in Fremantle had reported a Japanese aircraft/submarine anti-sub unit working the area, he was extremely careful not to give himself away. She was a tempting target, but Munson could not be certain how well armed she was. Besides, there was a good possibility the *Rasher* could be jumped by airplanes while shooting her up, so gun action was out of the question. Munson worked around and headed north; the trawler disappeared southwest into the haze.

In the afternoon, Munson surfaced the boat and proceeded up the Makassar Strait through the deep-water channel east of the Lima Islands. As usual, clots of native sailboats had to be avoided. He decided to delay passage through the Cape William choke point until after dark. He submerged to wait out what he called "plane business hours."

On 1 August, the *Rasher* cleared the strait and struck due north across the Celebes Sea for the Sibitu Passage in the Sulu Archipelago. There was enough aircraft activity during the run to suggest the possibility of an approaching convoy, but it never materialized. However, as the *Rasher* approached Sibitu at 2130, radar picked up interference wobble to the east. Munson's patrol report stated that the submarine

> Received proper challenge, replied, and exchanged calls and messages with the U.S.S. PUFFER by keying radar. Contact not made. He advised us he had sunk a ship that morning north of SIBITU, and that it might be warm. So it was, so it was.

Under a half moon, the *Rasher* entered the passage. The dank aroma of tropical vegetation reached the bridge as she skirted the coast of Tawitawi and North Borneo. No sooner had she reached the Laparan Island Passage than the accuracy of the *Puffer*'s message became apparent. Bill Norrington's diary described what happened next.

> About one hour later, met and avoided patrol boat. Was just getting well clear when we sighted a plane coming at us astern, flying up our wake. Gave left full rudder, changed course, then dove. Two bombs dropped as we passed 45 feet, one quite close. No damage to speak of. Bright moon. Plane dropped flare and it and patrol searched in vicinity. We pulled out and surfaced about two hours later. All clear. Whew! The PUFFER was right. The Japs must have been mad!

Ken Tate, back aboard for this patrol, sure thought they were.

Aug. 1, 1944: Just before getting all the way through Sibitu Passage we were sighted by a Jap patrol bomber. He was only about 3 miles away and we dove but only reached 45 ft. when he let go 2 bombs which jarred hell out of us. This was the first time we were ever bombed at night.

◆　◆　◆

Via the Sulu Sea, Munson made for the South China Sea. The *Rasher* submerged at 0700 on 3 August to transit the Mindoro Strait, staying well clear of dangerous Apo Reef. When she drew near Lubang Island, the boat surfaced and headed northwest. The next day she entered her assigned area.

Perfect weather and bright moonlight greeted the *Rasher* when she surfaced thirty miles south of Scarborough Shoal on the evening of 5 August to start a battery charge, dump the day's accumulation of trash and garbage, ventilate living spaces, and start a standard surface routine.

As was his practice, Hank Munson departed the wardroom after supper to prowl about his ship to see what might catch his attention and to talk with the watchstanders and off-duty sailors. He engendered an intimacy to which his men responded warmly. He loved to see what his motor macs, electricians, and torpedomen were working on. In addition, these strolls provided him an opportunity to get a feel for how things were, what the men thought, what they anticipated, how primed they were for battle.

Mostly, though, his time during patrols was spent in his miniature stateroom wrestling with paperwork and the myriad chores that fall to a warship's captain. A brilliant mathematician, he relaxed by posing and solving calculus problems, producing long, complex equations and scribblings on note pads that were decipherable only by him. But he always had cocked a seaman's ear for the boat, for what was going on around him. He sensed, as do all skippers, the change in a diesel's tune, any dissonant whine from a compressor or pump. And he felt in the sibilant hiss and slap of water along the hull the subtle changes in course and speed and the condition of the sea itself.

As he thrust his head from behind the green curtain in the doorway of his stateroom this night, Munson sensed a subtle fluctuation in the normal, smooth flow of the ship's pulse. He headed aft to the control room, passing the cribbage players in the wardroom engrossed in their game. By the time he reached the foot of the conning tower ladder he knew what it was.

"Radar contact! Sixteen thousand yards. Call the skipper!"

In a flash, Munson was hunched over the PPI scope looking at four bright pips, one larger than the other three, bearing 225° T.

From the bridge, Munson started an end around. The diesels throttled up, and the *Rasher's* bow cut around to the southeast to get in position on the targets' starboard flank.

By 0130, Munson had the *Rasher* where he wanted her. With the PPI keeping track of targets, it was like looking down on the convoy from above. Plot worked out their speed at eight knots on a base course of 155, zigzagging about 30 degrees every seven minutes.

The *Rasher* submerged, and Munson started his approach.

He identified his target as the 8,223-ton passenger-cargo ship *Kosei Maru*. She was escorted by a submarine chaser stationed to port. Two small transport-escorts of about 1,000 tons each were staggered on the *maru's* starboard flank.

Munson's next maneuver was incredibly daring. At 0211, when the leading escort was only 700 yards away, angle on the bow zero, Dead Eye headed straight at her, then ordered his helmsman to start swinging right slowly across both escorts' tracks as they approached (see diagram, page 223). When the *Rasher* was 1,350 yards from the target, he fired six torpedoes.

Munson demonstrated a cool, uncanny ability to outfox the Japanese:

> Timed five hits as we went deep to avoid being rammed. Target screws immediately stopped and loud and unmistakable breakup noises were heard in all compartments. Think the target went down faster than we did. Evaded easily by working into target's wake at high speed and deep submergence and then took courses up the reverse of the target's course. Escorts dropped four charges at a considerable distance and commenced an energetic but futile search using echo ranging and listening, never getting close.

But while the torpedoes were exploding against the target's hull, the *Rasher* came close to being sunk by her own hand.

Depth control was lost when two poppet valves in the forward torpedo room were accidentally held open too long. Unchecked, sea

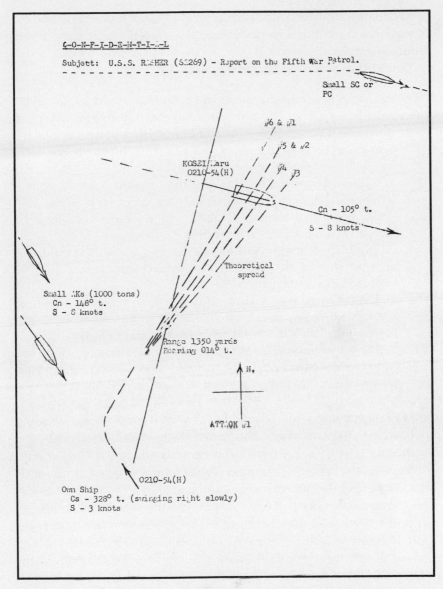

Attack No. 1
Diagram by Henry G. Munson
from his original patrol report.

water roared into the ship. Heavy forward and uncontrollable, the
Rasher nosed over and started down fast into the mile-deep South
China Sea Basin.

Bob Mathewson remembered it vividly:

> We had a new torpedoman aboard who had served on one of the
> older boats where they had had trouble with the ship's firing cir-
> cuits, and it was standard operating procedure to have a torpedo-
> man stand between the tubes and fire them by hand. We never
> found this necessary to do on the RASHER.
>
> Captain Munson elected to fire the forward tubes in reverse
> order, 6, 5, 4, 3, 2, and 1. When he gave the order to "Fire One," this
> torpedoman fired Number 1 tube by hand along with Number 6
> tube, and Number 2 tube with Number 5 tube.
>
> The torpedoman manning the poppet valve manifold was
> unaware that tubes 1 and 2 had been fired and did not close the
> poppet valves on these two tubes.
>
> These valves opened automatically when a torpedo was fired
> and vented the impulse air into the bilges to prevent an air bubble
> from rising to the surface and betraying the boat's position.
>
> These vent lines were about six inches in diameter, so we had
> two six-inch lines flooding the forward torpedo room under great
> sea pressure as we had gone to 300 feet and silent running.

Nine tons of water poured into the forward torpedo room bilges and
slopped over the deck plates. The *Rasher*'s heavy nose pulled her deep.

Bracing himself against the steep down-angle and casting a worried eye on the bathythermograph stylus, which wiggled off the scale
at 450 feet, and the control room depth gauge, which quivered at 460,
Pete Sasgen solemnly reminded Captain Munson that unlike his last
ship, the *Crevalle*, a thick-skinned boat, the *Rasher*'s test depth was
only 312 feet. Munson, ever calm and composed, gave orders halting
the plummet, then promised every man aboard membership in the
"Deep Dunkers Club." He himself, he said, was a charter member.

Exec Bill Norrington was hanging on in the conning tower when
the ship was finally leveled off by expert blowing and pumping. "She
didn't hardly leak at all," he noted in his diary. "Some boat!"

But despite all the rumbling and hissing of compressed air as the
submarine plunged more than 100 feet below her test depth, the
escorts could not find her. As for the target, Munson was sure of six
hits despite hearing only five. Since two torpedoes were fired
simultaneously, he reasoned that both had reached the target and

exploded at the same time. Regardless, his patrol report states:

> Surfaced with escorts milling around 8400 yards astern and cleared to the west.

Sent to the bottom was not the *Kosei Maru*, but rather the *Shiroganesan Maru*, 4,739 tons. Messages to convoy headquarters explained her whereabouts with the loathsome word used by the Japanese to describe the sinking of one of their own ships: *chimbotsu*.

The only damage the *Rasher* sustained was the flooding of the pitometer log and two sound head training motors. After a thorough fresh-water flushing and twelve hours of baking in the ship's oven to dry the equipment out, the electrician's mates had everything back in operation a day later.

◆ ◆ ◆

On 8 August, during a routine trim dive, a lookout broke his arm just above the elbow when he caught it between the deck and conning tower hatch seat as he scrambled below. It was a serious break that could not be set and splinted by the pharmacist's mate with the material on board. Munson radioed Fremantle requesting a rendezvous with the submarine *Hoe*, which was in an adjacent area and due to leave for her base in two days. The *Rasher* rendezvoused the next day south of Scarborough Shoal with both the *Bluefish* and the *Hoe*, and the patient was transferred in the *Hoe's* rubber boat.

After the *Hoe* departed, Munson worked out plans with Henderson via megaphone. They decided that the two boats should patrol fifteen miles apart running east and west in the traffic lanes forty miles south of Scarborough Shoal.

As the *Rasher* sailed to her station, she passed the location of her attack two nights earlier. She found an immense amount of wreckage and oil covering at least ten square miles. Bill Norrington went out on deck with a boathook to investigate:

> Saw three dead Japs and wreckage at spot of our attack. A boat, a busted life boat, an ice box, a vegetable locker, kegs, life jackets, wood, beer bottles, boxes all over the place. We spent about two hours investigating junk trying to identify the ship. About four of us were on the main deck looking things over with the ship lying to, with Manila only about 100 miles away. Perhaps we were foolish, but it was fun.

The next two days were uneventful. Patrolling in both deep water and coastal areas turned up only freight-hauling sampans and luggers. Late in the day on the eleventh, during a rendezvous with the *Bluefish*, radar made contact on two ships; they were chased down, but they turned out to be patrol craft not worthy of an engagement.

In the morning, dark clouds arrived from the west on a freshening wind. The gray South China Sea grew restive, with whitecaps building quickly to eight feet. About noon, large groups of sampans passed south, running ahead of the weather. As the wind picked up and the barometer plunged, it was apparent that a sizable storm was developing. As the day wore on heavy rain arrived. The ship rolled and pitched violently. A radio message from Task Force Seventy-one ordered the *Rasher* and the *Bluefish* to station themselves near Capones Island for weather reports and lifeguard duty in conjunction with air strikes on Luzon scheduled to commence on 13 August.

The thirteenth brought a full-fledged typhoon. This posed extraordinary dangers to a small ship like a submarine. The *Rasher* struggled through waves fifteen feet high and thirty feet across from peak to peak. Her propellers whirred like eggbeaters when the sea dropped away from her stern. Wind shrieked through the periscope shears and antennas; giant combers crashed over the bridge. Dressed in oilskins, Munson and his men crouched behind the bulwarks and held on for dear life. At noon Task Force Seventy-one wisely cancelled lifeguard operations; no planes could fly in such weather, anyway. Relieved, Munson resumed patrolling to the west and north with the *Bluefish*. It was miserable.

> Typhoon weather, sea force 5, much rain and mist, depth control difficult, visibility low and variable, torpedo performance doubtful.

Mountains of water, lashing rain, and blinding spume battered the ship as the helmsmen fought to stay on course. Below decks, torpedomen fretted over their torpedo stowage; a ton and a half of steel the size of a sewer pipe crashing around in the cramped space would spell disaster. To make matters worse, after the boat surfaced from a trim dive white water thundered down the conning tower hatch until it was ankle deep in the compartment.

The South China Sea heaved and thrashed all day on the fourteenth. Early in the morning of the fifteenth, radar managed to pick up recognition signals from the *Puffer* despite the ugly sea return generated by the storm.

The *Puffer's* Captain Selby reported that three days earlier he had attacked a convoy near Sibitu Passage and sunk a 5,000-ton tanker and damaged another, the *Shimpo Maru*. The skipper of the *Shimpo Maru*, he said, ran her aground off Cape Calavite on Mindoro Island. But the *Puffer* was out of torpedoes and could not finish her off.

Task Force Seventy-one was apprised of the situation and relayed instructions, via Munson, for Henderson and the *Bluefish* to do the job. For the *Bluefish*, it was a 400-mile round trip. The *Rasher* was left on her own. When Henderson shoved off he wished Munson good luck and good hunting. He had no idea how good both would be.

◆ ◆ ◆

As the war of attrition gained momentum in 1943, a grim scene unfolded each morning in Tokyo. In the staff room of the Japanese Combined Convoy Fleet Headquarters, a big map with red flags showed the positions of ships that had been lost during the night to American submarines. The flags were affixed each morning at 0900 after the bad news was assessed and positions accurately located. The staff officers were alarmed by the growing number of red flags that greeted them each day. It fell to a junior staff officer to call the ship section of the General Staff to apprise them of the number of ships sunk overnight. The chief of the section then had the unpleasant chore of reporting directly to the feared Gen. Hideki Tojo, who was Japan's premier, war minister, home minister, and chief of the Army General Staff.

Typically, upon hearing the latest news from convoy headquarters, Tojo immediately phoned Adm. Shigetaro Shimada, navy minister and chief of the Naval Staff, to lash him for the navy's failure to protect Imperial shipping. In his enraged state, Tojo may have suggested *hara-kari* as the only way for Shimada to redeem himself. (Ironically, Tojo himself would resign by the middle of July 1944, after the loss of the Marianas, which he had personally guaranteed would never be surrendered.)

With Tojo's fury still ringing in his ears, Admiral Shimada undoubtedly ripped into his subordinates. He ordered that henceforth all convoys must be protected from the submarine onslaught—no matter the cost.

Shimada's—and Tojo's—wrath was not wasted on the commanders who assembled Convoy HI-71 in late July and early August 1944. It was big, nearly twenty ships in all, and its cargo of food and military equipment so vital that it was accorded more than a dozen escorts. One of them was the largest and most important ship in the convoy, the 20,000-ton escort aircraft carrier *Taiyo*.

The 591-foot-long *Taiyo* was the former *Kasuga Maru*, a handsome passenger-cargo ship built in the late 1930s. In 1941, she was converted to CVE-1. Because of an incorrect English interpretation of Japanese characters found in captured documents, the *Taiyo* was also known as the *Otaka*, which in Japanese means "Great Eagle," certainly an appropriate name for an aircraft carrier. She could carry twenty-one planes and make a top speed of twenty-three knots. The *Taiyo* had led a charmed life, escaping many a torpedo attack. But her luck was running out.

HI-71 sailed for the Philippines from Takao, Formosa, on 16 August 1944. Its track southeast across the South China Sea and down the western coast of Luzon would take it into area Whitewash.

By the seventeenth, the storm had passed south; the barometer was on the rise. When the *Rasher*'s rolling and pitching subsided, routine returned below decks. Cribbage and acey-deucy boards reappeared, a sure sign that things were back to normal. But like everyone else, Ken Tate was ready for some real action.

> Aug 10–17, 1944: It has been raining heavily all week. (Typhoon weather) We've been patrolling from Manila to the top of Luzon from 4 to 5 miles off land. Nothing doing at Lingayen Gulf.

Two hundred and twenty-five miles north of the *Rasher*'s position was a wolf pack out of Pearl Harbor operating under the name "Donc's Devils." (Munson, not one to care for such things, had not bothered to name his own wolf pack.) The Devils were under the command of Lt. Comdr. Glynn R. "Donc" Donaho in the *Picuda*. The pack included the *Spadefish* and the *Redfish*, both of which were new boats.

On the evening of 17 August, despite the blinding rain and rough conditions, the *Redfish*, skippered by Lt. Comdr. Louis McGregor, made contact with a huge southbound convoy. It consisted of over a dozen tankers and transports. McGregor got off a contact report to his pack-mates and started a surface approach. By 0500 he was in position and ready to fire torpedoes at a transport when he saw an escort carrier. At the last possible moment he shifted targets and fired at the *Taiyo*. Great Eagle's luck held. The torpedoes missed.

◆ ◆ ◆

With the *Redfish's* contact report in hand, Munson studied the charts of the Luzon coast. If McGregor's coordinates were correct (in fact they were not, due to the typhoon that had prevented accurate navigational fixes for days), the convoy would be coming down the coast close inshore. Munson radioed the *Bluefish*, off to attend to the grounded *Shimpo Maru*, and the *Raton*, which was in an area adjacent to the *Rasher's*, and told them both to spare no turns to get there to help out.

During the night the *Rasher* had outrun a weather front moving in from the southwest. Now brightening skies in the morning forced her to submerge as she headed north to find the convoy. Intense aircraft activity along the coast suggested a possible ship movement.

When the *Rasher* reached the mouth of the Goba River just below Laoag City, Munson spotted an enemy airfield surrounded by barracks, hangars, and, at the north end of the field, radio towers. He watched planes practicing takeoffs, landings, and glide bombing runs. Other planes took off and headed north, while others returned from patrols. He took pictures of the base through the periscope, trying to capture as many details as possible.

Only one thing spoiled the view. As Number One periscope was being hoisted for a routine sweep, the elevation handle fell from its folded position and caught on the lip of the well, wrenching the scope out of alignment. When Munson ran it up, the scope vibrated so much it could not be used to search for aircraft or for photography.

As the *Rasher* pushed her convoy search north, the weather front, accompanied by unrelenting rain, overtook her.

By 1800, all hands, including Munson himself, were in a state of nervous expectation. The tracking party anticipated every rise of the periscope. Every quiver on the radar scope sent pulse rates soaring. The unrelenting tropical downpour made searching slow and tedious, requiring frequent and dangerously long periscope observations. Heavy rain beating on the surface of the sea hampered sound conditions. The ship was quiet; time passed slowly. At 1905, Munson surfaced the boat and headed for Cape Bojeador to sweep the area.

Chief Quartermaster James White was handling the navigation chores. He recalled:

> The radar operator, who knew that because of the weather we had not had a good position fix for some time, informed me that we were beginning to get some land or peaks on radar. I knew this could not be, as we were too far out for radar to pick up land. When

I got to the radar, numerous pips were showing up and could only be ships. I sounded the alarm and we tied into them.

Munson's patrol report recorded the time of the contact as 2009.

Made radar contact dead ahead at 15,000 yards on a 13 (approximately) ship convoy with about 6 escorts.

Two target groups totaling well over twenty ships were heading due south, and the *Rasher* was dead ahead of them! She'd just hit the submarine jackpot. Munson wrote:

The speed, number of escorting vessels, great size of this convoy and of the individual ships, plus the intense aerial activity proceeding its passage, convinced us that this was an exceptionally important convoy. This proved to be true.

The PPI displayed both groups in a line of close columns, the escorts arrayed in a conventional screening formation outboard. The first group was just as big as Munson described—thirteen ships and six escorts. A second distinct group of eight or nine large transports with escorts followed closely behind the first one. Convoy speed was twelve knots, base course 205, 10 degree zigzag to either side.
Munson noted:

The night was very dark, no moon, completely and thickly overcast with almost continuous rain—absolutely ideal conditions for a night attack.

At the airfield below Laoag City, a large searchlight pierced the darkness, pointing north to guide the convoy down the coast.
Munson wasted no time. Firing solution completed, skipper directing the attack from the bridge, the *Rasher* raced in on the convoy's starboard side, her four-engine roar all but drowned out by the whipping rain and wind.
Upon reaching the firing point 1,500 yards ahead of the starboard flanking escort, the radarmen were confronted with so many targets it was nearly impossible for them to isolate the one Munson had chosen to shoot. With the escort looming up 900 yards away, he ordered left full rudder and full power to turn out ahead of her, then steadied the rudder amidships on an outbound course until radar had the target bearing. (See diagram, page 231.)

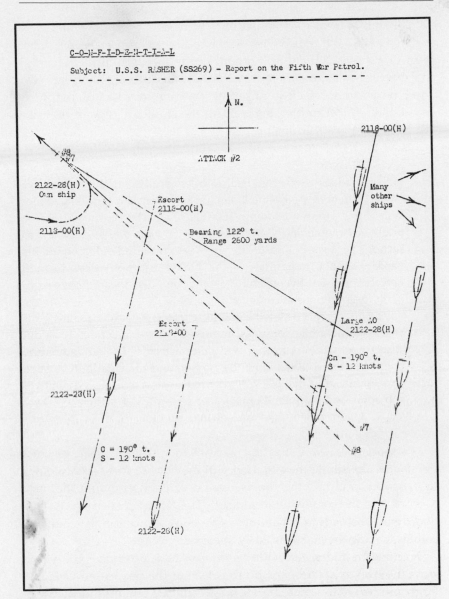

Attack No. 2
Diagram by Henry G. Munson
from his original patrol report.

"All stop"—the *Rasher* hauled down. Unable to see his targets in the pitch dark, and thus having to rely on radar ranges and bearings, Munson was set to fire four torpedoes from the stern tubes. After the first two fish were on their way, he held his fire on the other two while he confirmed their gyro settings. Meanwhile, he ordered flank speed and left full rudder, and ran up the starboard side of the convoy preparing to attack again.

Just as the *Rasher* steadied up, Munson reported,

> both torpedoes were seen, heard and correctly timed to hit a huge tanker, apparently gasoline laden judging from the appalling explosion with a column of flame 1000 feet high. The entire sky was a bright red momentarily and the target and the whole convoy was seen for an instant. Part of the ship blew off and landed about 500 yards from the remainder of the tanker and both parts burned fiercely for about twenty minutes and then disappeared from sight in one grand final explosion.

> The near escort decided something was wrong, he fired his guns at all points of the compass, reversed course and fiercely depth charged something or other two miles astern of us. Pandemonium reigned in the convoy, lights flashed on and off, side lights turned on, depth charges fell in every direction, gun fire broke out all over and some badly aimed 40mm tracer passed astern of us.. . . . Two ships appeared to indulge in a spirited gun duel for a few minutes.

Munson radioed a contact report to both the *Bluefish* and Fremantle, describing the situation. But the *Bluefish* was seventy miles to the south, and no other boats were near enough to join the fray: Munson had the convoy all to himself. The *Rasher* dashed up its starboard side, reloading torpedoes. The convoy obligingly changed course, making the end around even easier.

Tracking by radar and sound, Munson took position 5,000 yards from the convoy's starboard bow. Selecting the nearest and biggest target on the radar screen, he set up an attack from around the stern of a flanking escort. As the escort steamed out of the way, the PPI presented a picture beyond the wildest dream of any submarine skipper: at least eleven more targets surrounded the big one Munson had picked. He slowed, fired six bow tubes at her, swung hard left, fired four stern tubes at another large target steaming in a far column, then hauled off at flank speed to watch the fireworks. Ten torpedoes fingered out in the darkness. (See diagram page 233.)

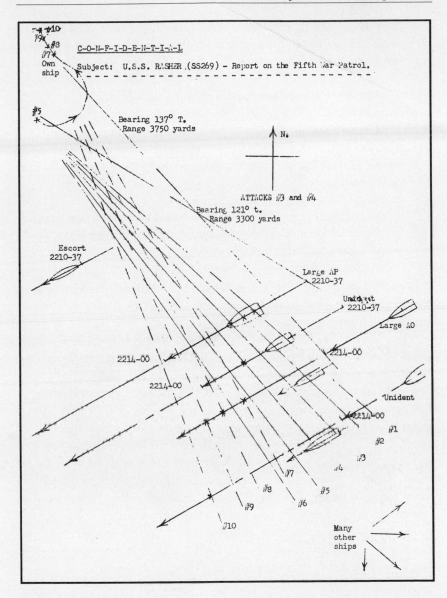

Attacks Nos. 3 & 4
Diagram by Henry G. Munson
from his original patrol report.

> Observed, heard, and timed three hits on the bow tube target. It immediately began burning and smoking heavily, and was seen to be a large transport.

In flames, the big *maru* dropped out of the formation.

Another hit!

A bow tube torpedo walloped an unidentified target beyond and ahead of the first one, lighting up ships and escorts alike. Twinkling red lifeboat marker lights began to appear around the torpedoed ships. More hits:

> Observed, heard, and timed two hits, heard and timed one more, on the stern tube target at the proper interval. These three hits with the large spread indicates that this target was very long.

Indeed it was very long. Hank "Dead Eye" Munson had torpedoed the *Taiyo*. The fourth stern torpedo ran on and exploded against an unidentified target beyond the aircraft carrier.

The convoy was devastated. And Great Eagle was on her way to the floor of the South China Sea. One can imagine the scene aboard the doomed ship. Three torpedoes had pierced her hull below the waterline (her conversion to a warship did not include the application of belt armor). Even as he tried to regroup the convoy, the *Taiyo*'s captain must have known his ship was mortally damaged. Evenly spaced fore to aft, the hits more than likely crushed crew-berthing spaces, wrecked the cavernous hangar deck, and destroyed the starboard after boiler room. So many sailors were undoubtedly killed outright that there were too few left to fight fires: almost instantly they burned out of control. In just a few minutes, water must have reached the overhead in the hangar deck and then flooded into adjacent spaces and compartments. The *Taiyo* went down so fast there probably was not even time to save the Emperor's portrait that hung on the bridge.

All around, chaos reigned. Munson's report noted:

> The usual depth chargings, gun firings and signalling began anew, with the escorts rushing around like rats in a cage.

The escorts were confused by Munson's rapid maneuvering and two attacks. As their convoy went up in flames, they opened fire on each other in their frustration. For sure someone would have to answer to Admiral Shimada.

Since Munson was almost out of torpedoes, he broadcast another contact report. Then, with only four fish forward and two aft, Munson looked for the best way to use them.

After the initial onslaught, the convoy split into two groups. Munson could not possibly attack both, but he hoped one might be fodder for the *Spadefish* when she arrived from the north. For his final attack, Dead Eye picked the larger of the two groups. It consisted of two big ships in column, a third large ship on the port quarter, and a solitary escort.

Soaked through despite his rain gear, Munson went below and huddled with the radar operator in the conning tower to study the targets' disposition. As he watched, they zigged right to 290, west-northwest, blundering right into the *Rasher*'s path. Confident of his approach, Munson returned to the bridge to direct the attack.

At 2327 the TDC had the solution; three minutes later he fired four bow torpedoes at the leading target. They left the tubes at eight-second intervals, the spread developed from aft forward to increase the fan effect. Number One hooked wildly right, out of control, however. (See diagram, page 236.)

Munson ordered right full rudder, brought the stern tubes to bear, and fired at the second ship in the column.

Three hits from the bow tubes! For an instant it was like daylight. A mighty explosion rocked the coast of Luzon as a huge munitions-laden transport was blown to bits.

Munson could do no wrong that night; the torpedo that had veered right found a 4,000-ton transport 1,400 yards beyond the vaporized munitions carrier. Exactly two minutes later, a big 10,000-tonner on station astern of the munitions ship caught both fish fired from the after tubes.

Munson reported:

> We hauled out to the west and stopped to collect our wits and estimate the situation.

While they did, a message arrived from the *Bluefish* detailing her attack on two tankers, part of the remnants of the convoy. Returning from her mission in the south, she happened upon them at a most fortuitous moment. Munson acknowledged Henderson's message and detailed his own situation. At midnight the *Rasher* headed back to the attack point to see if anything was still afloat there. The vessel that was hit by the stray bow torpedo had staggered south, badly dam-

C-O-N-F-I-D-E-N-T-I-A-L

Subject: U.S.S. RASHER (SS269) - Report on the Fifth War Patrol.
- -

#1

2333-25

#4
#3
#2

Escort

2330-28
Large Unident

Cn - 290° t.
S - 12 knots

2333-25

#10   #9

2330-28
Large AK

2333-25

Bearing 048° t.
Range 2100 yards

Cn - 300° t.
S - 13 kts.

Bearing 056° 30' t.
Range 2200 yds.

2330-28
Large AP

#2 #3
#1

2330-28(H)

↑ N.

Own
ship

#9   2333-25(H)
#10

ATTACKS #5 and #6

Attacks Nos. 5 & 6
Diagram by Henry G. Munson
from his original patrol report.

aged, the escort by her side. They were tracked until the *maru* disappeared from radar, possibly sunk. The target hit by the two stern torpedoes was limping for the beach at five knots to ground`herself. The *Rasher* followed to keep an eye on her. Yet another ship was tracked to the south, also heading for the beach; this was one of the ships damaged in an earlier attack.

For two hours, through an unrelenting downpour, Munson shadowed the cripple. Out of torpedoes, he considered using the deck gun to sink her, but the shooting would attract escorts. In fact, at one point the *Rasher* slipped unnoticed between two escorts that were searching for her four miles apart. Farther on she entered a long blanket of heavy oil alive with pathetic-looking Japanese sailors coated with black muck and clinging to swamped life rafts. To the north, two large, prolonged flashes lit up the sky and then settled to a steady glow: the *Spadefish* had arrived. She sank a troop transport fleeing from the *Rasher*'s attack. For the enemy, it was a nightmare in five acts.

At 0410, as the cripple approached the beach near Port Curimao, south of Laoag City, an escort joined her and

> suddenly illuminated the big fellow [the *maru*] with a large, high intensity searchlight. He didn't like it for he fired two shots from a large gun at what we hoped was the escort! We were delighted for we saw [that the cripple was] a large, two stack transport very low in the water.

The escort was mistaken for the killer submarine.

When the *Rasher*'s fathometer pinged once to get a depth sounding near the beach, the escort heard it and came tearing after her. Munson rang up flank speed and pulled away to the northwest for a few minutes, then came back around to a westerly course while the escort continued on in blind pursuit to the north.

By 0417, the only radar contacts left were the two cripples heading in to Port Curimao's beach. Munson followed as far as he safely could, then turned back to sea as dawn was breaking. Enough was enough: the four-hour battle was over.

◆ ◆ ◆

The *Rasher* went deep, her crew dead tired. But, to celebrate, a jubilant Munson passed the word for all hands to assemble in the control room to "splice the main brace." He congratulated each man for an outstanding job and passed out shots of medicinal brandy until it was all gone. It was a night they would never forget.

In the morning, the staff of the Japanese Combined Convoy Fleet Headquarters would be greeted by a thicket of red flags on the map. For all intents and purposes, HI-71, one of the biggest convoys ever assembled by the Japanese, had ceased to exist. Torpedoed with it was the plan to reinforce the Philippine garrison. By January 1945, the islands would be back in American hands.

Hank Munson did not know for certain how many ships had been sunk or damaged. What was known for sure was that on this patrol, twenty-four torpedoes were fired. By Munson's tally, twenty-two were hits, sixteen of them on HI-71. A review of the attack on the convoy confirmed at least two 10,000-ton oilers, two 10,000-ton transports, and one 7,500-ton munitions ship sunk; three unidentified 4,000-tonners, possibly more, were damaged. The rough tonnage totals for the night's effort worked out to 47,500 tons sunk and 12,000 damaged. The ship sunk on the morning of 6 August (identifed as the *Koesi Maru*) added another 8,223 tons, for 55,723 total tons sunk on the *Rasher*'s fifth patrol. Munson, not given to exaggeration nor wildly erroneous assumptions, entered these numbers in his patrol report.

The postwar JANAC scoring reduced the tonnage sunk but did not alter the impressive picture. The ship sunk on 6 August was not the *Koesi Maru*, but rather the *Shiroganesan Maru*, a 4,739-ton transport. The biggest bag from the attack of 18–19 August was, of course, the 20,000-ton *Taiyo* (*Otaka*). The *Teia Maru*, a 17,537-ton passenger-cargo ship, was the second-largest merchant vessel sunk by a U.S. submarine during the war. The *Teiyo Maru* was a 9,849-ton oiler. The *Eishin Maru*, a 542-ton transport, was the target run aground near Port Curimao. These five ships totaled 52,667 tons. And with damage totaling another 20,000 to 22,000 tons, it was the most successful patrol of the entire war—topping out at more than 70,000 tons sunk and damaged. (Following up the *Rasher*'s attack on HI-71, the *Bluefish* sank the *Hayasui*, a 6,500-ton tanker, while the *Spadefish* sank the *Tamatsu Maru*, a 9,589-ton passenger-cargo vessel. On the night of 18–19 August, the Japanese lost six ships totaling 64,017 tons. Many more were put out of action.)

Munson's comments at the end of his patrol report summed up the attitude of his crew:

> The crew is getting "fish happy." Patrolling more than a day or two on station without hearing torpedoes explode causes a general let

down in spirits. "Radar contact, 16,000 yards" spreads through the boat like wildfire and every man heads for his battle station with a gleam in his eyes. Fortunately, all hands heard plenty of explosions from hits; but they were not thoroughly satisfied—they wanted to reload 24 fish and sock the Jap again.

◆ ◆ ◆

There remain, however, questions concerning three ships that were part of HI-71. The 542-ton *Eishin Maru*, aground on a reef, may have been misidentified by Ultra intercepts and JANAC's postwar review of Japanese records. It is possible she was a different and much larger ship of the same name. The *Rasher*'s attack party had no trouble identifying ships and their relative sizes from the PPI scope, and 542 tons seems quite small for a ship assigned to such a large, fast, and important convoy as HI-71. The same question applies to the *Takatori Maru*, a very small (277-ton) transport reported by Ultra intercepts as also aground off Port Curimao and in critical condition. This ship was apparently keeping station on the far side of a primary target and was hit by one of the *Rasher*'s free-ranging torpedoes. Were these two vessels the ones JANAC said they were? We may never know.

Another ship, the *Noshiro Maru*, was reported damaged. However, after the war, Henry Munson, then a captain, visited the Philippines and saw her still beached, a total wreck. JANAC credited the *Noshiro Maru* not to the *Rasher* but to aircraft that bombed her on 21 September 1944, more than a month after she was beached. JANAC mysteriously placed the air attack many miles south of Munson's attack. Should Munson and the *Rasher* have been credited for "sinking" the *Noshiro Maru*? Fifty years after the attack, this question remains unanswered.

A final postscript involves the infamous *Awa Maru*. This was apparently the badly damaged two-stack transport that Munson followed toward the beach. Indeed, Ultra intercepts said she was aground on a reef. Towed into Manila on 21 August, the *Awa Maru* was repaired. In April 1945, dressed up as a hospital ship and granted safe passage, she was accidentally sunk by the *Queenfish*. But before that mishap, she would cross the *Rasher*'s track again.

◆ ◆ ◆

On 30 August, the *Rasher* entered Midway lagoon via the narrow, man-made channel. Flights of resident "gooney birds"—the glorious *Diomedea exulans*, the famous wandering albatross of the Ancient

Mariner—soaring effortlessly on outstretched wings spanning nearly eleven feet greeted the *Rasher* far out at sea and followed her all the way to her berth alongside a sub tender. Being rather curious and sociable creatures, they gathered round the fueling dock and watched as the *Rasher* was topped off for her 1,200-mile passage to Pearl Harbor. In eight hours she was loaded and headed east. Accompanying her on this leg of the trip was the *Pompon*.

On 3 September, the verdant headlands of Oahu appeared over the horizon. The island's subtropical green splendor glittered in the sun like an emerald. The *Rasher* and the *Pompon* joined the *Tang*, another submarine just returned from a war patrol. Together they rendezvoused with an escort assigned to lead them into the channel entrance to Pearl Harbor and through the anti-submarine nets. For a sailor, entering Pearl was always an exciting moment; stepping up from the sea could be seen Diamond Head, the bustling city of Honolulu, Aloha Tower, and King Kamehameha's statue.

The only event to sour the grand entrance occurred when Munson flashed a signal ordering the *Pompon* and the *Tang* to fall in astern of the *Rasher* for their arrival at the submarine base. As the senior skipper of the three, returning from a magnificent patrol, he felt entitled to the simple courtesy.

In addition, the *Rasher*'s crew was proud of the new battle flag she was flying. It had been whipped together on the way east by Chief White using the ship's hand-cranked sewing machine, which he kept stowed by the hydraulic trim manifold under a jury-rigged desk used for navigation in the control room. The flag was a four-by-seven-foot field of blue wool bunting surrounding a rather nasty-looking fish decked out in boxing gloves and sailor's white hat. He displayed two prominent rows of razor-sharp teeth surrounded by full, red lips. The fish and his hat had formerly been a white mattress cover; the red lips were made with a bottle of chart-correcting ink. Around this fellow were nearly thirty skulls representing the Japanese ships that had tasted the submarine's torpedoes. The *Rasher* was also festooned with her coxcomb of miniature "meatballs," as the Japanese flag was called. Munson wanted to make a splash when his submarine arrived at Ten-Ten Dock with a full section of his crew at quarters on deck and himself in crisp khakis and black tie.

But Lt. Comdr. Richard O'Kane, captain of the *Tang*, ignored Munson's blinker signals and skipped on ahead to get there first. O'Kane said the *Tang* kowtowed to no one, not the *Rasher*, not Hank Munson. Munson was furious. (The brash O'Kane would be credited with twenty-four sinkings, more than any other American skipper. A Medal of Honor winner, he was one of only nine survivors when one the *Tang's* torpedoes made a circular run and sank her on 24 October 1944.) But the *Tang* took a back seat when Admiral Lockwood and his staff immediately went aboard the *Rasher* to congratulate Dead Eye and his crew for one of the greatest submarine patrols ever conducted.

◆ ◆ ◆

An important footnote was later added to Munson's patrol report. On 16 August 1945, two days after Japan's surrender, the following report was submitted to Adm. Chester W. Nimitz, Commander in Chief, United States Pacific Fleet.

FF12-10(A)/A16-3(18) SUBMARINE FORCE PACIFIC FLEET
Serial: 02066 Care of Fleet Post Office,
  San Francisco, California,
  16 August 1945

CONFIDENTIAL
Subject: U.S.S. RASHER (SS 269)—Report of Fifth War Patrol
  (22 July to 3 September 1944)

Reference: (a) ComSubPac Third Endorsement FF12-10/A16
  3(15)/(16)

Confidential Serial 09154 dated 11 September 1944 to
  subject patrol report.

1. In reference (a) the RASHER was credited with sinking one large AO, 10,000 tons, Attack No. 4. Based upon information obtained from prisoner of war sources and further discussion of this attack with the commanding officer of the RASHER at the time, it is now confirmed that the ship sunk was an OTAKA Type CVE, 20,000 tons. Accordingly, all copies of reference (a) will be corrected to read as follows:

SUNK

1—AK (KOSEI MARU TYPE (EC) — 8,200 TONS (ATTACK NO. 1)
1—LARGE AO (EU) — 10,000 TONS (ATTACK NO. 2)
1—LARGE AP (EU) — 10,000 TONS (ATTACK NO. 3)
1—CVE (OTAKA) TYPE) (EU) — 20,000 TONS (ATTACK NO. 4)
1—LARGE AK (EU) — _7,500_ TONS (ATTACK NO. 5)
  TOTAL SUNK 55,700 TONS

DAMAGED

1—UN	—	4,000 TONS (ATTACK NO. 3)
1—UN	—	4,000 TONS (ATTACK NO. 4)
1—UN	—	4,000 TONS (ATTACK NO. 5)
1—LARGE AP (EU)	—	10,000 TONS (ATTACK NO. 6)
TOTAL DAMAGED		22,000 TONS
TOTAL SUNK & DAMAGED		77,700 TONS

G. C. Crawford
Chief of Staff

For comparison, JANAC's totals are:

1—AK SHIROGANESAN MARU	—	4,739 TONS (ATTACK NO. 1)
1—AO TEIYO MARU	—	9,849 TONS (ATTACK NO. 2)
1—AP TEIA MARU	—	17,537 TONS (ATTACK NO. 3)
1—CVE OTAKA	—	20,000 TONS (ATTACK NO. 4)
1—AK EISHIN MARU	—	542 TONS (ATTACK NO. 5)
TOTAL SUNK		52,667 TONS

◆ ◆ ◆

On 6 September 1944, the *Rasher* departed Pearl Harbor for the United States. It was Munson's last voyage as a wartime skipper.

Part 4

California and the China Coast

The Barbary Coast

The letter started, "My Darling Wife." It arrived in Evanston, Illinois, at the end of August, postmarked Fleet Post Office, San Francisco. From their prearranged code, Pete Sasgen's wife knew the *Rasher* was on her way home. On 1 September, the phone rang at her Dewey Avenue apartment. A friend of Sasgen's, a Navy chaplain who had that very day landed in the States from Fremantle, was calling to confirm that the ship was on her way to San Francisco, and Pete would call as soon as she got there.

The *Rasher* made her last position report to the Commander Western Sea Frontier at dawn on 11 September. She was a hundred miles from San Francisco Bay.

Following standard procedure for boats approaching the West Coast, Munson scrupulously maintained a speed of fifteen knots and followed the prescribed submarine route thirty miles south of the main east-west shipping lane to California. This procedure prevented attacks by friendly aircraft and ships and calmed jittery convoys, which, unlike the coastal defense commander, were unaware of the *Rasher*'s passage. At noon she reached the assigned rendezvous point off the Farallon Islands and was greeted by a patrol craft that flashed a "welcome home" signal. Falling in behind her escort, she followed the channel past Seal Rocks Beach and sailed under the famous bridge into the Golden Gate. To port were the Marin headlands, shrouded in white September fog; to starboard, rising sublimely from the edge of the bay, was the beautiful, sun-spanked city.

At North Point, a touch past Alcatraz Island, the *Rasher* turned into the southbound ship traffic lane. When the Ferry Tower was broad on the beam and the San Francisco-Oakland Bay Bridge overhead, she angled a bit to starboard. From there it was a straight shot south to the U.S. Naval Drydocks at Hunters Point. Across the bay was the

245

Alameda Naval Station, and beyond, the pastel blue-green hills of Oakland. The *Rasher* rounded Point Avisadero and maneuvered smartly toward the berths at South Basin, where a reception committee, complete with a band, waited to welcome her back to the United States. Flags flying and crew at quarters, Munson warped her in.

◆ ◆ ◆

The *Rasher*'s crew was split into two sections and rotated on thirty-day leaves. Within the hour, Pete Sasgen was on the phone making travel arrangements for his wife and son to come to San Francisco to live while the *Rasher* was overhauled.

Isabelle Sasgen immediately called her cousin, who was the executive secretary to the president of the Pepsodent Toothpaste Company in Chicago. The cousin knew Sasgen was serving in subs in the Pacific and had offered to help procure transportation to California should Isabelle ever need it. Despite the restrictions imposed on civilian travel by the priorities accorded to military personnel, her cousin's boss generously offered the use of his private Pullman compartment on the Santa Fe Railroad. Meanwhile, Sasgen found a small, cozy, furnished apartment on Van Ness Avenue near Market Street downtown.

Shortly before his family's arrival, Chief Machinist's Mate Sasgen received his much-anticipated commission as ensign, USNR, "one of the proudest moments of my life," he said. He was so big it took half the duty section to pick him up and throw him off the dock at Hunters Point in the traditional fleeting-up ritual. Since Sasgen was an old *Rasher* hand and veteran sub sailor, he knew his new duties as junior officer would include, in addition to the engineering department, the commissary department. So his first order of business was to authorize his personal use of some of the wardroom's silverware, dishes, and linens while the ship was torn apart. Thus, when his family arrived, everything was ready for them. The apartment's kitchen was equipped like a submarine galley, and many a fine meal would be served to visiting shipmates on *Rasher* china over the next two and a half months.

The Navy's fleet overhaul facilities at Hunters Point were massive. At the south end of the yard stood two mighty hammerhead cranes, each capable of lifting 400 tons. They served the adjacent dry docks, which were large enough to accommodate an aircraft carrier. At the north end were three smaller dry docks dedicated solely to submarine refits. In between, warehouses and low brick shipfitters shops lined the piers and bulkheads fronting the bay. Cable, wire, steel plate, pipes, anchor chain, engines, guns, propellers, and ship fittings of every conceivable type, shape, and size were stacked all over the yard on every square foot of space available. The place bustled with non-stop activity. Trucks, jeeps, and forklifts dashed every which way, sometimes causing traffic jams at the yard's major intersections. Like a busy city, Hunters Point hummed twenty-four hours a day.

Submarine refit work was administered from a stand of grim-looking barracks buildings and ship's offices tucked below Galvez Avenue. The barracks also served as a temporary home for the submarine crews. The supervisor of shipbuilding had a work schedule and 41-page Brief of Work and Costs for the *Rasher* that contained no less than 131 items scheduled for modification, outright replacement, or overhaul, from periscope to keel. This brief was presented at the overhaul conference. In addition, there was a list of repairs requested by the *Rasher's* department heads and her commanding officer. Modifications she was to undergo ranged from the insertion of longitudinal inside hull stiffeners to the installation of an ice cream freezer. Basic overhaul would be performed on such items as diesel engines, pumps, hydraulic system, valves, gauges, and compressors. And there would be a complete paint job.

Within a day or two Navy tugs moved the *Rasher* into one of the narrow dry docks adjacent to India Basin. As soon as she was blocked, a work gang came aboard and got down to business. There was no time to waste. The refits were complicated, and the inflexible schedule allowed little time for head-scratching.

The *Rasher's* duty section, consisting of those men not on leave, was assigned to the refit and moved into a living barge equipped with bunks, showers, and cooking facilities. The barge was moored in the adjacent narrow wet dock. The duty section's job was to stand security and fire watches during the overhaul. Next the *Rasher* was stripped of Title B gear, spare parts, tools, personal effects, office equipment, weapons, registered publications, and anything else that was loose. All this was moved to the barge for secure stowage. With that accomplished, the submarine was cold iron.

Workmen dismantled the *Rasher's* deck and removed two rectangular soft patches on her pressure hull, along with their canvas and rubber gaskets, to permit access to her innards.

Before the work could begin in earnest, an unexpected difficulty arose: no one could locate her plans and blueprints. It was essential they be examined before beginning internal modifications that entailed cutting into tanks, moving pipes, and rearranging equipment.

Every submarine in the Navy was issued a complete set of her builder's plans on microfilm in lieu of bulky, full-size paper prints. Correspondence between Hunters Point and Manitowoc revealed that the *Rasher* was an exception, and in fact had been supplied with a set of paper plans covering hull, machinery, and electrical installations. Still, no one could find them. More correspondence transpired, including a memo from Hank Munson to the Bureau of Ships in Washington, D.C., requesting that microfilmed plans be forwarded immediately. Meanwhile, critical work ground to a halt.

On 19 October, Munson received a memo via the morning guard mail.

(610e)	SS269(/31-3(610e)	17 October 1944.
To:	The Commanding Officer,	
	U.S.S. RASHER (SS 269).	
Subj:	Microfilm of SS269 Plans, Forwarding of.	
Ref:	(a) C.O. U.S.S. RASHER ltr SS269/12-2, Serial (304), to BuShips dated 20 September 1944.	
	(b) SupShip, USN Manitowoc, Wisc., ltr SS269/S1-3(303) to BuShips dated 4 October 1944.	

Encl: (S.C.)
(A)   1 Microfilm Cabinet with 2020 Slides
(B)   1 Federal Projector, Serial No. 2940

1. The above enclosures are being forwarded today by Express from the Washington Navy Yard, via Officer-in-Charge, Naval Overseas Freight Terminal, San Francisco, Calif.

2. Enclosure (A) contains the microfilmed plans for the SS269, arranged in the cabinet by Bureau Plan Number. The Index prepared by Manitowoc for use with the Microfilm is to be furnished you by SupShips, Manitowoc. An Instruction Sheet is enclosed in the cabinet.

3. Enclosure (B) is a projector for use with the microfilm. An Instruction Booklet is in the carrying case.

cc: CinC, NOFT, San Francisco, Calif.   Janet BOGARDUS
SupShips, Manitowoc, Wisc.   Lt.(j.g.) W-V(S) USNR
                                             BY DIRECTION

The day the microfilm arrived, the *Rasher*'s plans were found aboard the living barge.

◆ ◆ ◆

The Hunters Point overhaul was reminiscent of the Manitowoc building yards. Tangles of electrical cables and hoses were draped from dockside to the *Rasher*'s cluttered, dismantled topsides. Bottles of acetylene and oxygen fed sputtering torches wielded by men in coveralls and welding masks. Crates of gear were piled everywhere. Dirt and grime crunched underfoot. Ear-splitting noise resonated from below decks. Pipes, valves, and electrical conduit hung like spaghetti from the overhead. Uprooted decks exposed dank bilges. Shafts of sunlight slanted into spaces that had not seen any since the *Rasher* had been on the building ways. Pistons, connecting rods, liners, studs, and fuel injection equipment from dismantled diesel engines were strewn on the engine room flats beside air tools, wrenches, and boxes of new parts. Aft, motors and reduction gear innards lay exposed.

Acrid smoke from hot metal wafted up hatches. Air chisels chattered like machine guns as old equipment was removed from the control room and conning tower and new brackets and panels were welded in place for the air conditioners and upgraded radar stacks, cabinetry, and wiring. The bridge and conning tower fairwater was torched apart, its sections lifted away to make room for new armament and more antennas. Both periscopes lay in cradles waiting for self-propelled cranes to load them off to the optical shop for refurbishing. To the inexperienced observer, it must have seemed that the *Rasher*, her vitals scattered all over Hunters Point, could never put to sea again. Even the old salts fretted over this as work progressed, the surgery becoming more radical with every pop of the cutting torch.

While the refit progressed apace under the watchful eyes of the *Rasher*'s crew members detailed to supervise the work, many sailors attended schools and worked out on training devices to familiarize them with the new electronic equipment, radar, radio, gunnery, and machinery being installed. Torpedomen attended a special school to acquaint them with the new Mark-18 electric torpedoes being delivered to the fleet by their manufacturer, the Westinghouse Corporation of Sharon, Pennsylvania.

When first introduced in late 1943, the Mark-18, like most submarine ordnance, had serious problems associated with its performance. Unlike the steam-powered Mark-14s, the Mark-18s were powered by electric storage batteries. Consequently, they left no telltale bubble wakes on their run to the target, a tremendous improvement in the basic submarine weapon. But because the torpedoes were powered by batteries, they required frequent and time-consuming maintenance. The fish had to be pulled from the tubes for servicing several times a week.

A problem associated with the Mark-18's storage batteries was the generation of hydrogen gas and the ever-present possibility of an explosion from its accumulation inside the torpedo's body. Such an explosion could touch off the torpex warhead. To rectify this problem, submarine personnel designed a hot-wire hydrogen eliminator that burned up the gas as it was generated.

An even more dangerous problem was corrosion in the steel rudder-post bearings that sometimes made the rudders jam, causing erratic and even circular runs. (At least two boats—the *Tang* and *Tullibee*—were to find themselves on the receiving end of their own torpedoes. Seventy-six men were lost with the *Tang*, seventy-nine with the *Tullibee*.) Stainless steel posts fixed that defect.

The Mark-18's biggest drawback, however, was its slow speed. It was capable of thirty-two knots, versus the Mark-14's forty-nine knots. Mark-18s required far more accurate fire-control information than the current TDCs were able to provide, though with practice and a little fudging, most fire-control parties were able to adapt to the new torpedo's requirements.

Nevertheless, from the submariners' point of view, these flaws were overshadowed by the weapon's most important feature: the fact that it did not leave a wake to give away the submarine's position. By 1945, more than half of the torpedoes being fired were Mark-18s; they sent a lot of Japanese shipping to Davey Jones's locker.

One of the most fascinating devices installed in the *Rasher* during her refit was an ST radar periscope. As noted earlier, ST combined a miniature radar antenna and receiving unit with an optical system in an enlarged night periscope head. It allowed a skipper to obtain very accurate ranges and bearings on targets or on land while submerged without exposing the SJ antenna above water. As with other wartime innovations, this device was conceived, designed, developed, and deployed in just a matter of months. As the boats came in for overhauls, their old scopes were pulled and the new ones slipped in. Best of all, the ST needed little in the way of additional, complicating equipment, making it easy to maintain.

Another big improvement was in the gunnery department. Installed abaft the *Rasher*'s conning tower was a new Mark-17 5-inch gun designed expressly for submarine use. It was compact, powerful, and fully waterproof. It fired high-explosive and armor-piercing rounds and was ideal for attacking lightly armed patrol vessels and sampans. In addition, a Mark-3 40-millimeter gun was installed in place of the 20-millimeter mounted on the conning tower cigarette deck. Unlike the 20s, which had to be dismounted and stowed below, the 40-millimeter was cadmium plated and waterproof. It, too, fired a variety of potent projectiles that were especially devastating when used against small craft. More and more such boats were succumbing to submarine deck guns.

◆ ◆ ◆

While the *Rasher* lay in pieces at Hunters Point, her sailors enjoyed liberty in San Francisco. The city's population had surged from a prewar high of 400,000 to over half a million. Thousands of soldiers, sailors, and marines from the Presidio, Treasure Island, and dozens of other bases, as well as hoards of civilian workers, had swarmed into the bay area. Consequently, the bars lined up outside the main gate of Hunters Point never closed, nor did those in Bayview and Bayshore. Downtown there were great nightclubs. Finoccio's on Broadway was known for its chorus line of female impersonators; The Forbidden City on Sutter Street had a colorful show with exotic dancers and music; shot and beer joints such as the Irisher and Chez Paris stood shoulder-to-shoulder on Powell, open around the clock, offering a sailor anything he asked for, including a busted jaw from local toughs.

The *Rasher*'s experienced hands were quick to spot a good deal, too.

One day Lt. (j.g.), T.W.E. "Luke" Bowdler, who had served under Hank Munson on the *Crevalle* and on the *Rasher*, was collared by Lt. Arthur "Willy" Newlon in the ship's office. Bowdler recalled:

> Bill Newlon came in and said, "Luke, give me a hundred bucks." "What for?" I asked. Newlon replied, "Never mind; give me a hundred and you'll get it back." I gave him the hundred, and off he went.
>
> A few hours later Bill told me the nickel slot machine which we had jointly purchased was on the barge. "With the profits from the nickel machine we'll purchase a dime machine, then a quarter machine, and the profits will finance the ship's party before the

RASHER leaves for her sixth patrol." The yard workers spent freely on the one-armed bandits while they drank coffee from the pots nearby. Newlon's scheme was looking great.

As the slot machines produced, and with our stay at Hunters Point nearing an end, Newlon and I visited some booking offices to set up the entertainment for the party. While on leave from the RASHER, Newlon and I were reassigned billets and did not return. We were told it was a great ship's party.

The slot machine was sold to another boat when the *Rasher* left California.

◆ ◆ ◆

Hank Munson's presence during the early stages of the refit did not mean he would skipper the *Rasher* on her sixth run. On the contrary, he was due to be detached before the refit was completed. Therefore, the question foremost in everyone's mind was, who would replace this extraordinary officer? That question was answered at the end of November when thirty-year-old Lt. Comdr. Benjamin E. Adams Jr. reported aboard.

Adams was a big, friendly, good-looking man, known for his moody, introspective nature. He had graduated from the Naval Academy in 1935 and put the *Flier* in commission as her executive officer in October 1943. He was aboard when, under way for her first war patrol in mid-January 1944, she grounded on a reef outside Midway's harbor during a bad storm. Friction developed between exec and skipper, and while the *Flier* was in San Francisco for repairs, Adams was transferred to the *Albacore* as her number two. After her overhaul, the *Flier* was lost with nearly all hands when she struck a mine on 13 August 1944 in the mine-infested Balabac Strait. Meanwhile, after a tour aboard the *Albacore*, Adams found himself back in the United States as a prospective commanding officer in the fall of 1944.

When Adams accepted the *Rasher* from Henry Munson in a brief change of command ceremony, he stepped into a big pair of shoes that Munson left behind to fill—as did Laughon and Hutchinson. From his first day as skipper, however, Adams seemed to take little personal interest in the *Rasher*'s overhaul. He left it to Executive Officer Bill Norrington to handle daily routine and wrap up details. Meanwhile, Ken Tate chauffeured the captain and Mrs. Adams around San

Francisco in the big Buick sedan provided by Special Services.

In early December, Adams received a terrific shock when he learned the *Albacore* was listed as missing and presumed lost. It was not discovered until after the war that, like the *Flier*, she had struck a mine; it happened on 7 November off Esan Misaki, Japan. Adams had thus narrowly escaped death twice. The loss of those two boats affected him deeply. As a fellow officer said, he was a man who believed things came in threes.

◆ ◆ ◆

The *Rasher*'s overhaul completed, the crew, both veterans and newcomers—some hand-picked by the leading chiefs—reassembled and began the serious work of getting the ship ready for trials, training, and, once again, war.

Among the new hands carefully selected for duty was J. P. Paris, fireman first class, a sturdily built former Golden Glover from Alabama. He had just graduated from Navy electrical school. Like the other new men, he was proud and excited to be aboard the famous *Rasher* as she headed back to the war zone.

> I knew the RASHER's fine record when I found out I was to be sent for an interview. I was elated until I met the other man that was to be interviewed. He was older and had more education. His grades were better than mine and I figured I would be returned to the relief crew pool, but for some reason the chief selected me. That was one of the proudest days of my life. I never let him and the RASHER down.

After final inspection, Ben Adams got the *Rasher* under way for post-overhaul trials. This was no ordinary shakedown. A new skipper was aboard, with all the attendant changes that brings to operations and procedures. A lot of sophisticated and complex equipment had to be mastered. And the men fresh from sub school needed rigorous combat training. So there were long, tiring days ahead.

Accompanied by an escort, the *Rasher* nosed south of San Francisco through swirling fog and bright sunshine for the submarine operations zone. The ship traffic in and out of San Francisco Bay was heavy, and it took skill and careful navigating to avoid a mishap. When she reached the area, trials commenced immediately. As with her builder's trials, first came surface operation, then a controlled shallow dive, then a dive to test depth. Engines, auxiliaries, pumps, periscopes, bow and stern planes, torpedo tubes, and electronics were thoroughly tested and approved.

On this first outing, the new men performed like veterans, a tribute to the high level of training they had received on other submarines and at New London. The veterans were their usual expert selves. Adams, like his predecessors, showed he knew his way around the boats well enough, and once at sea proved to be a competent, if low-key, skipper.

Back at Hunters Point, minor repairs and adjustments were made; then, it was on to round-the-clock training exercises. During this intense period, Adams, unlike past *Rasher* skippers, often deferred to his junior officers to conduct the mock attacks and carry out exercises while he played the role of interested observer. Regardless, shake-down and training were completed in an efficient and comprehensive fashion.

The *Rasher* was scheduled to depart San Francisco on 20 December 1944. Once again, Christmas would be spent at sea. More upsetting than that, however, was the news that her big battle flag had been stolen from the equipment locker on the living barge and therefore would not be flying when she sailed under the Golden Gate Bridge. (Forty-three years later it reappeared in the collection of the Submarine Force Museum in New London, Connecticut, the gift of an anonymous donor.)

As the day for departure drew closer, loved ones said their tearful goodbyes. Isabelle Sasgen and her son vacated the apartment on Van Ness Street and returned to Chicago by train on 17 December. Pete Sasgen returned the china, linens, and silverware to the wardroom.

Before final loading and departure, the *Rasher* posed for identification photographs in San Francisco Bay. She looked brand new in her fresh coat of Measure 32 haze gray-and-black camouflage paint, a potent 5-inch deck gun aft, a 40-millimeter on the cigarette deck, and a forest of new antennas sprouting from the conning tower.

On 20 December, with a band playing "Anchors Aweigh," the *Rasher* backed from her berth at Hunters Point. Adams conned her out of the bay into heavy Pacific weather and pointed her bow south-west for a final round of departure exercises with aircraft and a PC escort. Late in the day he signaled his thanks to the escort and headed the ship west for Pearl Harbor.

Hutchinson, Laughon, and Munson had unalterably and forever formed the *Rasher*'s character. There were high expectations aboard as she set out on her sixth war patrol.

The Road to Tokyo

By Christmas 1944, the submarine offensive against Japanese merchant shipping was nearly over. Targets worthy of torpedoes were almost nonexistent. What was left of the enemy's once mighty fleet of oilers, transports, and cargo vessels operated principally in the Sea of Japan and the Yellow Sea, close to the home islands. In 1944 alone, more than 600 ships and 2.7 million tons—merchant and combatant—had been sunk. Strategically, things looked bad for the Japanese. January 1945 saw Leyte and Mindanao under Allied control. Worst of all, with the fall of Mindoro, and the westward retreat of the decimated tanker fleet, the flow of oil to the home islands from those conquered territories where beleaguered garrisons still held out had come to an end. Allied planning now shifted to the final phase of the Pacific War: Operation Olympic, the invasion of Kyushu, Japan, scheduled for November 1945.

In late 1944, Pacific submarine operations began moving forward from Pearl Harbor and Australia. Along with the move came a change in tactical emphasis. New bases were established many thousands of miles closer to Japan. This allowed the boats to reach their patrol areas in a day or two; it also increased the effectiveness of submarine lifeguard services for the B-29 strikes against Honshu. The first such advanced base had been built at Midway in 1942. Later came Majuro Atoll in the Marshalls. After that, bases were developed at Tanapag Harbor on Saipan and Apra Harbor on Guam, both fully equipped for submarine refits and services.

Meanwhile, in Australia, Ralph Christie was relieved by Adm. James Fife. Taking over in mid-December, Fife's first objective was to consolidate the Brisbane and Fremantle commands and move the combined operation to Subic Bay in the Philippines. It took the joint efforts of Navy Seabees and Army engineers to hack a base out of the Philippine jungle and clear the harbor; it was open for business by March. With his boats on Japan's doorstep, it was Fife's intention to track down and sink every last Japanese ship in the Pacific. When that was accomplished, he planned to use his submarines as gunboats to destroy the sampan fleet to keep food from reaching what was left of the Empire.

By early 1945, then, U.S. submarines crisscrossed the western Pacific in great numbers, equipped with the latest radars, ST periscopes, 5-inch deck guns, Mark-18 electric torpedoes, anti-submarine decoy devices, and "Cuties"—small, experimental homing torpedoes. The modernized submarine force had reached a new level of deadly efficiency.

Into the East China Sea

The *Rasher* skirted Hawaii and turned toward Oahu from the southeast. Rough weather and gray overcast had accompanied her all the way from California. Hundreds of miles out at sea, the sailors had listened to music and war news on Honolulu radio, KGMB. Closer to the islands, a welcoming committee of sea birds fell in astern to follow her in. She passed Diamond Head and Waikiki, picked up her escort, and made the turn at Barber's Point for the Pearl Harbor channel entrance. After the final turn at Ford Island, Adams brought her alongside a finger pier at the sub base, where line handlers were awaiting her arrival.

There were hardly any remnants of the old Navy the Japanese had surprised and devastated four years earlier. That Navy harkened back to the twenties and thirties, the Navy of Calvin Coolidge and Herbert Hoover. Now, the harbor was filled with a powerful fleet of modern carriers, battleships, cruisers, and destroyers, nearly all of them built since the beginning of the war. Every available berth was taken; many other ships were moored in the roadstead. Their overwhelming presence evoked a sense of impending victory.

The *Rasher* laid over in Pearl only long enough to complete a few minor repairs and refuel. Then she got under way with orders to arrive at Midway Island on 2 January. From there it would be on to Saipan.

Midway, too, was bustling with men and ships. The island had undergone vast changes in the four months since the *Rasher* put in on her way back to Pearl Harbor. New tank farms had sprouted alongside warehouses, offices, and barracks. Improvements to the harbor included a sand-filled sheet-metal breakwater to protect the boats from the strong winds that formerly made mooring impossible during stormy weather—as Adams knew only too well. And there were new piers and fueling facilities along the sandy spit that formed the north side of the harbor. Dozens of Quonset huts had been thrown up along the perimeter road between the piers and floating dry dock. When the *Rasher* reached her destination, a Navy pilot directed her into the channel and harbor, where she tied up to the tender *Sperry*.

Ashore, submariners and aviators alike shared Sand Island, where the sub base was headquartered. At one end of the island was the trans-Pacific cable station where lines from the United States and Hawaii were split off into cables linking the Far East. (Most of them had been cut.) At the other end of the island was the famous

"Gooneyville Lodge," the old Pan American Airways Hotel where officers were billeted. The hotel was a one-story affair of typical South Seas construction—airy and breezy. The enlisted men bunked at the new barracks and clubhouse built especially for them, complete with softball and soccer fields and refrigerators filled with cold beer. And since gooney birds were not subject to the perquisites of rank or rate, they resided at both locations and along the roads and beaches near the submarine piers.

In preparation for her sixth patrol, the *Rasher* underwent sixteen days of intense wolf pack training with two submarines. One pack-mate was the *Finback* (in September 1944 she had plucked a future president, Lt. (j.g.) George Bush, from the waters of the Bonin Islands after he ditched his Navy dive bomber), skippered by Lt. Comdr. Robert R. Williams Jr.; the other was the *Pilotfish*, skippered by Comdr. Allen G. Schnable.

Day and night, the three submarines practiced as a coordinated attack group. Ben Adams again deferred to his junior officers to conduct exercises. Submerged and surface drills, approaches and attacks were carried out with the assistance of an escort. When no other "target" was available, each submarine in turn played the role of an enemy ship. Wolf-packing with three boats proved to be much more complicated than it was with Munson's duo of the *Rasher* and the *Bluefish*; once again, communication was the weakest link. When there was a break in the exhausting workout, a day of tuna fishing provided relaxation. Adams, it turned out, was an avid angler who proudly hung his catch from the conning tower for display.

With the training finished, final loading was completed and more ordnance went aboard. Four new Mark-18 electric torpedoes were slipped into the after torpedo room. And since more attention was being paid to small craft, twenty-five extra rounds of 5-inch ammunition and eleven boxes of 40-millimeter were stowed in the magazines. At 0904 on 19 January the *Rasher*, the *Finback,* and the *Pilotfish*, with Commander Schnable as pack leader, departed for Saipan in the Marianas, where the trio would receive their operation orders.

The Marianas were north of Guam. Saipan, the center-most atoll in the chain, was nearly astride latitude 15° north, and a mere 1,300 miles from Japan. It had been secured by U.S. Marines in a bloody battle in June 1944. It immediately underwent conversion from a hunk of coral into a base for B-29 bombers. Rota and Tinian, also in the Marianas chain, were similarly transformed. At the war's present stage, the Pacific east of the Marianas was America's private lake, where her fleet could roam as it pleased, enemy opposition having virtually evaporated. With the Navy in control of those former Japanese perimeter islands, submarines would soon take possession of the Yellow Sea, the East China Sea, and the Formosa Straits.

◆ ◆ ◆

As the three submarines proceeded northwest for Saipan, they continued to drill and train their crews. When they were not running tracking exercises on each other, they maintained strict radio silence. The boats zigzagged and changed course often because there was always the possibility of an encounter with a Japanese submarine on a mission to rescue Imperial Army troops left stranded on one of the bypassed islands. Adams occasionally joined in wardroom card games, but for the most part, he kept to his stateroom.

At 0700 on 28 January, the submarines rendezvoused off Saipan with a patrol boat waiting to escort them and the submarine *Blower* through the coral reefs into Tanapag Harbor. Inside they moored in the nest alongside the tender *Fulton*.

On the island, construction continued apace. Bulldozers, trucks, and heavy equipment were at work around the clock enlarging the base and lengthening runways for the B-29s that roared off to targets in Japan every hour. The constant movement of construction vehicles stirred up clouds of white coral dust as fine as face powder. It covered foliage, vehicles, buildings, clothing, and even the submarines in the harbor.

Under the watchful eye of the Fuel King, Bob Mathewson, the *Rasher* took on 38,000 gallons of fuel to replace what had been used up on the nine-day trip to Saipan. The fresh water tanks were topped off too, and, as a last minute precaution, extra ingredients for the ice cream maker were rounded up on the *Fulton* and stowed in the submarine's freezer space. And, as usual, the SJ radar needed repair. On the way to Saipan, it had lost most of its ranging ability. The tender's repair crew disassembled the upper antenna and traced the problem to gobs of gasket cement on the wave guide. Once it was cleaned and reassembled, the *Fulton's* repair crew proclaimed it would work perfectly. Of course, the radarmen knew better.

Meanwhile, Adams joined Schnable and Williams aboard the *Fulton* to review their orders and get last-minute intelligence briefings.

Task Force Seventeen's Op-Order 34-45 called for the trio to form a coordinated attack group and patrol the southern part of the East

China Sea from about Hangchow Bay, China, to the Formosa Straits. Schnable elected to call the wolf pack "Schnable's Sharks," and the *Rasher* was designated "Shark No. 3." The patrol was to be terminated on or about 8 March, making for a forty-five-day run.

Many a hazard lurked in the East China Sea.

For starters, getting there was fraught with danger. The skippers were advised that during the Marine assault on Iwo Jima scheduled for 19 February, submarine safety lanes would not be in effect. That meant that if one of the boats had to make an emergency return from patrol during February, she would be subject to attack by friendly forces.

The East China Sea lapped the shores of mainland China on the west, Kyushu, Japan, and the southern tip of Korea on the north, and the Ryukyu chain and Formosa in the east and south, respectively. Any submarine crossing the confluence of 30° north longitude and 130° west latitude in the Tokara Retto, entering the East China Sea, was virtually on the Emperor's doorstep. A detour to Quelpart Island put one just a few miles from the heavily mined Tsushima Straits and Sea of Japan. These waters, once impregnable, would soon be breached by mine-detecting submarines.

Despite the proximity of the home islands, most of the boats patrolling the area returned to their bases with full torpedo loads. Ironically, at one time the problem had been a shortage of torpedoes; now it was a shortage of targets. Nevertheless, any skipper taking his boat into the East China Sea had to be very wary of the Japanese anti-submarine effort, and he had to constantly bear in mind the shallow waters in which he would be operating. The 100-fathom curve lay southeast of Shanghai and Kagoshima. Average depths north of the curve were only sixty fathoms. Naturally, the small convoys that dared ply the region hugged the shore for safety; there, the water was barely fifty feet deep in most places. According to skippers who had patrolled the southern part of the East China Sea, Schnable's Sharks could expect to find some *maru*s straggling up from the Formosa Straits, or crossing from China to Formosa. Naval units retreating from Java and Indochina might be caught making a dash for home waters, presenting an opportunity for an aggressive skipper.

The greatest danger the boats faced was from minefields.

As part of their briefing materials, Schnable, Williams, and Adams were given copies of bulletins prepared by the Joint Intelligence Center, Pacific Ocean Area (JICPOA) detailing Japanese minefields. Included in the bulletins were annotated chart overlays showing where the fields were. This information was based on intelligence estimates and captured "Notices to Mariners" that warned merchant ships to stay clear of certain areas.

The bulletins, bound with JICPOA's signature yellow covers, painted a chilling picture. A huge mine barrier had been sown seaward of the coastal *maru* routes from northeast Honshu to Formosa. The fields were constantly reinforced with thousands of new mines to strengthen the defenses and to replace those that broke loose from their moorings. While U.S. mines were rarely laid in water deeper than 60 fathoms, the Japanese had not only mined near the coast but had laid many anchored mines in water as deep as 250 fathoms, which meant that the 100-fathom curve was no guarantee of safety.

The Japanese mines were 33-inch diameter Type-93 horn-type contact devices similar to the U.S. Navy's Mark-6. When a horn was broken by contact with a vessel, acid was released, causing a chemical reaction with the detonator and setting off the mine.

More worrisome than sown fields were the floaters—mines that had broken away from their moorings. The Geneva Convention stipulated that mines were to be armed only when the pull and weight of the cable provided tension on the mooring spindle. Mines that came adrift were supposed to self-sterilize, but often they did not. Moreover, some Japanese mines had anti-recovery devices that set the mines off if they were handled. Thus, Schnable's Sharks faced considerable danger merely by venturing into their assigned area.

If he truly believed things came in threes, the JICPOA bulletins must have given Adams a sense of foreboding.

Regardless, he returned from the meeting and ordered the ship made ready for sea. The maneuvering watch was stationed, and at 1734 on 29 January, the nest breasted out for the *Rasher* to back clear. In company with her pack-mates and an escort, she passed through the submarine nets. Once clear of Saipan, Schnable's Sharks set a course of 275 and were under way for their station.

For several days, they patrolled unhindered on the surface in tropical warmth and sunshine. Numerous radar contacts were made on patrolling aircraft, but they were mostly identifiable as friendlies. The submarine *Sennet*, returning from patrol, was sighted and exchanged recognition signals with the pack. Adams held training dives and battle surface and gunnery drills—all to good purpose, for on 2 February, they sighted the first of many floating mines.

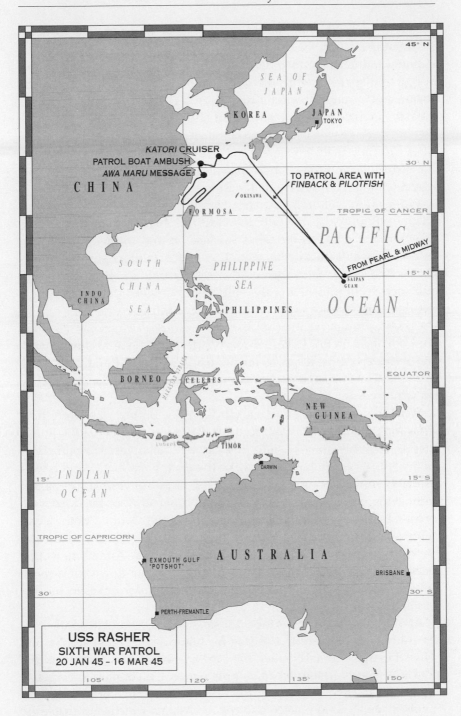

SEA OF JAPAN

KOREA

JAPAN
■ TOKYO

KATORI CRUISER
PATROL BOAT AMBUSH
AWA MARU MESSAGE

CHINA

TO PATROL AREA WITH
FINBACK & *PILOTFISH*

✈ OKINAWA

FORMOSA

TROPIC OF CANCER

PACIFIC

SOUTH

PHILIPPINE

FROM PEARL & MIDWAY

CHINA

SEA

SAIPAN
GUAM

INDO
CHINA

SEA

PHILIPPINES

OCEAN

EQUATOR

BORNEO

CELEBES

NEW
GUINEA

TIMOR

LOMBOK

INDIAN

DARWIN

OCEAN

TROPIC OF CAPRICORN

AUSTRALIA

EXMOUTH GULF
"POTSHOT"

BRISBANE ■

PERTH-FREMANTLE

USS RASHER
SIXTH WAR PATROL
20 JAN 45 – 16 MAR 45

It was an evil-looking horn-type laying in wait for some unwary vessel. It bobbed in the choppy water, one moment exposed, another moment hidden. Adams ordered the .50-caliber machine guns to the bridge to dispatch it while the ship was maneuvered to keep it safely abeam and in range. It was holed and sank without exploding. Late in the day, another one was sighted and shot up. It appeared to be sinking, but darkness fell before the submariners could be certain. The up-close meetings with mines were a grim reminder of the dangers to come during nighttime surface patrolling. In the dark there was no way the things could be sighted in time to maneuver to avoid them.

Winter returned on 3 February. Heavy weather rolled in from the northwest, and stiff, raw winds made the guys and antennas hum their familiar tune. As the wind worked around to the north, frigid gale-force seas battered the ship. The watchstanders shrugged into parkas and foul weather gear. Adams took the opportunity to exercise each section in diving the ship and changing depths in rough weather, which was good practice but demanding work.

Fighting rough weather all the way, the *Rasher* reached the fog-bound Tokara Retto. Here she ran headlong into snow flurries and hail the size of BBs; it rattled off the bridge fairwater and pelted the lookouts. The *Pilotfish* and the *Finback* had long before disappeared in the wintery mist.

With the ship at 30° north latitude, Yaku Shima was thirty-five miles off the starboard beam; Kyushu, the southernmost of the home islands, lay only another sixty miles north. Relatively speaking, the *Rasher* was within hailing distance of the enemy mainland, and it was strangely disconcerting to find no aircraft or patrol vessels strenuously blocking her advance. The only radar contacts were the dozens of small islands and rock outcroppings along the Osumi Shoto. Near noon, a huge four-engined Mavis-type float plane was sighted low on the horizon in the direction of Kusagaki-shima. Adams took the *Rasher* down to avoid being spotted and kept her down for a meal uninterrupted by flying plates, glasses, and cutlery caused by the snarling storm.

Another U.S. submarine, the *Silversides*, was spotted late in the day 200 miles west of the retto, heading for home, but SJ radar stubbornly refused to make contact on her. For perhaps the hundredth time in six patrols, the technicians spread its guts out on the conning tower deck to look for the problem, trying their best to keep the parts from sliding away as the ship pitched and rolled. Adams watched impatiently over their shoulders.

At daybreak, more mines were sighted and sunk, though not without difficulty. The .50-caliber rounds tended to ricochet off the mine's spherical shape, and it took a healthy dose of ammo to pierce the outer case and sink one. So far none of the mines had exploded. Adams suggested a way to deal with them, which he entered in his patrol report:

> Much difficulty has been experienced and a great deal of ammunition expended in sinking mines due to rough seas. It is believed that a .50 cal. single shot gun fitted with a telescopic sight and firing AP [armor-piercing] projectiles would save appreciable time and ammunition in heavy weather.

As the Sharks moved northwest, they kept their eyes open for more floaters. On 6 February 1945, Adams noted their position and search plan.

> Entered patrol area in assigned position, the center of which is Lat. 28°-55′ N, Long. 124°-10E. According to plan previously prepared prior departure Saipan, packs would sweep from north to south of patrol area from 6–15 February, remain in extreme southern portion 16–21 February, and then return northward 22 February to 8 March. FINBACK to have easternmost position, PILOTFISH central position, and RASHER to have the westernmost; each submarine assigned a daily area of 10′ of latitude by 20′ of longitude.

At 0900 on 7 February, Adams, Schnable, and Williams rendezvoused to confirm and coordinate their patrol and to accurately fix their positions. Sea conditions were still rough, but when the Sharks split up and headed for their patrol stations, the sun at last broke through the sullen gray overcast. Slowly but surely the weather cleared, promising a night sky filled with stars.

◆ ◆ ◆

Two days later, at 0430, Adams was summoned to the bridge by the officer of the deck. A lookout had spotted a strange red light on the horizon bearing 120° T. The *Rasher* came to a new heading to intercept it, and four engines went on line. Adams checked the time and noted that the Moon was due up any minute; the red light must be the curvature of the rising Moon. Still, he stationed the tracking party and commenced an approach. As the *Rasher* closed, they saw it was a brightly lighted Japanese hospital ship. Her markings were quite clear, and, every navigation light ablaze, she was lit up like an ocean liner. Adams broke off the approach. The Japanese ran many hospital ships between Japan and the occupied territories—so many, in fact, that Nimitz and others suspected they were using them to transport badly needed materiel to the home islands under the guise of mercy voyages. But little could be done to stop it. Unfortunately, in April, the practice would culminate in tragedy with the sinking of the *Awa Maru* by the *Queenfish*.

The *Rasher* resumed her patrol.

That night, the engineering gang prepared to change over the Number 4 Fuel Oil Ballast Tank to a main ballast tank—by now a routine event. And since Bob Mathewson was Fuel King, it was his job to make the conversion. He recalled:

> The skipper wanted the tanks converted back to ballast tanks as we could then ride a little higher in the water and gain an extra knot or so in cruising speed. As usual, this entailed crawling down into the superstructure at night with the proper wrenches for removing the heavy metal blanks from the vent risers and reconnecting the vent valve linkage, all of this with only the dim illumination of a blue-lensed flashlight.
>
> I put on foul weather gear as the water was cold and a life jacket which would undoubtedly have been useless if the boat was forced to dive.
>
> I had only been working a short while when Pete Sasgen dropped in beside me, stating he had come to help, as waves were washing into the superstructure and slowing down the work. He also brought with him several individual bottles of medicinal brandy to "warm me up." These I promptly drank. A short time later the engineering officer, Lt. Henry Hohwiesner, passed us several more bottles of brandy apiece which we quickly drank. About halfway through the job, the XO, Lieutenant Norrington, showed up with more brandy, as he apparently did not know about the previous bottles. Naturally, we did not enlighten him. Just before we completed the job and went below, the pharmacist's mate showed up with two more bottles apiece.
>
> By the time we finished the job and went below, Pete had a rosy glow, as he benefited by having eaten the evening meal before coming topside, while I had forgone the meal in order to get the job started. All that brandy on an empty stomach hit me as I went below, and I doubt if I could have hit my butt with both hands.

The next five days were uneventful. By 14 February, the wolf pack had worked south to Tung Yung Tau island off the coast of China, where more floating mines were sighted and destroyed. This time, however, some of the bigger ones blew up with such force that even from a distance they showered the ship with fragments. If a small, fragile ship like a submarine were to strike one of these mines, she would be totally destroyed. It also settled once and for all whether or not the mines disarmed when they went adrift.

Commander Schnable altered the pack's station assignments daily by radio as they searched on a broad front. He cautioned against being tempted to shoot up the large, two-masted junks that appeared from time to time; it wouldn't be worth giving away the pack's position. But it hardly seemed it would matter, for as they moved south toward the Formosa Straits, the sea was devoid of ships; for all intents and purposes, the enemy had disappeared. Local coastal traffic of sampans, junks, and small luggers was all that plied the waters between Foochow, Taipei, and Chi-lung. Occasionally an enemy plane droned by, but it was clear the Japanese perimeter had drawn inward, closer and closer to the home islands.

Finally, at 0319 on the fifteenth, radar made a solid contact just outside the Formosa Strait in a driving rain. From the size of the pip, the target was judged to be a large picket boat. Conditions were ideal for a surface attack. Battle stations torpedo bonged through the ship and all hands sprang to life, shedding the torpor of the pre-dawn hours. The target's range was 13,000 yards, and she was poking along at a shade less than seven knots. Adams got off a contact report to his pack-mates. He gave them the coordinates, then followed up with the message, "Am attacking."

He brought the *Rasher* onto a normal approach course on four engines. The tubes were ready forward. As she closed in, radar picked up a second target on the starboard quarter of the first one. Adams dropped down into the conning tower to study the PPI scope and mull over this development. The new pip was roughly the same size as the first one; it was undoubtedly another picket boat. But Adams did not like the setup he was facing. When the *Rasher* attained a 90-degree starboard track to shoot, the second target would be in a good position to launch a counterattack. Thus he hesitated.

In fact, it was not a particularly unfavorable setup, given the element of surprise and the weather. Granted, these were patrol boats, but Hank Munson never hesitated to attack on the surface across an escort's bow; Laughon, never shrinking from an opportunity, frequently sallied into the teeth of multiple escorts in both fair weather and foul. So did Hutchinson. Ben Adams, however, was a different kind of skipper.

First, he consulted with the radar operator. The radarman, despite Adams's doubts, assured him that, given its size on the scope, the target was worthy of torpedoes. Adams then took note of the Force 4 seas and their potential effect on torpedo performance. Back on the bridge, he overcame whatever concerns he harbored and finally ordered right full rudder to come about and bring the stern tubes to bear.

Without seeing the target, and relying solely on radar ranges and bearings, he fired the four Mark-18 electrics on a 2,800-yard run, then hauled out at flank speed. Sound reported the fish were running hot, straight, and normal, but at the end of the timed runs—nothing. The two targets continued on their way and were lost in the rain.

Adams was sure he had a perfect setup in the TDC. He concluded the misses were due to the torpedoes under-running the target, though the depth settings were four feet. In his patrol report, he noted:

> Target was evidently overestimated as to size and if true, he may have been a radar decoy with submarine or patrol craft stationed on quarter to counter an attack.

The latter was pure conjecture. At that time there were no credible reports of an anti-sub team operating in the East China Sea.

Adams was convinced the targets had been alerted to the *Rasher*'s presence. Again keeping to an ultra-cautious course, he decided against a follow-up attack. Some of the veterans grumbled that with the dearth of targets, they would have made another try.

A half-hour after securing from battle stations, the submarine tracked an identical contact on the same course and speed as the previous one. This time Adams declined to even attempt an approach, saying the target was too small, probably another patrol craft or picket, and not worth an attack. He ordered a course change due east toward Formosa and sent another contact report to the *Pilotfish*, which, along with the *Finback*, was now in position to the west. He advised that the target was a shallow-draft patrol boat and that the first attack had been unsuccessful. His pack-mates were to maintain their stations rather than come racing to join in.

By late morning, the Sharks had worked into the extreme southern part of their patrol area off the coast of Formosa near Taipei. Seas were still running at Force 3 before gusty winds out of the northeast. At noon they reversed course to patrol back toward the north. When Tungsha Tao was sighted, the *Rasher* turned west to patrol across the 110-mile-wide approaches to Formosa Strait. In the afternoon she was strafed by a Japanese Betty bomber. So much for the notion the Japanese were toothless. With SD being keyed only intermittently to prevent coastal homing on its signal, the Betty dove out of the overcast without warning and made three erratic passes while the *Rasher* dove. The strafing caused no damage, but after surfacing, power was lost on the port screw because of a burned-out overload relay. It took an hour to effect repairs by bypassing the fried relay. Meanwhile, the ship maneuvered awkwardly on the starboard shaft.

The day wore on, chilly, gray, drizzly. And boring.

At 2130, the radio room received a dispatch from Commander Schnable advising that Task Force Seventeen expected a Japanese task group of three capital ships and several destroyers to pass through their area, heading north at high speed. The report sent electricity surging through the ship.

Adams studied the charts. Task Force Seventeen's information, derived from Ultra intercepts, said that the enemy track was northeast. Their destination, reported Ultra, was probably the Tsushima Straits and the Sea of Japan. Less likely was one of the bases on the eastern side of the home islands. The question was, after leaving the Formosa Straits, would the enemy ships navigate the shallow coastal waters of China from Foochow to Wenchow, then turn northeast at Hangchow Bay, or would they immediately strike across the open water of the East China Sea?

The heart of the task group was the hybrid carrier-battleships *Ise* and *Hyuga*, based in Singapore. Because the Japanese were desperate for fuel, the two were loaded with drums of oil and ordered to run the blockade. Radio intelligence in Pearl Harbor had monitored Singapore's communications with the ships and thus knew their route and schedule. It was an excellent opportunity for Schnable's Sharks to smash a final, wild gamble to replenish Japan's dwindling oil stocks.

At 0507 the *Rasher* was cruising just south of Wenchow on alert. Then came the call: "Radar contact!"

There were three contacts nine miles astern, coming up fast. Adams looked them over and decided it was the enemy task force:

Three pips were so strong they scared the radar operator. Ahead full on four engines tracking ahead. At 12,000 yards radar signals were at saturation levels. Sent task force position to pack.

"Battle stations! Battle stations!"

The targets were on a heading of 030, making eighteen knots. Adams picked up the pace and tracked ahead at full speed on their coastal flank, intending to identify the ships when it was light enough in the east to silhouette them. Then he planned a periscope approach.

Suddenly a radar pip detached itself from the main group and veered toward the *Rasher*. Adams mentally tracked this new target, which he guessed to be a flanking escort that had zigged in their direction sniffing for a scent. From the interference on the SJ, there was little doubt the vessel was radar-equipped.

With no time to waste trying to identify targets, Adams put the rudder over full right on a port track and sent the lookouts below. The *Rasher* came around and drove head-on into a wall of rain, making the targets impossible to see.

Drawing closer, Adams pulled the plug and burrowed under, heading for radar depth.

The targets continued on their line of bearing steady on 030 at eighteen knots. Through the ST scope, in the rain, Adams could just make out the port bow wave on the nearest target but could not yet identify the ship. She was overlapping another large but indistinct target on her starboard flank 1,800 yards away; beyond them was yet another ship. Adams planned to fire a six-torpedo spread from forward to aft at the near target: the fish were set to run under and explode beneath the ships' armor belt blisters at the turn of the bilges. The skipper seemed determined to stick with the setup despite the hunting escort.

"Standby forward! Standby One!" he ordered.

All of a sudden the primary target took an unanticipated zig in the *Rasher*'s direction.

"Check fire! Shifting targets! He's zigged toward! New target... bearing—mark!"

"One-five-zero!"

"Range—mark!"

"Three-one-double-oh! Set!"

"Fire One!"

The submarine lurched at eight-second intervals, the torpedoes leaving their tubes aimed for the second ship in the group. Sound followed their warble and reported they were running hot, straight, and normal.

But in his haste to change targets and reset, Adams neglected to order a change in the spread. The fish all went out on the same course, with identical gyro angles, and missed. He watched the first target turn bows on until he could see both port and starboard bow waves. With a 10-degree port angle on the bow and the range less than a thousand yards and decreasing fast, the warship knifed right for the *Rasher's* periscope as though she knew exactly where the submarine was.

Adams took her deep, rigged for depth charge. As the *Rasher* swung sharply right to get off her firing point, the enemy ship loomed out of the dark at high speed, machinery roaring. Like a freight train, she barreled overhead from bow to stern right down the *Rasher's* center line, causing the sailors to duck instinctively. Adams's report stated:

> With a rising scream, the blowers and reduction gears of the near target went overhead followed by the thrum of fast screws going out at 170 relative.

The anticipated depth-charging never materialized.

Three minutes after the first torpedo was fired, men in the forward torpedo room reported hearing an explosion. But Sound reported the enemy ships' machinery declivity fading like a northbound express; if any were hit, they didn't slow for a second. Adams popped up the periscope and SJ radar mast for a quick look. All clear. A contact report to both Task Force Seventeen and the wolf pack gave the details of the encounter, and reported the enemy ships' northerly course for other boats up the line to try and intercept.

From Adams's review of the attack, it seemed reasonable to conclude that the *Rasher* had been detected either by her own radar emissions or by the enemy's. Hence, the close approach by both target and escort. Why there was no depth-charging was anybody's guess.

Because they had not heard the characteristic heavy screw beat of large warships, Adams believed they had merely encountered an advanced screen of the main task force. So rather than trying an end around on the ships heading north, Adams set off on a high-periscope search south toward the Formosa Strait in hopes of finding the main force. But the sweep was in vain. Only one radar contact materialized, and it developed into a small picket boat. Adams was forced to admit they had missed their chance.

A keen sense of disappointment altered the normally high-spirited mood aboard the *Rasher*.

Adams resumed patrolling in the vicinity of Tung Yung Tau as Schnable directed. Not a ship was sighted, however, not even a spitkit or sampan. On 18 February, the pack moved north to a new area. There the *Rasher's* gun crews exploded more mines; a few fragments landed on deck and became souvenirs. But all along the twisting coast of China and the confusing maze of outlying islands, from Matsu Dao to Dayu Shan, and across the East China Sea north of Formosa, they encountered not a single ship.

◆ ◆ ◆

It was during the noon meal on the nineteenth that the radio room picked up a plain-language message overlapping on the wolf pack frequency of 2006 kilocycles from a strong transmitter either on the Chinese mainland or Formosa. In both Japanese and Japanese-style English, it gave the position, course, and speed of the *Awa Maru*, now repaired and back at sea gussied up as a relief ship granted safe passage by the U.S. Navy. In fractured protocol, the message gave details of her location:

AWA MARU   X JRNR   X   NOON POSITION LAT   26R 17N LONG 122R 35E   X CO 235   X SPEED 15 MILES

Her position at that moment was less than sixty miles from Schnable's Sharks.

◆ ◆ ◆

In 1944, the United States had received information that detailed the brutal treatment Allied POWs were receiving at the hands of the Japanese. Through the Swiss, Japan was asked to deliver Red Cross packages to the prisoners. At first the Japanese refused. But since the shipping routes to Southeast Asia had been cut by submarines, the Imperial Staff realized they had been handed an opportunity to clandestinely transport badly needed military equipment to their troops. Quickly, they changed their minds and signaled their agreement.

To deliver the shipments, they selected the 11,249-ton *Awa Maru*, one of Japan's biggest and fastest transports. She was one of the ships that was run up on the beach after Hank Munson's attack shattered Convoy HI-71 in August of 1944. She had been towed to Manila, repaired, and recently returned to duty. She was loaded with crated aircraft, bombs, ammunition, and the 2,000 tons of Red Cross provisions. The *Awa Maru* left Meji, Japan, on 17 February, with stops planned for Singapore and Indonesia. She would return to Japan by way of Hong Kong and Formosa. It was obvious to the U.S. Navy that more than relief supplies were involved in this undertaking—after all, why use such a large ship for a relatively small cargo of Red Cross parcels? Nonetheless, Nimitz and Lockwood sent out a safe conduct message three times for three consecutive nights to all submarines in the area:

> AWA MARU WILL BE PAINTED WITH A WHITE CROSS ON EACH SIDE OF FUNNEL X CROSSES TO BE ILLUMINATED ELECTRICALLY AT NIGHT X WHITE CROSS ON TOP OF BRIDGE X WHITE CROSS ON SECOND AND FIFTH HATCHES X TWO WHITE CROSSES ON EACH SIDE OF SHIP X ALL NAVIGATION LIGHTS TO BE LIGHTED AT NIGHT

The *Awa Maru* picked her way through the minefields sown along the China coast and reached her southern destination safely. For the return voyage she was loaded with tons of raw rubber, lead, tin, and other materials in short supply in Japan. She also took aboard several hundred stranded merchant marine officers, military personnel, diplomats, and civilians.

At the end of March, the *Awa Maru* set out for Japan. Again Nimitz and Lockwood broadcast a safe conduct message to all submarines. Unfortunately, the message was mishandled by the commanding officer of the submarine *Queenfish*. On 1 April, thinking the *Awa Maru* was a destroyer, he fired four torpedoes and sank her. It was an error of circumstances—thick fog, a radar attack, and the *Awa Maru*'s failure to sound her fog horn. Nevertheless, the *Queenfish*'s skipper was court-martialed. Save for a lone seaman, the *Awa Maru* was lost with all hands.

◆ ◆ ◆

Schnable's Sharks scoured the East China Sea for enemy shipping. They moved north, encountering more mines, random aircraft patrols, and small craft. One morning the improving weather brought out sailing vessels of every description. Adams poetically described the scene as "a ghostly radiance of fog in which the sails of these vessels could be seen for over three miles." It looked like a Newport regatta.

At the end of the day on 22 February, the *Rasher* reversed her course to patrol to the south again. Schnable had deployed the boats so that the *Pilotfish* was patrolling in the northern sector of the area and the *Finback* in the west. The *Rasher* anchored the southern end.

She started out the morning submerged in the mouth of the Formosa Strait. At 0835, Sound reported the distant thunder of a dozen depth charges. They were followed by echo-ranging on a rough bearing of 220. Visual contact with an escort vessel was made at 10,000 yards. The *Rasher* went to battle stations and came around to a north-westerly heading. More distant thunder rumbled as the enemy ships tried to clear the route ahead of them of any lurking submarines. As the *Rasher* settled on an approach course in the direction of the thunder, Adams motioned for the ST periscope to be raised for a look.

A sense of anticipation electrified the submarine's crew. It was like old times again: the enemy approaching, the *Rasher* waiting for just the right moment to fire torpedoes. No doubt Japanese ships would soon be headed for the bottom.

The captain watched three transports approach. They were followed by two barge-like, shallow-draft landing craft. Four escorts—one on the point, two on either beam, one astern—provided protection. Every five minutes the escorts rotated their position counterclockwise around the *maru*s. Sound conditions in the strait were so good the soundman could tell when the escorts changed position. The convoy was steaming southeast through morning haze from Foochow on a course that would take them into Keelung on the northern tip of Formosa, forty miles away. The *Rasher* swung onto a parallel course of 129 and waited for a zig in her direction that would bring the targets closer.

ONI 208-J identified the three transports as the *Hino Maru No. 3*, the *Akito Maru*, and the *Eldorado Maru*. The escorts were three *Chidori*s and an old coastal gunboat. With ST radar faltering, Adams squinted through the scope and calculated ranges to the nearest escort using the stadimeter. "Mark—8,000 yards!" The scope dropped away; the tracking party huddled to look things over.

The *Rasher*'s position was abeam of the convoy, roughly midway between the coasts of Formosa and China. While this gave Adams plenty of room to maneuver, he faced three complications. First, with a convoy speed of nine knots, the ships were slowly pulling ahead. Unless the targets made a southerly zig to halve the range, a sub-merged approach was all but impossible before they reached port. Second, the setup, zig or no zig, posed exceptionally long torpedo ranges with little chance of a hit given the way the targets were dispersed. Third, the escorts were doing a good job of sniffing at the edges of the convoy.

To the plotting party, these complications were but minor annoyances easily surmounted by tenacity and skillful submarining. And since targets were scarce, Adams was urged to surface, work around fast, and attack.

Up went the scope. Adams studied the convoy, trying to decide what to do. Down went the scope. The plotting party awaited orders. Adams hesitated. Up went the scope. He asked a junior officer to take a look and give his opinion. Topside, seven ships advanced across a cheerless gray sea; time was wasting. "Attack now, Captain," he said.

But two D3A Val dive bombers arrived to shepherd the convoy into Keelung. Unable to surface, the *Rasher* had no chance to catch her prey. Adams secured from battle stations as the convoy steamed toward Formosa and disappeared. Once again, the *Rasher* had been skunked. Gloom descended on the ship.

Boredom set in. Cribbage and acey-ducey had lost their attraction. Drills, training dives, and torpedo maintenance did little to relieve the monotony of endless patrolling and the frustration of aborted attacks. The novelty of blowing up mines had worn off, yet the danger they posed had not, a fact made all too clear when the ship surfaced one evening and the OOD spotted a bobbing set of horns only fifty yards off the port bow.

Shortly after midnight on 24 February, another hospital ship was sighted. Lights ablaze like a city, she made such a good practice target that the tracking party eagerly went to work on her as she passed.

Before dawn the next day, a mysterious flash over the horizon, followed by a distant explosion, held out the possibility of some *real* action. But nothing came of it.

Following Schnable's orders, the patrol continued westward.

Days were gloomy, skies relentlessly, suffocatingly overcast. Adams kept to his stateroom, showing up in the wardroom only for meals. A pervasive mood of ennui gripped the submariners.

At 0855 on 27 February, with SJ radar still sputtering and the radarmen still cursing, a sharp lookout spotted what looked like a wildly zigzagging destroyer at a range of ten miles. The tracking party scurried to the conning tower. Every man jumped to his battle station, re-energized, ready for action.

Adams put the destroyer astern and started tracking from ahead, hoping she might turn out to be an advanced unit of a convoy. After running for several miles with nothing showing on the horizon,

Adams assumed they had pulled too far ahead and slowed down. Still nothing appeared, so he reversed course and went to full speed to try to relocate the destroyer.

Sound reported explosions coming from the direction of the target's last bearing. Was someone being depth-charged? In a few minutes Adams sighted the destroyer, all alone, her position barely fifty miles from the coastal city of Ningpo.

Watching her from the bridge through binoculars, Adams wondered what a destroyer was doing out there by herself. And where were the *Rasher's* pack-mates?

Most perplexing of all were the destroyer's actions.

> Regained contact bearing 019°T, range 18,000 yards and observed flashes of gunfire from target. The fall of shot was not observed. I am unable to explain the movements of the target as observed—one possible—a newly commissioned ship exercising guns, getting turning data at various speeds with varying rudder angles, compensating magnetic compass.

Adams radioed the Sharks a description of the unusual goings on, then stood off on the surface some distance away to watch.

A float plane flew lazy circles over the target. Depth charges thumped and thundered. When the plane edged a little too close for comfort, Adams didn't hesitate a second; he hit the diving alarm and took her down. When it was clear, he surfaced the boat, regained contact with the warship, and sent another report to Schnable, urging him to put on some turns.

At one point the enemy ship got under way and ran back and forth over short east-west course legs, dropping depth charges. Surface bursts could easily be seen through the high periscope. Another float plane appeared from the west. More depth charges rumbled. Or were they torpedoes from one of the Sharks? Was a Shark under attack? Adams pulled the plug and moved in closer to try and identify this odd enemy.

The ship was bigger than a destroyer and lacked the slender profile and low freeboard most Japanese destroyers had. Twin armored turrets were situated fore and aft; torpedo tubes were mounted parallel to the low after deckhouse abaft the bridge. From the look of things, the ship definitely appeared to be undergoing sea trials and training and launching and recovering her aircraft. From some angles she looked identical to a *Katori*-class light cruiser, and the plotting party was convinced she was. However, when viewed broadside she had a distinct separation between her forward superstructure and foremast, and her stack was much shorter than those shown in the ONI 41-42 identification profiles. She was fitted amidships with a scout plane catapult; though it was in use, it could not be seen because of all the loose gear cluttering up the main deck. Despite the preponderance of opinion that she was a cruiser, Adams remained unconvinced. She looked too small to him. He thought she might be a new type of ship unknown to ONI .

Regardless of her type, the tracking and fire control parties stood by waiting for orders to commence an approach. She was a sitting duck.

Adams motioned for the periscope to be raised for another look. Then he lowered it. He paused, then motioned for it to be raised again and ordered the *Rasher* planed up higher to give him a better look. He marked the target's bearing and range. He lowered the scope and studied the charts marked with the target's position. Adams noted with emphasis that she was technically in the *Pilotfish*'s area and was hers to attack. He debated the difficulties of getting in without being detected by the planes. He wondered aloud how many bombs they carried. All the while, the unrest in the conning tower grew. Here was an enemy warship lying to, just begging to be torpedoed, a submariner's dream. All it would take to blow her to pieces was to close in, point the bow and shoot.

Around the captain, men exchanged looks of disbelief and shook their heads in exasperation. Adams did not seem to notice as he maneuvered to maintain contact and worried aloud about being spotted by the aircraft.

With more depth charges rumbling from the direction of the cruiser, Adams opined that perhaps the *Pilotfish* had attacked and the depth charges were meant for her. Urged to investigate, he demurred, claiming the water was too clear and too shallow to maneuver closer.

Meanwhile, the enemy continued to launch and recover her planes, drop depth charges, and fire her guns, oblivious to the *Rasher*, 10,000 yards away and watching her every move.

Adams turned the conn over to his exec and instructed him to monitor the situation, not to close in, but to keep him informed. He then lay below to his stateroom. At regular intervals over the next two hours, he received reports there.

By 1700, it was obvious to all hands that Adams did not plan to attack. The men were tense, for it went against everything the *Rasher* embodied to stand by while such a prime target was within range of her torpedoes.

At 1736 the *Finback* was sighted. Adams gave his assent, and the *Rasher* surfaced to make visual contact with her. The *Pilotfish* was close by. Together, the Sharks began a confusing, disorganized, and dispiriting wolf pack attack, recounted in Adams's patrol report:

1830   Told FINBACK via radar that target was 15 miles north of FINBACK.

1930   Moonrise. Commenced closing.

1930   With target in sight from bridge and with periscope, SJ radar gave a maximum range of 11,800 yards.

   Either target is smaller than estimated or smaller target has interposed itself between us and our original target. Believe the former to be true. SJ radar range to FINBACK 9,000 yards. Commenced tracking target.

2030   Lost target. Asked FINBACK if she had contact.

2040   FINBACK said she had contact with an escort vessel. We headed north to regain contact.

2135   Regained contact bearing approximately 217°T, SJ range 11,000 yards. Course north speed 10 knots.

2140   From FINBACK "Numerous small radar contacts."

2155   From FINBACK "Three small ships course north speed 10."

2210   Lost contact. SJ had been unable to pick up target after previously ranging 9,000 yards on friendly submarine. Believed target too small for torpedo fire. Changed course to north and westward to regain contact.

2224   FINBACK dove for attack.

2300   Radar interference from PILOTFISH bearing 252° T.

2320   SJ radar contact on PILOTFISH bearing 252°T, range 7,800 yards. Changed course to north. Sent last known enemy position to PILOTFISH via radar.

0045   FINBACK sent "No Attack. Have you contact?" "Negative" from PILOTFISH and RASHER.

The ship had finished her exercises and slipped away. Aboard the *Rasher* the mood was glum. Back-to-back failures did not sit well with aggressive submariners. Snide comments added to the dark mood. The *Rasher*'s finely woven fabric of unity and camaraderie was unraveling.

◆ ◆ ◆

Early in the morning of 28 February, an accurate fix was taken from Yushan Liehtao near Ninghsien to pinpoint the *Rasher*'s position off the easternmost point on the China coast. With a week left to patrol the East China Sea, Adams pressed on with the Sharks.

For the next six days the routine of patrolling was interrupted only by an occasional sailboat, a plane, and sightings of the *Rasher*'s pack-mates. The weather turned raw and foggy again. Every morning, deadening overcast swept in from the west, coloring the sea a depressing blackish-green.

Then on 7 March, in gathering dusk, a small ship was sighted at a range of 11,000 yards. She was tracked on various courses at varying speeds, and radar reported intermittent flashes of interference from the general bearing of the contact—a dead giveaway she was a radar-equipped patrol boat. The target abruptly steadied up, swung around, and started echo-ranging. Adams put the rudder over, rang up four engines, and began ending around to the north; this time he was determined to mount an attack.

An hour after starting around, as the *Rasher* thundered along off the target's starboard beam, radar picked up a small sailing vessel dead ahead. Adams studied the situation in silence, as usual keeping his own counsel. Picket boat, he decided. As the *Rasher* slowed to track it, radar lost contact on the first target. But Adams was unwilling to let his quarry get away this time; he slipped around the picket, brought the ship back to a northerly heading, and pursued at full speed.

It took an hour to regain contact. Adams made up his mind that when the *Rasher* got ahead he'd dive to radar depth, close in until the patrol boat could be seen in the periscope, then complete the approach using ST radar. The charts warned of shoals off the coast near Nanji Shan, just north of the spot that Plot showed the intercept point to be. But the *Rasher* would be in position to shoot before reaching dangerous ground.

At 0005, the patrol boat was four miles off the *Rasher*'s starboard bow, invisible to the eye but showing as a bright green pip on the radar screen. Three minutes later, another vessel appeared, dead ahead, 4,000 yards away, lying to off Dayu Shan. She fired a challenge via blinker tube. Sensing trouble, Adams turned due east, putting the new contact on the port beam, and slowed down to look things over.

The ship, flashing more signals, got under way to close in; the target the *Rasher* had been chasing also turned due east, increased speed, and circled around onto a southeasterly course.

The *Rasher* was about to be boxed in by two enemy patrol boats, one closing in from ahead, the other from the port beam. To the north was Nanji Shan's shoal water; to the west, the coast of China and its reefs. The only escape route lay south.

Grasping the dangerous situation they were in, Adams asked, ". . . who has been tracking whom?"

It was a clever trap, considering Japanese anti-submarine patrols had been virtually invisible since the wolf pack had entered the East China Sea. The radar-equipped patrol boat had drawn the *Rasher* north, pretending to be unaware that the submarine was running up her flank. Now the target and her companion were trying to circle around and force the *Rasher* into shallow coastal water. But Adams turned south and made his getaway just as radar reported four more fast patrol boats boring in from the east. It was a close shave, but the *Rasher*'s powerful diesels left them miles behind.

At Taishan Liehtao, Adams cut away from the coast, turned north again, and at flank speed swung east of the area where the trap had nearly been sprung. At dawn the *Rasher* rendezvoused with the *Finback* and the *Pilotfish* in preparation for departing the patrol area, but not before evading submarine-hunting aircraft summoned by the patrol boats. Throughout the day the planes kept the boats down; one of them nearly bombed the *Finback* as she dove.

At 2200 on 8 March, ComSubPac ordered Schnable's Sharks back to Guam.

East of the Tokara Retto, headed for home, the *Rasher* exchanged signals and parlayed with the *Queenfish*, which was on her way to her fateful encounter with the *Awa Maru*.

Part 5

To the Shores of Japan

"Ace" Nace

When the submarine war moved west, Admiral Lockwood packed up his staff and moved SubPac's headquarters to Guam, where he set up shop aboard the tender *Holland*. Dredging, filling, and blasting had transformed Apra Harbor into a bustling Navy base that was approaching the size and complexity of Pearl Harbor. The submarine rest camp, Camp Dealy (named for the legendary submariner, Comdr. Samuel D. Dealy, who was lost with the *Harder* west of the Philippines in August 1944) was modern and well-equipped. It boasted two swimming pools (although one was merely a ragged hole blasted in the coral reef with a rusty shark net to seaward), a softball field, and a volleyball court, all of which were in constant use. As on Saipan, clouds of sere white coral dust covered everything.

Lockwood had come to Guam in order to be closer to the forces engaged in the final push to defeat the Japanese. With the Japanese merchant fleet decimated and their navy in ruins, and with B-29s able to reach targets in Japan almost unchallenged, it was clearly air power that now had the decisive role in paving the way for the Allied invasion of Japan. Consequently, the operational imperatives for submarines shifted to lifeguarding.

Rudimentary air-sea rescue operations had been undertaken earlier in the war—during the air raid on Surabaya in June 1944, for instance. But it was not until 1945 that rescue work became an operational priority and officially named the "Lifeguard League." Working with Maj. Gen. Curtis LeMay, commander of the XXI Bomber Command, Lockwood and his staff ironed out the details. With LeMay's B-29s bombing Japan from the Marianas, it was decided that Lockwood's submarines would be stationed along the Pacific approach and retirement routes to pluck downed aviators from the sea.

Such an operation required extraordinary cooperation from both fliers and sailors. It also meant that the Air Force had to trust the submariners to be there when needed. Aircrews were trained to nurse their damaged planes home rather than ditching. But a B-29 with part of a wing missing, a feathered prop or two, and a fuselage holed like Swiss cheese did not stand much of a chance. Therefore, it was clear from the outset that for lifeguarding to be successful on a large scale, submarines would have to stay on the surface while planes flew to and from the targets so the airmen and submarines could locate each other. Navigation for both planes and submarines alike was difficult: locating a small ship at sea was no mean feat; having a submarine in the right spot at the right time was a tricky proposition. The real key to success, however, was communications. Everyone knew that without good communications it would be impossible to direct the submarines to downed pilots or for pilots to be directed to a submarine waiting to rescue them, regardless of how much air cover the XXI Bomber Command provided to guide the participants.

In practice, however, reliable communications between aircraft and submarine proved difficult to establish. Problems arose with mismatched radio frequencies, improper authentication signals, and balky radio equipment both afloat and in the air. Poor communications grossly compounded the difficulties associated with finding downed airmen, as did errors in reporting their locations and the lack of reliable homing beacons. (The beacon problem was on its way to being rectified, however.)

Poor communications with the Air Force frequently left the lifeguarding submarines in the dark about such basic tactical matters as the timing of missions and their completion, weather conditions over targets, and, most basic of all, whether or not planes had gone down. Sometimes the only information a submarine would receive about the lifeguard mission for which she was standing by would come via ComSubPac. Sometimes the boats were left entirely to their own devices, wandering around off the coast of Japan, exposing themselves to danger needlessly, waiting for orders that never came.

From the submariners' point of view, lifeguarding was an important but thankless task. Ironically, the waning stages of the Pacific conflict had brought the submarine force full circle—from prewar fleet strategic unit, to independent offensive tactical unit, back to fleet strategic unit once again, this time working in concert with the Army Air Force. Regardless of the difficulties involved, more than 500 aviators were saved by submarines.

◆ ◆ ◆

The *Rasher* reached Guam on 16 March, ending a long, tiring, thoroughly frustrating patrol.

Ben Adams certainly seemed anxious to put it behind him. He departed the ship without the customary leave-taking as soon as he had his personal belongings packed and his patrol report in the hands of his division commander. In his haste, he neglected to report in person for a verbal debriefing—standard procedure for all skippers returning from a war patrol. When he did not show up, the division commander ordered the *Rasher*'s officers to find him. A day later they did.

Adams's patrol report was factual enough, but between the lines lurked a host of unanswered questions about the manner in which it had been conducted. Although the patrol officially received the positive endorsements of his superiors, he was relieved of command on 20 March 1945.

Once again the *Rasher* awaited a new skipper.

The post-patrol refit got under way immediately. It included the installation of new equipment designed specifically for lifeguard duty, the priority on the *Rasher*'s seventh run.

One such piece of equipment was a portable AU-1 direction-finder loop to assist in finding downed air crews. It homed in on signals broadcast from a "Gibson Girl" radio beacon (so-called because of its voluminous white cloth-like reflector) dropped from a plane to a lifeboat.

Also, a new piece of defensive gear, a TDM torpedo detector, was installed. Still in an early stage of development, it was supposed to detect torpedoes fired by an enemy submarine and display to the operator the direction from which they were coming. But it could be used only at slow cruising speeds because the ambient noise from diesel engines and rushing sea water deafened it.

Normal crew rotations and transfers had men on their way to the sub tenders or other veteran boats; for some it was new construction. Many new faces reported aboard. One of them was a handsome young lieutenant commander who arrived on 1 April. His name was Charles D. Nace, and he was the *Rasher*'s new skipper. He had graduated from submarine school in 1941, and now, at age twenty-eight, he was about to take command of one of the Navy's most successful and famous submarines.

Nace had completed six war patrols in the *Cero*, two as engineering officer and four as exec. He was promoted to lieutenant commander in March 1944 and a month later received the designation "qualified for command of submarines." In December, he returned to San Francisco with the *Cero* for an overhaul. Two months later, he was sent to Guam as a "prospective commanding officer" with orders to report to Comdr. Thomas Dykers, an old friend from New London and now the boss of Submarine Division 282. A few weeks after arriving the young officer found himself standing on the *Rasher*'s quarterdeck being addressed as "Captain." For Nace, having his own command—particularly a boat with the *Rasher*'s reputation—was the fulfillment of a dream.

> I was very fortunate to get the RASHER. She came with a history of great accomplishments achieved by a well-trained and competent crew. The more I became acquainted with the officers and men, the better I liked my first command. Old or new, these crew members exuded confidence and I quickly realized that I had inherited one hell of a fine ship.

Commander Dykers came aboard shortly after Nace's get-acquainted period. With Dykers along as a training officer, the *Rasher* shoved off for eight days of training, some of them spent with her old friend the *Bluefish*, which fired exercise torpedoes at her for TDM training. The *Bluefish* was under the command of Lt. Comdr. George W. Forbes Jr., who was Nace's Naval Academy classmate and his roommate at sub school. For the two men, it was like old times again.

Though Dykers and Nace were buddies, the commodore treated Nace like any other skipper. His training regimen was rigorous, and he saw to it that the *Rasher* was ready for unrestricted operations. Captain Nace noted one welcome difference, however:

> My experience had always been that upon completion of this type of training period, both the CO and XO, in particular, needed a rest, and they usually tried to find some sack time for the first couple of days en route to the patrol area. In this case, however, Dykers seemed to sense that RASHER had a damn fine, well-trained crew and that the new CO wasn't going to turn everything upside down. So he didn't keep us up all night every night as had been my experience with one previous training officer, and all of us seemed to be better off for it.

On 13 April (12 April in the States) radio broadcasts carried the news of President Roosevelt's death at Warm Springs, Georgia. The boats in the nests and along the piers in Guam lowered their flags to half staff. Officers and men crowded around radios to get what information they could about the events at home and to learn something of President Harry Truman. On that same somber day, the *Queenfish* put into Apra Harbor, where she had been ordered after sinking the *Awa Maru*.

After the usual loading and preparations for patrol, Nace backed the *Rasher* from her berth on 17 April and got under way to join the Lifeguard League assigned to LeMay's B-29s in the vicinity of Nampo-Shoto, off the coast of Japan in the Philippine Sea.

Her op-orders, No. 79-45, also directed her into the still-dangerous sector around latitude 32° north and longitude 139° east and, farther, into the Kii Suido, the channel leading to the Inland Sea between Shikoku and Honshu, to intercept any enemy naval sorties from the Inland Sea. From intelligence briefings and information extracted from the patrol reports of submarines that had previously operated in the area, Nace did not expect to encounter an abundance of enemy ships. Nevertheless, the *Rasher* left Guam with a "Cutie" on board.

The Navy's latest technological marvel, the Mark-27 electric homing torpedo, dubbed Cutie, reached the war zone with plenty of bugs still to be worked out but with great potential. Designed along the lines of the German *Zaunkonig* acoustic torpedo, the little fish was supposed to home in on the propeller noises of a ship and, no matter what course the target steered, follow the sound and explode on contact. Cuties were slow, however, and therefore useless against a ship making more than 8 1/2 knots. They were most effective against shallow-draft vessels such as patrol craft that were steaming slowly on anti-submarine search patterns. Cuties did not carry particularly powerful warheads, but they could inflict serious damage to a ship's propellers and rudder. Then the target could be finished off with a conventional torpedo or gunfire.

For obvious reasons, Cuties were always carried in the stern tubes and fired away from the submarine's direction of travel. Fired from between 150- and 200-foot depths, the torpedo incorporated a safety device to deactivate its acoustical sensors below 150 feet so that when launched it would not turn around and home in on the submarine that had just fired it. Unlike standard torpedoes, the Cuties were not fired by compressed air; instead, they "swam" out of the flooded tube under their own power. With Japanese shipping either sunk or holed up in port, the Cutie was eminently suited for the targets the *Rasher* would most likely encounter on this patrol—small, shallow-draft anti-submarine craft.

45° N

SEA OF JAPAN

KOREA

JAPAN

TOKYO

"CUTIE" ATTACK

PT BOATS

SURFACE GUN ATTACK

LIFEGUARD

30° N

TO MIDWAY

E A S T CHINA SEA

CHINA

OKINAWA

FORMOSA

TROPIC OF CANCER

SOUTH CHINA SEA

PHILIPPINE SEA

PACIFIC

INDO CHINA

PHILIPPINES

SAIPAN

GUAM

15° N

OCEAN

BORNEO

CELEBES

EQUATOR

NEW GUINEA

JAVA

LOMBOK

TIMOR

15°

INDIAN OCEAN

DARWIN

15° S

TROPIC OF CAPRICORN

AUSTRALIA

EXMOUTH GULF "POTSHOT"

BRISBANE

30°

30° S

PERTH-FREMANTLE

USS RASHER
SEVENTH WAR PATROL
17 APR 45 – 29 MAY 45

105°   120°   135°   150°

◆ ◆ ◆

Weather en route to the patrol area was pleasant. During the day the skies were hazy and visibility was fair. Moderate seas made surface cruising quite pleasant. Nace conducted daily drills and training dives. Homemade targets and balloons were used to practice with the 5-inch and 40-millimeter guns. The new skipper believed in being prepared in the event gun targets were encountered:

> Use of deck guns was left to the discretion of each skipper. My philosophy was to be well-prepared for a battle surface type of shootout, but use them mostly as a last resort. Each situation presented a myriad of considerations: was it early or late in the patrol when detection of our presence was less important; was it likely that no targets worthy of a torpedo were going to be encountered; was the prospective engagement decidedly favorable to the submarine, etc.? Many of the prospective targets were of minuscule importance to the total war effort, and many were no threat to the primary mission of the submarine.

Nace meshed nicely with his crew and they with him. The young skipper was well-liked and respected. However, he did exhibit one shortcoming that, if not corrected, would prove damaging, both personally and professionally, to a submariner, especially a crack commanding officer: Nace was woefully lacking in cribbage skills.

He had rightfully earned the nickname "Ace" for his poker artistry. Nace was widely feared for his coolness when faced with a bluff; he was rumored to be clairvoyant when it came time to pass or draw. But mastery of cribbage had somehow eluded the man, and he was easy pickings in the wardroom. Pete Sasgen knew the captain was a hard case, but nevertheless took him under his wing. Nace remembered:

> Without him, my life aboard the RASHER would have been a series of humiliating defeats during recreation in the wardroom. The other officers were beating me consistently until Pete became my guru.

Sasgen taught him well—but not too well. Pretty soon Nace could actually win a game now and again. Captain of the ship or not, he was given no special consideration as he limped his way around the cribbage board. He would, by God, have to compete in the toughest arena of all—the submarine wardroom. And there would be plenty of days ahead for concentrated study of the nuances of the game.

When the *Rasher* arrived at the southern extreme of her patrol station on 21 April 1945, she immediately received orders from ComSubPac assigning her to a lifeguard station the next day. Already, silvery B-29 Superforts were sighted en route to Tokyo and Yokahama, and later returning from their strikes. The radio watch listened in on the lifeguard frequencies in the event someone needed help, but there were no Maydays. On the way to her station, the *Rasher* sank a floating mine with the .50-caliber machine guns. All submarines working the western Philippine Sea had been duly warned that floating mines were everywhere.

By noon on the twenty-second, the *Rasher* was in position 120 miles off the Izu Peninsula, southwest of Yokahama, standing by for a flight of B-29s returning from a bombing mission. ComSubPac's orders required her to maintain station from 1330 to 1500.

Being so close to the enemy's vitals meant exercising extreme caution; the Japanese were still capable of unleashing potent anti-submarine attacks from land and sea. While searching for aircraft (friendly and otherwise), SD radar had to be keyed sparingly to avoid revealing the *Rasher*'s position to extremely powerful Japanese direction finders on the small outlying islands seaward of Honshu.

Once on station, Nace awaited protective air cover. Like all lifeguarding boats, the *Rasher* was assigned a B-29 to ward off possible enemy air attacks and to guide her to the pickup point should a plane ditch in her area. Though air cover for boats stationed to the north showed up on schedule, the *Rasher*'s cover never appeared. Her introduction to lifeguarding had left her feeling naked and useless.

Several B-29s and their P-51 Mustang escorts passed overhead on their way home, but no distress calls were addressed to the *Rasher*. At 1600 Nace headed north, anticipating orders to proceed to Hachijo Jima to search along the Nampo-Shoto chain toward Tokyo Bay for enemy vessels.

Patrolling the islands all night proved uneventful. After a morning trim dive, Nace maneuvered the *Rasher* east of Hachijo Jima, the biggest island in the chain. No ships were in sight, but there were plenty of floating mines riding the swift archipelago currents from the north to destroy. In the evening, Nace received new orders directing him to a lifeguard position north of Mikura Jima for the twenty-fourth and twenty-sixth; that would take the *Rasher* within sixty miles of the Japanese mainland.

Nace began heading for station. The submarine passed small islands that were little more than hunks of ancient lava sticking a few feet above the sea, part of the billion-year-old geologic formations that had thrust upward from the bottom of the ocean to form the rugged islands of Japan.

Nace was mindful of the three-knot local current drift that had to be fought to maintain course, speed, and schedule. The lookouts were warned to be extra alert for drifting mines. With bright moonlight and calm seas, there was every likelihood the mines would be spotted in time to take evasive action.

The men settled into a relaxed but watchful routine.

At a half hour to midnight, the bridge speaker blared, "Radar contact, bearing two-eight-zero! Range fifty-seven-hundred!"

A small patrol boat, or sea truck, could be seen from the bridge. Beyond her, radar had contact with a larger target, a big lugger of about 200 tons displacement bearing trapezoidal lugsails and jibs. Both vessels were making six knots. Nace decided that if he could get a good setup on the lugger he would attack; she was perfect for a Cutie. He ordered the rudder over and three engines on line to head up the target's starboard side to work around her.

As he did, radar sang out a third contact—another lugger, but hard to see against the dark background of Mikura Jima, which the *Rasher* was passing to the southwest. Yet a fourth radar contact materialized dead ahead, closing rapidly. Without warning, the *Rasher* was surrounded by so many contacts they impeded the attack:

> Our efforts to gain station in front of the target are blocked now by the contact dead ahead who is still closing rapidly. If we take time to avoid this contact and end around our target again we will be late in reaching our lifeguard station. Considered night surface gun attack but the odds appear to be 4 to 1 against us and we cannot be sure what the armament of these small craft might be.
>
> Passed our target 3500 yards abeam and confirmed identification, all hands agree he was a small lugger or a sea truck. Bright moon made visibility excellent.

Nace broke off the approach and shaped course for the *Rasher*'s station.

By morning, she was idling in position. Flights of B-29s were sighted heading for Tokyo. This time her air cover showed up as promised. Despite intense jamming from Japanese shore stations,

VHF voice radio contact was established with the orbiting bomber, and the *Rasher* settled down to wait.

At 1052, the radio watch received a position report from the B-29, but no information as to what was located there. This was followed by another message saying that ten aviators in lifejackets were down five miles south of the entrance to Suruga Wan, thirty-eight miles north of the *Rasher*'s present position.

In the radio room, the skipper donned a set of headphones and listened in. Japanese-language voice transmissions kept breaking in on the lifeguard frequencies, and Nace was skeptical the communications they had received were authentic. The Japanese did a good job of sending fake transmissions, complete with realistic-sounding jargon and radio protocols. Before he ran off into an enemy trap, the skipper wisely asked the B-29 for confirmation of the ditching position, how many men were in the water, and a repeat of the authenticator codes.

"Am searching right now. Will tell you as soon as possible," was the reply.

Shortly, more information crackled over the radio from the B-29, but with the wrong authenticator prefixes; then a chattering Japanese broke in on the circuit. Voice communications were garbled by jamming. Who the hell are we talking to? Nace wondered.

> We wanted to be sure we were talking to the right guy. Decided to wait until we received properly authenticated message containing a posit and information as to what was there . . . or until we received some information from ComSubPac.

It was frustrating work trying to save airmen.

> We were never certain that a ditching had occurred. Improper signals and changes in the downed position made it difficult to take aggressive action.

At 1350, a genuine message arrived from ComSubPac ordering the *Rasher* to search for a downed aircrew whose coordinates were twenty miles south-southeast of the coastal city of Hamamatsu.

On four engines, it took two hours to reach the location. The B-29 flying cover soon radioed that it had the downed aviators in sight and was circling them. Still, there was confusion: the B-29's coordinates did not match those given by ComSubPac; the position the pilot gave was not off Hamamatsu, but rather in the mouth of Suruga Wan.

Exasperated, Nace decided the plane's navigator knew where he was better than ComSubPac did, so he turned the *Rasher* north for the bay entrance. On the way, she was overflown by the Superfort heading south on an opposite course. The pilot radioed that he was low on fuel and was heading home. More alarmingly, he added that a small surface craft was five miles from the life rafts but not yet headed for them. The *Rasher* tore north at full speed to snatch up the men before the enemy did.

Already it was 1800; dusk was gathering as the *Rasher* neared the deep-set bay west of the Izu Peninsula. It was the closest she had ever been to Japan.

When the submarine was three miles from the reported ditching position, a two-engined Japanese bomber was sighted six miles away. Nace pulled the plug and closed in on the fliers' reported position at periscope depth using a high periscope. But where the rafts were supposed to be, the sea was empty.

A quick check for aircraft, and Nace surfaced the boat to search while there was still light. Nothing. Not even the vessel reported by the B-29 was in sight. With darkness descending, the quartermaster fired green Very rockets—a potential invitation to disaster, since they were likely to be seen by the enemy, but necessary. No reply. By 2122, Nace concluded the airmen had been picked up by the Japanese. He retired south, firing green Very stars at hourly intervals in hopes he would be proved wrong.

At 0233, a message from ComSubPac directed the *Rasher* to continue searching on a southeasterly track, which would take into consideration tide and current along the coast of Honshu. But weather was now a factor: a falling barometer announced the approach of a major storm front. By first light on 25 April, the seas had made up to Force 4; high winds whistled through the bridge overhead and periscope shears.

The only thing the search turned up was the badly decomposed body of a Japanese dressed in a leather flight jacket and white trousers. Other than the ghastly corpse, the sea was deserted. Even if the aviators were by some miracle located, Nace knew it would be nearly impossible to get them aboard in such sea conditions. As the search wore on, the wind worked around to the east-northeast; by nightfall, the *Rasher* was in the grip of a full-fledged storm, her bow rising and falling in sickening lurches.

At dawn, ComSubPac directed Nace to turn the search northward.

It was a decidedly difficult task, with the ship now being buffeted by winds of forty-five knots and hammered by Force 5 seas. This kind of weather was capable of sinking a small ship (and no doubt was tearing mines loose from their moorings along the coast).

ComSubPac advised that the *Haddock* had joined in the search east of the Nampo-Shoto, and that after sunset, the two were to break off the hunt. Nace did so at the appointed time. It was hopeless; men adrift in a life raft could not survive for long in such weather.

Seas moderated by the afternoon of the twenty-seventh. The *Rasher* patrolled near Mikura Jima. Since the typhoon-like weather had pushed them around relentlessly for two days, Nace tried for an accurate position fix on the island. But after the pounding the antenna trunks had taken from heavy seas, both the SJ and ST units were out of commission. Nace took the boat into the calm of deep water while the technicians dropped the trunks and pulled the power transformer and range indicator unit. The men worked all day, but both radars were out of commission when the boat surfaced at 2000 to charge batteries and resume patrolling. While the technicians sweated over the gear, Nace got under way for Hachijo Jima.

As the *Rasher* passed south of the rock-like islands, a small vessel, another sea truck, was spotted heading north toward Shikine Jima.

Pounding through heavy seas, Nace started ending around on three engines, relying on good old-fashioned visual plotting to get into position. Even though the storm had passed south, a gun attack was out of the question because the submarine was rolling badly in still-heavy swells. In addition, there was no way to tell how well-armed the target was. In these seas, without radar, even a torpedo attack would be difficult.

In the nick of time, the SJ radar went on line again. It confirmed the target's course to be nearly due north. When the *Rasher* was 5,000 yards ahead of the target, two more sea trucks were picked up on her port and starboard beams. Nace ordered battle stations submerged. It was Cutie time!

The skipper recalled the attack:

> The target was estimated to be too small for conventional torpedoes and the setup seemed perfect for one of these new weapons. We were at the prescribed firing depth with good contact on the target's screw noises. Everyone in the fire control party figured we had a perfect setup and tracking solution, but the Cutie did not hit the target. It's possible we fired too soon or too late. It's possible the

target noise level was not high enough to attract the torpedo. And of course, it's possible the torpedo didn't function as designed.

The little sea trucks disappeared into the night. When the Cutie reached the end of its run, it sank into the Sikoku Basin in 15,000 feet of water. Nace surfaced the boat and headed northwest for her new lifeguard station, which the *Rasher* would share with the *Haddock*.

At 0127, fifty miles west of Kozu Jima, two smallish sea trucks were sighted in moonlight and tracked by radar. This time Nace ordered the 20- and 40-millimeter gun crews topside.

As the *Rasher* closed in, all hands except the gunner's mates were behind the bridge's ballistic protection. At a range of 1,000 yards, Nace gave the order to open fire with the 20-millimeter on the smaller of the two targets.

Both ships were caught completely by surprise. Nace maneuvered adroitly to bring the 40-millimeter gun to bear too. From both ends of the conning tower, the night came alive with blinding muzzle flashes and red tracers. The smaller ship swung around to ram, but Nace pirouetted his boat, allowing the gunners to rake the hapless Japanese vessel with 20-millimeter shells as she passed close astern. Deadly slugs ripped into bulkheads, masts, ventilators, and cargo gear, reducing her topside to a shambles. Hunks of debris flew every which way.

Sparks spewing from her stack, engine room straining to put full power to the screw, the larger sea truck maneuvered wildly to escape the withering gunfire, but to no avail. Pressing the attack, Nace nosed the *Rasher* in close, and the 40-millimeter poured tracers and incendiary shells into her. A fire broke out amidships and spread rapidly. Round after round wrecked the deckhouse and bridge, leaving the craft dead in the water, burning and listing badly.

The smaller sea truck, heavily damaged, managed to flee into the darkness.

Drawing off, Nace secured the guns. It was over. Time to head for the day's lifeguard station.

At 1000, the *Rasher* rendezvoused with the *Haddock* off Cape Omae to await orders. Away in the haze, Honshu was a jagged line rising out of the sea; one hundred and fifty miles to the northwest was Tokyo. Mysteriously, friendly air cover had vanished. Both the VHF and lifeguard frequencies were eerily silent despite repeated calls from the *Rasher* and the *Haddock*. Nace noted in his patrol report that the boats felt a little naked.

On lifeguard station 10 miles south of Iro Saki. This is not a very nice place to be without fighter cover. Decided to stay on the surface, however, to be certain of getting any information from planes or ComSubPac.

All morning, unidentified SD contacts spiked the radar screen, keeping the lookouts, the OOD, and the skipper on their toes. Suddenly, a Japanese plane roared in on the deck from dead astern, forcing a quick dive to 200 feet. An hour later, Nace poked up the scope, then surfaced. No Japanese planes were visible, but there was still no air cover either. Feeling useless—and vulnerable—Nace called it a day at 1500.

Headed south. We have had enough. The strike must have been cancelled but apparently the zoomies did not put out the dope. We heard nothing at all on 4475 kcs and it looks as though we stuck our neck out all day for nothing.

Early in the morning on 30 April, ComSubPac ordered the *Rasher* to a new lifeguard position farther south.

Under a bright moon she worked down the western side of the Nampo-Shoto. At 0415, two vessels were sighted near Inamba Jima. They were so small they hardly gave back a radar echo. Even so, Nace started tracking: a target was a target.

From a distance the vessels appeared to have the low freeboard and sinister shape of PT boats. As the *Rasher* drew closer to investigate, the two vessels abruptly turned toward her. With a roar, huge bow waves exploded from under their hulls as they dug in at full throttle. Just like PT boats! The *Rasher*'s bow wave erupted, too, as Nace ordered flank speed, the rudder hard over to sheer away. The PTs raced within 1,200 yards before the *Rasher*'s four thundering engines pulled her off to the south.

Believe the heavy seas prevented them from chasing us at high speed. It looks as though the Nips were waiting for us.

◆ ◆ ◆

At daybreak the *Rasher* was back on station. Again Nace waited patiently for some official word about the strikes: again none arrived. At 1700 he quit station and headed north for Inamba Jima to search for ships. The lookouts kept an eye out for PT boats.

Patrolling around the island was routine and uneventful. The mine disposal team dispatched a floater, and the engineers made repairs to the bow plane hydraulics. Sub skippers were not exaggerating: there really were no targets left. But Nace had ideas:

> . . . we contemplate submerged patrol close to the coast of Honshu later when the nights are dark. The moon is too bright now to close the coast for a morning diving position.

At 2215, ComSubPac shifted the *Rasher*'s lifeguard station 200 miles west. She was to be in position during the night of 2–3 May. She got under way immediately on a course cutting due west across the Philippine Sea. The position coordinates were off the Kii Peninsula, due east of Kushimoto. The charts and the *Coast Pilot* showed small offshore islands and shoals were plentiful. With the swift littoral currents around southern Honshu, it would be a difficult area to work in.

On the way to her station, ComSubPac advised that air strikes would be delayed twenty-four hours because of bad weather. No one had to tell the submariners about the weather; by late afternoon seas were thrashing at Force 4, whipped up by thirty-knot gales. The storm proved to be short-lived, however.

> 4 May 0205. On station. Weather has moderated. SD contact 8 miles with IFF [Identification Friend or Foe]. We thought this might be our cover so we called him continuously but never raised him on either VHF or 4475. . . . We received no dope whatsoever. ComSubPac told us there would be moments like these and it certainly makes us feel rather useless.

At daybreak, skies cleared. B-29s were sighted, but not a one could be raised on voice channels. To banish a bad case of Pacific torpor caused by the tedium of steaming in circles waiting for something to happen, Nace conducted gunnery drills with improvised targets. In the wardroom a hotly contested cribbage match unfolded.

At 1600, with lifeguard channels still mute, Nace assumed the strikes were over and headed for the mouth of the Kii Suido. Opening onto Osaka Bay and the Inland Sea, the strait lay between the big island of Shikoku and the Kii Peninsula of Honshu. Minefields, both Japanese and U.S. (the latter courtesy of submarines and B-29s), abounded, making it a nightmarish place for a submarine. Intelligence reports indicated that remnants of the Imperial Navy were holed up in the Inland Sea and might be bagged as they ran the channel to sortie north or south.

Instructions in the *Rasher's* operation order pertaining to guarding the exit of the Kii Suido implied that Nace should concentrate his efforts near the center of the strait to maximize detection of enemy warships no matter which side of the deep-water channel they might use to exit. Easy enough to do, Nace knew, as the channel was not so wide as to prevent good coverage. At the same time the op-ord also encouraged aggressive operations against *any* target of opportunity. As an experienced submariner, Nace knew that merchant shipping would naturally hug the shoreline. To catch them would require coverage of the entire strait rather than just the main channel—a tall order considering the strait's width. These conflicting objectives—narrow coverage versus wide coverage—were to govern his strategy and tactics in the days ahead.

Because of the *Rasher's* lifeguard commitments, Nace had time only to give the place a quick once-over. Later, he planned to return for a more thorough sweep. On this night, nothing was sighted but sampans.

◆ ◆ ◆

From 5 May through 8 May, the *Rasher* was on station while heavy incendiary raids were carried out against Kyushu, Yokahama, Kawasaki, and Tokyo. Each day, B-29s and P-51s were sighted heading to and returning from their targets. No planes were reported down. In between assignments, Nace briefly reconnoitered the seaward approaches to Kii Suido and, farther south, the Bungo Suido. On the ninth, as heavy weather rolled in again, Nace turned southwest to investigate the Nampo-Shoto line near Hachijo Jima.

Because of the storm and the proximity of land, he decided to patrol the area submerged. During the noon meal of sandwiches—standard heavy-weather fare—a ship was sighted four miles away making for the exposed harbor on the northeastern side of Hachijo Jima. Bolting a ham and cheese, Nace took over the periscope to make the approach. He was determined to sink a ship this time.

The target's appearance was similar to that of an old-style 1,200-ton Japanese destroyer. She had been converted to a transport and refitted with an elongated deckhouse and other topside modifications. Thus nothing in the identification manuals looked much like her. She was zigzagging and pinging, and because of her high speed—fifteen knots—Plot confirmed she could not be intercepted before making port. But with the first truly torpedo-worthy target yet sighted, Nace was not ready to give up. With high, stormy seas lapping over the periscope and depth control difficult, he swung around to take a peek inside the harbor entrance.

> Closed the harbor to 2 1/2 miles and believe we saw him in there but the background of buildings and land made it difficult to be certain.

Nace tried to move in for a closer look. He knew it was too risky when the boat nearly broached. He decided to wait around and see if the ship—the "Tokyo Express," as he called her—might venture out.

For the remainder of the night and into the morning, the *Rasher* loitered off the harbor entrance in heavy weather. But the transport stubbornly stayed put. Finally, Nace decided to look for new opportunities to the north around the Boso Peninsula. By late afternoon the weather, if not the hunters' luck, improved as the storm blew itself out against Honshu.

◆ ◆ ◆

The *Rasher's* call sign turned up in the evening Foxes on 10 May. She was ordered to take up a lifeguard position eighty miles east of the Kii Suido and to stand by for early morning airstrikes. At sunset on 11 May, she was to relieve the submarine *Torsk* guarding the strait. With the position 280 miles away, Nace put three engines on and took a shortcut around Mikura Jima. It would bring the *Rasher* close to Hachijo Jima again, where she had waited in vain for the Tokyo Express to leave the safety of the harbor.

After the submarine surfaced at dusk north of the island, radar made contact with a small ship and an escort steaming for the harbor. Nace immediately started tracking. There was no time to waste; if the *Rasher* was to reach her lifeguard station on time, an attack had to be completed in one hour, no more. Good visibility dictated a minimum firing range of 3,000 yards. This was far from ideal, but if the *Rasher* went closer she would be spotted. Nace headed in. On the island, a navigation beacon flashed on for a few seconds to guide the ships as they neared the breakwater. The race was on.

The *Rasher* worked past the escort stationed on the *maru's* port side, then turned in, presenting as small a silhouette as possible. The target was a beauty, a new, 1,500-ton, 270-foot auxiliary transport. She and her escort were nearly overlapping when Nace gave the order to shoot.

Commenced firing six torpedoes forward using TBT bearings. All torpedoes could be seen leaving the tubes in the phosphorescent water and we believe they all ran normally. They were tracked . . . by sound. One minute and a half after firing the target was seen to turn towards. Whether he was due to zig or whether he was alerted we do not know. We continued to plot his track after shooting [and it] showed a [huge] 50° zig towards . . .

All torpedoes missed ahead.

Gunfire erupted from the target group. In a flash, Nace ordered right full rudder to turn off the track and pull away. Minutes later, three torpedoes slammed into the fringing reef and exploded.

A follow-up attack was impossible. Popping their guns in all directions, and with the entire island alerted, the target and escort sped past the breakwater into the harbor unscathed. Once again, despite a good setup, attack position, and fire-control solution, the *Rasher*'s efforts had fallen short.

After the stint of morning lifeguard duty, Ace Nace set a course southwest for the Kii Suido. He was determined to put a load of torpedoes into the bottom of a ship—any ship—flying the flag of the rising sun.

◆ ◆ ◆

On the surface by night, submerged by day, the *Rasher* patrolled north and south across the mouth of the strait. Every morning sailboats and sampans tacked inshore as they went about their business of tending nets and fishing, unaware they were being watched by a periscope just a few miles off the beach. But not a ship worthy of a torpedo was sighted.

Then at 1047 on 14 May, the periscope watch sighted the upper works of a ship rounding the point of Shiono Misaki from the northeast. As the tracking party sprang to work, Nace increased speed to close the beach from the *Rasher*'s position just outside the 100-fathom curve. He decided that this target of opportunity called for him to invoke the second part of his op-ord. "Battle stations submerged" bonged away.

"Up periscope!"

Nace had a nice view of a shallow-draft auxiliary transport much like the one he had missed near Hachijo Jima.

"Bearing—mark!"

"Zero-two-zero."

"Range—mark!"

"Five thousand."

"Angle on the bow, eighty port! Down scope!" The TDC whirred as the target information was cranked in. Nace gave the target time to clear the point.

"Up periscope!" He snapped the handles down with determination and took a long look.

The Japanese was not cooperating. "Damn it! We're too far out to get this guy. He's right on the beach!" Nace grumbled.

The enemy ship had doubled the point and turned into the bight, hugging the craggy coastline. Her skipper was no doubt confident he was safe from submarine attack. He was: the *Rasher* was 5,000 yards seaward. By the time she got into position to fire torpedoes, the target would be long gone.

Nace fit the camera to the periscope ocular and, instead of torpedoes, fired the shutter at the ship as she passed south. Then he took another quick look around before lowering the periscope.

"Got another target here! Possible patrol! Bearing—mark!"

"Three-one-zero."

"Range—mark!"

"About seven thousand."

"Down scope!"

The *Rasher* was right on the 100-fathom curve. Inside the curve the bottom rose up swiftly to less than ten fathoms—not a good place to take a submerged submarine. Complicating things was the Kuroshio current—the Black Stream. Its strong easterly set made forward progress difficult while running submerged. Still, Nace pressed ahead.

"Up scope!" He twisted the handles to their next detent to focus in high magnification; the ship leaped into view.

"Target's a large patrol boat. He's zigged in toward the beach, running parallel. Looks like he's heading for Shiono Misaki. Angle on the bow—make it sixty starboard. Down scope!"

Nace continued on an approach course of 320 for several more minutes, then motioned up for the periscope.

"Got another target! Small trawler! Angle on the bow—zero! Range—mark!"

"Four thousand!"

"Down scope! Come to course two-six-five!"

The Kuroshio was setting the trawler down on the submarine, forcing Nace to work around to the south. Once clear of the trawler, he planned to turn west to get back into position and regain contact with the auxiliary. Meanwhile, the large patrol boat remained well inshore, heading east.

"Up scope! Range to the trawler!"

"Fifteen hundred."

"Close! Too damn close!" Nace said. "Come left to two-three-zero!"

Five minutes later the skipper took another look. The trawler was closer yet, her screws plenty loud.

> Went deep and rigged for silent running. Put him astern. He crossed our stern and so decided to ease back up and try to regain our position. . . .

Nace took a look: there was the trawler, sitting on the *Rasher*'s starboard quarter, 1,500 yards away.

"Come to three-one-zero! All ahead one-third! Down scope!"

Keeping the trawler astern, Nace headed toward the beach to try and regain contact with the first target.

"Up periscope!"

To starboard, behind the promontory of Shiono Misaki, Nace sighted the upper works of another ship approaching from the northeast. Even though she was five miles away, the skipper could make out two king posts, one goal post cargo boom, and a stack aft belching black smoke from coal-fired boilers.

He gave up on the first target and started an approach on the new arrival—only to discover another small trawler dead ahead of the *Rasher*'s submerged position, blocking the way. To further complicate matters, a float plane winged over the point of Shiono Misaki, scouting ahead of the *maru*. To the seaward side of the target was the patrol boat that had worked her way down the coast earlier. She had been steaming out to meet the *maru* to escort her into the strait.

The *Rasher*'s situation was hopeless. She was 10,000 yards west of Shiono Misaki, submerged well inside the 100-fathom curve, 8,000 yards from the beach in shelving water, fighting a strong southeasterly current running at 1.5 knots. The trawlers had done an effective job forcing her south, away from the target. Perfectly orchestrated tactics had thwarted a submarine attack.

When the *maru* rounded the cape, Nace identified her as an *Amakasu Maru*-class, engines-aft freighter. ONI 208-J said she had a displacement of 1,900 tons. She was by far the best target Nace had yet seen. The skipper watched her go by close to shore, cussing himself for muffing it and cussing the trawlers for running such effective interference. As they took the *maru* under their wing and worked up the coast, Nace could only watch the target's stern disappear behind her smoke.

"Down periscope!"

◆ ◆ ◆

Early the next morning, the *Rasher* poked her bull nose close to the beach at Ichie Saki for another look-see. Sampans and a few other small boats raced along the coast. At 1000, three large motor sampans were wandering along the 100-fathom curve; they seemed to be patrolling. The periscope watch kept an eye on their erratic maneuverings.

At 1112, a mast was sighted close to the coast off Ichie Saki. Nace draped himself on the periscope and studied the small ship that hove into view from the Kii Suido.

"It's our friend from yesterday!" the skipper announced.

It was the patrol boat that had escorted the *maru* into the strait. Anticipating the same tactics he'd encountered the day before, Nace moved in close, halfway between Ichie Saki and Shiono Misaki. Sure enough, a second mast appeared astern of the escort.

"Same routine. Small target . . . maybe a sub! Down scope!"

Here was a fresh opportunity—and a submarine to boot. Every man was poised for action; they eagerly anticipated the skipper's juicy description of an RO- or I-class submarine.

Nace started the approach and thumbed up for the periscope. "Range to the escort—mark!"

"Eight thousand."

"Still can't see enough of the target to get his range!"

Plot estimated the escort's speed was nine or ten knots. Nace rotated the scope: one of the motor sampans sighted at 1000 hauled into view from the northwest, patrolling down the 100-fathom curve. She passed between the *Rasher* and the target group and continued south without detecting the submarine.

With the patrol boat looming ever closer, the skipper ran the periscope up and down every few minutes, trying to get a look at the trailing target. At last Nace was able to see it. Some submarine it turned out to be!

> Tentatively identified target as similar to one of our landing craft, disgustingly small. Continued approach in hopes he might show up to be worthy of torpedoes.

At last, Nace could see that the target was in fact a small trawler bobbing up and down in the heavy swells making up from the north-east as an approaching storm blackened the sky:

> Decided that both these guys were escorts and that since this was the same time the escort came by yesterday to pick up his ship off SHIONO MISAKI, that they were heading down to pick one up today. Decided to wait close to the beach for their return trip as nei-ther of these escorts were worth a torpedo. Apparently we were not detected. We heard no pinging.

Putting the escorts astern, Nace went as deep as he dared in the shallow water, rigging for depth charge and silent running just in case. Unaware of the *Rasher*'s presence, both escorts steamed by and disappeared into sheets of rain walking up the coast. By 1400, with nothing in sight and with seas heavy and visibility less than half a mile, Nace headed for deeper water.

At 2100, the *Rasher* surfaced into a full-fledged, fast-moving storm. Before the turbos could get her fully blown up, torrents of water crashed over the bridge and roared down the open hatch into the con-ning tower. In an instant, sailors were sloshing around in a foot of water. Orders flew left and right; hatches slammed shut; bilge pumps started; screaming turbos blew ballast tanks dry. In a few minutes everything was back under control. The night was spent headed into the wind to ride out the blow. At the height of its ferocity, the for-ward marker buoy socket came adrift (the buoys themselves had been removed for war patrolling) and banged around on deck, making a terrible racket. By morning, seas had calmed and winds had abated. A fix showed the *Rasher* had been blown well east of Shiono Misaki.

With cable cutters in hand, a work party inched forward on the seesawing bow to cut loose the marker buoy socket and ditch it. In the radio shack, freshly decoded Fox skeds brought good news: ComSubPac ordered the *Rasher* to end her patrol and depart for Midway on 21 May. With only five days left to bag a ship, Nace returned to the strait to resume patrolling. Beautiful weather found the coast of Japan alive with sampans and coastal luggers. But for three days no ship worthy of a torpedo was sighted. Time was run-ning out.

During the noon meal on the next to last day in the Kii Suido, the periscope watch sighted two trawlers west of Ichie Saki. They were steaming erratically—like bloodhounds trying to pick up a scent.

When a submarine chaser joined them and the three ships began working in the direction of the *Rasher*, Nace took the conn and headed around them to the east and south to get back to the 100-fathom curve in case the submarine was discovered and forced to go deep.

While Nace kept an eye on the anti-submarine team astern through the periscope, something caught his attention. Six thousand yards away, rounding the point, another auxiliary transport steamed into view. This one was diesel-powered and turned out in a jagged camouflage paint job that made her very difficult to pick out against the rocky coast. But forced south by the escorts, the *Rasher* was too far away to get back in and attack. The Japanese had thumbed their noses at him again, and Ace Nace's luck had flat run out.

On 21 May, the *Rasher* departed for Gooneyville.

Gooneyville

Midway wasn't Hawaii, but Chuck Nace wasn't fussy.

> As far as advanced bases go, Midway was one of the best. But I had great concern for my crew because this was their second advanced base refit in a row. I'm sure consideration was given to bringing us back to Pearl Harbor; however, it was another 1,200 miles to the east and the overall requirements for submarines on station apparently outweighed the additional 2,400 miles of transit time to enjoy a refit in paradise.

Statistics told the story of the *Rasher*'s seventh patrol. As testimony to the dearth of targets, she returned with fifteen torpedoes, claiming not a single hit. Forty-three days were spent at sea—thirty-two of them in the patrol area. Guam to Midway, she had steamed 9,836 miles and burned up 111,350 gallons of fuel.

While the Submarine Combat Pin was not authorized, Nace was praised by his superiors for a thorough and aggressive patrol and a well-conducted gun attack on the two picket boats; the *Rasher* was given credit for sinking one and damaging the other. After reading Nace's descriptions of lifeguard communications difficulties, Capt. Charles W. "Weary" Wilkins, CO of Submarine Squadron Twelve, recommended joint communications schools for aircraft and submarine personnel. (The war would be over before the schools could be set up.)

Captain Vernon. L. "Rebel" Lowrance, CO of Submarine Division 121, added his personal endorsement to Nace's report:

> The administrative Division Commander congratulates the commanding officer, officers and crew for the completion of a long and arduous patrol and regrets that more enemy targets were not available to this splendid fighting ship.

As a rookie skipper, Nace had done an excellent job, given the difficulties he faced. Said Lowrance:

> The patrol was carried out in a thorough and aggressive manner but unfortunately, resulted in few torpedo target contacts. The majority of the patrol was spent in lifeguard duty.

The *Rasher* was turned over to the refit crew of the tender *Griffin*. Ashore, shipmates said their goodbyes; with the war drawing to a close, it would be the last time many of them would see each other. After normal rotations, the only members of the original commissioning crew that remained were Pete Sasgen, Max Lytle, Chester Kenrich, Charlie Reuff, Len Peterson, and John Owens. Of all the men who had served in the *Rasher*, only Sasgen and Lytle would be able to boast that they had been aboard on all eight war patrols—a singular distinction and rare circumstance in the submarine navy.

◆ ◆ ◆

By late spring of 1945, ComSubPac, with Admiral Lockwood as the prime mover, had finalized plans—code-named Operation Barney—to penetrate the last bastion of the Japanese Empire: the Sea of Japan. The problem, as always, was how to get in and get out safely, for the way was blocked by formidable minefields.

Several points of entry and exit existed, most of them unsuitable for one reason or another. The Tatar Strait in the far north was icebound much of the year. When not frozen, transit was forbidden because it lay in Soviet territorial waters and the Soviet Union was still neutral in the Pacific War. La Pérouse Strait, where the *Wahoo* had been lost on an earlier foray, was not only mined but heavily patrolled by enemy ships and aircraft. Because it was used by Russian shipping as a route from the Sea of Okhotsk to Vladivostok, its use posed political problems as well. Farther south, both the Tsugaru Strait and Shimonoseki Strait were narrow, heavily fortified, and heavily mined deathtraps. That left the Tsushima Straits, the narrow waterway located between Kyushu and the Korean Peninsula.

The key to the operation would be the newly developed mine-detecting QLA sonar gear. Lockwood believed that a small group of submarines equipped with the apparatus and operated by properly trained crews could locate the mines, slip through the Tsushima Straits into the Sea of Japan, raise havoc with shipping, then make a quick escape on the surface through La Pérouse. The Russians, Lockwood sniffed, could protest all they wanted about territorial sovereignty.

The hunting promised to be good in the Sea of Japan, but the real value of the operation, Lockwood maintained, was the terrific psychological blow it would deal to the enemy. It would demonstrate that no part of the Empire was safe from attack. He hoped it would torpedo whatever confidence the Japanese people retained in their leaders.

Parallel to the Sea of Japan submarine operation, plans were being implemented for an attack on the Japanese mainland by Adm. William F. "Bull" Halsey's Third Fleet. The armada would sortie from Leyte Gulf on 1 July. Battleships would bombard targets ashore while naval aircraft attacked cities on Honshu and Hokkaido, including Tokyo. The attacks would be the preamble to the invasion of Japan itself.

While these plans were refined and the forces gathered, scientists in Alamogordo, New Mexico, prepared to detonate an atomic bomb.

For the submarine force, the unrestricted war of attrition against Japan was virtually over. The once-busy merchant shipping lanes of the Southwest Pacific were no more. Routes from Singapore, Halmahera, Luzon, Surabaya, Celebes, Ambon, and Tokyo were merely faded lines on Imperial maps. Thousands of malaria-ridden Japanese troops awaited rescue on remote islands that the American advance had bypassed. Tons of materiel and food lay mouldering in abandoned staging areas because there were no *marus* left to carry them home. So sparse were submarine targets that only four enemy vessels, totaling barely 4,000 tons, were sunk in all of May 1945. By the middle of June only one sizable ship had been sunk. (How many sampans, luggers, and coastal craft were sunk could only be guessed at.) The once-ubiquitous *marus* had literally vanished from the sea: those few naval vessels still afloat were low on fuel and ammunition and without sailors to man them. Yet even in the face of imminent destruction of all that was left of their army, navy, and homeland, the leaders in Tokyo equivocated rather than capitulating.

Submarines dispatched for lifeguard duty were being heavily armed for surface gun attacks on the sampan fleets along the coasts of China and Japan. These motley craft were the last purveyors of food and vital supplies to the Empire. Thus, when the *Rasher* stood out of the lagoon at Midway bound for Saipan on 23 June 1945, she had two potent 40-millimeter guns mounted fore and aft on her conning tower. She was now one of Fife's submersible gunboats.

With the war rushing to conclusion, Nace set a course due west.

The Setting Sun

On the way to Saipan, Nace conducted daily training dives and fire-control drills. Balloons were sent aloft from the bridge and the gun crews shot them down. The drills were taken seriously; they were essential, especially for the new men. But there was less urgency about them than there might have been had the Japanese still posed a serious threat. In fact, along the way calls were exchanged with U.S. submarines operating freely on the surface heading to and from Saipan and Guam, a sure sign that the Pacific was indeed an American lake.

Meanwhile, Chuck Nace continued his cribbage tutelage under Pete Sasgen and was on his way to rehabilitating his wardroom reputation at the board.

> He taught me the fine points of the game and in effect made me a little more "street smart." Pete had some great expressions for developing me to a higher plane of gamesmanship such as "peer-less pegging," "cagey crib," and "clever cut." But while he raised the caliber of my play so that I became competitive in the ward-room, I don't recall that I ever beat him.

Sasgen was a good teacher—but not too good.

On 2 July 1945, the *Rasher* moored alongside the submarine tender *Orion* in Tanapag Harbor, Saipan. Nace reported to the operations office and received his patrol orders. Destination: the waters off southern Formosa. Mission: lifeguard duty for the Luzon-based planes hammering the island. Not what he had hoped for, but important duty nonetheless. Minor voyage repairs were completed in one day, and the *Rasher* departed for her assigned station in company with the *Sea Fox*.

On the eighth, she passed between Diogo and Batan Islands south of Formosa in the Luzon Strait. Nace radioed Task Force Seventy-one, under whose orders the *Rasher* was operating, that she was in position and requesting orders.

Just after midnight Task Force Seventy-one sent a reply: Report to Subic Bay in the Philippines for new orders.

◆ ◆ ◆

Subic was the bustling headquarters of the commands that had made up the former Fremantle and Brisbane submarine bases. It was a hot, humid jungle facility replete with malaria and monsoon rains. The harbor had been cleared of wreckage and sunken ships, and now repairs went on day and night. The rest camp, Camp Coe (named for Lt. Comdr. James W. Coe, lost with the *Cisco* in September 1943), was big and modern but surrounded by a sea of mud. Australia, the down-under paradise, was a world away and was sorely missed by the submariners.

When the *Rasher* joined the other boats alongside the sub tender *Gilmore*, Admiral Fife came aboard to meet Captain Nace and look over the famous *Rasher*. When he had last seen her in Brisbane, she was a new boat fresh from the States.

She was reassigned to Task Force Seventeen and issued a new set of operation orders. Her patrol station was now an area southwest of Formosa, where she would relieve the *Cabrilla* as a lifeguard. Nace was also apprised of the scope of U.S. fleet surface and air operations in the region so he could avoid blundering into a friendly task force and being attacked. (This had happened to four other boats, with near disastrous results.) There were also indications that Japanese fleet units might make a final all-out *banzai* attack, though it was not likely to come in the Formosa area. Nevertheless, all submarines were ordered to be on the alert.

Fife himself supplied Nace with one last-minute piece of information. There was the possibility a Japanese submarine might be encountered near Takao, Formosa. The Japanese were using their boats to evacuate high-ranking military personnel from territories in the south, and Fife told him to keep his eyes open.

◆ ◆ ◆

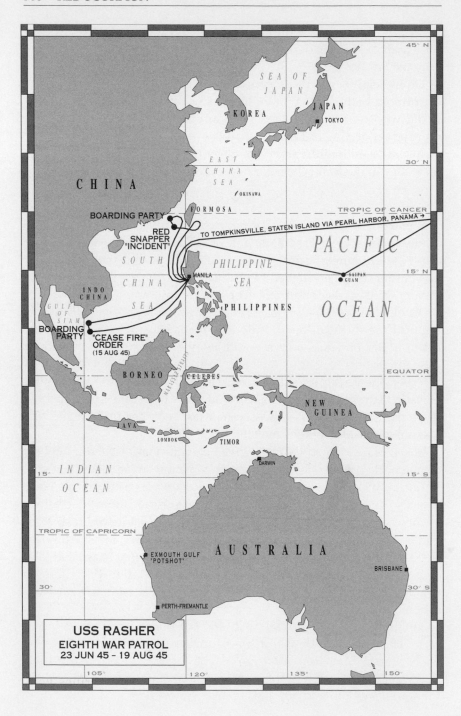

45° N

SEA OF
JAPAN

KOREA   JAPAN

TOKYO

30° N

EAST
CHINA
SEA

CHINA

OKINAWA

FORMOSA   TROPIC OF CANCER

BOARDING PARTY   PACIFIC

RED
SNAPPER   TO TOMPKINSVILLE, STATEN ISLAND VIA PEARL HARBOR, PANAMA →
"INCIDENT"

SOUTH   PHILIPPINE

CHINA   SEA   MANILA   SAIPAN   15° N
                                                    GUAM
INDO
CHINA   SEA

GULF   PHILIPPINES   OCEAN
OF
SIAM

BOARDING
PARTY   "CEASE FIRE"
ORDER
(15 AUG 45)

BORNEO   CELEBES   EQUATOR

NEW
GUINEA

JAVA

LOMBOK   TIMOR

INDIAN   DARWIN   15° S

OCEAN

TROPIC OF CAPRICORN

AUSTRALIA

EXMOUTH GULF
"POTSHOT"
                                                BRISBANE

30°   30° S

PERTH-FREMANTLE

USS RASHER
EIGHTH WAR PATROL
23 JUN 45 – 19 AUG 45

105°   120°   135°   150°

En route to the patrol area, Nace was determined to remain on the surface as much as possible to increase area coverage and to facilitate communications with the Air Force and ComSubPac. On 13 July, the *Rasher* arrived on station twenty miles south of Formosa in the Bashi Channel and settled into the numbing routine of a lifeguard.

Voice communications were established with her air cover, a PBY. Then came the wait as the Fifth Air Force pounded what was left of the Japanese air force and its bases in and around Takao and Tainan. Early in the afternoon, the *Rasher*'s air cover informed her that no U.S. planes were down and that her services would not be needed until the next day. With that, Nace moved eastward to patrol.

The next two days were uneventful. Air raids started early and were over by afternoon. No planes were lost. The nightly Foxes sometimes sparked a little interest. One advised that the Japanese submarine, an I-boat, was heading for Takao, and the *Rasher* should be alert. But it provided no time or date for the sub's arrival.

From late evening until the next morning, Nace patrolled the waters west of Formosa up to the Pescadores Islands, which sat like sentinels in the mouth of the strait. He idled in the area, sometimes submerged, sometimes on the surface, all day in hopes the submarine or a ship might appear. But nothing was seen except a small sampan.

The next day, the fifteenth, was also uneventful. Two Japanese PT boats were sighted sweeping a channel from Takao south at high speed, but they did not come near.

Since there were no calls for the *Rasher*'s services, Nace patrolled from Takao southwest in the direction of Pratas Reef and then doubled back. To pass the time, sailors turned to submarine qualification studies, routine maintenance, card games, and extra sack time. The officers gathered in the wardroom for the *Rasher* cribbage championship.

Lt. (j.g.) Howard Geer was a participant in these hard-fought battles:

> The big talk and ribbing that went on were beyond description. Pete Sasgen's claim to the championship of the Southwest Pacific was hotly contested by whoever he was playing with. When a breakdown occurred in the engine room, he was out like a shot and everyone knew that all would be well. Pete's puns, which were many, spiced up the atmosphere but were always greeted by loud groans. What a personality!

Nace was pegging madly around the board when he got a call: "Captain, we've got a ship in sight!"

The *Rasher* was northbound, seventeen miles west of Takao, when a smoke smudge 35,000 yards away was spotted through the high periscope by a sharp-eyed quartermaster. Nace ordered the ship to battle stations and commenced tracking.

It was a *maru*. From the vessel's position to port, it appeared she had come out of the Pescadores Channel heading for Takao, which put her on a base course of 150.

"Come to course three-zero-zero, all ahead full!" Nace ordered.

Two more engines rolled over on the starting bottles and rumbled to life; the *Rasher*'s wake churned up froth as she swung onto her new heading and picked up speed.

The *maru* zigged left, then left again, making for the harbor at Takao. Nace altered course to close as rapidly as possible. But since the sun had not yet set, and with landfall only minutes away, he knew they would have to dive or risk being sighted. The *Rasher* pressed in until the coast was only ten miles distant, then dove. When Sound reported a pair of high-speed screws, Nace raised the periscope to see what was going on.

> Sighted two PT boats, range about 7,000 yards, headed NW in the general direction of the target. They were making 15 knots. These were the same boats we saw yesterday. It appeared they may be going out to bring the ship in and so we continued to close the track on which they had come out. We continued to search for the target but never saw him again. It was getting dark rapidly now, but a half-moon would enable us to see anything that came by.

Nace caught a glimpse of the PT boats heading toward shore.

> PTs passed us at 2,000 yards and we tracked them at 15 knots. It appears they either went out to tell our target of our presence or else were looking for us, as we were probably sighted from the beach before we submerged.

Nace searched for the target, but she had vanished into the night.

◆ ◆ ◆

The next day was uneventful. The *Rasher* provided lifeguard services on the eighteenth, but no planes went down. Afterward, Nace decided to move around to the east coast of Formosa again, and the next morning the *Rasher* ran up the coastline three miles from the beach. But other than an occasional small boat, the area was absolutely deserted.

The long, boring days consisted of trim dives, exercises, and an occasional battle surface drill to fire the guns. Nace moved back over to the west coast of Formosa to patrol. More empty seas. The Fifth Air Force seemed to have forgotten all about the *Rasher*. Radio traffic was filled with routine messages, but none were addressed to her. The diesel engines droned on hour after hour. Time stood still. Nace recalled:

> For sure we did a lot of surface running during this patrol and without question the Japanese knew we were out there. They just didn't have adequate forces to constantly stay on top of us and keep us down. At this stage of the war, their total military resources in Formosa were probably ebbing rapidly. The noose was closing slowly but surely.

The *Rasher* surfaced from a trim dive late in the afternoon of 28 July. She was midway between the coasts of China and Formosa. With two engines on propulsion, a course was shaped for the strait while thoughts turned toward the evening meal. The exec's voice on the bridge speaker broke the reverie. He advised the skipper that the periscope watch had spotted masts ten miles away. Nace stationed the tracking party, and five minutes later the target developed into a sailing junk heading east. More speed was rung up, and the *Rasher* was swung toward it. Nace ordered battle stations surface. In short order, ammunition was passed up, small arms broken out, and the 40-millimeter guns manned.

The skipper decided to come alongside and board the vessel. A boarding party was quickly organized, armed, and told to stand by in the conning tower as the *Rasher* overtook the junk.

She was a badly weathered craft with bluff lines, a high poop, and overhanging stem. Two Chinese flags flew from the stays. Nace angled the *Rasher* in toward her and fired a few 40-millimeter rounds across her bow. The frightened crew immediately doused the sails.

Boarding such a vessel demanded expert seamanship in close quarters to prevent damage to the submarine's hull. Nace reported:

> Came alongside junk and sent boarding party over. There was a crew of nine men aboard and at least six were definitely Chinese.

The other three men were of questionable character. None spoke English. There was nothing aboard in the way of cargo, charts, etc. There appeared to be no food aboard, so we left them two bags of canned goods.

Pete Sasgen was in charge of the boarding party. When he and his shipmates went over, they kept their eyes and ears open for trouble.

I wore a pair of shorts and a .45 and sheath knife on my belt. I was 225 pounds, over six feet tall and must have looked like a giant to them. The skipper said that if he had to dive while we were aboard the junk, to stay aboard and he would return as soon as possible. I told him I'd get back aboard the sub if I had to climb down the periscope.

After the inspection, the *Rasher* backed off and headed east toward Takao.

Following the successful test of the atomic bomb in the New Mexico desert on 16 July 1945, the nuclear triggers for two bombs were delivered by the cruiser *Indianapolis* to a secret B-29 unit, the 509th Composite Group, at North Field on Tinian. The bombs were assembled, then scientists and aircrews stood by for orders from Washington. The Japanese were warned of the consequences if they did not soon surrender unconditionally, as demanded by the Potsdam Declaration of 26 July.

◆ ◆ ◆

Late in the day on the twenty-ninth, the seas began making up. And for the next two days the weather was squally and overcast. Junks and sampans vanished. Once or twice a day SD radar contacts were made on unseen, unidentified aircraft. On 1 August, the *Rasher* dutifully orbited a Fifth Air Force lifeguard station in rough weather for two hours. Then Nace went back to the tedium of patrolling west of Formosa.

Shortly after the noon meal on the fourth, another junk was sighted. Again the word for battle stations surface was passed. The *Rasher* moved in; Nace ordered a 5-inch shell fired across her bow. When the junk's crew saw a water spout erupt close aboard, they lowered the sails and ran up a Chinese flag.

The captain did not call away a boarding party this time, but he looked things over as the submarine came alongside.

> There was nothing on board except a pile of fishing nets. They were very humble, on their knees, and by sign language indicated that they needed water. Gave them food and water and departed friends.
>
> We also made a swap, giving them some old khaki uniforms in exchange for a good size load of red snappers which I knew were good eating from my experiences in Key West in the old R 2.

That evening a delicious meal of red snapper fillet was served up. Captain Nace knew how to run a submarine.

The *Rasher* continued her patrol west of Formosa.

The nightly Foxes had two messages for the *Rasher*. One of them brought cheers: Task Force Seventeen advised that she would be relieved by the *Cobia* in three more days, 8 August, and would return to Subic Bay. The second message said the Fifth Air Force needed her services thirty miles south of Formosa.

Would the war last three more days? That was the question on everyone's mind as the *Rasher* came about and headed south. Armed Forces Radio news reports vividly described the decimation of Japan's military and the destruction of her cities by incendiary raids.

The *Rasher's* track took her toward Mao-pi T'ou, the southern peninsula of Formosa. Pete Sasgen had the watch at 2052 when a problem developed.

> It was customary for the cooks to place the garbage in gunny sacks weighted with tin cans and used engine parts to ensure the bags would sink so the enemy wouldn't know we were in the vicinity. At night on the 1800-2000 watch, they would request permission to come on the bridge to dump garbage.
>
> I had the watch this particular night and we were on a zigzag course. When turning to starboard, the garbage was dumped on the starboard side and when turning to port, it was dumped on the port side to prevent it from getting caught in the ship's screws. They made the mistake of dumping on the wrong side and one of the bags became entangled in the port screw. The entire boat vibrated

and I immediately shut down the port propeller shaft. Captain Nace came topside immediately and asked what happened. After explaining, he attempted to free the propeller without success. I told him I'd go over the side and cut the bag loose. He agreed and I stripped to my shorts with a belt and knife. [With the ship] laying dead in the water, I dove over the side and cut the bag free.

After that, the ship was maneuvered at various speeds to check things out. Everything seemed normal, though the noise level from the port propeller was reported higher than usual. But Nace felt the situation did not warrant heading for Subic early with a casualty.

◆ ◆ ◆

At 0245 on 6 August 1945, the *Enola Gay*, a B-29 piloted by Col. Paul Tibbets Jr., took off from Tinian with an atomic bomb aboard. His target was Hiroshima, Japan. At 0815, the bomb was dropped over the city. At an altitude of 1,890 feet it exploded with the force of 20,000 tons of TNT and devastated nearly five square miles. At approximately 1100 Washington time, the White House press secretary made the announcement. Returning from the Potsdam Conference aboard the cruiser *Augusta*, President Truman had received a coded strike message from Tinian. Exultant, he eagerly awaited the Japanese response.

◆ ◆ ◆

Off the coast of Formosa, the night of 6 August was clear and dark. Suddenly, two explosions boomed astern, and twin plumes of water flew in the air. A huge Japanese flying boat roared up the *Rasher*'s port side: it was low enough for the watchstanders on the bridge to see its markings and the blue exhaust flames flickering from its engine nacelles. The bombs did no damage, but it was a reminder that the war was not over yet.

We had no indication of airborne radar, our SD was secured, and our SJ was being operated intermittently [Nace reported]. We have had good results picking up planes with our SJ, but missed this one.

After the *Rasher* reached her station, the Air Force cancelled the day's strike.

The final lifeguard call came on the eighth. The *Rasher* was on her way to her station off Mao-pi T'ao in seas turned rough by a typhoon passing to the west when a twin-engine fighter plane was spotted diving out of the clouds, closing fast. While the boat was passing thirty feet on a hard dive, the pilot dropped two bombs. They missed by a wide mark. Nace, watching the plane through the periscope, could see that it had dropped its payload and was headed back to Formosa, so he surfaced the boat and stood in to their station. When the B-17 air cover informed the *Rasher* there was no work for her, Nace quit the area and headed for Subic Bay.

The patrol was over, but he was not happy.

> On the way back to Subic, I agonized over the fact that we had nothing to show for our long patrol. And so I requested a short stopover period in the Gulf of Siam on the way south to Australia. I wanted to give our crew an opportunity to see some sort of action and hopefully gain for those who had not made earlier patrols the authorization to wear the submarine combat insignia. My request was granted.

◆ ◆ ◆

On 9 August 1945, *Bock's Car*, a B-29 piloted by Maj. Charles Sweeney, lifted off from Tinian with an atomic bomb, nicknamed "Fat Man." It was even more powerful than the one used on Hiroshima. Sweeney's primary target was Kokura, but weather conditions forced him to make the drop on his secondary target, Nagasaki, instead. The blast leveled about 44 percent of the city. Despite this destruction, Gen. Korechika Anami, the war minister, and his two chiefs of staff, Gen. Yoshijiro Umezu and Adm. Teijiro Toyoda, were determined to fight to the death: they believed the unconditional surrender demanded by the Allies was too dishonorable.

◆ ◆ ◆

The *Rasher* rendezvoused with the destroyer escort *Woodson* and the submarine *Boarfish* on 10 August. Together they entered Subic Bay.

The submariners knew the war was drawing to a close. Yet their emotions were mixed. Despite the satisfaction of having defeated the enemy, there was the empty feeling that came from returning with full torpedo loads at both ends of the boat. However, because Nace was as eager as any man aboard to add another Japanese ship to the *Rasher*'s superb record, there was the prospect of one more opportunity. Morale soared. While the *Rasher* was refueled and reprovisioned, rumors of large-scale attacks on Hiroshima and Nagasaki and of peace overtures were thick. But there was also sobering talk of an impending—and bloody—amphibious assault on the home islands. In the afternoon, celebratory gunfire erupted from the ships in the harbor when a false alarm spread through the base that the war was over. J. P. Paris was among those who thought it was.

> A group of us younger ones were partying at a place in the end of the bay when we got the word. We went back to the ship and most all of the crew was back so we celebrated most of the night on deck. Early the next morning Captain Nace had us awakened with the news that war was not over and we were shipping out on patrol immediately.

Nace had the *Rasher* back at sea the next day, 11 August, headed southwest at full speed, hoping to get on station before world events overtook her. The Gulf of Siam lay between the coasts of Cambodia, Siam, and the Burma-Malay peninsula. Not many boats had operated there during the war because the gulf was so shallow. It was also mined. But Nace wanted one last shot.

◆ ◆ ◆

In Washington, the President and his advisers waited for word from Tokyo. Finally, a message arrived via the Swiss saying the Japanese would consider surrender if the Emperor was neither dethroned nor charged with war crimes. But the twelfth and thirteenth passed without a definitive answer for the Allies. At the last minute several members of the Emperor's cabinet had balked. Admiral Toyoda was one of those who held out. He reasoned that the Emperor, being a living god, could not be subordinated to a position of capitulation to mere mortals. Unimpressed, President Truman ordered the resumption of B-29 raids.

◆ ◆ ◆

Since it was a three-day run to the Gulf of Siam, there was some urgency to the *Rasher*'s last mission. On the morning of the fourteenth (the thirteenth, east of the International Date Line) she was a hundred miles southeast of Cochin China.

◆ ◆ ◆

Reporters jammed the White House press room on 14 August 1945, waiting for an announcement. Throughout Washington, expectant crowds gathered in the summer heat. Lafayette Square was filled with thousands of people keeping a vigil. A message from the Japanese government, one that had been drafted only after the Emperor himself had taken the initiative and overruled his still-divided ministers, arrived at 1605. The Swiss charge d' affaires in Washington delivered the text of the message to Secretary of State James Byrnes, who took it at once to the President. At 1700, Truman announced what the world had been waiting to hear: the Japanese had surrendered. The war was over.

◆ ◆ ◆

15 August 1945

> 1200(I) Position
> Lat. 7-33 N
> Long. 107-23 E
> Patrolling in the SIAM GULF

0725 Submerged 8 miles north of GREAT REDANG ISLAND.

0925 Sighted sail bearing 339°T.

1010 Surfaced. Headed for sailing junk sighted at 0925.

1023 Went to battle stations surface.

1031 Fired 2 shots across bow of sailing junk. Junk doused his sails.

1036 Came alongside junk and sent boarding party over. Discovered cargo of rice aboard and commenced to jettison same. The crew of the junk was composed of Malayans, and their papers indicated they were working for the Japs.

1101 Sighted 2 planes bearing 180°T, range 12 miles. Cleared the bridge.

1120 Planes out of sight, commenced circling junk and forced natives to jettison the remainder of the cargo which amounted to about 2 tons of rice.

1235 Headed up the GULF OF SIAM toward the fishing fleets.

1400 Received serial Love from CTF 71.

CEASE OFFENSIVE OPERATIONS AGAINST JAPANESE FORCES X CONTINUE SEARCH AND PATROLS X MAINTAIN DEFENSIVE AND INTERNAL SECURITY MEASURES AT HIGHEST LEVEL AND BEWARE OF TREACHERY OR LAST MOMENT ATTACKS BY ENEMY FORCES OR INDIVIDUALS

It was over. Aboard the *Rasher*, jubilation broke out. Some men wept. Chuck Nace remembered:

We were cruising on the surface, looking forward to our forthcoming trip "down under" to the west coast of Australia since it was now apparent there were no targets in this area worthy of a torpedo or gun action. When the message arrived that the Japanese had surrendered, it brought forth a great mixture of emotions. I can remember being a little shocked and unbelieving at first. How could it have ended so quickly? We knew about the attacks on Hiroshima and Nagasaki, but we knew nothing at all about the atomic bomb. So we were expecting a long and bloody invasion of Japan. But when it sank in that it was truly over, everyone was absolutely ecstatic. It meant that we were going home. It had been a long war and for many of the old-timers on board, it seemed they had been fighting this war for most of their lives.

My deepest feelings when it finally sank in were very much the same as every member of the crew. I had some other thoughts but they did not override the homeward bound ones. I said to myself, here I am a professional naval officer in command of a submarine in the combat area; this may be the most exciting job I will ever have for the rest of my Navy career. What could surpass this?

Pete Sasgen's feelings were similar.

For me the end of the war brought no particular elation, joy, or celebration. Maybe it was because we were so successful on our eight patrols and assured of finishing off the Japs. Oh yes, congratulations were in order aboard ship among the officers and crew for a job well done. The skipper issued a ration of hospital brandy to each crew member. The thing utmost in our minds was that the war was over; we could relax and look forward to going home to our families.

Others were giddy with joy. But after the initial euphoria wore off, the veterans reflected on the terrible losses the submarine force had suffered. For many of them it meant the deaths of shipmates and close friends. For Chuck Nace, it was the loss of Naval Academy classmates and officers and men with whom he had "grown up" in submarines.

In forty-four months of combat operations, the force had lost fifty-two submarines and more than 3,500 officers and enlisted men, a higher percentage of personnel than any other branch of the military service. But the submarine force had dealt the Japanese a blow far out of proportion to its size: 1,323 ships totaling 5.6 million tons had been sent to the bottom.

A day or two after the cease-fire order, Task Force Seventy-one began pulling the boats back from their patrol areas. To Nace's consternation, the *Rasher* was recalled to Subic Bay.

> I reached the conclusion that this foray into the Gulf of Siam was one of those times when I shouldn't have volunteered for a damn thing.
>
> There we were about half way around the world and a smidgen north of the equator. The instructions we received were for all submarines north of the equator to proceed to Subic Bay; those south to Australia.
>
> I pleaded our case, pointing out that my crew had been to two advanced bases in a row, but to no avail. It was back to Subic for the RASHER.

In busy Subic Bay, the *Rasher* joined dozens of submarines tied up in nests alongside the tenders, the boats flying their battle flags and coxcombs in a colorful victory display. Submariners visited each other and relaxed on deck in the sun and swapped war stories.

Nace, meanwhile, wrapped up his patrol report and submitted it to the CO of Submarine Squadron Twenty-two, Comdr. Edward S. Hutchinson, the *Rasher*'s first skipper. Thus had the war come full circle. Her eighth and final war patrol report ended simply:

> 19 August 1945
> > 1200(I) Position
> > Subic Bay
> 0915   Moored to U.S.S. GILMORE.

A proud Hutchinson attached his endorsement to the report:

> Commander Submarine Squadron Twenty-two takes great pleasure in welcoming the U.S.S. RASHER alongside and with the greatest of pride congratulates the Commanding Officer, officers and men in the RASHER's outstanding contribution to the successful conclusion of the war.
>
> > > > > > E. S. Hutchinson

After completing minor repairs, the men waited impatiently for a flotilla of boats to assemble for the trip home. Subic itself had little to offer a restless submariner. After the obligatory trip to Manila to view the unbelievable devastation visited on the Philippine capital and take a few tourist snapshots, sailors hung around the ship restlessly awaiting departure orders.

When the time came to select a homecoming port in the United States, Nace asked the chief of the boat to canvass the crew and report to him their first choice from the list of cities available. It was unanimous: New Orleans. But when Nace submitted his request he was promptly turned down. Berths in New Orleans, he was informed, were already filled by boats with skippers senior to him. There were few, if any, skippers junior to Nace. Still, he got his second choice: New York City. When he announced their destination to a crew with a hankering for home, the men, though disappointed, were anxious to get under way.

On 3 September 1945, surrender documents were signed aboard the battleship *Missouri* in Tokyo Bay. The following day the *Rasher*, in company with the tender *Orion* and thirteen submarines, departed Subic for the long trip to the States via Pearl Harbor and the Panama Canal.

The voyage gave all hands ample time to relax and to anticipate the joyous reunions that awaited them at home. Everyone was in high spirits. Sasgen, a little 35-millimeter folding camera in hand, clambered through the ship snapping pictures and clowning with the men he'd come to know so intimately and with whom he had shared the greatest adventure imaginable.

In no time at all, Mauna Kea, Hawaii, appeared on the horizon to the southeast. The fleet of submarines met their escort off Ewa Beach in Mamala Bay and glided into Pearl Harbor. The base was alive with activity. More than half the Pacific Fleet was assembled there undergoing demobilization and overhaul. Already a steady procession of warships was headed for the West Coast to disembark crews, the ships to be mothballed.

A band was on hand at the submarine base piers to greet the boats. It was a short layover. Reprovisioned and refueled, the boats were serenaded again the next day as they left. For the submarines heading for the West Coast, the band played "California Here I Come"; for those heading to the East Coast, it was "Give My Regards to Broadway."

At sea again, east of Pearl, Sasgen could feel the war, the Navy, and the submarine he loved and had served on for twenty-nine months all slipping away. And he reflected on the quintessential spirit, the compelling essential character, at the heart of wartime submarine service.

There is a certain feeling that comes over you when you are standing the midnight to 4 AM watch on the bridge of a submarine in the
Pacific Ocean, miles from land. It is absolutely dark, no lights to be
seen except the bright stars overhead like the Southern Cross which
you feel you can reach up and touch. At first you feel so small and
insignificant in this great body of water with no sound except the
occasional splashing of water along the hull and the muffled roar of
the diesel exhaust.

Then you realize you must make the correct decisions at all times.
There is no time for daydreaming. You must be fully alert. The safety of the boat and the 80 men aboard are depending on you. This
gives you a feeling of pride and inner strength because you have
achieved this position of responsibility through your own efforts.
And you believe you can lick the whole Jap navy by yourself.

This overarching sense of personal responsibility and self-reliance
was a principle Sasgen and many of his shipmates would cherish for
the rest of their lives.

The *Rasher* cut southeast, traversing the vast Central Pacific Basin.
At night, she and her companions steamed with running lights
ablaze, an experience totally foreign for men used to stealth and con-
cealment. Skirting the coasts of Mexico, Honduras, Nicaragua, and
Costa Rica, the boats entered the Gulf of Panama.

Right on schedule, the *Rasher* arrived in Balboa. As a brand new
ship from Wisconsin, she and her young crew had undergone combat
training here two years earlier. Now, after a hearty liberty in Panama,
her war veterans topped off her tanks and enjoyed the slow, lazy passage through the canal to Coco Solo.

Once in the Caribbean, the *Rasher* struck out on the final 2,400-mile
leg to New York Harbor. Nace steered her east through the pass
between Santo Domingo and Puerto Rico, where once Sir Francis
Drake had hunted Spanish galleons. From there her rhumb line lay
slightly west of due north up the coast of the United States. For Nace
and his crew, it was the longest part of the trip. They were headed for
Tompkinsville, Staten Island, where a shore command had been
established to service the many submarines coming into New York.

As the boats swept north through the chilly Atlantic Ocean the
radiomen piped in commercial radio stations over the 1MC, priming
the sailors for their stateside arrival with advertisements for soap
powders and headache remedies and the latest popular music.

North of Atlantic City, New Jersey, the *Rasher* picked up the twin
lights at Atlantic Highlands and made the final course adjustment at

Sandy Hook for the turn into New York's Lower Bay. To the right was Brooklyn; dead ahead, The Narrows between Fort Hamilton and Fort Wadsworth. Beyond, up the Hudson River, stood the Statue of Liberty and the mighty spires of Manhattan.

Now the long voyage from Manitowoc to Brisbane, Ambon, and Fremantle; Darwin to Halmahera, the Celebes, the Makassar and Lombok Straits; Luzon, Formosa, and the Kii Suido, and every imaginable place in between was almost over.

It was a chilly and dreary October morning when the *Rasher* put in. Steam from the diesels' exhaust fled on wind gusts whipping off The Narrows to the Bay Street waterfront's tangle of wharves and barges. When she reached the Navy piers, Nace took a hard look at the murky water rushing by.

> The current was running strong and it would make turning into the narrow slips a hazardous operation. I knew one of my former skippers in the old R 2 would be on the dock since he was assigned to the submarine command in Tompkinsville, so I got ready to make my best landing ever.
>
> Actually we had to go like hell to keep from getting swept down the river, but we knifed on in and then that great bunch of electricians in the maneuvering room gave me the big backing bell we needed and made me look good.

After two and a half years of dodging Japanese planes and depth charges, the *Rasher* was home safe and sound. From fitting out to Tompkinsville, she had steamed 122,655 nautical miles.

A wonderful surprise awaited Chuck Nace.

> As the line handlers sprang into action, I was able to finally divert my eyes for a few seconds and lo and behold, standing there was my little bride, Pat.

For the skipper, his crew, and the USS *Rasher*, the war was truly over.

◆ ◆ ◆

Pete Sasgen lingered in the tiny stateroom he and another officer had shared. His gear was packed and deposited topside. He took one last look around to make sure he hadn't forgotten anything. Yes, he had his celebrated cribbage board. The photo of his wife and son he'd kept taped to his locker door for all those months was in his uniform breast pocket. The American flag flown from the conning tower staff when the *Rasher* entered Pearl Harbor from Subic Bay was folded regulation-style and tucked away in his bags. Satisfied that all was in order, he snatched his cap off his bunk and headed aft.

In the deserted control room he stood at the foot of the conning tower ladder and made a final inspection. How many times had he manned his battle station there? How often had the compartment been a blur of furious activity as Hutchinson, Laughon, Munson, Adams, and Nace barked orders? How many dives had he witnessed? Five hundred? Eight hundred? A thousand? He lingered briefly, musing on the places he'd seen, the battles he'd fought, the submarine he loved, and, most of all, the men who'd touched his life. Time to go. In one fluid motion he heaved himself up the ladder into the conning tower and went topside.

The submarine's black deck was wet with drizzle; a raw wind snapped the union jack. At the brow, Sasgen paused for a moment. Then he saluted the colors and went ashore, hefted his bags, and walked up the pier without so much as a backward glance. He never saw the *Rasher* again.

Epilogue

Hard by a pier jutting from the banks of a slough in Portland, Oregon, lay a black submarine. Time and the elements, to say nothing of faithful service as warship, radar picket boat, and training vessel, had not been kind. Now, she was an obsolete relic. Her curved ballast tanks were oil-canned, each frame standing out in bold relief like the ribs of a junkyard dog. Over the years she had suffered the indignities of coarse alterations and modifications. From her deck, hull, and superstructure sprouted odd brackets and crude stanchions welded on for some long-forgotten purpose. Cables and rusty wire rope were draped from lifelines; discarded gear and ground tackle lay about topside. Her streamlined conning tower had ugly little bridge wings to port and starboard, and the half-sphere of a plexiglass sprayshield was still in place. Big white numbers adorned her sail's waffled sides: "269."

Her 1940's fleet submarine profile—for that's what she was, despite the modern getup—was longer now than when she left the builder's yard many years ago. It would take a knowledgeable eye to discern the precise location of the thirty-foot section inserted into her hull when she was cut open to rearrange her guts. But a crusty old submariner, maybe one who remembered her glory years, would spot it in an instant. Despite the disfigurement it had wrought on her slim lines, he would no doubt find her beautiful still.

In late 1971 she lay in that backwater, unwanted, waiting to be towed to her last port for final disposition under the cutting torch. Soon she would be scrap for a steel mill somewhere in the world—maybe even, irony of ironies, in the very country whose merchant navy she once helped destroy.

But if you stood on her deck and listened closely, you could hear them—thrumming diesels and the roar of a klaxon. Look carefully and you could see it—a long, black, wraith-like shape knifing across the sea, its sibilant passage cleaving the surface. Then, with a swirl of bubbles and a whisper of foam, it swiftly disappeared beneath the waves, leaving not a trace.

Appendixes

Appendix 1

THE *RASHER*'S COMMANDING OFFICERS

EDWARD SHILLINGFORD HUTCHINSON
1904–1961
Commissioning and First War Patrol

Edward Shillingford Hutchinson was born in Philadelphia, Pennsylvania, on St. Valentine's Day, 1904. He was the son of a successful businessman and the grandson of Edward T. Stotesbury, a wealthy Pennsylvania industrialist.

An alumnus of Germantown Friends School, where he captained an undefeated football team in 1922, he was graduated from the United States Naval Academy in 1925. In 1938, he and Mary Elizabeth Lane of Paris, Texas, were married in Coco Solo in the Canal Zone.

Hutchinson skippered the *Grampus* and the *Rasher* and sank five Japanese ships in three war patrols. In November 1943, he became commanding officer of Submarine Squadron Twenty-two and joined the staff of Rear Adm. Ralph W. Christie, Commander Submarines Seventh Fleet.

After the war Hutchinson served in the office of the Chief of Naval Operations in Washington, D.C., rising to the rank of rear admiral. He retired in 1956. He won two Navy Crosses, the Legion of Merit, and a Presidential Unit Citation.

On 12 March 1961, at age fifty-seven, he died at Bethesda Naval Hospital. Admiral Hutchinson was buried with full military honors at Arlington National Cemetery.

WILLARD ROSS LAUGHON
1911–
Second, Third, and Fourth War Patrols

Willard Ross Laughon was born in Princeton, West Virginia, on 29 January 1911. He entered the United States Naval Academy in 1929. Under his stern portrait in the "Lucky Bag" of 1933 it was noted that the young midshipman was well read, "his dissertations ranging from Aesop's Fables to Kant, expounded with cold logic, heated interest and an admirable choice of words." It was also noted that he had a good mind for the practical, especially for intricate electrical hookups.

Laughon's first tour of duty after graduation was aboard the battleship *Arkansas* on reserve cruises up and down the West Coast. In 1934, he was transferred to the *Idaho*. Two years later he married Alice Mellot of Salisbury, Maryland.

His next assignment was the Submarine School at New London, Connecticut, after which he reported for duty on the China Station in 1937. In 1940, he helped recommission the *R 1*. He made eight patrols with her out of Bermuda, the last four as her commanding officer. After PCO school he took command of the *Rasher* for three war patrols, during which he sank nine ships. Laughon was awarded two Navy Crosses, a Presidential Unit Citation, and two Commendation Ribbons.

In the summer of 1944, he was detached from the *Rasher* for a tour of duty with ComSubSeventhFlt. After Germany surrendered in May 1945, he was sent to Londonderry, Ireland, to bring back to the United States the *U-1407*, one of the German Type XVIIB Walter boats. Back in the United States, he worked on their evaluation. Later, he had a tour of duty with the University of Texas ROTC.

In 1948, he returned to submarine duty as Operations Officer of Submarine Squadron Four in Key West, Florida. In 1950 he joined the staff of Commander Second Fleet, then moved on to the position of Commander Landing Ship Flotilla Two at Little Creek, Virginia, where he attained the rank of captain.

After retiring from the Navy in 1963, Laughon and his wife moved to Stuart, Florida, and established Anchor Real Estate. Until recently he also operated Anchor Fishing Fleet, which had two 40-foot Sportfisherman boats.

A self-described workaholic, Captain Laughon is busy with many projects, among them a book he is planning to write about his submarine experiences.

HENRY GLASS MUNSON
1909–1975
Fifth War Patrol

Henry Glass Munson, one of the most highly decorated submarine officers of World War II, was born on 31 December 1909, in Manila, Philippine Islands.

Munson was descended from an illustrious family that included such luminaries as Lawrence Washington, the grandfather of the country's first president; Francis Lightfoot Lee, a signer of the Declaration of Independence; and Thomas Munson, who settled in the Bay Colony in 1621, founded the city of New Haven, Connecticut, and was the first warden of Yale College.

Henry Munson's maternal grandfather, Adm. Henry Glass, was commandant of the U. S. Naval Academy and later commanded the Asiatic Squadron. His father, Capt. Francis Merten Munson, conducted yellow fever experiments under Walter Reed and wrote a standard text on tropical diseases.

A Rhodes Scholar, Munson was educated at the U.S. Naval Preparatory School in San Diego, California, and was graduated third in his class from the Naval Academy in 1932. He received a master's degree in nuclear physics from California Polytechnic Institute in 1952.

In August of 1942, while in command of the *S 38*, he attacked a Japanese convoy and sank a troop transport, earning the nickname "Dead Eye." The other five ships in the convoy fled back to Rabaul, stymieing an attempt to reinforce the embattled garrison on Guadalcanal. Later, in command of the *Crevalle*, he sank two more Japanese ships.

But it was while in command of the *Rasher* during her famous fifth war patrol, when he sank four Japanese ships, including the escort carrier *Taiyo*, in a single engagement that Munson's reputation as a top sub skipper was forever fixed. Thus, his and the *Rasher*'s name are virtually synonymous, the two being among the top scorers in every category for tonnage and number of ships sunk. His combat decorations included three Bronze Stars, a Presidential Unit Citation, and three Navy Crosses. He was twice nominated for the Medal of Honor. Later, he was decorated by the governments of Japan, Korea, and Brazil.

After the war, Munson headed the school of electrical engineering at the submarine base in Groton, Connecticut. During his tenure he wrote what is considered the definitive text on fleet submarines. From 1952 to 1956, he was an assistant to Adm. Hyman Rickover and was responsible for the development of the Mark-45 torpedo and nuclear depth charge. Munson was a member of the team that planned and directed the first underwater circumnavigation of the North Pole by the nuclear submarine *Triton*. He then headed the technical group that investigated the loss of the *Thresher*. Munson was hydrographer of the Navy from 1957 to 1959 and, later, commodore of the Third Destroyer Squadron in the Pacific.

Upon retiring from the Navy with the rank of captain, he became a senior research associate in the advanced military weapons division at the David Sarnoff Laboratory of RCA, Princeton, New Jersey. In later years, he taught physics at the Princeton High School, where he developed an advanced course in college-level physics for gifted students.

Captain Munson died on 16 July 1975, at the age of sixty-five. He is survived by his wife, Anna Marie Munson; a son, Christopher James Munson; and a grandson. His ashes were placed beneath the high altar of St. Thomas Church on Fifth Avenue in New York City.

BENJAMIN ERNEST ADAMS JR.
1914–1965
Sixth War Patrol

Benjamin Ernest Adams Jr. was born in 1914. After graduating from the U.S. Naval Academy in 1935, he served aboard the battleship *Texas* until 1940. After graduating from submarine school he reported for duty aboard the submarine tender *Holland*. In 1943, he put the *Flier* in commission as her executive officer. He later was transferred to the *Albacore* as her executive officer, then took command of the *Rasher*.

After the war Adams completed a tour of duty at the Philadelphia Naval Shipyard. Subsequently he was assigned to the Far East as British liaison officer under ComNavFive. He served as assistant planning officer in the Thirteenth Naval District before going to the amphibious force flagship *Eldorado* as her executive officer. In 1955, he joined the staff of ComPhibPac in Coronado, California. He was awarded a Bronze Star with "V," a Presidential Unit Citation with star, and the Army Distinguished Unit Emblem.

Adams retired from the Navy in January 1957 with the rank of captain. He and his family settled in Guadalajara, Mexico, where he died on 14 January 1965 at the age of fifty-one. He was buried with full military honors at Arlington National Cemetery. He is survived by two daughters, Sara Catlett and Margaret Dudley, and a son, Benjamin Ernest.

CHARLES DERICK NACE
1917-
Seventh and Eighth War Patrols

Charles Derick Nace was born in Philadelphia, Pennsylvania, on 27 January 1917. He was graduated from the U.S. Naval Academy in 1939. He served aboard the battleship *California* until 1940. After a brief stint in the destroyer *Mugford*, he received orders to report to submarine school in New London, Connecticut. After graduation in March 1941, he served in the submarine *R 2* until 1943, when he was transferred to the *Cero*. He made six war patrols as her engineering officer and then executive officer.

In February 1945, he was assigned to Submarine Division 282 as a "prospective submarine commanding officer." He assumed command of the *Rasher* on 1 April and was her commanding officer for her final two war patrols and her return to the United States and decommissioning.

Nace was an instructor and head of the Electrical Department at the Submarine School until June of 1948, when he assumed command of the submarine *Ronquil*. From 1950 to 1953, he was attached to the Bureau of Naval Personnel in Washington, D.C., after which he attended the Armed Forces Staff College in Norfolk, Virginia. He joined Submarine Squadron One as operations officer and, in June 1954, became Commander Submarine Division Seventy-two. In 1955, he became operations officer on the staff of Commander Submarine Force Pacific Fleet.

Nace attended the National War College in Washington, D.C., then served as administrative aide and assistant for JCS matters to the Deputy Chief of Naval Operations (Plans and Policy). In 1960, he assumed command of the attack transport *Pickaway*. A year later, he was assigned to advanced studies at the Center for International Affairs, Harvard University. Upon completion of his program he was designated a Fellow of the Center.

His next assignment was in 1962, when he became Commander Submarine Flotilla Seven in Yokosuka, Japan. From 1964 to 1965, he saw duty in the Strategic Plans Division of the Office of the Chief of Naval Operations and with the office of the Secretary of the Navy's Retention Task Force.

Nace was selected for the rank of rear admiral in 1965. He was assigned to the Bureau of Naval Personnel as special assistant for retention matters and later became assistant chief of naval personnel for plans and programs. In 1967 he assumed command of Submarine Flotilla Two. He also served as the second senior member of the Court of Inquiry into the loss of the submarine *Scorpion* in 1968. In June 1969, he reported aboard as Commander of U.S. Naval Forces, Southern Command, in Panama.

Admiral Nace retired in 1971. His awards include the Distinguished Service Medal; the Legion of Merit; the Bronze Star with Gold Star and Combat "V"; the American Defense Service Medal; Asiatic-Pacific Campaign Medal with Silver Star (five operations); American Campaign Medal; World War II Victory Medal; National Defense Service Medal with Bronze Star; the Philippine Liberation Ribbon; the Philippine Republic Presidential Unit Citation Badge; and the Brazilian Navy Order of Merit.

Admiral Nace and his wife, Pat, presently live in Virginia Beach, Virginia. They have two daughters, Stephanie and Christine.

Appendix 2

WORLD WAR II U.S. SUBMARINE JANAC TONNAGE STATISTICS

Total tonnage sunk: 5,586,400 gross tons—merchant and naval.

Total merchant tonnage: 5,005,774 gross tons—1,178 ships over 500 gross tons displacement.

Total naval tonnage: 577,626 gross tons—214 ships, including 1 battleship, 4 aircraft carriers, 4 escort aircraft carriers, 3 heavy cruisers, 8 light cruisers, 43 destroyers, and 23 submarines.

Appendix 3

USS *RASHER* OFFICIAL STATISTICS, 1942–1971

Keel laid: 4 May 1942

Launched: 20 December 1942

Commissioned: 8 June 1943

Total number of war patrols: 8

Total number of days on patrol: 401

Total tonnage sunk: 99,901 (JANAC)

Tonnage damaged: 64,481 (ComSubPac)

Number of ships sunk: 18 (JANAC)

Special missions: Mine-laying off Cochin, China, 4 January 1944

Wolf packs: with *Bluefish*, January 1944; with *Raton*, February 1944; with *Bluefish*, August 1944; with *Finback* and *Pilotfish*, February–March 1945

Total nautical miles steamed: 122,655

Number of torpedoes fired: 165

Total number of dives: approximately 861

Decommissioned: 26 June 1946

Recommissioned: 22 July 1953, as SSR 269 (Migraine III radar picket conversion)

Decommissioned: 27 May 1967

Stricken: 20 December 1971

Appendix 4

USS *RASHER* PRESIDENTIAL UNIT CITATION

THE SECRETARY OF THE NAVY

WASHINGTON

      The President of the United States takes pleasure in presenting the PRESIDENTIAL UNIT CITATION to the

UNITED STATES SHIP RASHER

for service as set forth in the following

CITATION:

      "For outstanding performance in combat during her First, Third, Fourth and Fifth War Patrols in enemy Japanese-controlled waters. Operating dangerously in bold defiance of watchful and aggressive enemy air patrols, the U.S.S. RASHER penetrated deep into forward areas to cover the enemy's vital supply lanes, tracking her targets relentlessly and striking hard at heavily escorted convoys. Fiercely opposed by hostile air and surface units, she launched her torpedoes accurately despite unfavorable attack opportunities and inflicted tremendous losses on the Japanese in thousands of tons of valuable shipping sunk or damaged. Tenacious in pursuit, devastating in her fire-power and highly successful in evading the enemy's persistent depth-charging, the RASHER has given striking evidence of her own readiness for battle and of the gallant fighting spirit of her officers and men."

For the President,

James Forrestal

Secretary of the Navy

Appendix 5

USS *RASHER* CITATIONS AND AWARDS

Presidential Unit Citation for Patrols 1, 3, 4, 5

Seven Battle Stars: Patrols 1–5

Iwo Jima Operation; Okinawa Gunto Operation

Four Navy Crosses

Twelve Silver Stars

Sixteen Bronze Stars

Six letters of commendation

One Navy and Marine Corps Medal

One Legion of Merit

Appendix 6

USS *RASHER* JANAC TONNAGE TOTALS

Name	Type	Date	Tonnage
FIRST PATROL—HUTCHINSON			
1. *Kogane Maru*	Passenger-Cargo	9 October 1943	3,132
2. *Kenkoku Maru*	Cargo	13 October 1943	3,127
3. *Koryo Maru*	Tanker	31 October 1943	589
4. *Tango Maru*	Tanker	8 November 1943	2,046
SECOND PATROL—LAUGHON			
5. *Kiyo Maru*	Tanker	4 January 1944	7,251
THIRD PATROL—LAUGHON			
6. *Tango Maru*	Cargo	25 February 1944	6,200
7. *Ryusei Maru*	Passenger-Cargo	25 February 1944	4,797
8. *Nittai Maru*	Cargo	3 March 1944	6,484
9. *Nichinan Maru*	Cargo	27 March 1944	2,750
FOURTH PATROL—LAUGHON			
10. *Choi Maru*	Cargo	11 May 1944	1,074
11. *Anshu Maru*	Converted Gunboat	29 May 1944	2,601
12. *Shioya*	Tanker	8 June 1944	4,000
13. *Koan Maru*	Cargo	14 June 1944	3,183
FIFTH PATROL—MUNSON			
14. *Shiroganesan Maru*	Cargo	6 August 1944	4,739
15. *Eishin Maru*	Cargo	18 August 1944	542
16. *Teiyo Maru*	Tanker	19 August 1944	9,849
17. *Taiyo*	Escort Aircraft Carrier	18 August 1944	20,000
18. *Teia Maru*	Transport	19 August 1944	17,537
		Total	99,901

Appendix 7

USS *RASHER* CREW LIST

Following are the names and rank or rate of all personnel known to have served in the *Rasher* from commissioning in Manitowoc, Wisconsin, on 8 June 1943, to decommissioning in New London, Connecticut, on 26 June 1946. Those men who were members of the commissioning crew are noted with an *. Crew members who are known to be deceased are marked with a †.

ADAMS, Benjamin Ernest Jr. † .... LCDR
AHART, Joseph Leo Jr. † TM3c
AKINS, Harold Laddie * MoMM3
ANDRACHIK, Joseph M. * SM1c
ARCONA, Otto Milton Bkr3c

BALL, David * .... CCK
BARTOLUCCI, Joseph Raymond † SM3c
BASKETT, Reavis Porter TM1c
BAUER, Joseph LaVerne * EM1c
BAUN, Clyde Richard * GM2c
BENSON, Orville Clarence MoMM3c
BENTLEY, Neil Benjamin RT1c
BERG, Andrew Halfdon Jr. *† .... CRM
BILLBURG, Clarence D. † RT2c
BIRD, George Robert MoMM2c
BITTS, Paul D. F1c
BLACKWOOD, James Riggs FCS1c
BLATCHFORD, Donald B. MoMM3c
BOEHNE, Fred H. * S2c
BOLTON, Levi .... —
BOWDLER, Thomas W. E. .... LTJG
BRADY, Cyrus T. SM2c
BRANZELL, Howard Stratford SC1c
BREDING, Harold F RT2c
BREWER, James Robert * FCS2c
BROOKS, Dean Cline * RM1c
BROWN, David Paul * SC3c
BROWNING, James Auswell EM2c
BRYANT, Edward L. Ck3c
BURGIO, James R. S1c
BURR, Robert William * .... CSS

CAIN, Mat M. .... LCDR

CARBLOM, Vernon Ralph F2c
CARLSON, Albert Frank † MoMM2c
CARPER, Stanley Ray EM3c
CARTER, Burdell Richard S. * TM1c
CARTER, Ross Moore GM3c
CASHEL, Robert Lester EM3c
CASSELS, Kermit † .... CRM
CHAMBERS, Roy A. .... LT
CHAPPELL, Cluff Edward MoMM3c
CLAYPOOLE, Richard Ray FCS3c
COATES, Robert Louis F1c
COLEMAN, John Gilbert QM2c
CORLEY, Albert Julian TM1c
CUNNING, Ursle Floyd * EM1c

DAVIS, Waymon * StM1c
DEAN, Clifton L. F1c
DEARDORFF, Merril C. F1c
DENFELD, Robert Richard * MM1c
DREWRY, Alexander Moseley * S1c

EDWARDS, George Custis † .... CMoMM
EUSTACHE, Robert Lee TM2c

FENN, Arthur Ernest Jr. S1c
FEUERBERG, Myer S2c
FOLEY, William John FCS3c
FOX, Earl George SM3c
FRANK, Robert Bailey * MoMM1c
FRAZIER, Wesley Allen *† .... CTM
FUTRELL, Sysler Brown EM2c

GALLI, Ferdinand Alfred *† .... CGM
GARRETT, Ralph D. MoMM3c
GEER, Howard E. .... LTJG
GILSHENAN, Eugene Anthony Jr. MoMM1c
GIMBER, Stephen H. * † .... LCDR
GOETZ, Ralph D. S1c
GOODELL, Paul Richard S1c
GOODMAN, Albert Morris TM3c
GRAHAM, Warren Richard * EM1c
GREFE, Theodore F. *† .... LT
GRIGSBY, Leighton Francis † .... CMoMM

HARALBAKIS, Alexander S2c
HARDESTY, Kenneth Clovia S1c
HARLEY, Bert Dunning TME3c
HARPER, Carl Edward MM1c

HARRIS, John Junior † (Lost on USS *Bullhead* Aug. 1945) QM3c
HEISSER, Melvin Ck2c
HELM, Clarence W. * F3c
HERRMANN, Thomas Warren * .... CTM
HETTIGER, Kurt Karl *† .... CMoMM
HILCHEY, Alvin William TM2c
HOHWIESNER, Henry G. Jr. .... LT
HOLMES, Billy Frank Y2c
HOLMES, Elmer .... —
HOLMQUIST, Robert William RT1c
HUDSON, George William † F1c
HUNT, James K. * S1c
HUTCHINSON, Edward Shillingford *† .... CDR
HUTCHISON, Robert Lester * .... CEM

INSKEEP, William Freeman * S1c
IRRGANG, Lyman C. TM1c
IVERY, Clarence *† .... CEM

JACKSON, Harry N. .... LTJG
JACOBS, Howard Lester F1
JARAMILLO, Nicholas Ramirez S1c
JUMP, John Michael QM2c

KAPLAN, Abraham Bkr3c
KARR, William Garrard RM3c
KENRICH, Chester Metcalf *† RT1c
KIRK, Charles Patterson * EM3c
KLEIN, Delmer Benton † S1c
KOEHLER, Kurt E. .... —
KURZ, Edward Alfred RM3c

LANINI, Harold Montgomery MoMM1c
LAUGHON, Willard Ross .... LCDR
LEBED, Alfred Joseph TM2c
LEE, Robert Hugh * TM1c
LENNON, Francis D. TM1c
LESLIE, Rex Otto MM1
LIBBEY, Raymond Edward TM3c
LOBER, Peter N. * .... ENS
LOEBACK, Henry J. † GM2c
LOFSTROM, William Axel † .... —
LONGMUIR, Donald William † S1c
LOREN, W. EM3c
LOWERY, Stanley D. .... —
LUBRICO, Leon Calarito St1c
LYNE, Fritz L. † .... ENS
LYON, Patrick G. .... —
LYTLE, Max Stevenson * † MoMM1c

McCARTY, Clifford Bowman MoMM1c
McKINLEY, John W. * .... ENS
MAIN, Kenneth † MoMM1c
MARTIN, Armor William * EM2c
MATHEWSON, Robert Wayne * MoMM2c
MATHIS, Hermele S1c
MENDENHALL, George TM1c
METERAND, William J. SoM3c
MICHAELS, Michael S1c
MILLER, Raleigh William TM1c
MILLER, Richard C. F1c
MOFFIT, Robert RM1c
MOHR, Kenneth Roy S1c
MONTE, Joseph James * Y2c
MONTGOMERY, John Lewis * GM3c
MOORE, Richard L. .... —
MORRIS, Robert MoMM1c
MORRISON, Daniel Theodore QM2c
MUELLER, Robert LeRoy * TM1c
MULLEN, James R. F1c
MULLER, Walter E. .... LTJG
MUNSON, Henry Glass † .... CDR
MURNANE, James Joseph S1c

NACE, Charles Derick .... LCDR
NATIONS, Fred "K" * S2c
NAU, James N. Y3c
NELSON, John Joseph MoMM1c
NELSON, Wiley .... CMoMM
NEWLON, Arthur W. * .... LT
NIESS, Albert Erich .... —
NORRINGTON, William E. * .... LT

OLIVER, James Dorsey St2c
ORR, Ellis B. * .... LCDR
OSBORNE, Cedric Henry PhM1c
O'SHAUGHNESSY, Edward F. F1c
O'TOOLE, Francis D. Bkr1c
OWENS, John Paul SC1c

PACE, Robert David *† TM2c
PARIS, "J. P." F1c
PARTIN, Marshall Furman *† TM2c
PASCALE, Charles J. RM3c
PAVELKA, L. R. .... ENS
PENDLETON, Henry C. FCS1c
PENNINGTON, Coy Elmer *† TM1c
PENNYMAN, Timothy Matthew St3c
PETERSON, Leonard August * .... CEM

PHILLIPS, Glenn P. F1c
PIERCE, Billie Gordon S1c
POGGI, Serafine R. * MoMM2c
PONTILLO, Michael MoMM1c
POPE, Lucius Ballenger Jr. S2c
PURCELL, John W. .... —

RABUN, Charles Luther MoMM3c
RAKICH, Charles L. TM3c
RAYL, Robert John Bader *† .... CMoMM
REA, Fielding Jr. S2c
REINHARD, George A. MoMM3c
REUFF, Charles Glenn * EM2c
RHYMES, Ralph Willard EM1c
RICE, Howell Barbee .... CRM
RIOS, Alfredo Alfonso † MoMM1c
ROGIN, Edward Anthony * MoMM2c
ROLEY, Warren A. Y2c
ROSENBROOK, Merle William * MoMM2c
ROWBERRY, Jay Edward S1c
ROWE, Des "C" * TM1c
RUNGE, Herbert Lewis * TM2c

ST. PETER, Joseph Marcellus † RM3c
SABIN, Robert O. MoMM1c
SAMPSON, Ansel Earland *† EM1
SASGEN, Peter Joseph *† .... ENS
SCHACK, Edward William MoMM2c
SCHAUMBURG, Ferdinand O. EM2c
SCHILLER, Arthur F. † S1c
SCHRAVESANDE, Leonard William SC2c
SCHULTZ, Harry B. * S2c
SCOTT, Frank Niels * RM2c
SEARS, Philip C. TM2c
SENNA, Norbert Edgar S1c
SHARP, Richard Milton PhM1c
SHILMOVER, Samson .... —
SMITH, Howard Ralph MoMM2c
SMITH, Maurice Glenn *† MoMM1c
SMITH, Stephen W. * S2c
SOUCY, Roland Joseph * MoMM3c
SOVERN, Roy Orville EM2c
SPINK, Robert Henry F1c
STICKLE, James E. S1c
STOEBER, Warren F. .... CPhM
STOKER, Dickson L. S1c
STRUCK, Elmer P. * F3c
STURTEVANT, Joseph W. * QM3c
SUTTON, James P. S1c

SZYSKO, Michael .... CCS

TATE, Kenneth Edwin * TM2c
THURNAU, Glen Andrew * F1c
TILLO, Bernardo Ck1c
TRACEY, Joseph Patrick EM3c
TUBBS, Donald William *† QM2c

UNGER, George Washington Jr. RM1c
USHER, Robert H. * MoMM1c

VIOLET, Edward Archie † MoMM2c
VRONA, Edward Victor * † MoMM2c

WADE, Russel F. .... LTJG
WALKER, Hestel EM3c
WARD, James Andrew RM3c
WARNOCK, Robert Joseph S1c
WASHINGTON, James C. StM2c
WATZKA, Byron Joseph † MoMM2c
WEIGEL, Lyle Albert * .... CWO
WEIGHILL, Walter Irvin .... CCS
WESTERHUIS, Louis Joseph *† S1c
WHELEN, John Kenneth *† .... CPhM
WHITAKER, Eugene Reuben GM3c
WHITE, Charles James † F1c
WHITE, James Allen .... CQM
WILCOX, Gifford .... LTJG
WILCOXSON, Alfred Anson † MoMM1c
WILLIAMS, Clayton Edgar * TM3c
WILLIAMS, Samuel "L D" GM3c
WILSON, Alton William Y2c
WILSON, Melvin Lamar EM1c
WILSON, Norval Dellon * .... CMoMM
WINDSON, Herbert S. FCS2c
WISE, Terry Edward F1c
WOODBURY, Ralph E. .... LTJG
WOODE, Wallace D. .... CMoMM
WOODWARD, John Fredrick F1c
WOODWORTH, Dale Eugene SC1c
WRIGHT, W. R. .... LTJG

YATES, Cyril B. † .... —
YODER, Donald H. F1c

ZIEGELMANN, Frank E. F1c
ZIER, Harry Franklin Joseph F1c
ZONE, Pio J. F1c

Glossary

Acey-deucy: Sailors' version of backgammon.

After battery compartment: Main section of a submarine behind the control room; houses battery cells and crew living and dining spaces.

AK: Cargo vessel.

Angle on the bow: Angle between the fore and aft axis of the target and line of sight from the submarine, measured from the target's bow to port or starboard.

Annunciator: An electro-mechanical signaling device for sending orders to an engine room.

AO: Oil tanker.

AP: Transport.

Ballast tanks: Tanks used to submerge and surface a submarine by filling them with water or blowing them dry.

Banca: Small native outrigger.

Bathythermograph (BT): Device used to measure underwater temperature variations.

Boatswain (Bosun): A sailor whose main duties pertain to deck and boat seamanship.

Bulkhead: Vertical partition separating compartments in a ship.

BuOrd (Bureau of Ordnance): Navy department responsible for weapons and ordnance.

BuShips (Bureau of Ships): Navy department responsible for the building and maintenance of all naval vessels.

CA: Heavy cruiser.

Chidori: Japanese anti-submarine vessel; a type of torpedo boat.

Chief of the Boat: Senior enlisted man aboard a submarine.

Christmas tree: Hull opening indicator panel.

Clamp down: To wipe a deck with a moist swab.

Commissioning pennant: Narrow red, white, and blue pennant with seven stars.

Conning tower: Horizontal cylindrical compartment above the control room; used for navigating and directing attacks.

Control room: Compartment directly below conning tower; submarine's operating center.

Cribbage: A card game for two to four players; various combinations of cards are formed to score points. A board with holes and pegs is used to keep score.

Cutie: Passive homing torpedo.

CV: Aircraft carrier.

CVE: Escort aircraft carrier.

DD: Destroyer.

Displacement: The weight of water displaced by a vessel, expressed in tons.

Distance to the track: Range in yards from a submarine to the target's track or course line.

ECM (Electric Coding Machine): Standard submarine coding-decoding device. When operating in shallow coastal waters, the ECM was sometimes left ashore to prevent its falling into enemy hands should the submarine be sunk and salvaged; usually a simple strip cipher device was substituted for the ECM.

Fleet-type submarine: Attack submarine used by the Navy in World War II; approximately 250 were built between 1940 and 1945.

Flood valves: Large Kingston valves located in the bottoms of ballast tanks to admit water; valves were removed for wartime patrolling.

Forward battery compartment: Main section of a submarine ahead of the control room; mainly housed battery cells and living quarters.

Fox schedule (skeds): Submarine radio communications network.

Fuel King: Enlisted man whose duties include fueling operations and associated record-keeping.

Gyro angle: Angle between fore and aft axis of the submarine and track of torpedo measured clockwise from the submarine's bow.

I-boat: Class of 2,100-ton displacement Japanese submarines.

Limber holes: Sea water drain holes in a submarine's superstructure.

Lubbers line: A fixed line on a compass aligned with a ship's longitudinal axis.

JANAC: Joint Army-Navy Assessment Committee. Official body charged after the war with according credit to submarines for enemy sinkings.

JK-QC sound gear: Dual-head, passive/active retractable submarine sound gear.

JP sound gear: Passive, single fixed-head sound gear installed in submarines beginning in mid-1944.

Junk: A type of sailing vessel found in Asian waters.

Kedge: To carry out an anchor, then by taking in the chain, hauling the ship up to the anchor.

Maru: Japanese merchant vessel.

Negative buoyancy: A condition attained when a submarine weighs more than the water it displaces, thus causing it to submerge.

Negative Tank: Floodable tank used to impart negative buoyancy to a submarine to make it dive rapidly.

Neutral buoyancy: A condition attained when a submerged submarine's displacement equals the weight of the water it displaces, thus requiring only small inputs from the diving planes to maintain trim.

Night Orders: Commanding officer's written orders to the officers of the deck while the ship is under way at night, including proper speed and course and what to do in emergencies or if contact is made with the enemy.

1MC: Shipboard announcing system.

ONI: Office of Naval Intelligence.

Operation Order (Op-Ord): Secret instructions and restrictions governing a submarine's war patrol.

Outer doors (shutters): Streamlined movable covers over torpedo tube muzzles.

Periscope shears: Upright supports around the periscopes where they protrude above the conning tower; lookouts are stationed on horizontal platforms mounted on the shears.

Pipe down: Instructions passed over the general announcing system (1MC) to commence an activity.

Pitometer log (pit log): A device used to measure a ship's speed through the water.

Positive buoyancy: Condition a submarine is in when its submerged displacement weighs less than the water it displaces, thus causing it to rise to the surface.

PPI (Position Plan Indicator): Radar scope display showing own ship and her position relative to other radar contacts.

Q-ship: A warship disguised as an unarmed vessel; used to decoy submarines into gun range.

Range: Distance in yards from periscope to target (2,000 yards equals approximately one nautical mile, or 6,080.20 feet).

Reduction gears: A gear train used to reduce the input speed from main propulsion motors to a lower output speed to a ship's propeller shafts.

Rhumb line: A course on a compass bearing.

RO-boat: Japanese 900-ton displacement submarine.

S-boat: Class of 800-ton displacement submarines built for the U.S. Navy in the 1920s. A few saw service in World War II.

SD radar: Submarine air search radar.

Sea (land) return: Radar interference caused by return echoes from sea or land. Sometimes called "grass."

Shakedown: Testing and training period for a ship and her crew after launching or overhaul.

SJ radar: Submarine surface search radar.

Sonar: Device used to detect underwater objects by means of sonic waves deflected back from the object. Can be used in passive (listening) mode, or active (sending and listening) mode.

Spitkit: Small, ramshackle vessel.

ST radar: Miniaturized radar unit installed in periscope head.

TBT (Target Bearing Transmitter): Binocular-like device on bridge used to transmit target bearings directly to the TDC while on surface.

TDC (Torpedo Data Computer): Analog mechanical fire control computer used to integrate target's and submarine's positions relative to each other; automatically computes torpedo gyro angle.

Top hamper: A ship's superstructure and rigging.

Torpex: A type of explosive packed in torpedo warheads.

Track angle: Angle between fore-aft axis of target and torpedo track as measured from target's bow, port or starboard.

Trice up: Bunks pushed up into their stowed positions.

True bearing (T.): Angle between actual (not magnetic) north-south line and line of sight measured clockwise from north.

Tumble home: Upward convex curve of a ship's side above the waterline.

Ultra: Name given to the breaking of Japanese merchant marine codes.

Union jack: Flag consisting of the union of the national ensign; flown from the bow of a moored or anchored ship.

V-boat: Class of large fleet-type submarines built for the U.S. Navy in the 1930s.

Variable ballast tanks: Tanks used to control a submarine's overall trim.

Watch: A sailor's duty period. Watches ashore and under way are normally stood for four hours, followed by eight hours off duty. Standard navy watches are: first watch 2000-2400; midwatch 0000-0400; morning watch 0400-0800; forenoon watch 0800-1200; afternoon watch 1200-1600; first dogwatch 1600-1800; second dogwatch 1800-2000.

Way: A ship's movement through the water.

Sources

Alden, John D. *The Fleet Submarine in the U.S. Navy*. Annapolis: United States Naval Institute Press, 1979.
———. *U.S. Submarine Attacks During World War II*. Annapolis: United States Naval Institute Press, 1989.
Beach, Edward L. *Dust on the Sea*. New York: Holt, Rinehart, Winston, 1972.
———. *Run Silent, Run Deep*. New York: Henry Holt, 1955.
———. *Submarine!* New York: Henry Holt, 1946.
Behr, Edward. *Hirohito: Behind the Myth*. New York: Villard Books, 1989.
Blair, Clay Jr. *Silent Victory*. Philadelphia: J. B. Lippincott Company, 1975.
Brooks, Lester. *Behind Japan's Surrender*. New York: McGraw-Hill, 1968.
Dull, Paul S. *A Battle History of the Imperial Japanese Navy*. Annapolis: United States Naval Institute Press, 1978.
Fahey, James C. *The Ships and Aircraft of the United States Fleet*. All editions. Annapolis: United States Naval Institute Press, 1938-1988.
The Fleet Type Submarine. NavPers, 1946.
Fluckey, Eugene B. *Thunder Below!* Chicago: University of Illinois Press, 1992.
Friedman, Norman. *Submarine Design and Development*. Annapolis: United States Naval Institute Press, 1984.
Galantin, I. J. *Take Her Deep! A Submarine Against Japan in World War II*. New York: Pocket Books, 1987.
Grider, George. *War Fish*. New York: Ballantine Books, 1958.
Holmes, W. J. *Double-Edged Secrets: U.S. Naval Intellegence Operations in the Pacific During World War II*. Annapolis: United States Naval Institute Press, 1979.
Hoyt, Edwin P. *Bowfin: The Story of One of America's Fabled Fleet Submarines in World War II*. New York: Avon Books, 1983.
Japanese Naval Vessels of World War Two. Annapolis: Naval Institute Press, 1987.
Kahn, David. *The Code Breakers*. New York: Macmillan, 1967.
Kaufmann, Yogi, and Paul Stillwell. *Sharks of Steel*. Annapolis: United States Naval Institute Press, 1993.

Knight, Austin M. *Modern Seamanship*. New York: D. Van Nostrand, 1945.

Lockwood, Charles A. *Sink 'Em All: Submarine Warfare in the Pacific*. New York: E. P. Dutton & Co., Inc., 1951.

McCullough, David. *Truman*. New York: Simon & Schuster, 1993.

Maloney, Elbert S. *Chapman Piloting: Seamanship and Small Boat Handling*. New York: Hearst Marine Books, 1983.

Mendenhall, Corwin. *Submarine Diary*. New York: Workman Publishing, Inc., 1991.

Mosely, Leonard. *Hirohito, Emperor of Japan*. Englewood Cliffs: Prentice-Hall, Inc., 1966.

Mueller, A. J. *Black Cats With Wings of Gold*. Philadelphia: SED Press, 1992.

Navy Year Book. New York: Duell, Sloan and Pearce, 1944.

Nelson, William T. *Fresh Water Submarines: The Manitowoc Story*. Manitowoc, Wisc.: Hoeffner Printing, 1986.

O'Kane, Richard H. *Clear the Bridge! The War Patrols of the U.S.S. Tang*. Chicago: Rand McNally, 1977.

————. *Wahoo: The Patrols of America's Most Famous WWII Submarine*. Navato, Calif.: Presidio Press, 1987.

Parillo, Mark P. *The Japanese Merchant Marine in World War II*. Annapolis: United States Naval Institute Press, 1993.

Phillips, Christopher. *Steichen at War*. New York: Harry N. Abrams Jr., 1981.

Pictorial History of the Second World War. All Volumes. New York: William H. Wise and Co., Inc., 1947.

Roscoe, Theodore. *United States Submarine Operations in World War II*. Annapolis: United States Naval Institute Press, 1949.

————. *United States Destroyer Operations in World War II*. Annapolis: United States Naval Institute Press, 1953.

Rousmaniere, John. *The Annapolis Book of Seamanship*. New York: Simon & Schuster, 1983.

Spector, Ronald H. *Eagle Against the Sun: The American War With Japan*. New York: The Free Press, 1985.

Stern, Robert C. *U.S. Subs in Action*. Carrollton, Texas: Squadron/Signal Publications, Inc., 1983.

Storry, Richard. *A History of Modern Japan*. Hammondsworth, Middlesex, England: Pelican Books, 1960.

Terzibaschitsch, Stefan. *Submarines of the U.S. Navy*. London: Arms and Armour Press, 1991.

The Bluejackets' Manual. Annapolis: United States Naval Institute Press, 1943.

United States Submarine Losses World War II. Washington, D.C.: Naval History Division, Office of the Chief of Naval Operations, 1946.

Wheeler, Keith. *War Under the Pacific*. Alexandria, Va.: Time-Life Books, 1980.

Winton, John. *Ultra in the Pacific*. Annapolis: United States Naval Institute Press, 1993.

Wyden, Peter. *Day One: Before Hiroshima and After*. New York: Simon & Schuster, 1984.

Miscellaneous sources:

United States Naval Institute *Proceedings*.

Horie, Y. "The Failure of the Japanese Convoy Escort." (October 1956): 1073-1081.

Davis, H. F. D. "Building Submarines in World War II." (July 1946): 933-939.

Ruhe, W. J. "The *Rasher's* Fifth." (September 1983): 78-81.

Transactions of the Society of Naval Architects and Engineers.

McKee, A. I. "Development of Submarines in the United States." (Issue of 1945): 344-355.

————. "Recent Submarine Design Practices and Problems." (Issue of 1959): 623-652.

Dictionary of American Naval Fighting Ships. Vol. VI. Washington, D.C.: Naval History Division, Department of the Navy, 1976.

Articles from various sources on sonar, radar, torpedoes, ordnance, diesel engines, bathythermographic devices, radio, communications, weather, hydrography, mapping, navigation, etc.

Ships' Orders. USS *Rasher.*

An invaluable source of information on submarine procedures and terminology. The orders—over 100 pages—cover everything from the issuance of liberty cards to operating diesel engines to diving the boat. Copy in author's files, a gift of William Norrington.

The patrol reports of the USS *Rasher,* eight volumes.

Primary source material. The reports detail combat operations at sea in patrol areas. Appendixes to reports provide highly detailed information on torpedo attacks, weather, ship and aircraft contacts, and much more. Submarine war patrol reports are available on mocrofilm from the Naval Historical Center in Washington, D.C. Paper copies of the *Rasher's* reports are in author's files.

The personal accounts of former *Rasher* crew members, from their letters, diaries, and conversations. Photographs from their collections.

Letters were the primary source for the quoted material; originals in author's files. Material was extracted from Peter J. Sasgen's memoir; copies are available from the author. Though personal war diaries were forbidden (in the event of capture by the enemy, they could potentially provide valuable information), Norrington and Tate each kept one. A photocopy of Norrington's diary can be obtained from him; Tate's original hardcover diary is in his possession. Rough notes of conversations were made by the author and integrated into the text. The bulk of the photographs are in the collection of Peter J. Sasgen. The photos gave the author a visual sense of some of the events described.

Index

About the Author

Peter T. Sasgen was born in Evanston, Illinois, in 1941. A graduate of the University of the Arts in Philadelphia, he holds a degree in design and illustration. After serving in the U.S. Navy as a staff artist with *All Hands* magazine from 1965 to 1967, he began his career as a freelance graphic designer and photographer in Washington, D.C. Presently he and his wife, Karen, operate a design studio in Philadelphia.

Sasgen has had a lifelong interest in submarines and the war in the Pacific. His research for *Red Scorpion* took him from old family records in Florida, to the National Archives in Maryland, to the abandoned dry docks of Hunters Point in California. In the process he developed close friendships with many of his late father's former shipmates from the *Rasher*. He is currently working on a novel about submarines, World War II, and present-day Japan.

1,7
4
___
6,8